Dixie Rising

DIXIE RISING

How the South Is Shaping
American Values, Politics, and Culture

PETER APPLEBOME

TIMES BOOKS

RANDOM HOUSE

Grateful acknowledgment is made to the following for permission to reprint previously published material:
W CLARK BUCHANAN: "The King's Prayer" by W Clark Buchanan. Copyright © 1993 by W Clark Buchanan. Reprinted by permission.
FRED MOORE: "Home Sweet Mobile Home" by Fred Moore. Reprinted by permission of Fred Moore.
WARNER BROS. PUBLICATIONS: Excerpt from "The Tulsa Shuffle" by Steve Ripley. Copyright © 1994 by Warner-Tamerlane Publishing Corp. (BMI) and Boy Rocking Music (BMI). All Rights o/b/o Boy Rocking Music administered by Warner-Tamerlane Publishing Corp. All rights reserved. Used by permission of Warner Bros. Publications U.S., Inc., Miami, FL 33014.
WORD, INC.: Excerpt from "America Again" by Carman and Michael O'Martian. Copyright © 1993 by Some-O-Dat Music (admin. by Word, Inc.), Middle C Music and Edward Grant, Inc. All rights reserved. Used by permission of Word, Inc.

Photographs by Alan S. Weiner

Library of Congress Cataloging-in-Publication Data
Applebome, Peter.
Dixie rising: how the South is shaping American values, politics, and culture / Peter Applebome.
p.   cm.
ISBN 0-8129-2653-6 (hardcover)
1. Southern States—Politics and government—1951–   2. Southern States—Civilization—20th century.
3. United States—Politics and government—1989–   4. United States—Civilization—1970–   I. Title.
F216.2.A67   1996   973.929—dc20   96-16080

Random House website address: http://www.randomhouse.com

Printed in the United States of America on acid-free paper
468975

Book design by Jane Fay

For my parents, Jerome and Sydel Applebome

Acknowledgments

One of the best reasons to write a first book is for the opportunity to thank people in print you've never sufficiently thanked in person. So, my appreciations here extend both to those who helped with this book and those who helped me get to the point where I could write it.

I first need to thank Steve Harrigan, Alamo-ologist, bard of Austin, and perhaps the best writer I know, who helped get me into this, encouraged me when I had no idea whether it was going to work, and served as an inspired editor and sounding board via daily E-mail over the course of the project. Also of immense help was John Egerton, whose life and work represents the best of the South. Others who offered invaluable editorial comments on the manuscript or individual chapters included Nick Lemann, Merle Black, John Hope Franklin, Jack Bass, Adam Nossiter, Frye Gaillard, Alston Fitts, and Amy Kurland.

At *The New York Times,* where I've worked for the past decade, I first need to thank Joseph Lelyveld, who, despite his instincts to not leave people in one place for too long, allowed me to stay in Atlanta long enough to write this book and then let me stay awhile longer. Also due thanks is his predecessor, Max Frankel, who encouraged me to write the series that helped lead to this book. I'm at least as indebted to

Nancy Sharkey, my current editor and one of the all-time classiest people I've known in journalism, who gave me the breathing room to get this done. On the National Desk, I've worked for four extremely capable and extremely different editors–Dave Jones, Soma Golden, Linda Mathews, and Dean Baquet. In different ways I'm indebted to all of them. I also owe a particular debt to editors and friends over the years on the National Desk like Bill Schmidt, Paul Haskins, Carl Lavin, Dennis Stern, Phil Taubman, and the late Jeff Schmalz. Among the many extraordinary reporters I've worked with over the years at *The Times,* I owe a particular debt to John Crewdson, who worked to get me hired long ago, back when I had hair, and Bob Reinhold, journalism's last gentleman, who did national reporting as well as it could be done and who was the perfect person to start out with in *The Times'* Houston Bureau. I'd also like to thank my friends and colleagues in *The Times'* Atlanta Bureau, Ron Smothers, Rick Bragg, Kevin Sack, and Uncle Ed Gargan, our honorary Atlantan, who helped prod me into doing this during his extended visit. No words can express how much I owe the amazing Susan Taylor, who somehow keeps all the trains on track. Special thanks also to Alan Weiner for his wonderful pictures here and his welcome, cranky companionship at various jaunts and disasters over the years. And thanks also to Louise Moreland, Mary Lu Mitchell, Andy Peters, and Deavours Hall for their help in the bureau.

In earlier stops on the way, I was able to work with and learn from friends and colleagues like Steve Blow, Stuart Wilk, Scott Parks, Bob Compton, and the late Buster Haas at *The Dallas Morning News,* and Mike Levy, Greg Curtis, Joe Nocera, Paul Burka, Peter Elkind, Harry Hurt III, Alison Cook, Mimi Swartz, Dominique Browning, and various other amazingly talented people at *Texas Monthly* magazine.

It's impossible to name all the people who gave of their time to make this book possible, but among them are Mark Gibbs in Cobb County; Charles Bonner in Selma; Leon McElveen, the world's most honorable Confederate, in Atlanta; Percy Reeves in Charlotte; Kathy Lamb in Belton, South Carolina; Margaret Gail Rogers in Mullins, South Carolina; Linda Pearce in Wilmington; Tim DuBois and Marty Stuart in Nashville; and Willie Morris in Mississippi.

My agent, Esther Newberg, was as good as everyone said she was, even when I made her nervous at the beginning. At Times Books, Peter

Osnos saw a book here before I was sure what it was; Geoff Shandler was a calm, skilled, thoughtful editor, Kate Scott and Dennis Ambrose did a meticulous job of copyediting, and Marty Blake and Robbin Schiff are due particular thanks for the amazing job they did on the cover.

My biggest debt goes to my parents, Jerome and Sydel Applebome—who have always been there beyond the call of duty in big ways and small ones—and to our extended Tanners Road family: my brother, Woody; sister, Louise; the I's and B's, and, yes, you too, Captain.

Finally, this book would never have happened without the support, forbearance, and patience of my wife, Mary Catherine, and the daily miracle of the crown jewels, Ben and Emma, my two little Southerners even if their daddy is not. My thanks to all. Any failings are my own.

Contents

Dixie Rising

Chapter 1

THE SOUTHERNIZATION OF AMERICA

T HEY CAME IN MIGHTY CHARIOTS TO THE SEA-GREEN OASIS OF THE Georgia Dome in downtown Atlanta proclaiming victory.

They came in humongous white Winnebago Chieftan 27s from Illinois, in Bibleland Travel charter buses, in the Chevy van from the Cross Roads Baptist Church of Easley, South Carolina, and in an ancient Lincoln Continental from Washington with home-schooling bumper stickers and pipe-cleaner hearts strung together hanging from the rearview mirror. They had Dr Peppers and Cokes in the coolers and Christian music by the Fairchilds or the Happy Goodman Family in the tape decks. They had Christian fish symbols, American flag decals, and bumper stickers reading GOD SAID IT. I BELIEVE IT. THAT SETTLES IT. or SAVE THE BABY HUMANS. STOP ABORTION.

They came in the shimmering heat of June 1995, on the 150th anniversary of the founding of the Southern Baptist Convention, to celebrate the past and contemplate the future of that most Southern of institutions, which now, with 15 million members, was the largest Protestant denomination in America.

There were great lacquered helmets of Jimmy Johnson hair, thick gray thatches of Newt Gingrich hair, breathtaking swards of Ronald Reagan hair, swept-back evangelist big hair that looked like it had been styled with a power blender and laced with Elmer's Glue. There were young Nordic Track bodies and bodies with bellies like canteloupes, honeydews, and watermelons. There were blond baby linebackers built like bowling balls being pushed in their strollers and toddlers in their Sunday-best white lace dresses with pink bows in their hair. There were incessant swelling hymns of praise ("Sing it one more time with all you have! The King is coming soon!") bouncing off the 750-foot-long, cable-supported, Teflon-coated fiberglass roof and beaming out of the dozens of Sony televisions jammed between billboards advertising Hooters girls, Doritos, Napa Auto Parts, Delta Airlines, and Coke. There was Good News without end.

Indeed, both the Good News of Jesus and the good news of this mortal coil was everywhere to be seen. Born in part out of support for slavery and nourished for generations in Bible-thumping, true-believing churches on small-town Main Streets throughout the South, the confederation of Southern Baptists always summed up the feverish religiosity, righteous probity, and confining insularity of the South. It was a world of tent revivals, riverside baptisms, and Main Street piety, a world sketched in shades of gray by Southern writers like Erskine Caldwell and Flannery O'Connor, a world where, as the writer Marshall Frady, himself the son of a Southern Baptist minister, put it, "The Old Testament and the Crucifixion always seemed to count for more than the New Testament and the Resurrection—a dire melodrama of thorns and betrayal and midnight anguish, with nothing in the life of Jesus mattering quite so much as his suffering and his death."

Now, both the president and the vice president, like the only other Democratic president of the past quarter century, were Southern Baptists—if not quite the Southern Baptists most of the messengers in Atlanta would have chosen—and the Republican road to oppose them was certain to run right through the heart of the South, its conservative values and the evangelical community of which the Baptists are a vital part. Indeed, the great conservative tide of the past quarter century had brought the values of Southern Baptists, and of millions of their brothers and sisters in other evangelical denominations and the new nondenominational Christian churches proliferating in shopping-mall-like churches across the country, from the fringe of the Bible Belt to the very center of national life.

Furthermore, in a way that once would have seemed a contradiction in terms, Southern Baptists were no longer geographically Southern Baptists. Beginning in 1942, when they spread to California, Southern Baptist congregations have set up shop in every state in the Union; now there are 1,900 black congregations, 3,000 Hispanic ones, and 800 Korean ones, a denomination speaking 101 languages endlessly morphing and reproducing itself across the country, like a Southern gene, bringing both the Good News of Jesus and the conservative values of the small-town South with it. Thus, in addition to the big hair and lime-green jackets of the white Southern Baptists, participants in the convention included Southern Baptists like Harriet Nelson, a black woman born in the Virgin Islands who now belonged to the largely black Peaceful Baptist Church in Miami, or like Billy Rios, pastor of the largely Brazilian First Portuguese-Speaking Baptist Church of San Francisco. Amid the sea of religious books could be found Bibles and religious texts in Chinese, Japanese and Korean, *La Biblia al Minuto, Dios Habla Hoy,* and Billy Graham's *Paz Con Dios.*

Make no mistake: despite the usual resolutions and witnessing about social issues like abortion or pornography or social decay and a rather extraordinary vote by the convention to "repent of racism of which we have been guilty" and to apologize and ask forgiveness from "all African Americans," this was a gathering about religion, not politics. But it occurred to more than a few of those present that the denomination's remarkable growth had parallels that went beyond religion, that the Southern conservatism these people grew up with had spread its reach beyond anything they could have imagined years ago. So when Billy Graham ended the convention by proclaiming, "Let the light shine. Let's light a candle that will banish moral and spiritual blight in America and around the world," there was reason to believe it could happen.

"Across our country there's an undercurrent that is not only conservative but also is very Christian," said Eugene Greer, the sports evangelism consultant for the Baptists' Foreign Mission Board, who helps send Southern Baptist athletes around the world to play, preach, and proselytize. He was standing in the Foreign Mission Board booth, surrounded by straight-arrow Baptist missionaries from Oklahoma and Texas who were wearing native garb from the Yucatan or Kenya and who looked vaguely as if they were at a costume party. "And I think the guts of it, the roots of it, is the stuff we always had in the South, what I grew up with in my little small church in Griffin, Georgia."

There's ample evidence that he's right. Indeed, the most striking aspect of American life at the century's end—in a way that would have been utterly unimaginable three decades ago at the height of the civil rights era—is how much the country looks like the South. In 1957, at a time when the New Deal legacy seemed utterly triumphant in American life, fourteen Southerners contributed essays on the region to a collection called *The Lasting South*. Here is the columnist James J. Kilpatrick in the final piece:

> The Southern States at mid-century find themselves very nearly alone in fighting this rear-guard action against the legions of Change, the armies of a supposed Enlightenment. They represent, collectively, the last and best hope of conservatism in the American Republic. If the conservative cause is to survive at all in the United States, as a political philosophy, as an approach to the perplexing problems of our rootless and edgy civilization, it will be largely because a body of tradition exists within the South and will not lie down.

Conservatism, of course, has prospered to a degree that almost no one would have predicted three or four decades ago and along with it so has the South. The two developments are not unrelated.

It's not just that the South has been the key to the nation's presidential politics since the development of the Republican Party's Southern strategy, first laid out in detail in Kevin Phillips's *The Emerging Republican Majority* in 1969 and then turned to political reality in Richard Nixon's presidential election campaign in 1972. It's not just that in every one of the nine elections between 1932 and 1988 in which one party captured all or nearly all the Southern electoral votes, that party won. It's not just that the two most successful Republican strategists of recent years, Newt Gingrich and Lee Atwater, rose to power from bases in the South nor that the 1994 Republican takeover of Congress for the first time in forty years reflected the transformation of white Southerners from diehard Democrats to reliable Republicans more than any other single factor.

It's not just that evangelical Christians like the faithful at the Georgia Dome account for one third of the Republican party membership and half the Republican primary vote in many states or that it's estimated they played a significant role in 120 congressional districts and were pivotal in Republican victories in 30 races in the historic 1994 Republican sweep.

The South's political ascendance reached a new peak in May 1996 when Bob Dole stepped down as majority leader of the Senate leaving two Republicans from Mississippi, the most Southern state of them all, fighting for his job and the President, Vice President, Speaker of the House, House Majority Leader, House Majority Whip, and Republican Party Chairman all from the South. But the South's influence can be seen throughout the nation's political culture.

Think of a place that's bitterly antigovernment and fiercely individualistic, where race is a constant subtext to daily life, and God and guns run through public discourse like an electric current. Think of a place where influential scholars market theories of white supremacy, where the word "liberal" is a negative epithet, where hang-'em-high law-and-order justice centered on the death penalty and throw-away-the-key sentencing are politically all but unstoppable. Think of a place obsessed with states' rights, as if it were the 1850s all over again and the Civil War had never been fought. Such characteristics have always described the South. Somehow, they now describe the nation.

Partly, this simply reflects the fact that so much of America's population and wealth have moved South—with no end to the movement in sight. For the past two decades, ever since the word "Sunbelt" entered the nation's lexicon, various trendmeisters have noted the shift of the population toward the South so often that it's become a stale truism, replaced on the fashion rack of ideas by newer, sexier models. But in fact, while the idea has lost its novelty, the trend itself is incontestably, demonstrably true. Along the way, demography, as it always does, has proved to be destiny.

Between 1970 and 1990, the population of the eleven states of the Old Confederacy, Virginia, North Carolina, South Carolina, Georgia, Florida, Tennessee, Alabama, Mississippi, Louisiana, Texas, and Arkansas, plus Kentucky (a fairly conservative notion of the South), grew by 40 percent—more than 20 million people—twice the national growth rate. The population of Florida grew by 76 percent, Texas by 46 percent, Georgia by 38 percent. All but Kentucky and the Deep South laggards of Louisiana, Mississippi, and Alabama grew faster than the national average, and even forlorn Mississippi has been one of the nation's economic success stories so far in the nineties. In 1970, the region accounted for about a quarter of the nation's population. By the end of the century the portion will be almost a third. The Census Bureau says that of the ten states that will add the most residents between 1993 and 2020, six are in the South: Texas, Florida, Georgia, North Carolina, Virginia, and Tennessee. Using the Census Bureau's broader definition of the South, which runs from Maryland to Texas, in 1990–91 alone the region attracted 370,000 new residents from the Northeast.

The population increase has enormously increased the political clout of the South. The eleven states of the Confederacy plus Kentucky and Oklahoma now elect 137 members of the House of Representatives–17 more than in 1960–while Northern states like New York and Massachusetts have lost representation at the same time.

The population shift to the South, and to the West, has been so stark that a presidential candidate could now win by carrying exactly the same states that Richard Nixon carried when he *lost* to John F. Kennedy in 1960. Going back further, under the same electoral calculus, the fire-and-brimstone populist, William Jennings Bryan, would have been an easy winner in 1896. More than two decades ago, the famous curveball artist and demographer Satchel Paige allowed: "You give this country twenty or thirty more years, everybody's got any sense is going down South." It looks like he was right.

As a result, the South in the first half of the nineties was transformed from the nation's economic outhouse, famously proclaimed by F.D.R. in 1938 to be the nation's number one economic problem, into its main engine of economic growth. In fact, if the eleven states of the Confederacy were a separate country, it would have the world's fourth-largest economy. In 1993, over half of America's new jobs were created in the South. During the same time, eight of the top ten states in terms of growth in manufacturing plants were in the South. Cities like Charlotte, Nashville, and Raleigh-Durham were experiencing labor shortages, and businesses in Nashville were advertising for workers from as far away as Puerto Rico. Atlanta added more jobs than any other city in the nation during 1993, '94, and '95. Lazy resort towns like Myrtle Beach, South Carolina, and once godforsaken Appalachian and Ozark hollows like Pigeon Forge, Tennessee; Branson, Missouri; and Eureka Springs, Arkansas, were transformed almost overnight into booming middle-class country-music and family-values vacation havens–the Coney Islands and Catskills of the nineties.

Conversely, in a way that parallels the evolution of evangelical Christianity from a distinctly Southern phenomenon to a national one, the region's influence on the nation was also reflected in the great and only dimly understood exodus of people *from* the South during the half century from 1910 to 1960, a migration virtually without parallel in American history. Most obvious was the migration of nearly 4.5 million blacks from the South, most of them to cities in the North, a development that changed forever the nature of urban life and American politics, turning race from an issue that defined the politics of the South into an issue that defines the politics of the nation. But just as important, if far more elusive, was the exodus of almost 4.6 million whites: Okies trekked to Bakersfield, California; poor whites joined poor blacks in the exodus from Mississippi and Alabama to Chicago; Tennesseans, Kentuckians, and West Virginians migrated to Ohio—so many Kentucky mountain people went to work in the auto plants of Ypsilanti, Michigan, that they still call the place Ypsitucky. Like the carriers of a dominant gene, they didn't stop being Southerners. They brought their music, their values, their evangelical religion, their history as the people of the nation's most violent region, and a whole panoply of Southern-fried virtues and sins.

On the face of it, the idea of the South as the home of quintessential Americana does not compute. Ever since the prologue to the Civil War, the South's stock in trade has been the myth and reality of its distinctiveness: the only part of the nation with institutionalized apartheid; the only part of the nation to know the crushing burden of losing a war; a place congenitally geared to looking toward the past in a nation rushing headlong into the future; a region whose holy vapors of evangelical religion, crushing poverty, and indelible sense of history made it if not quite a separate country, as close to it as this nation has ever known within its borders. When Quentin Compson's Harvard roommate in William Faulkner's *Absalom, Absalom!* requests of Quentin, "Tell about the South," he gets hundreds of pages of response that end with a resigned "You can't understand it. You would have to be born there." That distinctiveness never seemed more apparent than during the civil rights era just three decades ago.

But if Southern exceptionalism was and is real, it also hid as much as it revealed. To a large degree, the story of the nation is a mating dance between the North and the South, its history an index of which region was dominant. Over the years, the rest of the nation has Ping-Ponged between views of the South as a hellhole of poverty, torment, and depravity and as an American Eden of tradition, strength, and grace.

H. L. Mencken lampooned the South as the "bunghole of the United

States, a cesspool of Baptists, a Miasma of Methodism, snake-charmers, phoney real-estate operators, and syphilitic evangelists." Rhett, Scarlett, Melanie, and Ashley played out the ultimate pageant of grandeur and romance. Erskine Caldwell's grotesque cavalcade of rural lowlifes and losers picked at the scabs of what he called "a retarded and thwarted civilization" at the same time an endless parade of Depression-era musicals like *Hearts of Dixie, Hallelujah, Steamboat 'Round the Bend, Mississippi,* and *The Little Colonel,* portrayed a happy-go-lucky plantation paradise of grinning, dancing, banjo-playing darkies, gallant colonels and cavaliers, and delicate Southern belles in hoopskirts and lace. There is Carl Sandburg, the quintessential poet and singer of America's song, who deserted Chicago for the Blue Ridge Mountains in 1945, where he became a passionate adoptive Southerner; and there is the South that a reviewer in *The Nation* at roughly the same time described as "so sick from its old infections of prejudice and poverty that it is a menace to the nation." Hollywood has forever bounced back and forth serving up at one moment the murderous rednecks of *Deliverance, Cape Fear,* and *Easy Rider* and at the next the blissful grace and uplift of *Places in the Heart* or *The Trip to Bountiful.* Look one way, the South is the heart of darkness in *Mississippi Burning.* Look the other, it's the embarrassingly stereotypical but oddly redeemed drama of family values, roots, racial peace, and national healing of *Forrest Gump.*

Given the South's ability to evoke America in extremis, it's no surprise that American film as an art form began with *The Birth of a Nation* and the quintessential American film remains *Gone With the Wind.* Or, for that matter, that even if you discount William Faulkner, Eudora Welty, Richard Wright, Ralph Ellison, William Styron, Walker Percy, Robert Penn Warren, Thomas Wolfe, and the rest of the familiar pantheon of Southern authors, probably the two most prototypically American literary creations, Tom Sawyer and Huckleberry Finn, were the creations of an author, Mark Twain, who came from a slaveholding family in a Southern-sympathizing community and who enlisted in a Confederate volunteer unit when the Civil War broke out.

As recently as the civil rights era three decades ago, the differences between the South and the North seemed so glaring that it was easy for Northerners to cluck and grimace at the spectacle of depravity playing out in Selma and Birmingham and Jackson as if it reflected a realm of evil separate and apart. But even then the distinctions had a tendency to melt away. The historian Howard Zinn, who taught at Spelman College in Atlanta during the height of the civil rights era, began his evocation of that time in a book called *The Southern Mystique* with an almost stereotypical Yankee's view of entering a strange land.

> There was something about Georgia, the Carolinas, that marked them off, as with a giant cleaver, from the rest of the nation: the sun was hotter, the soil was redder, the people blacker and whiter, the air sweeter, heavier. But beyond the physical, beyond the strange look and smell of this country, was something more that went back to cotton and slavery, stretching into history as far as anyone could remember—an invisible mist over the entire Deep South, distorting justice, blurring perspective, and, most of all, indissoluble by reason.

But after seven years in Atlanta, he concludes that the South is different only in degree, in style, in the naked and terrible way race plays out there—not in the nature of the problem. Indeed, he finds himself viewing the South not as an aberration, but as "the essence of the nation." The South, he wrote in 1964, in a remarkably prescient passage,

> is not a mutation born by some accident into the normal lovely American family. It has simply taken the national genes and done the most with them. . . . And it may be important, exactly at this moment in our history when the South is going through the early stages of a kind of shock therapy, for the rest of the nation to understand that it stands by not as an administering doctor but as the next patient in line.

Indeed, three decades later, the region outside the South is the sicker patient; furthermore, most of the prescriptions for change are coming from the South, not the North, and they are coming almost exclusively from the right.

There is historical precedent for this. No one alive remembers a time when the South dominated America, so it is easy to forget that this was ever the case. But, of course, the first permanent colony in North America was Jamestown, Virginia, in 1607. Southerners wrote the Declaration of Independence and the Constitution. For forty-nine of the nation's first seventy-two years, more than two thirds of the time until Abraham Lincoln's election, a slaveholding Southerner was president of the United States. During that period, in Congress twenty-three of the thirty-six Speakers of the House and twenty-four of the presidents pro tempore of the senate were Southerners. On the Supreme Court, twenty of the thirty-five justices appointed until 1861 were Southerners.

The secessionist firebrand William Lowndes Yancey may have been more propagandist than historian when he proclaimed on the eve of the Civil War, "As for our history, we have made about all that has glorified the United States." But, now that the dogma of states' rights echoes through Washington like an old alarm clock that suddenly begins ringing after a long silence, it's worth remembering that John C. Calhoun, the South's preeminent political thinker, who lived from 1782–1850 and who framed the states' rights doctrine prior to the Civil War, had a vision of American politics that's startlingly relevant now. Not only did Calhoun, the tall, gaunt, brilliant, humorless son of the South Carolina upcountry near Abbeville, lay the intellectual groundwork for a defense of states' rights and the need to set limits on the power of national majorities and the federal government, he also laid out the strategy for the South's political triumph—knowing full well that secession could light a blaze that would render politics, for a time at least, secondary to force. The historian Richard Hofstadter, among others, has pointed out that Calhoun didn't want the South to leave the Union—he wanted the South to dominate the Union.

Well before the Civil War, Calhoun predicted an alliance between conservative forces in the South and the rest of the country as well as the agrarian interests of the South and the West. His impeccable logic was that the South, united on slavery, increasingly self-conscious as a region forged by myth and folk wisdom, and seeing itself under siege, was being cemented into a unified bloc in a way the North never would be. That's precisely what happened.

It was Southern Democrats and Northern Republicans who stopped the New Deal in its tracks—not to mention the Fair Deal, the New Frontier, and the Great Society. It was Southern Republicans and Northern Republicans who eviscerated Bill Clinton's legislative agenda in the spring of 1994; more than any other factor, the apparent shift of white Southerners from yellow dog Democrats to staunch Republicans created the tidal wave of the 1994 elections.

A perpetual debate goes on about how much of the real South is left—is it still distinctive or is it now just Topeka with more fried food, road kill, heat, and history? At the endless stream of conferences in which scholars and politicos philosophize about the region, John Shelton Reed, the witty sociologist and author from the University of North Carolina, often represents the notion of the enduring South, and Hodding Carter III, the writer and former Carter Administration spokesman, enjoys playing the role of Mr. The-South-Is-Dead. Indeed, it's mostly liberals and writers who don't live there anymore who tend to present the more-Southern-than-thou case that without segregation, one-party politics, and one-crop agriculture, the real South no longer exists. "The South is being etherized," intoned Frady in 1972, in the funereal tones with which the region has been repeatedly interred and reinterred for a century, "subtly rendered pastless, memoryless and vague of identity. What we are talking about is the passing of a sensibility—an event perhaps too wispy to define, but no less seismic.... The old pipe-organ range of prodigal possibilities for life there—both gentle and barbarous, good and evil—has contracted to the comfortable monotone note of middle C."

The South isn't what it was any more than New York is the city of Gene Kelly and Frank Sinatra in sailor suits singing "New York, New York, it's a wonderful town," in *On the Town*. But that utterly misses the point.

Rather than being pastless, the South is a place that at the end of the twentieth century, amazingly, is still fighting most of its oldest battles—over states' rights, the Confederate flag, integration, the meaning of its own history. Rather than memoryless, it's a place where blacks and whites compulsively reenact their separate histories as if to forever reconfirm Faulkner's famous remark that the South is a place where "the past is never dead, it isn't even past." Rather than neutered, it is still the most conservative part of America, still drenched in religion, still carrying the banners of the antebellum Old South states' rights crusades and the New South booster ideology of the 1880s, still in thrall to individualism in its most extravagant sense. Rather than without identity, it's still shaped by the endless sultry summers, voluptuous foliage, and wild, romantic excesses of spring colors and summer monsoons that some historians have cited as the most important factors in molding the identity of the South and creating a worldview at odds with its Northern neighbors.

Back in 1973, John Egerton, who writes from Nashville on the two great Southern verities of race and Southern cooking of the six major food groups—sugar, salt, butter, eggs, cream, and bacon grease—published a book called *The Americanization of Dixie: The Southernization of America*. People remember the first half of the title, but it's in the second half that he was really onto something. Egerton noodled around with the ways the South was disappearing, and good Southern boy that he is, he saw plenty. No one who compares the segregated, largely rural South of just three decades ago and the strip-malled South of Tex-Mex chains, bagel shops, and designer coffee kiosks today could fail to see that the South now is part of a national commercial culture in a way that it never was in the past. But Egerton also envisioned something else, a nation in which the South wasn't merely melting into the national stew but leading in the creation of a new one through a process in which North and South were exchanging not strengths but sins, "exporting vices without importing virtues." Rather than a disappearing South, he saw a "modern, acquisitive, urban, industrial, post-segregationist, on-the-make South...coming back with a bounce in its step, like a new salesman on the route, eager to please, intent on making it."

I'm not sure the transaction is so bleak—it is probably producing a less insular South and a less arrogant North. But where the South remains the most preaching, believing, testifying, proselytizing, evangelizing region of the country when people are looking back for the sense of roots, connections, and history—mythic or real—that the South represents, its success in closing the sale is no surprise.

The nation is too volatile and diverse, its culture too mercurial, to confidently look from any one moment and see a straight road stretching into the future. Less than two years into the 1994 Republican "revolution" of conservative social policy, fiscal conservatism, and power devolving to the states, Newt Gingrich and the Republican Robespierres of 1994 had the look of card players who had overplayed their hand, forgetting that you can capitalize on the throw-the-bums-out spirit of one year and be the new bums in the next. Indeed, it's clear that the one thing most likely to derail the nation's drift to the right in the short run is if the Republicans sing too loudly from the unadulterated Old South hymnal, like their disastrous attempt in 1995 at showing that the South's old game of nullification—or its new variation, shutting down the government—could work as a governing philosophy.

As evidenced by the frantic backtracking at the 1996 Republican

Convention, where the religious right and the Republicans' dubious record on race were stashed out of sight, even some Republicans realize the Revolution of 1994 could turn out to be not a watershed victory, but the South's new Gettysburg, a disastrous incursion too far into enemy territory. After all, on many social issues and in some ways on race, much of the nation has become more liberal while the political culture has lurched to the right. But if the South's conservative revolution shows signs of ebbing, it comes only after three decades of gains that have turned Nixon administration Attorney General John Mitchell's famous boast that "this country is going so far to the right that you won't recognize it" into political reality.

And at a time when a Democratic president like Bill Clinton is coming out for school prayer, going along with sweeping Republican legislation shredding welfare and taking his cues from a consultant, Dick Morris, who formerly worked for Southern arch-conservatives like Jesse Helms and Trent Lott; when race is a fractious national obsession; when the nation's population is moving steadily South; when the Supreme Court is acting as if Jefferson Davis were chief justice; when country music has become white America's music of choice and even stock car racing has become a $2 billion juggernaut; when evangelical Christians have transformed American politics; when unions are on the run across the nation much as they always have been in the South; when whites nationwide are giving up on public education just as so many Southerners did after integration—in times such as these, to understand America, you have to understand the South.

You have to understand how the howls and rebel yells of the Wallace campaign seeped into the nation's soul and exactly what Pat Buchanan was doing bragging about his Confederate ancestors and contributing regularly to one of the contemporary Lost Cause journals still refighting the Civil War. You need to make sense of mythic Southern places like stodgy old Natchez, Mississippi, with its dazzling planters' mansions and endlessly layered choreography of race, and of the odd mix of anywheresville suburban and rock-hard Southern values in places like Cobb County, Georgia, Plano, Texas, or suburban Birmingham. You need to make sense of the bizarre mixture of third-world tin-roof squalor and Las Vegas neon luxury coexisting in the Mississippi Delta; of Charlotte, North Carolina's, Wizard-of-Oz downtown and look-at-me boosterism; of the David Duke posters on weathered barns that pop up like a flashback from a train wreck just when you think the Cajun country around Breaux Bridge, Louisiana, is just about the greatest place in the world; of the evil eye and baleful glare the wary blacks give the rare white boy who wanders into Mosses, Alabama; of the great heart of Atlanta Congressman John Lewis; of Richard in Sweethome, Hobbes, Big Heat, and their front porch cyberchatter on the Internet Bubba list; of the way Patrick Lanzo's proposed Last Chance Beer and Pawn Shop, a nude dance club featuring Klan memorabilia, became the Georgia Peach Museum near Dallas, Georgia.

Maybe you don't need to make sense of Three States, the rural hamlet, which produced the fabulous Brown family—the late brothers Thester and Lester and Thester's son Chester—which staggers around the point on the map where Arkansas, Louisiana, and Texas intersect in the heart of the Ark-La-Tex region. You probably shouldn't worry too much about figuring out Helen, the supremely stupid ersatz German village plopped into the North Georgia mountains; or the towns of Nail, Yale Ben Hur, Oil Trough, or Egypt in the lonely Ozark reaches of northern Arkansas. The future of the country may not rest on fully comprehending the 1996 gathering of Christian nudists in Ocean City, North Carolina, or just what Joe Buddy Caine and Junior Bright had in mind when they decided to play the game of rattlesnake catch that left Joe Buddy dead of snakebites and Junior hospitalized in Anniston, Alabama, in September 1995.

But surely you would need to try to make sense of the insane jumble of progress and stagnation that is the South three decades after the civil rights revolution petered out. Indeed, there's probably no better place to start trying to understand race in America than to make sense of the utterly unexpected way the civil rights revolution turned out to be the best thing that ever happened to the white South, paving the way for the region's newfound prosperity, but a mixed blessing for Southern blacks, who won a measure of integration into a white world at the expense of some of the enduring and nurturing institutions of their old black one.

This book is both journalistic—because I've spent most of my adult life writing about the South for *The Dallas Morning News, Texas Monthly* magazine, and *The New York Times*—and personal, because in very conflicted ways what has happened to the country feels like what has happened to me. I'm not a native Southerner, but like a lot of people I wandered down here thinking of it as an interesting detour and ended up living here for most of my life. If it were up to me, I wouldn't leave.

Along the way I've eaten chow mein with David Duke, checked out Lester Maddox's tape deck (lots of Liberace and Lawrence Welk), and toured the Elvis-A-Rama in Branson, Missouri, the Cyclorama in Atlanta, and the Confederama in Chattanooga (which has since inexplicably been renamed The Battle for Chattanooga Museum). I've communed with people who found Jesus in a Pizza Hut sign and have done my best to digest both *Southern Partisan* magazine's collection of Confederate homages, *So Good a Cause,* and the epochal, unknown Dixiephobic screed, *How the South Finally Won the Civil War–and Controls the Political Future of the United States,* by Charles Potts, a real-estate broker, poet, toastmaster, and amateur historian from Walla Walla, Washington. I married a woman from Louisiana whose Great-aunt Linda (sister of her grandfather Daddy Boy) was married to Mississippi's infamous pot-bellied, jug-eared bigot, Senator Theodore Bilbo, giving me a branch on the outermost tendrils of my family tree whose existence I could not have imagined in a zillion years.

I'm not claiming any of that makes me a real Southerner, although at a time when two Yankees ran in 1994 for governor of Tennessee, Southern political powers like Newt Gingrich and Dick Armey aren't native Southerners, and country music stars are coming from places like Windsor, Ontario, and Princeton, New Jersey, it's no longer very clear exactly what a real Southerner is. Instead, my history has made me something of a schizophrenic, someone who thinks he's a Yankee but hasn't lived in the North for twenty-one years, doesn't want to go back, and has come to the point where Southerners look normal and Yankees seem weirdly out of touch–among them, people who actually thought Michael Dukakis could be elected president of the United States.

Out of habit or ancestral loyalties, I still vote Democratic and root for the Celtics and the San Francisco/New York Giants of the world of my father and grandfather. I hate football. I find stock-car racing unfathomable. I don't have a bass boat, a pickup, a gun, or a taste for bourbon. I've never read *Gone with the Wind* and fell asleep the only time I went to the movie. I don't even root for the Atlanta Braves. But, like countless people before me, I know I've been seduced. The weather is warmer, the people nicer, the traffic milder (well, don't hold me to this one), the prices lower, the pace of life saner, the greenery lusher, the history richer. Even the race relations are better.

I do not approach the fervor of the late Southern humorist and savant Brother Dave Gardner, who once allowed: "I love everything about the South; I even love hate." But when I trek out to the Civil War battlefields at Kennesaw or Vicksburg or Chickamauga with my nine-year-old son, Ben, or when my six-year-old daughter, Emma, and I dance around to Dwight Yoakam's "A Thousand Miles from Nowhere," or any of the other slick, suburban country music that Nashville cranks out these days, capturing the mood of the moment as the Brill Building in New York or Motown in Detroit captured the mood of a time long ago, the North seems a thousand miles from nowhere and the South feels like America.

This book doesn't pretend to be one of those encyclopedic attempts to stop for an RC Cola and Moon Pie and pick up country witticisms at every truck stop and boiled-peanut stand along the road. And it makes no pretense of capturing all the diversity of a region that, most broadly defined, encompasses El Paso and Miami, the bluegrass country and coal hollows of Kentucky, the yuppie suburbs of northern Virginia and the Cajun-Mediterranean insane asylum that is New Orleans. Instead, I've chosen to roam in the crevices and around the edges of the belly of the beast, the Deep South and Upper South from the Carolina Piedmont to the Mississippi Gulf Coast. The chapters attempt to evoke a place and an idea that says something about the region and, usually, something about the nation as well: the burgeoning suburban South of Newt Gingrich's home turf in Cobb County, Georgia; the mixed legacy of the civil rights movement in Selma, Alabama; the New South booster ethos of Charlotte, North Carolina; the startling nostalgia blacks have for the segregated schools of the 1950s in Wilmington, North Carolina; the new Tin Pan Alley of Nashville; the overheated combination of cottonfield gambling palaces, Elvis cultists, and hard-right politics that is Mississippi.

Ultimately, this book is an attempt to make sense of what the South's ascendance says about America and to figure out what kind of a place this South is, anyway. The South of Jimmy Carter or of Newt Gingrich? The South that elects more blacks to office than anywhere else in America or the South that elects so many of them from places where they have more political power and less economic opportunity than anywhere else in America? The South where Atlanta managed to put on the ultimate show of the South's renaissance–the 1996 Olympics– largely by selling itself and the contemporary South as a model of inter- racial harmony or the South where black churches were being torched by arsonists with terrifying frequency, like a macabre nightmare from the past? The South that, for my tastes, still elects all the wrong people for all the wrong reasons or the South where I've lived for half my life, where my kids were born, where I'd just as soon stay, the South that feels like home?

Looked at one way, it's a place of grace and faith that has purged most of its old sins while maintaining most of its old virtues, a place that for all its bloody past and the ambiguities and unresolved issues of the present offers the nation's best blueprint for racial peace. Looked at another way, it's a Potemkin Village of mirrors and trap doors, where old inequities are cloaked in new forms, a chameleon South changed only on the surface, now pumping old poisons into new veins, a place where even in the most neutered suburbs, what was still lives, beating insistently away like Poe's telltale heart.

Once when I was driving through the Florida panhandle, I stopped to check out the roadside artistry at a squat yellow tourist emporium with two signs out front. One read FACTORY OUTLET, CONCRETE SOU- VENIRS. The other read BUMBLE BEE REALTY. Gold streamers glistened in the wind and United States and Georgia flags hung out front. True, this was Florida, but the proprietors obviously figured that they got more bang for their buck with the Georgia flag with its gaudy Confederate Battle Flag design than they would with the more prosaic Florida one, featuring the more muted Confederate design of a red Saint Andrew's cross and the state seal against a white background.

The wares consisted of concrete yard art without end–revolting flying-bulldog gargoyles with spiked collars; sated nymphs; stern Indian chiefs; flamingos, dolphins, and seahorses; three-foot-tall cowgirls with long blond hair; sweet-faced seraphim; happy Buddhas and coiled dragons from the inscrutable East; handy funeral urns; trusty old black Sambos chowing down on watermelon and faithful black lawn jockeys ever ready to guard your Bermuda grass against unseen evil; jaunty derby-wearing Irish frogs, raffish stud-muffin frogs leaning seductively on their elbows, miserable frogs huddled on park benches looking as if they were about to be boiled alive. They don't call the panhandle L.A.– Lower Alabama–for nothing.

But drive on for a few miles and you're in the relentlessly tasteful *Architectural Digest* dreamland of Seaside, the instant Dixie Cape Cod of cobblestone streets, white picket fences, widow's walks, langorous front porches, and New England cottages in Bermuda pastel shades of pink, yellow, and blue where platoons of Atlanta lawyers and squadrons of Birmingham doctors' wives alight each summer to eat designer corn chips with peach melba salsa, drink piña coladas, and take seaside yoga classes. In the South these days, it always helps not to be too sure you know where you are.

"Southerners are very aggressive about their beliefs; it's almost like war with them," Diane Lacock was saying back at the concrete souvenir stand, where she was the salesperson on duty. "No wonder they're taking over everything." Thirteen years ago, her uncle, Robert Russell, an anthropologist and herbalist, came down from New York. Though he had always complained about the Southern politicians, he never left. Instead, after discerning that the family's genetic weakness was in the liver, he spent much of his time enjoying the sun and beach and concocting vitamin and herb combinations.

When he died in 1995 at the age of seventy, Diane came down from Colorado to settle his estate but soon moved into his yellow-pine house in the woods, where she listens to the cardinals and blue jays and orioles and smells the magnolia perfume and figures she'll leave someday– but then again, maybe not. "They'll probably convert us all or get all of us down here before it's over," she said and trundled off to the wholly owned subsidiary next door that sells campers and trailers, where the sign out front reads GOD IS THE CALM IN OUR STORM.

We all need a calm in our storm, divine or otherwise. In ways both real and illusory, the South these days seems to promise one. It offers a sense of history, roots, place, and community when the nation desperately is seeking all four. It has a bedrock of belief–religious, cultural, political, and racial–that has enormous power and appeal at a time of national drift and confusion. It is the purest kernel of conservative values and politics in a conservative era it has largely created. The South's golden moment has so often been glimpsed or predicted, only to recede like a mirage, that only a fool could look around now and say the South's time had incontrovertibly arrived, now and forever, amen. "It's America's will-o'-the-wisp Eden," a skeptical historian once said.

Still, there was another gathering in downtown Atlanta a year after the Baptists encamped that made a rather resounding statement about the South's new prominence in American and international life. In the end, the 1996 Olympics turned out to be a lot like the South, at turns glorious and tawdry, full of moments of soulful inspiration and searing tragedy. At their most bombastic, the games reflected the overreach of Southern boosterism run amuck. But for all the corporate clutter and commercial overkill, they also reflected the weird degree to which the South reborn was still the South. The most affecting moment of the whole two-week extravaganza didn't involve gymnastics or swimming or sprinting. It came on the Tuesday morning when Centennial Olympic Park reopened after the pipe bomb attack that killed one person and injured 111 others. Without a word of introduction, a lone black man walked to the middle of the huge Olympic stage. It was Wynton Marsalis, the great New Orleans trumpeter. He lifted his trumpet to his lips and in a mighty whisper and a gentle roar, he played the old hymn "Nearer My God to Thee"—"Just a closer walk with thee/Precious Jesus hear my plea"—in a New Orleans jazz funeral for the world. Beyond the quiet pathos of the moment and the noisy clamor of the rest of the games was a simple truth: risen again, the South had turned out to be not America's insular kingdom of the eccentric, forlorn, or exotic, but a place that had managed to maintain its identity while also putting its fingerprints on almost every aspect of the nation's soul, from race, to politics, to culture, to values.

"Southerners can never resist a losing cause," Margaret Mitchell once said. The question now is what they're making of a winning one.

Chapter 2

COBB COUNTY, GEORGIA
Newtland

K ENNESAW MOUNTAIN IS A HUMPBACKED RIDGE ABOUT TWO MILES long and seven hundred feet high that rises in Cobb County, Georgia, like a natural citadel between the mountains of north Georgia and the fine, green Southern metropolis of Atlanta. When William Tecumseh Sherman, the high-strung, leather-faced, motor-mouthed Union general, first pondered its modest grandeur in June 1864, he cabled to Washington: "Kennesaw is the key to the whole country." He was talking about the likelihood that he would face a Confederate stand at Kennesaw before getting his chance to fight, march, and burn his way through Atlanta, but metaphorically, maybe Uncle Billy, as the blue-clad Yankee reenactors always call their commander at the Civil War reenactments, was onto something else, too.

In fact, when Newt Gingrich comes home to orate to the adoring masses at the Cobb County Republican party breakfast at Vittle's restaurant, down the road in Marietta, when I drive around the spanking new subdivisions popping out of the red Georgia hills, when I check out the mix of Civil War memorabilia and neo-Nazi literature at Wildman's Civil War Surplus next door to the friendly all-American Big Shanty Cafe on Main Street in the town of Kennesaw, at the foot of the mountain, I often find myself thinking of Sherman's remark, like a bad song you can't get out of your head. By any measure—politics, culture, demographics, the city of Kennesaw and Cobb County look a lot like what America is coming to. Where that brings us is another question entirely.

To the Southern expatriates swapping lies over expensive bourbon in bars in Manhattan, Cobb County is to the real South as Kenny G is to real jazz, a limp, shriveled dessicated version of the genuine item too pale, pathetic, and lame to even bear serious comparison. With its expanses of glitzy malls and mirrored-glass office parks, its endless subdivisions sprouting from the bulldozed remains of pine and hardwood forest, its Anywhere U.S.A. corporate iconography of Bennigan's and Blockbuster Videos and Taco Bells, its F-15 Eagles screaming overhead on training flights from Dobbins Air Reserve Base, Cobb County is exhibit A for the case for the South's death by bleaching. But Flannery O'Connor, perhaps the foremost chronicler of an archgothic South drenched in sin and redemption, knew better when she said the identity of the South is "not really connected with mocking-birds and beaten biscuits and white columns anymore than it is with hookworm and bare feet and muddy clay roads. . . . It is not made from what passes, but from those qualities that endure." For all the changes in Cobb, the qualities that have endured in the end count for more than those that have passed.

The phrase "New South" may be the most overused and meaningless regional designation on the American landscape. When introduced during the 1880s by the Atlanta newspaper editor and regional promoter Henry Grady, it denoted a South eager to move on after the Civil War, a South that was seeking Northern investment and capital by offering up a let-bygones-be-bygones view of the "late unpleasantness" in the interest of economic progress. Grady's vision was based on the idea that Southerners would gladly provide cheap labor for Northern capitalists as long as the Yankees would pretty much let the South do what it wanted about race, a deal that turned out to be just fine with the North. Over time, the term has come to be used as an all-purpose, slightly condescending designation of approval, denoting a South where people don't go barefoot, don't join the Klan, don't go around lynching people. It's enough of an empty cliché that the novelist Walker Percy once groused, "My definition of a new South would be a South in which it never occurred to anybody to mention the New South."

Cobb is not the South that was, but it isn't that vaguely idealized New South either. It's the South of Gingrich's pugnacious sound bites, not Jimmy Carter's peanut country drawl; of white wine, not bourbon and branch water; of tidy air-conditioned suburban churches, not hardshell backwoods ones; of the gladiolus gardens and lemon meringue torte recipes in *Southern Living* magazine, and Newt-clone suburban Republicans with look-alike helmets of hair. It's the South of Chevrolet Suburbans with Christian fish symbols and of Chevy pickups with PRAISE THE LORD written in lacy script above the grille and where the bumper stickers in the mall parking lots read, RUSH IS RIGHT, VOTE CON-FEDERATE, and IMPEACH CLINTON AND HER HUSBAND TOO. Oddly, it's a new suburban South where blacks and whites don't have the proximity to each other that defined the South even during segregation; its an odd amalgam of the racial context of the North and the history and mores of the South. And it's one where for all its generic suburban qualities, history travels in a remarkably consistent straight line from one era's battles over culture and race to another's.

Cobb County usually hits the news as an example of what once passed for right-wing nuttery and now increasingly seems like main-stream politics and culture. In 1982, the town of Kennesaw briefly became famous when, in response to a gun control law in Morton Grove, Illinois, it passed an ordinance *requiring* every householder to own a gun. That the mayor walked around with a gold name tag depicting a brace of pistols, the pastor of the Gospel Light Baptist Church owned five guns himself, and the town's most conspicuous business was Dent Myers's shop trafficking in Civil War memorabilia and white-supremacist Klan and neo-Nazi literature only helped add to the notoriety.

There was an even bigger moment in 1993, when the Cobb County Commission passed a resolution condemning the "gay lifestyle" as incompatible with community standards, a resolution that led the Olympics to pull its volleyball competition out of Cobb and put Cobb, quite happily, in the front line of a national antigay backlash.

Cobb at times may sound like a goofball outpost of mossbacks and Neanderthals, but in reality it turns out to be the perfect distillation of the two trends driving American demography. The first is suburbaniza-tion. The second is Southernization. The 1990 census showed that for the first time there were more Americans living in suburbs than in either rural areas or cities. Between 1980 and 1990, the South's popula-tion grew by 21 percent, or twice the nation's growth rate. That repre-sented 10 million additional residents, or almost half the nation's total population growth. Cobb County alone has grown from 196,793 residents in 1970 to more than 500,000 in 1996. Between 1980 and 1990 it grew by 50.4 percent, compared to 9.8 percent for the nation.

Until his death in 1983, the man who represented much of the county in Congress was Dr. Larry McDonald, a Democrat and the former national head of the John Birch Society. McDonald, whose name graces the stretch of Interstate 75 that runs through the county, gained a reputation as the quintessential, out-of-the-loop crank in Congress. He spent much of his time reading archconservative tracts into the Congressional Record back in the pre-C-Span era, when it didn't make any difference, and once joked at a John Birch Society meeting that homosexuals should be assessed a "user's fee" to pay for AIDS research. In his medical practice as a urologist he was an enthusiastic booster of laetrile as a cure for cancer. To this day, his death, which occurred when a Soviet fighter jet shot down Korean Airlines flight 007 with himself and 268 other persons on board, is still viewed by some on the right as part of a plot by a hushed-up, Soviet Union–led one-world-government cabal. Now most of Cobb County is represented in Congress by none other than Newt Gingrich, architect of the Republican takeover of Congress in 1994. Make of that what you will.

Gingrich likes to cite Cobb County as an entrepreneurial, technologically savvy model for a Republican America of economic prosperity and conservative values. Mark Gibbs, a thirty-nine-year-old home builder and construction supervisor with sleepy eyes, thick dark hair, a soft, measured voice, and the disarming sincerity of an earnest young preacher, doesn't think much in political terms, but in his own way he shares Gingrich's vision of Cobb County as a special place. In fact, he believes that God brought him by design to the greatest place in America to live his life, raise his family, and do God's work.

Gibbs doesn't know for sure why the Lord led him to Cobb County, but he knows when his life changed forever. It was the Sunday morning in 1988 when his twenty-nine-year-old wife, Kim, suddenly collapsed in a grand mal seizure on the bedroom floor of their rented Cape Cod cottage on Granny White Pike in Nashville, her eyes rolling around back in her head like marbles, her teeth clenched so hard she almost bit his thumb off, her blond hair flying and body convulsing like an electric current was running through it. One minute she had handed him a diaper as he stood by their nine-month-old baby, Alyssa, as they were getting ready to go to church. The next he felt her body fall against his leg as if she'd been struck by lightning. When the convulsing stopped, he laid her limp body out like a pancake on the tan carpet, without the slightest idea whether she was likely to live, and waited for the E.M.T.s, who arrived a few minutes later.

Before long they managed to bring her to the outer edges of lucidity. One of them pointed to Mark and asked Kim who he was. She stared blankly at him, shook her head, and mumbled that she didn't know. He broke out in tears, and all he could think was, "Here I am with a nine-month-old baby and a wife who doesn't know who I am."

But during the twenty-five-minute ambulance drive to Vanderbilt University Hospital, his thoughts turned from terror to prayer. He acknowledged his helplessness before God and beseeched Him over and over to heal his wife. After filling out the insurance forms and paperwork at the hospital, he made his way to the small hospital chapel. "If you'll heal my wife, I will be yours; I'll accept you as my Lord," he prayed, and a few minutes later was ushered into his wife's room. She burst into tears of recognition, he did too, and his life was never the same again.

He doesn't necessarily think of that moment every Sunday at the Mount Paran Church of God, where he joins almost three thousand worshipers in a shiny new mall-like sanctuary whose amphitheaterlike design features klieg lights, bare white walls and TV monitors poking out of every corner. But it's never too far from his mind as the pivotal moment in his life, the moment he accepted Jesus Christ into his life. And he knows that all the blessings in his life—a wonderful wife and two great kids, a growing real estate business in the most prosperous part of the South, a life filled with faith and good friends and with love—stem from that decision.

It's a very Southern story, one of redemption through faith, in a region where there was a solid religious South before there was a solid political one. "The South is by a long way the most simply and sincerely religious country that I ever was in," the Englishman Sir William Archer wrote near the beginning of this century. "It is a country in which religion is a very large factor in life, and God is very real and personal." About sixty years later, H. Louis Patrick, the minister of Trinity Presbyterian Church in Charlotte, North Carolina, writing in the *Forum for Contemporary History,* updated the same idea. "Religion is what really makes and keeps the South a separate, solid and stable culture," he wrote. "The New South does not exist. And as long as the religion of the Southern Protestant Church remains what it is, nothing new will be conceived in, or issue from, the Southern womb."

Religion is as much a part of Southern life now as it was then, but Mark Gibbs is an unlikely person to represent it. Born in Philadelphia, raised in Chicago by a Presbyterian father who never went to church and a Catholic mother who went only on Christmas and Easter, Mark Gibbs grew up as far from charismatic Christianity and the red-hot fevers of Bible Belt faith as one could be. He couldn't care less about the Confederate flag or Deep South history, but he has lived half his life in the South, his kids share the soft Georgia inflections of their mother, who drives them home from church in the family's green Ford Explorer van, and, though he doesn't have the popular bumper sticker SOUTHERN BY THE GRACE OF GOD on the back of his car, he believes the phrase is true in the most literal sense.

Cobb County's Georgia red clay soil and hardwood and pine forests sit at a transitional geographical region where the North Georgia mountains meet the Carolina Piedmont. Its first inhabitants were the Creek Indians and then the Cherokee, who roamed its rolling foothills, lush valleys, rocky slopes, and the streams and tributaries of the Chattahoochee River and whose villages became important trading posts. They left behind the Indian names that still define the area's towns and streams–Kennesaw, Allatoona, Nickajack–but they weren't allowed to leave much else. Largely because of gold fever sweeping the South after it was found in the Carolinas, President Andrew Jackson ordered the Indians off the land six years after the county was formed in 1832. Soon the Cherokee were on their way to Oklahoma along the "Trail of Tears" and the Indian land was awarded to lucky settlers by lottery. The gold fever in Georgia came to naught, and the settlers created a culture of small farms rather than the plantations of the Black Belt to the south, in Georgia, Louisiana, Alabama, and Mississippi.

The county's first major moment in American history came in the Civil War, when William Tecumseh Sherman, marching south from Tennessee with a hundred thousand men and 254 pieces of artillery, realized that if he wanted to get to Atlanta, the manufacturing and rail center of the Confederacy and the path to burning, raping, and pillaging his way through the South's interior, it looked like he would have to somehow take Kennesaw Mountain. In the 100-degree heat of June 27, 1864, about three thousand Union soldiers and one thousand Confederates lost their lives finding out whether he could do it.

The Battle of Kennesaw Mountain, Sherman's worst defeat in the Atlanta campaign, was one of the basic slaughters of a war that set a new standard for the use of humans as cannon fodder. This was not a subject that Sherman seemed unduly torn up about. Amid the merriment of the Atlanta campaign, he dashed off a missive to his wife saying, "I begin to regard the death and mangling of a couple thousand men as a small affair, a kind of morning dash."

Like much of the war, Kennesaw Mountain was pretty straightforward, very bloody, and in the end utterly pointless. Still, the battle, short as it was, had a remarkable amount of the routine drama, pathos, eloquence, stupidity, courage, and irony that makes thousands of grown men collect Southern Blood Comic Books ("the first and only historically accurate Civil War comic series ever created") or cough up $410 for a Richmond Armory musket or $92.50 for a plain vanilla, seven-button Confederate economy frock coat or sleep in the mud so they can get up and reenact Civil War battles.

Throughout the war, the farm boys from Illinois, New York, and Ohio found ample reason to remember how much they had in common with their peers from Georgia, Arkansas, and Texas, and Kennesaw Mountain was no exception. At one point, as John Newton's IV Corps of Union soldiers was attacking one of Patrick Cleburne's Arkansas regiments, scores of injured Yankees lay unattended as the battle roared around them at the foot of the mountain. In the midst of the battle, gunfire ignited the underbrush, and a grass fire flared up, fatally burning some of the wounded and threatening to catch some others. Suddenly, the Confederate firing stopped and their commander, Lieutenant Colonel William H. Martin, commander of the consolidated 1st and 15th Arkansas regiments, called for a truce while the wounded could be taken away and the fire put out. While the battle raged along the rest of the line, men in blue from Illinois and in gray and butternut from Arkansas stamped out the fire and carried the wounded back behind the Union lines. After the area was cleared a Union major gave Martin a pair of matched Colt revolvers as a token of respect and appreciation and the men retreated to their lines and then went back to the humdrum routine of killing each other.

The worst fighting occurred at a place called the "Dead Angle," where Union troops advanced up six hundred yards of rocky slope and then across an open field in one of the war's classic doomed slaughters, much like Pickett's charge at Gettysburg. The Union forces lost nearly 1,800 men there in less than half an hour. Two days later, the stench of the dead and dying was so sickening that both sides called another seven-hour truce, during which men in blue and gray dragged the bloated, rotting, stinking corpses into deep trenches. While the work continued, the soldiers on both sides traded coffee and tobacco and amiably compared notes on the battle and the war. Some of the Union soldiers clambered around to Confederate General Benjamin Franklin Cheatham to get the autograph of the man who commanded the rebel forces at the Dead Angle.

In the end, none of it made a rat's ass of difference to the course of the war. Even before the battle began, the Union general, John M. Schofield, had established a position beyond the Confederates' southern flank. Instead of fighting his way over Kennesaw Mountain, Sherman only had to go around it. The Confederates, after tenaciously holding Kennesaw for two weeks, turned around and left it behind like a spent cartridge. Then they fell back closer to Atlanta, near the tail end of the four-month-long series of engagements and flanking movements that eventually gave the world the burning of Atlanta, Sherman's famous March to the Sea, *Gone With the Wind,* and a 1992 casting call in which 410 would-be Scarletts–black Scarletts and white Scarletts, fat and thin Scarletts, Scarletts from the Bronx and Scarletts from the sticks–gathered in Atlanta to try out for the lead role in the TV movie of Alexandra Ripley's lame sequel, *Scarlett.*

A half century after the battle of Kennesaw Mountain, Cobb County became even more famous. It was here that one Mary Phagan was born on a tenant farm outside Marietta in 1900 and was buried thirteen years later after being beaten and choked to death at the National Pencil Factory in Atlanta on Confederate Memorial Day, April 26, 1913. Southerners in increasing numbers were beginning to migrate from farms to cities to work in the mills and factories, and there was a widespread fear that the social fabric and traditional values were being cast aside in the process. Children worked sixty-six-hour weeks, crime and disease were rampant, and people feared that all the values they had grown up with were under assault by forces beyond their control. The murder of Mary

Phagan would have plugged in to all those fears even if the man arrested and charged with the crime had not been Leo Frank, the twenty-nine-year-old Jewish superintendent of the plant where she worked. Amid anti-Jewish hysteria, Frank, who was raised in New York, educated at Pratt Institute and Cornell University, and was pale and thin with bulging eyes and a nervous demeanor, was charged with her murder. He was soon convicted and sentenced to death by jurors who heard the crowd outside through the open courthouse windows chanting, "Hang the Jew."

Three quarters of a century later the case remains a tantalizing riddle. There is enough circumstantial evidence pointing to Frank to indicate that he could conceivably have done it. But the most damning testimony against him came from a black sweeper named Jim Conley, who repeatedly changed his story to police and was identified in a 1982 affadavit as the man who carried Phagan's limp body into the factory cellar, where it was later discovered. Most experts on the case believe the preponderance of evidence points to Conley, who at twenty-nine already had a lengthy arrest record, as the more likely killer. At the time the evidence was so ambiguous and the testimony against Frank so suspect that Governor John Slaton, convinced that Frank was innocent, commuted the sentence to life in prison, thus ensuring his own political doom with the stroke of his pen. Two years later, on August 16, 1915, with hysteria about the case still hanging in the moist summer air, at least five model Ts loaded with perhaps twenty-five armed men set out from Marietta at dusk and headed through cottonfields over dirt roads toward the prison, 175 miles away, where Frank was held.

Rather than the rabble of lynch-mob lore, they included many of the most respected citizens in town, including a clergyman, two former superior court justices, and a former sheriff. They set out by different routes so as not to draw undue attention, and cut telephone and telegraph wires leading to the prison. When they arrived, they overpowered guards sleeping on the porch, carried Frank, still in his nightclothes, to the backseat of one of the cars, and drove him back to Marietta, with the intention of carrying out the sentence the state had failed to.

On the way, Frank convinced some of his abductors that he really was innocent, and a debate broke out about just what should be done. In the end the abductors would not be swayed. Frank was blindfolded, marched to an oak tree not far from the gin house of former Cobb County Sheriff W. J. Frey, and told to stand on a table. A manila rope fashioned into a hangman's noose was tied around his neck, the table was kicked out from under him, and the deed was done.

The body, a blindfold over the face, the bare feet manacled together, swayed in the hot summer breeze for more than two hours as over six thousand people turned out to gawk, take in the festivities, and be photographed in front of the body. Some snipped off bits of Frank's nightshirt as a keepsake of the grand occasion. Others made off with pieces of the rope. Still, despite at least one man's efforts to mutilate the body, the citizenry's behavior met the standards of the *Marietta Journal and Courier*, which reported approvingly: "We are proud, indeed, to say that the body hanged for more than two hours amid a vast throng and no violence was done. Cobb County people are civilized. They are not barbarians."

For years, picture postcards of the body hanging from the tree were a hot-selling souvenir item in Marietta stores. It was one of the most infamous cases of anti-Semitism in American history, a case that was credited with reviving the Klan and sparking the founding of the Anti-Defamation League of B'nai B'rith. Frank was posthumously pardoned in 1986, but not before the original pardon request in 1982 brought out two hundred robed Klansmen and jackbooted Nazis to Mary Phagan's grave in Marietta for a protest rally and white rights gathering.

Cobb's most important moment wasn't either of these events, however. In 1941, the county purchased six hundred acres of land with the idea that it would build a municipal airport to rival what is now Harts-field Airport in Atlanta. In 1943, the Bell Aircraft Company leased the land to assemble B-29 bombers for the war effort and Cobb was never the same again. Defense spending helped create much of the modern South, and in Cobb County, the decision to assemble the B-29s there began its transformation from a farming community to a suburban area. Some 29,000 workers were needed at the plant, but Marietta was a city of less than 10,000 people. Most of those who came to work at the plant stayed in Cobb County. The Bell plant closed in 1946, but five years later, what was then the Lockheed Aircraft Company took over the same facility to modify the B-29 for the Korean War. Lockheed and the adjacent Dobbins Air Reserve Base have been the county's biggest employers ever since, and one of the most dramatic examples of how defense dollars increasingly have come to the South. At its peak at the end of the Vietnam era, Lockheed employed 33,000 people. With Pentagon cutbacks and corporate downsizing, employment has since dropped below 10,000. But the company, now Lockheed Martin Aeronautical Systems Company, a division of the $30-billion Lockheed Martin Corporation, remains one of the big winners in the shrinking defense industry. In 1991, it was awarded a third of the $70-billion contract to design the Air Force's F-22 advanced tactical fighter and also produces giant C-130J transport planes and P-3 maritime patrol planes. While defense plants like Lockheed's old factory in Burbank, California, or the Grumman Corporation plant that was once the biggest employer on Long Island, New York, have closed, defense spending increasingly has moved South. As is happening with manufacturing jobs in general, defense weapons dollars have shifted to states like Georgia, Louisiana, Florida, Mississippi, and Colorado, states offering cheaper wages, fewer unions, and less regulation. As a result, the Southeast and Rocky Mountain states have doubled their share of federal weapons dollars since 1976 while the Northeast and Pacific Coast have lost 15 percent or more. Lockheed no longer dominates the Cobb economy to the extent it once did. Still, as a gorgeous, glossy history of the county written for the fiftieth anniversary in 1992 of the Cobb County Chamber of Commerce puts it, in a sentence that may have been written by a weapons designer, "Lockheed is immersed in and permeates every facet of life in Cobb, working and caring with unparalleled largeness."

But people come to Cobb County for more than a chance to build airplanes. During the 1950s and 1960s, when integration came to Georgia, Cobb became Atlanta's prime white-flight suburb, a place which to the point of monomania defined itself as being whatever Atlanta, increasingly black, was not. During the era of segregation, Cobb had a substantial black population, most of them descendants of the 3,819 slaves enumerated in the 1860 census. As recently as 1930, its population was 18 percent black. But from 1950 to 1970, when its population swelled with whites fleeing Atlanta, blacks accounted for just 2 percent of Cobb's growth.

After a hundred years of sharing everything from trolley lines to water mains with Atlanta, after integration Cobb did everything it could to define itself as a world apart, becoming ever whiter, whereas the growth of other suburban counties like De Kalb County included large numbers of blacks as well as whites. When other area suburban counties joined the regional transportation authority, Cobb refused, largely because of fears that mass transit would make it easier for blacks to come to Cobb. One former Cobb County commissioner, Emmett Burton, said he "would stock the Chattahoochee with piranha" to keep rapid transit out. Joe Mack Wilson, a state representative who later became the mayor of Marietta, said in 1975 of the Chattahoochee, which separates Cobb from Atlanta: "They love that river down there [in Cobb]. They want to keep it as a moat. They wish they could build forts across there to keep people from coming up here." No one had to ask which people he was talking about.

During integration Cobb was a hotbed of Klan activity, with cross burnings and firebombings directed at blacks; its racial environment has continued to be so hostile that when Cobb got its first black dentist, Dr. Arva Lumpkin, in 1987, the headline in the Atlanta *Constitution* read: COBB'S FIRST BLACK DENTIST: MOVE TOOK NERVE. As late as 1986 the county had a single black doctor. Racial change has been slow, hard, and minimal, from school integration to hiring black teachers to the seven-year struggle that was needed to form a modest Cobb County Community Relations Council to air racial issues. Even today, two thirds of blacks seeking housing in Cobb County receive different information and get different treatment than whites, according to Joe Shifalo, executive director of Metro Fair Housing, which monitors housing discrimination in the Atlanta area. "If it were still legal to pass a referendum against black folks, Cobb County might do it," he said.

Of course, Cobb is not a monolith. For years the traditional breakdown has been "east of the chicken" or "west of the chicken," the bird in question being the big chicken, the fifty-six-foot-high metal rooster S. R. "Tubby" Davis built in 1963 to promote his Johnny Reb's Chick-Chuck-'N'-Shake restaurant on Highway 41 at Roswell Road, where you could get a three-piece box plus potatoes, slaw, and a dinner roll for a dollar or a pint of chicken gizzards for sixty-five cents. The original design was for a technological marvel with a beak that opened and shut and a comb that dipped in the breeze. When the magic moment came for the motor to be turned on for the first time, the building shook, the tables rattled, and all the windows in the restaurant shattered, so instead the chicken has stood proud and regal but immobile ever since.

Predictably, Johnny Reb's turned into a Kentucky Fried Chicken franchise. The monumental chicken out front was stripped down and rebuilt in 1993 after three decades of wind, rain, and pigeon droppings had rusted out its steel frame, but it still remains Cobb's most distinctive landmark and essential compass point. "West of the chicken" traditionally meant pickups with gun racks, old Marietta, Dobbins and Lockheed, and rock-ribbed conservatism. "East of the chicken" meant new cul-de-sac subdivisions, Saabs and BMWs, and the corporate transplants and endless sprawl of state-of-the-art suburbia. To some degree the distinction still means something. But as East Cobb has begun to run out of developable real estate, developers are increasingly building west and north in the county, making the east-west breakdown less definitive. And, though they sometimes fight different battles and affect different styles, there's not much that the west Cobb pickups and the east Cobb Beemers don't agree on these days. In addition, the south end of the county across from Atlanta increasingly attracts not just blacks but Hispanics and Asians to low-rise apartments.

Mark Gibbs and I met at his office at the rear of the Chastain Center office park, a typical low-slung suburban development about twenty-three miles north of downtown Atlanta off Interstate 75. The room was full of rolled-up architectural drawings and plat maps and on the wall next to his desk were various plaques and mementos, including a picture of the first house he built, the first dollar bill he earned, and a passage from Psalms: "Unless the Lord builds the house, those who build it labor in vain." Prominently displayed was a trade magazine ad with the headline NEVER GLIB, GIBBS, and copy reading "Mark Gibbs, President of Oakley Homes, knows the importance of adjustable cabinet shelves, hidden hinges, and just as importantly...relationships." The seven promises from Promise Keepers, the Christian Men's group he participates in, hung nearby.

Like most immigrants, Gibbs came South for economic reasons and soon found himself pinballing around a world circumscribed by the hot growth markets below the Mason-Dixon Line. By osmosis and by marriage, he got Southernized in the process. After graduating from the University of Illinois in 1978, he went to Houston, where the action was in the middle stages of the oil boom. His degree was in civil engineering, but while working as an engineer he began studying real estate and working toward an M.B.A. In 1983 he went to work for Gemcraft

Homes, one of the most aggressive home builders during the boom, which thudded to bankruptcy a few years later when Houston's boom went bust. Before that happened, he went to work for a developer and builder named Ken Berg, who in 1985 sent him to check out development possibilities in Atlanta. He stayed only a year, but during that time he met Kim, while both were on blind dates with someone else. A year to the day after they met, they were married in the church her family had gone to since she was a girl.

After Berg, he went to work in 1988 for the nation's biggest developer, the Trammell Crow company, first in Nashville, then in Atlanta. When he hit Atlanta the market was soft. In fact, despite being in Southern growth cities, he'd never quite managed to hit the right job at the right point in the market cycle. He tried commercial real estate with a company called Anderson Properties and then in 1992 went back to residential with Arvida/JMB Partners. In October 1992, his boss called him from Florida and said to meet him for dinner. When he arrived he found out his boss had just been fired. Soon he too was gone.

At that point he decided to go into business for himself. He says now he didn't have enough money to do it, and his wife was scared to death, but it felt right, so he put his jeans and boots back on, and started building houses. In 1993, spurred by the upcoming Olympics and Atlanta's phenomenal job growth, the market suddenly took off. After chasing bad markets for years, he hit the north Cobb market at just the right time. He built seventeen houses worth $4 million in 1994 and was hired as the development manager of Legacy Park, a 660-acre master-planned development where he and two partners will also develop a community of custom homes, 62 in a first phase, 126 altogether.

We drove out one day to look at Legacy Park with Richard Sellers, a residential construction banker with SouthTrust Bank, and Mark Carruth, one of his partners. Sellers wore a starched white shirt and dark tie, Gibbs and Carruth wore knit shirts and khakis. The sun was shining, it was late March and eighty-five degrees. We drove past the dense bare stands of oak, hickory, beech, poplar, and dogwood, the pinkish purples of the redbuds the first hint of the riot of color that was about a week away. The idea was for a half dozen or so builders to construct 1,300 new homes, all built around a densely wooded hundred-acre park, wooded creek, and wildlife sanctuary. There would be nature trails, a storytelling circle, a bandstand, tennis, volleyball, baseball fields, and a swim center. Houses would go for $100,000 to $300,000.

"For everyone who believes a magnificent, sun-filled park is part of their American heritage, your legacy is now in the making," read the brochure, which featured pictures of shaggy dogs, Little League kids, and riverfront picnics. "With our 117-acre TownPark recreation center, miles of tree-shaded parkpaths and hand-holding sidewalks, plus eleven exciting neighborhoods by Atlanta's most respected home builders, Legacy Park is unlike any community you have ever seen before. Unless, perhaps, you still dream of yesterday." It's typical home-builder hype, but it also rings true. If this isn't what America wants, suburbia the way God meant it to be, it's hard to imagine what America does want.

Gibbs began attending a Catholic church not long after arriving in Houston but didn't get serious about Christianity until he came to Atlanta for the first time. He became used to his real estate friends asking where he went to church, whether he read the Bible, whether he was a Christian. At first he answered yes, a little puzzled by the question. He was a Catholic, so he was a Christian. He didn't quite understand what they were getting at. But then they asked him whether he read the Bible and he had to answer, no, he didn't. They asked whether he had ever read the Bible, and he had to admit, no, he'd never read it. Indeed, he soon realized that he was a Christian in the sense that he wasn't a Moslem or Jew, but he was not a Christian in the way most of his friends were–people who had found Christ and whose lives were informed on a daily level by His presence.

Slowly, over time, the difference between him and his friends took on added importance. He started to read the Bible while he was in Houston, and when he moved to Nashville, he started to attend Sunday school classes at the nondenominational church he was attending. He went to some evangelical events too, but he found them more interesting than transforming. Still, something was going on. Gibbs would be the first to admit that if he's anything, he's breathtakingly ordinary. "I've always been a nice guy, everyone will tell you that," he said with a shrug. He was wearing a cotton shirt in a dark paisley pattern, khaki pants, and tassled loafers. A James Taylor tape was in the tape deck of the Explorer van.

Thinking back, he realizes that something was building that he didn't quite recognize. Between his wife's Christianity, his friends, his church, his Bible reading, the whole culture of religion and conservative values that stretched rather uniformly from Houston to Nashville to Atlanta, he was changing in ways he didn't quite recognize until his wife's seizure brought everything into revelatory focus. To this day, he doesn't know for sure what happened other than that God was behind it. She had never had health problems before the seizure. Three months after her seizure she felt fine but tests showed extremely abnormal brainwave activity, as did tests after six and nine months. They took tests after a year, and this time, miraculously, she was entirely normal, as if she'd been completely healed. She was taken off medication and has never had a problem since. "There's no explanation for why it happened," he said. "No explanation how she was miraculously healed. But I believe there's a purpose for everything. I believe God had a purpose in healing her. I believe it was a miracle, and I see that on a daily basis."

For several years Kim worked with a group of Christians called Concerned Women of America. Now she is leading a Bible study group for teenage girls. Mark leads a Christian Fellowship men's group ("Looking for fellowship with other businessmen? Join us!") that meets every Friday morning at seven A.M. at the TGI Friday's at Windy Hill and Power's Ferry roads. He also works to promote Promise Keepers, which fills up arenas like Texas Stadium outside Dallas or the Georgia Dome in downtown Atlanta for Christian men's revivals, where sixty or seventy thousand men gather to sing, pray, praise Jesus, and talk about what it means to be a Christian man at the end of the twentieth century. In some ways, Mark can sound almost New Age-y. "I've always been a social person who has always appreciated good friends. To this day, I have friends in Houston that I love to death, friends in Chicago, in Nashville, in Atlanta. Guys are finally realizing that relationships are important, that we need each other, that it's a tough cruel world out there, and it's a whole lot easier to go through it when you've got someone to help you through it, even if it's nothing other than someone who can listen and understand."

Fifteen or twenty years ago, when the demographic and generational tides were bringing boomers like him to California, such sentiments could have brought him to the Esalen Institute, or various other nodes of the human potential movement. But these days he is a parent, a businessman, a taxpayer, a Christian, and a Southerner, so nothing in the world seems more natural than putting his left arm around his wife's waist as they stand in church, closing his eyes, raising his right arm in the air as if using it as an antenna to soak up the holy spirit, and singing along in a deep, peaceful voice. "You're my Lord, you're my Lord, You have risen from the dead and you're my Lord. . . ."

Even for those who haven't found Christ, it's easy to see the case for Cobb County. You can buy your slice of the American dream for a quarter of what it costs in Larchmont or Bethesda or Winnetka, and you get better weather, nicer people, less crime, and a better economy. Median household income in Cobb, which is 90 percent white, is $41,810, compared with a national average of $33,178. Two thirds of the housing units are single-family homes. There are plenty of high-end half-million-dollar homes, but most new homes range from as low as $70,000 in the blue-collar towns of south and west Cobb to $200,000 in the more affluent areas of east Cobb. The county has added 100,000 jobs over the past decade and seen the number of housing units jump from 113,271 in 1980 to 189,872 in 1990. The Atlanta metro area has led the nation in job growth for the past three years, but it's not Atlanta that has been growing like a weed, it's suburban Cobb and Gwinnett and Cherokee counties.

Barbara Wolfe, a thirty-nine-year-old mother of two, grew up in Baldwin, Long Island, and came to Cobb from Fort Lauderdale. She is, God forbid, a liberal, who was so appalled by the antigay resolution that she joined the Cobb Citizens Coalition, a group organized to oppose it. But most people don't choose where they live on the basis of the pre-vailing political currents. When Barbara Wolfe talks about life in Cobb County, she sounds like a booster too. Well, mostly. She loves the hills and trees, the dazzling display of spring when the Bradford pear, aza-leas, dogwoods, and camellias burst out in color, the friendliness of the people, the good schools, the affordability of housing—even, to a point, the Sunday-school manners and well-scrubbed sensibilities.

Like a lot of Yankees she was still not entirely used to the yes ma'ams and no ma'ams of the kids, the effusive greetings and "Ya'll hurry back"s in the stores. But she was a child of the suburbs, and who needs to pay four times as much to shovel snow and fight the Long Island Expressway for what you can find in Cobb? "I like that people are more down to earth, more polite, that you don't have to walk around screaming and yelling and being rude, you know, the whole New York thing," she said. "It seems crazy listening to myself say this, but sometimes I think that a lot of the characteristics that come from some of this fundamentalist religious stuff that I hate also cause it to be so pleasant here. If they didn't make it political it might be perfect. But it's not."

One reason it's not is the way she always knew on some level that she was on someone else's turf. It was the way she was reluctant to walk into her daughter's elementary school and say, "Excuse me, but my daughter's Jewish and you're only teaching about Christmas." It was the way none of her liberal friends felt comfortable putting up Democratic party yard signs or talking politics with their neighbors. "There aren't a lot of liberals in Cobb County," she said with a sigh. "I'm not sure you're allowed to use the word."

Indeed, when the opponents of the antigay referendum looked around for a spokesman they found that almost no one wanted to come forward. Some gay men did speak out, but gays were unlikely to generate much support. Before long, almost by default, leadership fell to Rabbi Steven Lebow of Temple Kol Emeth, a fourteen-year-old congregation whose five-year-old synagogue across from Eastminister Presbyterian Church is meant to look as though it was built from Jerusalem stone. Rabbi Lebow's congregation was a mishmash of rootless transplants and Southern Jews who often turned out to be more Southern than Jewish. "I call us the rock 'n' roll temple," he said. "We're sort of reconformadox."

Rabbi Lebow wasn't much of a crusader by nature. A small, balding man from Fort Lauderdale, Florida, with a modest mustache and a singsong, slightly whiny voice, he too had reason to keep quiet. In his ten years, Lebow has seen the best and worst of Cobb County. For years, while building itself up to the point that it could erect its own synagogue, the congregation had been taken in and was given space to worship by non-Jewish groups across the county. It met back then at a bank and a day-care center, at the Mount Zion United Methodist Church and the Chestnut Ridge Christian Church. There were plans to expand its existing sanctuary building, but on the High Holy Days, when worshipers outnumbered seats in its sanctuary, it met at the Catholic Church of the Transfiguration—the church covered the nine hundred–pound cross with a shroud so the Kol Emeth congregation could feel comfortable worshiping.

On the other hand, Temple Kol Emeth also had to deal with six separate incidents of vandalism and defacement when it built its own synagogue which finally ended when what Lebow calls "the Jewish good ol' boys" in his congregation organized a Jewish Defense League–style patrol that carried their shotguns and .22s and finally chased off a bunch of neo-Nazi kids who'd been responsible. Still, there was one last coda. On the week they opened in December 1991 someone spray-painted in German: Jews are not wanted here.

You didn't have to look hard to see how close all the volatile issues in Cobb's past were to its present. Rabbi Lebow recalled going to a meeting of the Kiwanis Club where a reporter from the *Marietta Daily Journal* spoke on the Leo Frank case. "Leo Frank is normally about as far from my mind as whether the Braves are going to play–I've basically given up and don't even think about them," he said. It was the middle of the 1995 baseball strike, and we were at Kurt's Deli, which was started by a born-again Christian, who sold it to the Holocaust survivor who had been his counterman, who sold it to Barbara and Eric Gillman, who had moved down from New York.

"Leo Frank, what is it, eighty years ago? Seventy years ago? It's not relevant to modern Jewish life. And I go to this Kiwanis meeting and Bill Kinney stands up and he gives this harangue about the Leo Frank case and you can see people holding the tables and their knuckles are turning white! And I guess you could have picked my jaw up off the ground, because I'm thinking, 'This shit really riles them up, doesn't it?' And I'm the Jew in the room and to me it's, whatever, let it go. It's like blaming me for killing Christ. But these guys, it's like their Grandpa said he was one of the ones or great Grandma was there when they hung him. It's ingrained in their family history. It still pushes all their buttons."

On purely practical grounds, having a rock 'n' roll rabbi from Fort Lauderdale stand up for the gays in Cobb County wasn't exactly the perfect recipe for a groundswell of popular support. But no one else wanted to put himself on the line, so Lebow said he'd do it. He began lining up clergymen for a letter opposing the referendum–about thirty agreed to participate–but before it was even out, he received a call from a prominent minister. "He said, 'I want to know the names that are going to be on the resolution, because my denomination stands firmly against homosexuality and anyone whose name is on your resolution, we're going to see they pay the price.' And then he said, 'You can get your thirty, but I can get three hundred.' I said this wasn't a competition. I know there are plenty of Baptists and Methodists out there, I know you're going to beat me, that's not the point. In fact, we came out with our thirty, they came up with their three hundred, I got death threats and harassing calls and I'm still glad I did it. I don't have a hobby. I have this."

Lebow wasn't exactly a raging liberal. He had given sermons in favor of the death penalty. He agreed with half of what he heard Rush Limbaugh say. He described his own politics as "passionate moderation." The truth is that while there are a few "liberals" in a place like Cobb County, there aren't many liberal issues likely to galvanize more than a tiny sliver of support. On some issues, like abortion, there's a sizable pro-choice constituency. But aside from something that's mostly reactive, it's hard to know what a liberal agenda would be. IMAGINE NO LIBERALS, said the popular bumper stickers on the tailgates of the west Cobb pickups and the east Cobb Beemers. In Cobb, it wasn't very hard to do.

It was Newt Gingrich who codified that utter contempt accorded views opposed to his in his now famous maybe-it's-a-course-maybe-it's-not televised lectures that began at Kennesaw State College near Marietta, where he decreed that he would allow "liberals but not liberal ideas" into the classroom. Like most Cobb folks he was from someplace else, of course—an Army brat who came closest to finding a home in Columbus, Georgia, and who represented a largely blue-collar district south of Atlanta before taking advantage of redistricting to move toward the safely Republican environs of Cobb. Now, you could find him most weekends at events like the Cobb County Republican breakfast at Vittle's restaurant, where it was impossible to be too far to the right, or at gatherings like his sort-of-annual birthday party barbecue at Fuller's Park in east Cobb, where he and Jack Kemp threw around a football while a Newt staffer in a purple Barney outfit with a blue and white NEWT'S FRIEND bumper sticker sweated in the summer sun. Newt, as might be expected, was making the case for Cobb as his vision of America's future.

"These people want safety, and they believe big cities have failed and

are controlled by people who are incapable of delivering goods and services," he said as the 1994 congressional races were just getting
underway. We were standing by a wooden fence at the edge of a paved
path, and he'd greet his followers one by one as they came or left and
then go back to talking in his now familiar nasal stream of consciousness. At the time, taking over Congress and ascending to the speaker-
ship seemed the longest of long shots. Newt was still relatively new to
his district, so rather than being a big deal, the cookout attracted maybe
a hundred folks, most of them party activists who knew him well. He
was wearing khakis and an open-necked shirt, looking like the host at a
backyard suburban barbecue. All he was missing was one of those white
aprons tied at the back and reading CHEF NEWT.

"What they find here is a sort of Norman Rockwell world with fiber-
optic computers and jet airplanes. But the values that would have been
the *Saturday Evening Post* of the mid-fifties are the values of most of
these people now." Soon he was on a roll, contrasting the pristine work
ethic of Cobb versus the "welfare state" values of Atlanta, a pitch as old
as the South. Fifteen years ago even a Strom Thurmond or Jesse Helms
would have been leery of using the most transparent of codes to stigma-
tize a whole race. But the South they grew up in was one where blacks
and whites always, on some level, had to confront one another. Cobb's
past was full of the starkest issues of race, but in Cobb now blacks
were largely symbolic rather than real–representing the unseen menace, horror, and decay of Atlanta, 70 percent black, just across the
Chattahoochee–so Gingrich's words flew out in his usual, breezy, unfiltered flow.

"People in Cobb don't object to upper-middle-class neighbors who
keep their lawn cut and move to the area to avoid crime," he went on.
"What people worry about is the bus line gradually destroying one
apartment complex after another, bringing people out for public
housing who have no middle-class values and whose kids as they
become teenagers often are centers of robbery and where the schools
collapse because the parents that live in the apartment complexes don't
care that the kids don't do well in school and the whole school
collapses."

Over the years, few politicians have been as comfortable at stringing
together sweeping generalizations and non sequiturs as seamlessly as

Gingrich, and soon he was in full flight. "To say you can't have the Ten Commandments on the wall because it might threaten somebody where you have a country where O. J. Simpson may well have killed his wife is crazy," he said. It was the day after White Bronco Day, and it was not clear what O. J. maybe having killed his wife had to do with nine of the Ten Commandments, but Gingrich kept going, in love as ever with the sound of his own voice. "I deliberately strung together in my speech at the '92 convention 'nihilistic, multicultural, hedonists,' and the point I was trying to drive home was that these are the people who believe the surgeon general is sick. They think the elite has lost its mind. They also believe that the world market exists. This is probably the Number One Internet county in the state."

Like his famous classroom lecture that veered from the alleged inability of women soldiers to stay in a ditch for thirty days without getting infections to the way men are biologically driven to go out and hunt giraffes, there was no telling what would come next. But it was all delivered with such self-assured, matter-of-fact moral certainty that if he ended up by saying, "... and that's why I'm a Marxist," you'd just nod your head in agreement. Of course, he ended not with a conversion to Marxism but with a ringing endorsement of his constituents. "It's the places like Cobb that are entrepreneurial, that have weak unions, that have a strong work ethic, that are going to do well," he said. "Low tax, low union, strong work ethic, strong commitment to family and community." He didn't finish the sentence. He didn't need to.

Still, there were a few discordant notes in Cobb's symphony of entrepreneurial suburban virtue. The first was that just as the South benefitted more than anyplace else in America from the programs of the hated big-government New Deal, Cobb turned out to be one of the hungriest hogs at the contemporary federal trough. A 1993 study published in *Common Cause* magazine found that Cobb took in $3.4 billion in federal funds in 1992 and ranked third among suburban counties nationally in the amount of federal aid it received in 1992. The only counties ahead of it were Arlington County, Virginia, just outside Washington, D.C., and Brevard County, Florida, home of the Kennedy Space Center. Of the top ten suburban counties in federal dollars, eight are in the South or in the border state of Maryland. Overall, Cobb received 41 percent above the average for all 3,042 counties in the

United States. As House Speaker, Gingrich in 1994 lambasted New York City as a "culture of waste," hopelessly addicted to the federal dole. But Cobb residents, it turns out, get far more federal aid per capita than New York City residents: $9,878, or about $4,000 more.

Indeed, Cobb's prosperity is strikingly tied to federal spending, particularly defense spending. The foremost example is Lockheed, first the beneficiary of a billion-dollar bailout in 1971 that probably saved the company, and since then a bulwark of the defense economy. Defense contracts to Lockheed and Dobbins in 1994 came to $2.7 billion, or more than half the federal dollars flowing into Cobb. When defense cuts slashed employment in half during the early 1980s, the government spent $2 million to retrain 3,700 workers, most of whom remained dependable Cobb taxpayers.

Other than Lockheed, what has really made Cobb boom has been its location at one of the key junctures of the interstate highway system, where I-75 running south from Detroit intersects with the loop around Atlanta, I-285. Where they meet is an area of malls, high-rises, and high-tech businesses called the Platinum Triangle, where the federal government spent $73 million on road improvement between 1989 and 1994. According to the analysis in *Common Cause* magazine, the federal government spends $14 million on education in Cobb, with beneficiaries ranging from school-lunch and breakfast programs to Life College, the world's largest chiropractic school. Cobb is counting on the federal government to fund up to 90 percent of $20 million of expenditures in airport improvements. The federal government paid 80 percent of the start-up costs when Cobb started its own transit system to stay independent of Atlanta and bailed out three failed savings and loans when they collapsed in 1991. Small-business loans, insurance, and federal guarantees for mortgages came to $629 million in 1994.

The second discordant note was that, to a degree that was truly spooky, Cobb was home not just to suburban Republicans but to a stunning array of those at the furthest fringes of the far and religious right, who floated seamlessly in and out of the mainstream of county life. Lester Maddox, the former segregationist governor, now viewed as something of a respected elder statesman, still lived there, periodically venturing out to ride his bicycle backward in local parades. So did J. B. Stoner, a convicted church bomber, former Klansman, virulent anti-

Semite and lifelong white supremacist who once ran for the Georgia senate under the subtle slogan: "You cannot have law and order and niggers too ... Vote white." Stoner was viewed by law enforcement officials across the South as one of the most dangerous racists of his time, who had over the years shown an unerring ability to be in the vicinity when bombs went off.

At seventy-one, Stoner saw life these days as a good news/bad news joke. The bad news was that even a place like Cobb wasn't what it used to be. "It's going down—too many niggers and Asians," he allowed one steamy morning as he waited for a Klan rally to start in nearby Forsyth County. "I'd like for it to be all white. There was a time when there weren't any nigger lovers in the South—none that would admit it, anyway. That's the way things should have stayed." He was sitting in a red pickup chomping on a king-sized Zero candy bar, wearing a blue denim cowboy hat with a thunderbolt insignia (a symbol taken from Hitler's Waffen-SS), a blue seersucker jacket with a thunderbolt pin, striped gold and blue tie, and gray slacks—looking like a jaunty retiree on his way to a big night of church bingo.

On the sunny side of the street, as he saw it, at least the blacks were about to get theirs. Literature for his Crusade Against Corruption explained that blacks have the Gc-1 fast gene, which makes them susceptible to AIDS, while whites have the Gc-2 gene, which leaves them relatively immune. "We white racists are now on the winning team," he explained, "because with AIDS God is killing off the Jews, part Jews, niggers, part niggers, and queers. Like I say, if you lie down with dogs, you get up with fleas. If you lie down with Jews, niggers or queers, you get up with AIDS. All I can say is, thank God for AIDS."

Another slugger on the winning team was Dent Myers, who sold Klan, Nazi, and white supremacist literature at his picturesque Wildman's Civil War Shop on the friendly little main street of Kennesaw. In recent years Cobb has been a center of skinhead activity, but far-right activity often took more mainstream forms. Sam G. Dickson was a prominent lawyer with an office on Marietta's town square, a longtime supporter of David Duke, and a prominent member of the Holocaust Denial movement. Over the years he had brought leading Holocaust deniers like John Tyndal and David Irving to Cobb and had regularly represented white supremacists and Klansmen. "If you're a Scot, you should be a Scot and not a Frenchman," he said. "If you're black, you should be a black and not a wannabe."

And then there was Dr. Ed Fields, a nonpracticing chiropractor and publisher of the newspaper *The Truth at Last*, which regularly offered up neo-Nazi fare under headlines like OVER 50% OF CLINTON'S MAJOR APPOINTEES ARE ZIONIST JEWS. Fields has spent most of his life in Klan, white supremacist, and anti-Semitic organizations and in 1958 had founded with Stoner the neo-Nazi National States Rights Party. When he was in high school in Atlanta, he joined a neo-Nazi group called the Columbians whose members wore brown shirt uniforms with thunderbolt armbands and patrolled white neighborhoods to keep blacks out. At the height of the convulsive racial tensions that led to the church bombings and racial violence in Birmingham, Alabama, in the 1960s, he and Stoner set up a "white man's bookstore" in suburban Bessemer to help "save Alabama and the nation from Jew Communists and their nigger allies."

The Truth at Last was the successor to *The Thunderbolt–The White Man's Viewpoint,* which was first published in August 1946 and for a time was identified largely with Stoner. According to the Anti-Defamation League of B'nai B'rith, until the late 1980s it was "the most widely read publication among the Klans and other hate groups." Fields still had the first issue, with its front-page picture of Columbians founder Emory Burke saluting the statue of Tom Watson, the famous populist Congressman turned racist, who kept Georgia in a lather over the Leo Frank case. "The long awaited white man's movement to save first the south and then the nation has at last begun," the lead on its front page begins. "The object and purpose of the movement is to encourage our people to think in terms of Race, Nation and Faith, and to work for a national moral reawakening in order to build a progressive white community that is bound together by a deep spiritual consciousness of the past and determination to share a common future."

Fields saw himself as a gentleman "racialist," a proud inheritor of the best traditions of the South's past, segregation among them. "We bend over backwards not to appear radical," he said of *The Truth at Last* and his other endeavors. "Of course, in the nineteen-forties, fifties, and sixties, none of this was extremist whatsoever, and I hope people don't take it that way now."

We were at Shillings, a mock English pub on Marietta's town square.

There was a 120-year-old bar, mock Tiffany glass, old-timey light fixtures, and autographed pictures on the wall of Alex Trebeck of the television show *Jeopardy* ("To Dave, best wishes") and golfer Larry
Williams ("To Dave, Great Putt"). The Muzak was playing Motown,
the O.J. trial was on CNN, and two waitresses were trading horror stories about the North, trying to decide which was worse, the weather or
the rudeness. Dr. Fields showed up a few minutes after me in a gray
wool sweater with a white shirt and a blue tie underneath it, and
checked slacks. His sharp features were flushed, his hair was dyed a red-
dish brown that made it look like a bad wig, and he spoke with an
affected, clenched-jaw, upper-crust accent, which gave him a slightly
seedy faux-patrician air.

He had brought along the latest issue of *The Truth at Last,* which is
sent free to every white member of the Georgia Legislature. It was
pretty typical white supremacist fare. There were two pages of crime
and race news that reported only on crimes by blacks against whites
under headlines like WHITE FAMILIES DESTROYED BY NEGRO MURDERS;
ANOTHER WHITE LIFE LOST!; SLAUGHTER OF WHITES BY NEGROES! A typical story began: "The Negro war on White people continues to esca-
late." There were sociological asides such as, "The wild and backward
ways of Africa and Haiti are commonplace today in areas of the U.S.
infested by Blacks." The issue was weak on anti-Semitism but otherwise
there was the usual mix of rabid antiblack stories, intriguing letters like
that from F.H. in Houston, containing the suggestion that Massachusetts be turned into a separate, independent, black nation, and advertisements for books with titles like *The Case for the Relocation of the American
Negro to Africa.*

"I hate to say it, but we're probably the only segregationist paper left
in the country," he said in a chagrined tone, as if mourning the disap-
pearance of a grand old tradition like the corner soda fountain. "There
are plenty of good conservative papers like *The Spotlight,* but they don't
go into segregation and the race question the way we do." Overall,
however, he felt things were turning his way. "The country is getting
more conservative, the races are separating more all the time. Look at
The Bell Curve. The fact is the blacks have been promised total equality
with the white people, and they're not capable of reaching total
equality. The result has been a breakdown of society. People in America
generally are afraid of the blacks, and when you talk about how nice,

peaceful, and quiet things were under segregation, not too many people would disagree with you."

After lunch we went to our cars, which turned out to be parked next to each other on the square. I followed his cranberry Buick Century out from the square on West Dixie Avenue then crossed over the railroad tracks and doubled back. The homes were the old frame houses of small-town Marietta, not east Cobb suburbia. There was a train whistle in the distance. The radio was playing Arlo Guthrie's version of "The City of New Orleans." We soon turned into the old city cemetery. He was taking me to Mary Phagan's grave.

It was a cold February day and the blue sky was streaked with delicate plumes of white clouds as we got out of our cars. He was making the case for Frank's guilt as we walked. "You hear about his posthumous pardon," he said. "A lot of people objected to it, but the pardon was granted because he was not able to complete all his appeals, not because they thought he was innocent. To straighten this out the city of Marietta erected this plaque." We both read: "Celebrated in song as Little Mary Phagan after her murder on Confederate Memorial Day, 1913, in Atlanta, a day marked by C.S.A. veterans in 1915; the tribute by Tom Watson set in 1933. Leo Frank sentenced to hang [but] granted clemency before lynching August 1915. 1986 pardon based on state's failure to protect him and apprehend killers, not Frank's innocence." Fields repeated the last line, "not Frank's innocence," with satisfaction, as if repeating history's verdict. (Apparently, even in Marietta, history's verdict isn't so clear. The city changed the plaque to a more generic historical marker later in 1995 after Jewish groups raised the issue.)

Across from the marker the white headstone read: "Born June 1, 1900, died April 26, 1913. In this day of fading ideals and disappearing landmarks, little Mary Phagan's heroism is an heirloom than which there is nothing more precious among the old red hills of Georgia. Sleep little girl. Sleep in your humble grave. But if the angels are good to you, in the realms beyond the troubled sunset and the clouded stars they will let you know that many an aching heart in Georgia beats for you and many a tear from eyes unused to weep has paid you a tribute too sacred for words."

We read it silently and then got ready to leave.

"Our message is finally getting out," Fields said jauntily, as if renewed by his visit. "We're selling Confederate flags all over, books on the Civil War. I'm speaking to a meeting in Chicago March 25. It will be a packed hall. People think maybe the South had the right answers on the race problems after all."

If they knew his full program, most people in Cobb County would probably dismiss Ed Fields as a racist creep obsessing on the past and Stoner as a loathsome throwback to a time best forgotten. But the surface appeal—fear of blacks, a longing for a safer past and older values, law and order, "Race, Nation, and Faith" as the Columbians put it—dovetailed with most things going on in the county. Often the racism was anything but subtle.

Once I went to a Confederate memorabilia show at the Cobb Convention Center with two of my neighbors. Like other such conventions, it combined history, Lost Cause nostalgia, and contemporary conservative politics in a seamless blend, like different chapters in the same textbook. The bumper stickers reading IMPEACH CLINTON or IF I HAD KNOWN THIS I WOULD HAVE PICKED MY OWN COTTON were as much a part of the show as the Stonewall Jackson portraits, antique rebel spittoons, and Confederate cavalry sabers. On the way back we stopped for lunch at Carey's Burgers just down from Dobbins on one of Cobb's main drags. There was a great hard-core, seven-plays-for-one-dollar country jukebox whose offerings included Ray Price's "For the Good Times," Faron Young's "Hello Walls," Patsy Cline's "Crazy," and Hank Williams's "Your Cheatin' Heart." In the middle of it were two less celebrated songs by a group called the Trashy White Band. One was called "Alabama Nigger." The other was called "She Ran Off with a Nigger." I punched up the first one, and the music filled the room, "I'm an Alabama nigger, and I want to be free. To hell with the N double A C-P . . . I want to eat where the white folks eat, 'cause I'm white on the heels of my feet. . . ."

Apparently it had been there for years and no one had ever tried to raise the point that perhaps it wasn't entirely appropriate.

As extreme as Fields's broader agenda was, on most of the issues of the day he was swimming in hospitable seas. When *Nightline* aired a report on the antigay referendum, whom did it find to interview but Ed Fields, identified as just another Cobb resident. When Newt Gingrich in 1992 faced a Democratic opponent, attorney Tony Center, for the first time in the Sixth District after barely squeaking by in his first Republican primary, Cobb residents received a flyer from Dr. Fields in the mail. It was headlined TONY CENTER—SECRET JEWISH CANDIDATE. Addressed "Dear Fellow Christian," it accused Center of hiding his religion from the public and asked, "Do we want a Congressman to represent our 6th District who does not hold the same basic Christian values as do the Christian majority here?" When Governor Zell Miller tried to change the Georgia state flag, with its Confederate emblem, the Cross of St. Andrew, Fields was one of the founders of an organization to retain the flag, an effort that easily prevailed. He bragged that he and a group of pickets on Marietta's square were responsible for getting Gingrich to back off from his early support for changing the flag.

Ed Fields is probably no more mainstream than Keith L. Maney of Marietta, who addressed the Cobb County Commission on the antigay resolution by saying: "Men and women who have abandoned normal relations and have chosen an unnatural lifestyle of homosexuality, those who have become God haters in their wickedness, evil in their perversion, as well as those who approve of such men and women doing these things, deserve to be put to death, according to the Holy Bible"; or the Christian Reconstructionist supporters of the referendum who advocated a Christian theocratic republic; or the creeps who defaced Rabbi Lebow's temple; or the students who defaced the office of a black professor at Kennesaw State with swastikas and racist graffiti. But in a place where the political spectrum runs from center right to extremist right, you never know how far to the right things will go and you can never underestimate the ability of those outside the mainstream to shape the public debate. "We got a lot of calls of support, but we also had people call and say things like 'I'm going to drag you outside and slit your throat and watch your queer blood run in the street,'" said John Greaves, a thirty-six-year-old credit analyst who was the most visible gay opponent of the resolution, but who left the county when he was threatened and harassed. "You can't live that way. I got exhausted by it. Cobb County is like a boat where all the people have run to the right side. You get enough people on the right side, eventually the boat just tips over."

Cobb isn't likely to tip over, but it's hard to see what will move anyone to the left side of the boat anytime soon. Like most of his friends, Mark Gibbs doesn't think of himself as a political person. When he thinks about what he wants to do with his life, what he really hopes is that after he's dead and gone, he'll have made some great friends who know he made a difference in their lives and that his wife and children will speak more highly of him than anyone else around. He doesn't have the hard-right animus toward Bill Clinton that many in Cobb have. Indeed, in his instinctively personalized view of things, he said that if Bill Clinton were sitting in the room, he'd probably find him "a good guy." But he thinks Clinton's social agenda goes contrary to his faith. He's not sure the Republicans know what they're doing, but he feels he pays too much tax, government does too much too badly, and the Republicans deserve a chance. He's sorry the county's antigay resolution caused such ill will, but he thinks homosexuality is wrong, and he's glad the county came out against it. Mostly, he thinks the country has lost its moral moorings, it's become unglued, and he's thankful that God has allowed him and his family to find his island of warmth, prosperity, and peace in suburban Georgia.

He finds a particular measure of peace each Sunday at his church, Mount Paran, which sits on sixty-five wooded acres out where the subdivisions of suburbia are rapidly overtaking the fields and houses of what not long ago was rural Georgia. Mount Paran is one of five non denominational churches that form a twelve thousand–member congregation that dates back to 1919. As we waited in the pews, a pianist played soft, ethereal piano music that wafted above the murmur and bustle as people flocked in. Most were white, but there were a fair number of blacks as well, and the church's literature took pains to show black faces in what seemed like a fairly unusual gesture toward inclusion. Then a twenty-piece orchestra broke into what sounded like the upbeat overture to a Broadway play, a seventy-five-voice choir sang the opening hymn, and the service began. Both the music and the service had the comfortable, seductive feeling of something that was both spiritual and familiar, religious and suburban at the same time.

Near the end of the service, Mark went to the front vestibule to man the Promise Keepers table and Kim remained behind. She was wearing a white sweater and long white skirt and a string of pearls, and her blond hair fell down on her shoulders. From the pulpit, Pastor Mark L. Walker, the son of Paul Walker, the senior pastor of the Mount Paran congregations, got very serious, almost anguished. The shimmering piano figures and show-band excitement of the opening of the service were long gone. He said he had something critical to say and he didn't want anyone to leave. He said he was calling for the congregation to dedicate the year to the theme of "advancing the kingdom through prayer" and wanted members to commit to it if they were able.

"Now, listen to me," he said. He was a tall, handsome man of thirty-five with a thick helmet of coal-black hair, who had taken up his father's mantle in the church after an older brother, Paul Dana Walker, a young minister and evangelist, was killed in an automobile accident. Though he had begun in business, working for a computer company, he had the preacher's ability to make his message so personal that each congregant felt he was being let in on a momentous secret. "If you have made this step to accept the call to prayer, if you've made that step, now hear me, I want to pray a prayer to anoint you to that task. This is not something to enter into lightly because the Enemy is not going to like it."

Pastor Walker asked each head of household, whoever it was—man, woman, single parent, whatever—to come forward. He had already enunciated the Four C's of his prayer program: collective individual needs, community needs, church needs, and country needs. In a moment the aisles and stairways were jammed with people—their arms raised straight up in the air, hands outstretched with palms up, heads bowed or eyes closed—who had surged forward to accept the challenge. Kim was near the right of the pulpit, her right arm in the air. "I'm desperate for You, God," Walker said, his voice breaking. "I'm desperate for You. I'm desperate for You in my home, I'm desperate for You in my personal life, in my business, I'm desperate for You in my community, I'm desperate for You in my church, I'm desperate for You in my country, I'm desperate for You in this world, God. Hold forth Your spirit. Give me the anointing. Give me the anointing. Give me the anointing."

He prayed for every head of household, for every man struggling to be a good father, for every single parent, for every single person and young person. "The time is short, Father," he said, and there were "Amens" throughout the church. "We want this city for You. We want our neighborhoods for You. We want our schools back, God. We want our schools back. We want our government back, oh, God. We want the rule of this land to be a godly rule, God." There were murmurs of "Yes," not the loud, sharp call and response of the black church, but deep, pained sighs of longing. People were crying throughout the building, mothers holding tight to babies, people holding hands or standing in prayer with their eyes closed and their upraised arms swaying like reeds in the wind. "Hallelujah," moaned Pastor Walker. "Hallelujah. Hallelujah. Hallelujah."

Chapter 3

SELMA, ALABAMA
Crossing the Bridge, Calling the Roll,
Keeping the Faith, Thirty Years On

ONE SUNDAY AFTERNOON IN FEBRUARY 1963, CHARLES BONNER and Cleophus Hobbs, sixteen years old and best friends, were pushing Bonner's old green 1954 Ford south along Church Street in Selma, Alabama, where it had broken down, when a slender young black man they had never seen before walked over and offered to help. He was light-complected, his skin the color of a paper bag, and was neatly dressed in a sport coat, yellow button-down shirt, and dark tie. Pinned to his shirt was a button showing two hands, one black and one white, reaching out and grasping each other, and the letters S-N-C-C. Bonner and Hobbs only had to take one look at his confident, self-assured, vaguely hip demeanor to know this was not someone whose life experiences were limited to the crushing indignities they took for granted as the price of growing up black in Selma.

As he pushed, the man started telling them an intriguing story. He said his name was Bernard Lafayette, he was a minister and the field secretary for a group they had never heard of called the Student Non-violent Coordinating Committee, and he wanted to enlist their help in a crusade to transform the lives of the black people of Selma and the Alabama Black Belt. As they soon learned, SNCC, whose leaders over the years included James Forman, John Lewis, Bob Moses, Fannie Lou Hamer, Julian Bond, and Stokely Carmichael, had a reputation for providing the shock troops of the civil rights movement—younger, tougher, less patient, more inclined to prefer action over theory or lawsuits than the N.A.A.C.P. or Martin Luther King's Southern Christian Leadership Conference (S.C.L.C.).

Like most poor black people in the South at the time, Bonner and Hobbs had only the vaguest notion of the civil rights movement. They had heard something about Freedom Riders, and they knew a little about the Montgomery bus boycott fifty miles away, but Selma was still an isolated, segregated Old South trading town. The most dramatic civil rights events in Alabama had yet to play out, and the notion of a world different from the apartheid of Selma was as foreign as one where people spoke Greek and walked the streets in togas.

After they pushed the car into Bonner's driveway, the three of them sat on the ample front porch of the big yellow duplex where Bonner lived with his mother and grandmother. Lafayette was twenty-two years old and had come to Selma from Atlanta two weeks after George Wallace's famous "Segregation now, segregation tomorrow, segregation forever" inaugural speech in January 1963. His was the thankless task of trying to organize the divided, intimidated, powerless black residents of the Alabama Black Belt, the desperately poor, rural counties named for the color of their soil, not the black people brought in to pick cotton. He told them of the sit-ins in Nashville, South Carolina, and Atlanta, of the theory and practice of nonviolence, of his plan to recruit students to organize voter registration drives in Selma, where in 1963 of the more than 15,000 blacks of voting age less than 250 had been certified as eligible voters by the white registrars.

The two students listened in rapt excitement like kids who had grown up in a desert hearing for the first time about life in a rain forest. "What Bernard was telling us," Bonner said later, "was like opening a window to an entire new world." They may not have known anything about the civil rights movement, but they knew enough about Selma to be instant converts. They knew they hated to go to the back door of the Thirsty Boy restaurant to ring a bell and get food handed out a window while the white kids sat with their girlfriends inside. They knew they hated sitting in the buzzard's roost, the balcony reserved for blacks at the Wilby and Walton movie theaters, where white kids would hassle them and throw things at them. They hated having to call white kids their own age "Mister." They hated the way there was only a single store downtown, S. H. Kress, that had a "colored" restroom. They hated the ever-present fear that one look at a white woman taken the wrong way could land you in a creek with a rope around your neck.

When Bonner worked in the cotton fields where his uncle, A. C. Parnell, sharecropped near the town of Orville, about twenty-five miles west of Selma, he would say to Parnell, "You tell us that Abraham Lincoln freed the slaves, and here you're living in a house with no paint, working in the cotton fields in the hot sun, and the guy who's going to get most of the cotton lives in a big white mansion. His kids go to a beautiful school while we go to a one-room shack from first to sixth grade and sit around a pot-bellied stove. How can you tell me Abe Lincoln freed us?" His uncle would just smile and say, "This is just the way of the world," and they'd go on picking cotton.

So when Bernard Lafayette said that the world didn't have to be that way, Bonner leaped at the chance to see whether if, as he puts it, there was "light at the end of the apartheid tunnel." He, Hobbs, and a third friend named Terry Shaw became the initial young core of the SNCC faithful in Selma, first organizing and recruiting their fellow students at black R. B. Hudson High School, then organizing marches and demonstrations and sit-ins for desegregation and voter registration. Before long they were skittering around rural Wilcox, Hale, Greene, and Perry counties, in cars with the headlights on and the taillights disconnected, sleeping on the floor of sharecroppers' shacks with a gun at their side, preaching voter registration and civil rights in the heart of the rural South at a time when people were routinely killed for less.

Eventually, Bonner got kicked out of Selma University for organizing a walkout during a church service and migrated to California, where he is now a civil rights lawyer in Sausalito. Hobbs joined the army, moved to New Jersey, learned to be an electrician, came back home, and now lives alone in an old farmhouse near the Sardis community outside town. Shaw moved to Detroit in 1967, where he now works as a body-shop repairman for Chrysler. Though it was all long ago, three decades now, they all live half in the present and half in the past, a time when they and other ordinary young people became a part of something so big, empowering, and transforming it will remain a part of their lives forever.

On the weekend of March 3–5, 1995, they all came back to Selma to commemorate the thirtieth anniversary of Bloody Sunday, the infamous police riot on March 7, 1965, in which mounted white lawmen swinging billy clubs and bullwhips and spraying teargas surged into a column of demonstrators on the Edmund Pettus Bridge, chased them down, and beat them as they attempted to stagger to safety. Hobbs, Bonner, and Shaw were all there, about a quarter of the way back in the line led by Hosea Williams and John Lewis, and were among those gassed and then herded like cattle back to Brown Chapel Church after they attempted to march from Selma to Montgomery to demand the right to vote. Televised around the world, Bloody Sunday became one of the unforgettable images that, like the water hoses and police dogs of Birmingham or Martin Luther King's "I have a dream" speech, defined its time and signaled the inevitable end of the South's empire of Jim Crow.

Many of the aging lions of the civil rights movement–John Lewis, Joseph Lowery, Hosea Williams, Coretta Scott King, James Bevel, Jesse Jackson, and James Forman–also came back for what was billed as the 1995 Bridge Crossing Jubilee. Also there were dozens of people whose names only historians or movement veterans now know. Scott B. Smith, Jr., known to all as Scottie B, an SNCC wild man from the Southside of Chicago, who used to wear a bone around his neck as a kind of strength-giving talisman, showed up. So did Bettie Fikes, Matthew Jones, and Chico Neblett of the Freedom Singers, who sang at marches and demonstrations across the South. Bob Mants was there; he had marched over the bridge in the second row, next to Albert Turner and behind Lewis and Williams. He stayed to do civil rights and economic development work in the former Klan stronghold of Lowndes County. Jimmy Rogers, who came to the movement in Selma and Lowndes via Brooklyn and Tuskegee Institute (now Tuskegee University), came in from Oakland, where he's a probation officer. Charles Mauldin, the main high school student leader a few years after Bonner, Hobbs, and Shaw, came over from Birmingham, where he's in reservoir management with Alabama Power. All came to sing the old songs, to feel the old spirit, to celebrate what had been won and ponder what had not been won.

In fact, there had been a lot of both. Eight days after Bloody Sunday, amid national revulsion against the brutality of Selma, President Johnson gave the most impassioned civil rights speech of his presidency. "At times," he said, "history and fate meet at a single time in a single place to shape a turning point in man's unending search for freedom. So it was last week in Selma, Alabama." He proclaimed, "We shall overcome," and demanded the passage of new civil rights legislation, which almost five months later, on August 6, produced the landmark Voting Rights Act of 1965.

Though no one knew it then, that great moment was the apogee of an arc, not the rising tide it seemed. Five days after the Voting Rights Act was passed, Watts erupted in the first massive urban riot of the sixties, signaling the shift in the nation's racial battleground from the de jure segregation of the South to the more diffuse de facto segregation and racial division of the rest of the country. In the sixties, steamy little Selma was transformed into a mythic place that defined a rare moment in American race relations when who was right and who was wrong, which tactics made sense and which did not, had a moral clarity as transcendent as scripture. In the nineties, as the veterans of Bloody Sunday returned, Selma was a reminder that the civil rights paradigm of the sixties—the glories of the movement—still reigned partly as a tribute to what happened then but also partly because nothing in three decades had come along to replace or replenish it.

In some ways, the Selma reunion was a monument to the incalculable changes that had come to the South largely because of the sacrifices young people like Bonner had made thirty years ago. Where blacks were once beaten and shot for attempting to vote—until the sixties no black had even attempted to register in Lowndes County in the twentieth century—they now controlled most of the governments of the Black Belt. Indeed, the Black Belt and the equally poor Mississippi Delta had more black elected officials than any other region of America. Legal segregation, of course, was all gone, and in Selma, at least, there was a small, growing, black middle class.

But if, beneath the glitzy suburban Beemers, Bennigans, and Blockbuster environment, Cobb County was still indelibly the white South, Selma was still in the Black Belt, and felt less like a place transformed than one where the dead still walk and history has played out in a series of cruel feints and sly role reversals. Most of the schools are still segregated; the old white public schools are virtually all black and the whites are now in private academies. The racial violence of the past is gone, replaced by an ugly tide of black-on-black crime that dwarfs the violence of Jim Crow. Many of the civil rights leaders of the 1960s are now the entrenched political class, but the state-mandated tax code still protects the interests of the white landowners who preceded them, and

virtually all the major employers–businesses, stores, banks–are owned
by whites. Lumber has replaced cotton as the region's main crop, but is
controlled by either the whites who owned the land then or giant
lumber companies that own it now, and the lumber business had no
more need than cotton farming did for most of the blacks rendered
obsolete by mechanized agriculture.

And as it was then, the Black Belt, now 66 percent black, remains
one of the poorest places in America. Though the South led the nation
in population growth in the 1980s, the ten Black Belt counties saw
population fall by 7.4 percent, to 187,994, with a net migration out of
the Black Belt of 29,052 persons. In what is already one of the nation's
poorest states, per capita income in the Black Belt fell from 67.2 percent
of the state average in 1979 to 65.1 percent of the state average in 1989.
In 1989 the median family income of $18,349 compared with $28,688
for Alabama and $35,225 for the whole United States. In Dallas County,
where Selma is the county seat, median household income for whites is
$27,886; for blacks, $9,077. The percentage of families headed by a
single parent, usually a black woman, rose to 40.9 percent.

Thus, especially for those who have stayed to fight the fight, like Bob
Mants, who bears the physical scars from Bloody Sunday and the
mental scars from thirty years of ill-fated efforts at economic development, the present often looks like the past in disguise: new words, but
the same music.

"You have black faces in high places in public office, but people may
be poorer now than when I came here in 1965," Mants told me when
we first spoke, a half year before the reunion. "I thought back then if
there was anyplace I wanted to raise my kids it would be here, because
they could see black people moving forward, advancing themselves as a
race. I was naive. The progress hasn't taken place."

Actually, there was nothing in the history of Selma or the Black Belt
that would have led to the conclusion that history could easily change
course, any more than it would have made sense to think that the
Alabama River, which runs through town would one day decide to flow
upstream to the east rather than downstream to the west. Instead, in
the dense stands of pine, the old white mansions and sharecropper
shacks–the routine landscape of sun-baked rural torpor–almost everything about the Black Belt speaks more to intractable continuity than

sudden change. Near Lownesboro, a town twenty miles east of Selma, buried in ivy and weeds and moss, stands an old antebellum mansion named Dicksonia. Built in 1830 and remodeled in 1856, it was built as a grand two-story white mansion, accented in front and on one side by a colonnade of massive fluted Doric pillars. Surrounding it were ornate gardens and grounds of boxwoods and camellias and moss-draped oaks. One morning in 1939 a fire lit in the fireplace around four-thirty flared out of control, climbed a wall, and set the place ablaze. In a half hour the house was destroyed. A few years later it was rebuilt in concrete and steel in the image of the first. One morning in 1964, a lit cigarette left in a stuffed chair in the only room in the house with wood paneling set off another blaze. It burned down again. It still stands today, a ghostly ruin baking in the Alabama sun, not quite living, not quite dead, as the past lingers across the Black Belt long after it should be gone.

Selma, fifty miles west of Montgomery, was established in 1819 as a slave market and cotton center and soon became the unofficial capital of the Black Belt. Named for the royal fortress described in William McPherson's "Songs of Ossian," its first white settlers were mostly Presbyterians of Scotch-Irish descent, most of them farmers deserting the exhausted soil of the Piedmont for the rich black humus farther west. Selma's first black residents were, of course, slaves, Africans at times brought in by the hundreds. A local history explained: "Several large buildings were erected in the town especially for the accommodation of negro traders and their property.... [One was] a three-story wooden building, sufficiently large to accommodate four or five hundred negroes. On the ground floor, a large sitting room was provided for the exhibition of negroes on the market, and from among them could be selected blacksmiths, carpenters, bright mulatto girls and women for seamstresses, field hands, women and children of all ages, sizes and qualities."

Prior to the Civil War, Dallas County produced more cotton than any other county in Alabama, sending 63,410 bales to market in 1860. During the war it became a critical part of the Confederate war effort with an arsenal that produced ammunition, a naval yard building warships, and a Naval ordnance works that produced artillery for shore defenses and the Confederate Navy. No sacrifice for the cause was too great or too small: in October 1863 the agent for the Confederate Nitre and Mining Bureau asked the ladies of Selma to save the contents of their chamber pots, since urine is a rich source of nitrogen, necessary in making gunpowder.

Despite being defended by the legendarily ferocious Nathan Bedford Forrest, the slave trader, demon warrior, and eventually the first grand wizard of the Ku Klux Klan, the city fell to the Union general John Harrison Wilson's raiders on April 2, 1865. During Reconstruction, when a Union army briefly occupied Dallas County and its presence and Republican rule allowed blacks to vote, Selma and Dallas County elected two black U.S. Congressmen, a black state senator, and a black criminal-court judge, as well as five black city councilmen, five black county commissioners, thirteen black state legislators, a black tax assessor and a black coroner. One of them, Benjamin S. Turner, became the first person from Selma ever sent to Congress. His platform called for "universal suffrage and universal amnesty," and the first bill he introduced was to grant amnesty to all the Confederate leaders disenfranchised by the Fourteenth Amendment. "Let the past be forgotten," he told Congress in his maiden speech, "and let us all, from every sun and every clime, of every hue and every shade, go to work peacefully to build up the shattered temples of this grand and glorious republic."

It was a moment that quickly faded. The withdrawal of federal troops in 1874 meant the withdrawal of protection for black citizens. Soon blacks were driven from office. By the 1890s, the antiblack fevers were so intense that even some whites were taken aback. "Why, sir," said the former governor and Confederate colonel William C. Oates, "now, when the negro is doing no harm, why, people want to kill him and wipe him off the face of the earth!" In 1901, virtually all blacks were officially disenfranchised through a variety of measures in the new state Constitution. In 1900 there were 9,871 black voters in Dallas County and 181,471 in all of Alabama. After the Constitution was enacted, 52 were left in Selma and 3,654 in the state. From then until the revolution of 1965 blacks lived in circumstances that waxed and waned in degrees of repression from relatively benign paternalism to overt terror.

Despite its infamous place in civil rights lore, Selma didn't quite represent the worst brutality of the segregated South. Selma's aristocrats prided themselves on their ability to maintain their power without the crudest forms of violence. They worked hard, for example, to keep the Klan out of the city in the twenties and to keep a lid on violence during the civil rights era. And it was both Selma's virtues and vices that made it attractive to the civil rights movement. Selma was once known as the Athens of Black Alabama because it has had two black colleges since 1889 (not always the same ones), which provided King with a middle-class base and students likely to be supporters.

But moderation only went so far. Between 1882 and 1913, for example, there were nineteen lynchings in Selma's Dallas County. And, if Selma likes to see itself apart from its less-refined neighbors in the Black Belt, history will likely lump them together as an area that created as many civil rights martyrs as anywhere in the South. Jimmie Lee Jackson, a black twenty-seven-year-old pulpwood cutter, was shot in the stomach by state troopers on February 18, 1965, at Mack's Café in nearby Marion after he tried to protect himself and his mother from the clubs of law officers who had broken up a civil rights demonstration. He died March 26, and his death provided the impetus for the Selma-to-Montgomery march. The Reverend James Reeb, a white Unitarian minister from Washington, D.C., was greeted with taunts of "Hey, you niggers!," attacked by four white men, and viciously beaten with a heavy club on March 9, 1965, after he and two other ministers left a black café two days after Bloody Sunday. He suffered a massive skull fracture and died two days later. Viola Liuzzo, a thirty-nine-year-old white mother from Detroit, was shot to death by Klansmen on March 25, 1965, while helping drive marchers back to Selma after the completion of the march that finally made it from Selma to Montgomery. Jonathan Daniels, a twenty-six-year-old white seminary student was shotgunned to death on August 20, 1965, by a highway department employee and honorary deputy sheriff named Tom Coleman when he, a fellow minister, and two black teenagers tried to buy a soda at a grocery store in Hayneville in Lowndes County, where Mrs. Liuzzo was also killed. The deaths and well-documented horrors made history, like Selma's infamous Sheriff Jim Clark, yelling, "Get those god-damned niggers! And get those god-damned white niggers!" as he led his mounted posse against the demonstrators on the Edmund Pettus Bridge. But the small barbarisms directed not just at civil rights demonstrators but those who tried to tell their story, linger with as much force. Wendell Hoffman, a CBS news photographer wore a jock strap with a protective cup in Selma because whites tried to hit him in the groin with sticks while he worked. Richard Veleriani, an NBC correspondent, beaten bloody in the riot where Jackson was fatally shot, looked up to find a white man asking him if he needed a doctor. Dazed, he nodded yes. "We don't have doctors for people like you," the man replied.

The ugliest racial violence of the past is long gone, replaced, for the most part, by the compulsive surface cordiality of Southern life. Bonner can now buy his mother a house in a neighborhood where he couldn't even walk when he was a kid. There are black clerks in the banks, stores, and offices downtown where only white faces were allowed when he was growing up. In fact, carping on the past drives many people, particularly whites, crazy, as if no matter what happens, no matter what grievances are redressed, no matter how many riots there are in L.A. or how bitter, institutionalized, and impacted racial division remains in a place like New York City, when people hear the word "Selma" they immediately think of the place where those nitwit Southerners showed us all the face of bigotry.

The gripe is not without merit. Blacks and whites certainly deal with one another more intimately and have more shared experience in Selma than in New York City. But in their heart of hearts, people have to know that race will always be Selma's claim to fame and that how well it solves racial problems will be its path to grace or perdition. Like an indelible stain, race pervades every aspect of life in the Black Belt, now as in the past. How could it not? During the civil rights era, places like Selma looked like the locus of a revolution. Now they look more like places where the civil rights era was merely a very short, evanescent moment in a long continuum, an upheaval that ended one world but never could create a new one.

The two racial poles of the new Selma can be glimpsed at the low-slung, light-colored brick headquarters of the black law firm of Chestnut, Sanders, Sanders, & Pettaway, on Jeff Davis Avenue, and in the cluttered Broad Street office of Joe Smitherman, the mayor of Selma during Bloody Sunday who is mayor of Selma today.

That there's a powerful black law firm in Selma—known, in one of Selma's routine, rich ironies, as "the Jeff Davis crowd"—is a sign of remarkable progress. Back when J. L. Chestnut, Jr., was growing up in Selma in the thirties and forties, the best most blacks could aspire to would be to become a personage on the Drag, the three-block-long strip of cafés, dance halls, gambling dives, and bootleg joints on Broad Avenue between Tabernacle Baptist Church and Jeff Davis Avenue.

Black men would hang out at the Roxy Theater, the White Dot Café, Bro Fields Café, Jabbo's, or Stella Brown's chicken shack, drinking, playing poker, Georgia Skin, or Tonk, shooting dice and trying to steer clear of the swaggering white cop they called Mr. Craw (as in "sticks in your craw"), who patrolled the street. Chestnut grew up idolizing the men of the street, but before long he realized there was no future on the Drag. He went to Talladega College in Alabama, then graduated from Dillard University in New Orleans and went on to Howard University Law School in Washington. He graduated in 1958 as the first ripples of the civil rights movement were shimmering across the South, and drove back over the Edmund Pettus Bridge on a warm night in June 1958 to become Selma's first black lawyer since Reconstruction and one of only five in all of Alabama.

Chestnut's autobiography, *Black in Selma,* is a splenetic, depressing document, part history, part screed, that chronicles his progression from a lonely drunk so cynical he didn't expect the civil rights era to produce anything that mattered in Selma, to one of the most powerful figures in the Black Belt, perhaps in Alabama. His law firm, usually called just Chestnut, Sanders, is the largest black law firm in Alabama. It represents many of the municipal and school boards of the Black Belt. Hank Sanders is Selma's first black state senator since Reconstruction. Rose Sanders is a civil rights dynamo, the force behind the National Voting Rights Museum and Institute in Selma, which occupies the brick building that used to house the segregationist white Citizens Council. Chestnut's book seems to be more about what has been won than what has been lost, but it's so drenched in Selma's bitter history of race and so full of anger that in the end all he sees is confrontation and strife without end. His bleak conclusion:

> Everyone in Selma is warped by race in some way. The white people who run the town see themselves as superior and uniquely suited to rule. . . . They think they know what's best for everybody. They remain dedicated to maintaining white control because they believe black people can't run things as well as they can. They're warped in that way. It's hard to persuade me that any white person in power wants to be fair and work on an equal basis with black people. I assume otherwise. In my experience, they want you to agree with them and let them continue to be in charge of everything. It takes a lot for me to overcome my built-in suspicion. I suppose I'm warped in that way.

Chestnut can be amiable and conciliatory at times—he and Smitherman seem to enjoy battling in public and then posing together like old warriors connected at the hip by Selma's history. But Chestnut remains so vituperative that much of what comes out of his mouth can be described in one word—"racist." For example, he wrote a letter to Alvin Benn—a fair, hard-nosed, white reporter for the *Montgomery Advertiser,* who has taken his share of abuse from whites as well—that was printed in the *Advertiser* on February 26, 1992. In the letter Chestnut complained about an article Benn had written concerning the Alabama Bar Association's failure to respond publicly to complaints filed the previous year about Mrs. Sanders. Chestnut called Selma "this racist cesspool of a town," accused Mayor Smitherman of calling a black woman a "black bitch," and said, "her husband should have gone immediately to the mayor's office and shot the bastard between his damn eyes." The letter continued:

> If you ever write a page of scurrilous, deliberately imbalanced crap about my black wife to satisfy a bunch of low-life, white, racist, rednecks in Alabama, I will find a thousand ways to fix your ass good, election or no election. You can't fool me with lame, self-serving explanations. It is insulting as hell to have some white son-of-a-bitch piss in my face and claim it's rain. You are clowns and racists of the first order.... If you knew what else these greedy, WASPish motherfuckers say behind your back, you would get up off your knees and quit kissing all their raw, pink asses.

These days, the most conspicuous member of the Chestnut firm is often Rose Sanders. Like her husband, Hank, she's a graduate of Harvard Law School who could pretty much have written her own ticket at a big law firm in New York, Washington, or Atlanta but came to Alabama because that's where she felt she could do the most good. When they signed their first partnership agreement in 1972, she and Hank agreed to a salary of $25 a week. Rose Sanders is a striking, slim woman with luminous eyes and is given to brightly colored African robes and head wraps. She seems to be in constant motion, racing around town in her Toyota Avalon filled with plaques and African art and posters for one event or another, marching into hearings or city council meetings with her arms full of legal documents or petitions, dashing across the Black Belt to work with youth groups, or flying off around the country. In recent years she has battled cancer, but if you ask her how she's doing, she just swats the question aside with a "Psssshhhooo, I'm too busy to worry about that." Indeed, she's too busy to spend much time anguishing about anything, including the past–it's not her style and she has too much else to do. But like so many powerful black people in Selma she's constantly torn between how much has been accomplished and how much has not been. When we met one afternoon on the upper floor of the National Voting Rights Museum and Institute, which she more than anyone else willed into operation, she spoke in a steady *rat-a-tat-tat*, like a woman who had more thoughts than time to utter them.

"When the civil rights movement ended, institutional building didn't begin," she said. "If the civil rights movement had expanded to the point of building institutions or of improving institutions to take care of the needs of the people, then I don't think you would have the violence and despair we have today. Instead, people were so elated to have the victory, to have the president of this country say, "We shall overcome," that many people thought the battle was over. That's where we made our critical mistake. Now, for the majority of the people in the Black Belt, who are black and poor, their lives have not significantly changed. There's been a reduction in the number of economic institutions that serve their needs. You don't find any black farmers anymore, for instance. So in many instances, the quality of life is worse because of the onset of drugs and crime. I have personally been burglarized around fifteen times at my home and business. You have murders, black children killing black children like we never had before. We had two kids killed here two weeks ago, just murdered like dogs in their home. Do you know we had two mothers accused of murdering their children here last year? In the Black Belt? That's incredible."

She's far too savvy to vent her rage the way Chestnut does, but her political approach is not too different–she figures it will take black people working with black people to move blacks forward. "What you have in the Black Belt," she said disdainfully, "is what you call white-black coalitions. When white people realized their power base was threatened they looked around at the black community and decided, now who is the lesser of two evils? And they formed coalitions with the groups that were most aligned with white interests to make sure the white agenda was served. When white people realize they can gain some advantage by aligning with the black vote, it has become a very dangerous situation in the black community and the brown community to make deals with the white power structure to win office." I said that some people might think that's what is needed, white people and black people finding common ground to move both forward. "Whites would never do that," she said. "A white politician would never do that. Common ground must be principled ground."

For many blacks the epitome of the wrong kind of coalition building is the persistence in power of Smitherman, a former appliance salesman who was raised by a widowed mother on welfare, began in politics as a segregationist, and has hung on for three decades as one of the shrewdest Southern politicians of his time. Born in 1929, the youngest of six children of a sawmill worker who died when Smitherman was two months old, he began in politics as a young, skinny, jug-eared kid from the wrong side of the tracks. From the start he was a master at finding the seams of the political landscape. In his first campaign for mayor, he galvanized the resentments of whites who felt they'd been shut out by the blue bloods who had always run the town, positioned himself as a "responsible" segregationist rather than a Klan type, and became the town's first twentieth-century mayor to be picked from outside its business elite.

Now, at sixty-seven, he's still politically astute and compulsively garrulous, a salesman to the end. In his days as a vacuum cleaner salesman, he'd throw a penny on the rug, suck it up with a vacuum, and then dig through the bag to retrieve it—a way, he said, to elicit sympathy from potential customers.

To Chestnut, Smitherman's main salesman's trick as mayor has been his mastery of the first law of the new racial politics of the Black Belt: "If you give a little, you won't have to give a lot." Over the years, to the dismay of many blacks, he has consistently managed to attract enough black support to win in a city that's now 55 percent black, tacking to the right against conservative white challengers and providing enough new paved roads, neighborhood centers, or city hall jobs to black allies to beat back black challengers.

"You're probably looking at the last white mayor of Selma," Smitherman said, as he sat at his desk, wearing a yellow windbreaker and chain-smoking Winston Light 100s, amid thirty years' worth of civic proclamations and photos of himself with luminaries and former mentors like George Wallace and former adversaries like Jesse Jackson, stacked-up shotguns, old cigar boxes, an antique cash register behind him, a Bear Bryant houndstooth-check hat next to it. "But if a black is elected, the whites will determine which black is elected. It won't be somebody Rose [Sanders] or the Jeff Davis crowd will pick. Chess is a great attorney. He's got a lot of bitterness, but he can be amusing, he can be nice. He's made a lot of gains here. But Rose is different. Rose doesn't like any whites, and she doesn't like most blacks unless they are completely on her side. She's a straight racist, black racist."

Smitherman went on in that vein for a while, but soon tacked back to a more cynical view of things: the racial politics of the nineties in Selma is just the old racial politics with a more diverse cast of characters on the stage. "They're just doing what we did—using race as a rallying cry to feed on the ignorance, the poverty, just like white politicians like George Wallace and Joe Smitherman did. Wallace didn't believe what he was saying. He wasn't a racist and he wasn't a bigot—he didn't hate. He knew the political winds, and he believed in segregation, just like I did. But sometimes, you put a politician on the stump, he's liable to say anything. And then when you go home, you think, 'Why did I say that?' "

It's a remarkably charitable reading of Wallace and rests on a duplicitous comparison: that the racial tirades of Chestnut are analogous to the brutal, often deadly, lengths whites holding the reins of all the political and economic power of the Black Belt went to to maintain a morally bankrupt system of white supremacy. It may be a flawed parallel, but it has remarkable resonance for whites in Selma these days, if only because many whites now often say, with some justification, that they too know what it's like to be a victim in the Black Belt's endless racial wars.

Their cause célèbre played out at the end of 1989 when the Selma Board of Education, in a 6–5 vote that went along strict racial lines, voted not to renew the contract of the city's first black superintendent, Dr. Norward Roussell. That spring, in 1990, the Alabama River reached its highest level in one hundred years. There was widespread flooding in Selma and nearby towns, and at the height of it, a number of recently buried coffins rose up from the waterlogged depths of Elkwood Cemetery, the city's second oldest, and then were carried along by the floodwaters like a ghoulish armada of the dead. Like the coffins of Elkwood, the ghosts of Bloody Sunday came back to the surface that spring as well.

Roussell, a smart, self-assured educator from the sophisticated black-Creole world of New Orleans, had been appointed amid much fanfare and optimism in 1987. Roussell had developed a reputation as a hard man to get along with in his hometown, and his personality was prickly enough that even Chestnut described him as "somewhat arrogant." At first, whites greeted him more warmly than black and Roussell's record of hiring more white teachers than black and his election as the first black to join the Rotary Club left many in the black community suspicious.

But the tables turned when Roussell began taking steps to dismantle a system of student placement that allowed a much larger proportion of whites than blacks to take honors courses on the basis largely of subjective teacher evaluations rather than objective test scores. There are arguments to this day over whether the tracking was as rigid and widespread as Rose Sanders and her crowd alleged: in effect, blacks charged that the schools were integrated but the classes were largely segregated, and it's clear that the system that was in place left whites disproportionately in the top classes. As far back as 1987, blacks had formed an organization called BEST—Best Education Support Team—to dismantle the system.

At the time, Selma had one of the few integrated school systems in the Black Belt, which was a source of pride for many blacks and whites. Like most communities, Selma had its own "seg" academies, Meadowview Christian, which had a largely blue-collar clientele, and the more prestigious Morgan Academy, west of town near the all-white Selma Country Club. But the public schools remained 30 percent white and the feeling in town was that if you wanted the best education, the honors classes, the advanced-placement courses, the place to go was Selma High. There was even a spirited bumper sticker war in the white community. Parents of children in the public schools, who took to calling Morgan "Moron Academy," would drive around with bumper stickers reading, MY HEART IS IN THE PUBLIC SCHOOLS AND SO ARE MY CHILDREN. The Morgan crowd had bumper stickers reading, MY CHILDREN ARE MY HEART, AND THEY ATTEND MORGAN ACADEMY.

When the board voted not to renew Roussell's contract, enraged blacks, led by the Jeff Davis group, threatened to shut the city down unless the contract was extended and the six white members of the board were fired. Blacks staged boycotts of local banks and businesses and a takeover of City Hall, in which protesters camped out for more than two weeks on the City Hall grounds. At one point, a wild melee broke out at Smitherman's office and four black protest leaders, including Rose Sanders, were arrested and carried from the building. Fights and disruptions at the high school and middle schools led to their closure, meaning that five hundred white kids and three hundred black kids could not attend school. Blacks sang freedom songs, staged marches, and made constant references to the sacrifices of "Bloody Sunday," whose twenty-fifth anniversary celebration was being mapped out by Chestnut and Sanders in the midst of it all.

With public schools still closed, white parents, turning the turmoil of the 1960s on its head, asked for federal protection for their children to attend school. The Alabama National Guard was called out to make sure schools could reopen. "If the federal government could send troops so that eleven black kids could attend high school in Little Rock," a businessman named Otey Crisman asked, "can't it also send help so that five hundred white kids can attend Selma High?"

The schools finally reopened, and Roussell was not rehired, but the rancor and distrust continued. The turmoil ended with the old end-game of racial division—resegregation. Over the next year or so, almost all of the whites left the high school, and even many of the parents who had once ridiculed Morgan Academy decided to send their children there.

Rose Sanders, for one, sees the uprising of 1990 in much the spirit of the uprising of 1965, one in a long series of steps needed to root out the institutionalized inequalities of the Black Belt. "We went twenty years with one black valedictorian even though the school was seventy per-cent black," she said. "What does that tell children? If you went into the classrooms you saw all black and all white. How do you think a child feels who enters a building with a white child every day and they go to separate and unequal courses of study?"

But many blacks and whites look back on the school wars as a dis-aster—an exercise in overkill in an endless war that killed integrated edu-cation in Selma for the indefinite future. Alston Fitts III is a local

historian and the director of information for the Edmundite Missions, a
Catholic missionary group with a long history of social service in the
Black Belt. He's a former English professor whose interests run to black
studies and Shakespeare. If there's such a thing as a white liberal left in
the Black Belt, he's pretty close. He kept his kids in the public schools
after most of the whites pulled out, but in the fall of 1991 he borrowed
money from his sister and sent his two daughters to an integrated
boarding school near Birmingham. Now he veers between regret and
something close to bitterness.

"Selma's pride for so long was that there was still significant school
integration," he said when we talked in his cramped little office. "Now
we're separated the way we always were, only the difference now is that
the shiny new public schools belong to the blacks and the second-rate
private schools belong to the whites. My biggest happiness coming out
of integration was that I thought my children were growing up more
freely than I ever could. They went to school with black kids, they
made their first communion with black kids, they learned their cate-
chism from a black woman who's one of our neighbors. And I guess the
greatest disappointment to me was the way all that was swept away by
the debacle. I remember my friends telling me in great distress that their
children, who had been injured physically or psychically during this,
were now more racist than they, their parents, had ever been, because
they were not making comments out of ignorance but out of bitter
experience that they were generalizing and making absolute."

Still, Fitts has few illusions about the purity of his own beliefs. "If
Jesus Christ returned, if the Second Coming took place here in Selma,
the news coverage would start with a thirty-second clip of the troopers
chasing the demonstrators across the bridge. You know, I've accepted
that more or less. But when they show it now it's always with someone
saying, it's so many years since then, and every bank in town is still
white. Oh golly, I didn't know we were supposed to give them a bank.
But then, of course, I was always a very middle-class member of the
movement, if I could even claim to have been that."

Selma, which today has about 23,000 residents, about 55 percent
black, is not as vital as it once was, but it doesn't look much different on
the surface from how it looked back in 1965. The streets are now paved
in the poor parts of town. The clean, low-rise, redbrick public housing

is an improvement over the worst of the old shacks of the black poor. There's a modest little forty-store mall, none of it more upscale than the JCPenney that's the one big national department store, and a strip of fast-food joints. The huge old redbrick Hotel Albert, modeled after a Venetian palace, is gone. So are some of the most infamous hangouts of segregated Selma, like the Silver Moon Café, which the men who killed Reverend Reeb had just exited, which stocked bottles of whiskey and boxes of cornflakes on the shelves and had a tin channel spittoon running the length of the floor below the counter.

But from the crest of the bridge, when you come in from the east, Selma sits atop the river like a vision of small-town repose, its sturdy array of nineteenth-century brick buildings unsullied by any shiny new interloper or monument to growth. Much of the area on Water Avenue along the river—prime redevelopment property if Selma ever came alive—molders in sullen dilapidation, although there are persistent plans to restore the old St. James Hotel, a structure built in 1837, which once housed travelers from Alabama River paddle wheelers and steamboats. The few exceptions include the restaurant Major Grumble's—Mayor Smitherman's favorite hangout—named for the leader of an 1830s militia that marched eleven miles to Selma to battle an imaginary slave rebellion, and the felicitously international La Petit Shoppe, a little yellow gift shop poised above the river.

The main drag, Broad Street, though not as busy as it was thirty years ago, is still fairly vital, having thus far escaped the Wal-Martization that's killed so many small-town downtowns. On the streets to the west are some of the grand, white-columned antebellum mansions, like the glorious Sturdivant Hall, one of the best-preserved Greek Revival buildings in the South, and handsome brick and frame cottages that once housed all of Selma's elite and now house the ones who haven't moved out to the new subdivisions and huge lots farther west. But most of the streets meander eventually into rows of modest frame houses or brick cottages or dismal vistas of weathered shotgun shacks or tumbledown frame houses with peeling paint and yards with old cars up on blocks, where black kids pedal bikes or practice baton twirling on a fall afternoon.

I drove out one day from Atlanta to meet Cleophus Hobbs. It was a chilly November morning just past Halloween and every third car

seemed to have burnt-orange-and-blue Auburn University regalia–
tiger's feet, WAR EAGLES written in white shoe polish on rear windows,
orange flags and pennants and wind socks hanging from the radio
antennas–all on their way to Auburn, twenty miles in from the state
line, for the homecoming game against mighty Northeast Louisiana.

There were no such big doings going on in Selma, where the main
excitement seemed to be the crowd hanging out outside It's a Hair
Affair and More (BEAUTY IS OUR BUSINESS) next to the 80 East Wash
(CLEANEST WASH IN TOWN) just before the bridge. We drove to Lannie's
Bar BQ Spot, a Selma institution, offering soulful spicy barbecue and on
the counter a huge jar of Penrose Big Mama cook-cured, bone-in pigs'
feet, pickled in the standard ominous pinkish-purple ooze. Like the
equally appetizing Texas specialty, cow's stomach soup, pickled pigs'
feet are the opposite of an acquired taste: unless you're born eating it,
you never will.

Hobbs was smaller and slighter than Charles Bonner, whom I had
met earlier. Bonner is tall, dark-skinned, and rather debonair. He talks in
crisp, carefully crafted sentences as if he's constantly explaining an
important point of law in court, whereas Hobbs is quieter and less decisive on the surface. Hobbs wore an old plaid work shirt over a gray
T-shirt, black jeans, work boots, and wire-rimmed glasses. His hair was
liberally flecked with gray and curled out from under his Hyperformer
Soybean Seed cap. His most striking feature was his long, thin, bony,
weathered hands, like hands in certain civil rights–era photos of black
life in the South. In the 1970s, Hobbs formed a group called FOCUS,
Friends Organized to Create a United Society, to do voter registration
and community work in the area outside town where he lives. They
were able to get a fire truck and form a volunteer fire department, but it
had been hard to keep up interest. Hobbs now found himself wondering how things had moved so far backward.

"It's hard to even talk to kids now," he said, as we drove around
town. "They don't have any purpose other than to make a fast dollar,
and they don't care how they do it. Some of these kids would be as
likely to kill you as to kill a snake. It's sad. When we met Bernard
Lafayette, we never gave any thought to standing up to white folks. We
were scared of white folks. If they said jump, we'd say 'How high?' But
he was able to awaken something in us that we didn't know was there. I
don't know how you do that with kids today. I wish I did."

We drove out to an area called "Slave City," just outside the city limits, where some of Selma's poorest blacks live in cinder-block bunkers without indoor plumbing. It's the kind of numbing rural poverty you see in all the little towns of the Black Belt but it is usually not quite such a presence in larger towns like Selma. Back in town we looped around some of the haunts of Hobbs's youth like the Tabernacle Baptist Church—with its broad dome, four white pillars, and the basement meeting room where Lafayette held his organizing sessions—and R. B. Hudson, now a middle school. We drove past the Bottoms, another patch of dilapidated housing that's just up the street from the elegant homes of Church and Mabry streets, a reminder of how close rich and poor, black and white, always were even in the segregated South. Then we headed out to the rambling new ranch houses west of town, where many whites have gravitated in Selma's small contribution to white flight.

Like many blacks, Hobbs is now caught between his instinctive suspicion of whites and his distaste for much of the black leadership. He sees the Chestnut-Sanders group as flagrant self-promoters who use the movement he helped start to further their own interests, but he also assumes the tracking grievances were valid. He is stunned and disgusted by the lack of respect and the absence of values he sees in many young blacks and their parents, but also thinks much of the plight of blacks is a function of what is essentially a white plot to destroy the black community through drugs. "The system got smarter," he said, "and we didn't stay on top of it. We let them sneak in another tactic against us. They supply the dope, and they give it to the kids on the street, and those are the ones who go to jail. It's not the big suppliers who go to jail. If they want to stop it, they could stop it. But they don't."

Hobbs these days is probably part of a great muddled middle, black and white, who'd like to get past the same dead-ends of race but don't quite know how. Some are trying. There are assorted leadership groups like One Selma, an interracial gathering of community leaders trying to bridge the divide. At the mall in a little office just before you come to the JCPenney store is something called the Selma Do Something Fund, one of three national pilot programs in leadership training and community development, run locally by a twenty-five-year-old teacher named Meria Carstarphen, the daughter of the town's only black pharmacist.

Carstarphen is among those who think that the turmoil of 1990 was an unnecessary disaster, and she's still not sure how real the issue was. She was an honors senior the year before the turmoil, and half or a third of the students in her classes were black. "It's still confusing to me. And I look at it and see a tragedy. Let's face it, this community can't go forward if we're forever polarized. What we're trying to do is get people to sit together at the table and have an honest dialogue. It happens in pockets, but it's like a disjointed conversation. It never flows into a solid paragraph. It's more like a sentence or two, here or there. The rest of the world is moving toward unity, and we're still stuck in the past. But we don't need to be. There's a Bosnian student here. His name is Marco Matic. His father's a doctor. Everyone asks him, of all the places you could live in the United States, why are you in Selma? And his answer is, he really likes Selma. He likes the people. He likes the town. He likes the South. I wish more people could think like that. I'm not saying we've got everything together or that we're perfect. But we've got a lot to work with if we only give it a chance."

I wandered around downtown late in the afternoon. It was a chilly day and the streets were almost empty. There were elaborate Halloween displays, ghosts and skeletons and old farmer's carts full of pumpkins, hay bales, bright-colored gourds, and Indian corn in front of the grand Victorian, prairie-style, and Greek Revival houses on the west side of town. As the sun began to set, I walked over the bridge facing incoming traffic on the pedestrian walkway on the side of the bridge the Bloody Sunday marchers were on. If you looked upstream, to the east, a harvest moon was rising in the late-afternoon chill. If you looked downstream, to the west, the setting sun cast blinding ripples on the river. The rising moon was easier on the eyes, but the sunset dancing on the water was so riveting and powerful you couldn't take your eyes off it. In much the same way, what was—searing, blinding, unforgettable— holds the eye in Selma more than what's on the horizon.

That night Selma's twenty-fourth African Extravaganza, yet another Sanders production, was held at the performing arts center in what used to be the old segregated Walton Theater, now restored. Inside the lobby perhaps a hundred fifty or two hundred people, virtually all of them black, milled around and lined up for the collard greens, rice and raisins, mashed potatoes, and chicken served with ladles out of huge iron pots. Many people, like Rose Sanders and her daughter Maleika, were in beautiful African robes, and the gathering had the warm air of a community gathering—Southern in the best sense.

The program began with ten African students from Concordia College singing the African national anthem followed by four young girls from Selma doing an African dance. The main attraction was a performance of *Pain's Heaven,* a play cowritten and codirected by Sanders's son Kindaka and performed by students from the alternative school Sanders had founded for kids kicked out of the public schools. It began with a dirgelike song sung by an offstage choir with the lyrics, "Pain's heaven. Pain's heaven. Pain's hell would be a better place for me." A black teenager playing an old drunk shuffled out carrying a bottle of whiskey and announced, "If you're black, I know y'all know what pain's heaven is all about." Most of the action that followed took part in a stylized urban ghetto block with graffiti on the walls where young blacks talked trash and sold drugs, where women were bitches and hos, and where the only adult was the drunk, Preacher Man, who implored the young people to make something of themselves while he drank his life away.

After a very long, tendentious first act, there was an intermission, which honored some of the community adults who worked with children and some of the teens who are members of Sanders's 21st Century Youth Leadership Conference. The teenagers shouted out slogans of unity and pride and then made a circle around their elders and recited together: "I want to lift my elders up. They are not heavy. I want to lift my brother up. He is not heavy. I want to lift my sister up. She is not heavy." If the question is how to reach young black kids, Rose Sanders apparently had found a way.

The second act began with more of the same meandering street talk and directionless soul-searching, followed by a drug bust of some of the kids. At the police station they were yelled at and threatened by three black kids playing cops. The action didn't strike me as comic, but the audience roared with laughter as the kids were manhandled as if there were something inherently funny about the familiarity of it all and the idea of black kids in cops' uniforms getting to play the Man. In the finale, the most troubled of the youths wanders into an unfamiliar part of town. The first white presence in the play, a stylized honky voice offstage, calls him a nigger, tells him his kind used to be lynched

for coming around this part of town, and then steps onstage in a spec-
tral white person's mask, like a combination of the Phantom of the
Opera and Jason from *Friday the 13th*. The black kid finally charges into
him and knocks him to the ground, but the white man pulls out a gun
and kills him.

The surviving black kids return to find out the white man has been
hailed in the newspaper as a hero who defended himself against black
gangsters. The injustice of it all finally leads the blacks to see they have
to mend their wayward ways and work together. "We must march on
like we did in the sixties," one announces. Shouting, "No justice, no
peace," they get out picket signs that read UNITED WE STAND and EYES
ON THE PRIZE. They throw the symbols of their wayward lives—their
whiskey bottles, their dice, their hot pants—into the dead boy's coffin.
And galvanized by the need to fight white racism, they are cleansed
at last.

Actually, virtually all of the dozens of young blacks killed in Selma in
recent years have been killed by other blacks, not by white racists. The
fifteen burglaries Rose Sanders complained about were almost certainly
the work of her neighbors in the black community, not of avenging
white rednecks. It's hard to imagine that the John Lewises and Martin
Luther Kings of the world, were they in Selma in 1995, would find this
play quite the right metaphor for the perils and pitfalls of the world
around them. But, now as then, it's the imagery of the Movement—the
bridge, the beatings, the past—that endures.

People evoke Bloody Sunday and the civil rights era for many reasons. Some do it because, for all the change that has occurred, the
enduring imagery of white racism and black struggle has the same
metaphorical power—and perhaps historical and institutional truth—as it
did then. They do it to teach their children, to honor the astounding
courage of the people who got their heads cracked and their souls
jarred, to remember the past, to tap into its energy, to pay homage to
what was won, to mourn for what was not. But mostly they do it
because Selma reflected the apex of a startlingly short-lived moment
where the lines between good and evil, right and wrong, seemed as
stark as the great bluffs above the Alabama River, and the prospects for
shimmering, incandescent, healing change seemed just over the
horizon. "If Negroes could vote, there would be no [Sheriff] Jim Clarks,"
Martin Luther King, Jr., told an audience at Brown Chapel Church a

few weeks before Bloody Sunday. "There would be no oppressive poverty directed against Negroes, our children would not be crippled by segregated schools, and the whole community might live together in harmony."

The words seem as ancient as Crete but the spirit they evoke still has the healing power of the gospel. So the aging warriors who returned to Selma for the thirtieth anniversary of Bloody Sunday, though looking to reminisce, to touch the past, to see old friends, to sing old songs, came back mostly to see how much of the spirit of Selma still lived and whether it was possible to rekindle its flames.

Their first impressions could have been a lot better. Rose Sanders and the Jubilee organizers had put together an ambitious program of activities, beginning with a February 19 Memorial Day for Jimmie Lee Jackson, whose death in Marion had set in motion the sequence of events that led to Bloody Sunday. Events included a Miss Jubilee Pageant at Wallace Community College in Selma (named, of course, for George Wallace, the movement's Antichrist in the sixties), a youth conference, a legal conference, a women's conference, parades and balls, a Jubilee Parade, interfaith services, and of course a recreation of the historic march itself.

Most people showed up Saturday afternoon, March 4, in time for the Bridge Crossing Jubilee Festival, a street fair and party at the foot of the bridge in front of the Voting Rights Museum. Rap and funk musicians bumped and thumped away and a troupe of drummers and dancers from Detroit played traditional African music from the Mali and Gambia regions of the Ivory Coast. Black kids, who looked like hip city kids anywhere in their baggy hip-hop pants and silver-and-black L.A. Raiders jackets and baseball caps—eons away from the wide-eyed farmboys of Bonner and Hobbs's day—milled around, sitting on the historical markers overlooking the river as rap from boom boxes competed with the music on stage. Vendors hawked civil rights memorabilia— SELMA-MONTGOMERY THIRTIETH ANNIVERSARY hats, caps, coffee mugs, and T-shirts ($10 in white, $12 in black)—plus barbecue, souvlaki, Mr. Ricky the Rib Master's ribs, funnel cakes, and chicken sandwiches.

Most of the SNCC veterans found their way to the Voting Rights Museum, ground zero of the celebration, where Bob Mants had set up his own personal civil rights museum within a civil rights museum on the second floor. The collection included strategy memos and photos of heroes of the past: Stokely Carmichael, Rap Brown, Marion Barry, John Lewis, Julian Bond, and Malcolm X. One photograph showed an old road sign reading NIGGER FOOD ROAD NEXT RIGHT. There was a history of the way the Black Panther party began in Lowndes County and pictures of the tent city where blacks gathered when they were kicked off the farms where they sharecropped after they attempted to vote.

Many of them had not been back in three decades, and they greeted one another with great, exultant roars of delight and ferocious, teary bear hugs. One of these was Scottie B, who wandered around bleary-eyed, partly from a nip or two, partly from the emotion of it all. "I was with Jonathan Daniels when he died, when Tom Coleman shot him down, and I haven't been back in twenty-eight years," Scottie B said. "I was run out of Tuskegee after we closed the school down and held the trustees hostage after King was killed. The sheriff told me, 'The first bird you see flying in any direction, you go in that direction and don't come back.'

"We was known to go into a place, get the sheriff all flipped out of his mind and by the time they looked up we'd be gone. And, man, you better have been gone. You went to jail and then somehow, you'd fallen downstairs or had an accident. One of their favorite things was to put a phone book on your head and beat you with one of those blackjacks on your head. What it does, it causes your brain to swell, but there's no bruises. You want to talk about pain. Man, that was pain."

"You come tonight to White Hall, you'll see what it was like," said Bob Mants, drawing a map in my notepad of the route to the municipal building in the small Lowndes County town called White Hall where a former SNCC member is now the mayor in what used to be the staunchest Klan county in the Black Belt. "We gonna have a real SNCC wang dang doodle and drink some of that Black Panther piss. Come on out. You'll see."

While we talked another old friend he hadn't seen in decades named Cornelius Jones came up to Scottie B and the two of them stared at each other for a moment in shock, like folks encountering the dead. They embraced and talked for a while, telescoping eras in a few phrases until Jones, who works with kids in Jackson, suddenly turned serious, as if remembering what this whole thing was supposed to be about.

"You know," he said, "we need to get with these young people about this whole thing of drugs and violence. The more I talk to them the more I understand why it really is necessary that our stories be told. That they know about heroes, the kind of heroes these kids need. Talk about courage. Talk about commitment. Talk about sacrifices. We were human, but we did some things."

"We were crazy," Scottie B said.

"We were human; that wasn't craziness."

"Things we did, I don't understand."

"You're denigrating something that really speaks to what people are supposed to be about."

"Standing in the middle of train tracks. Stopping trains. Man, I don't know how we did what we did."

Soon they ventured downstairs to the street, where they ran into Bonner, Shaw, and Hobbs, who were watching the celebration glumly, with barely concealed irritation, all thinking the same thoughts.

"This is not a circus, this is real," Shaw said, looking out disdainfully to the stage where masses of kids were crowded in listening to rap music. "You know, everyone should be here for the same purpose, to pay tribute to what happened here. But it's only the older people who feel goose bumps. Why did we march in the first place? For rap music? For this? It ain't right. I was with Jimmie Lee Jackson when he was killed. I don't think he died for hot dogs and rap music and carnivals. Right now is the time every young kid here eighteen or older should be registering to vote. You know what I'm saying? Here they have a thirtieth-year anniversary and the same mayor as when we started and there's not even someone registering people to vote. This isn't what it's about. This is a showboat. And when it's over, there won't be one new neighborhood center. There won't be one new youth program. This shouldn't be no circus. This is real."

The main events for the night were an "Invisible Giants" banquet and the "Red, Black and Green Ball" at the Elks Club in Selma. But that wasn't where the SNCC crowd was heading. Instead, they took U.S. Highway 80 toward Montgomery and hung a left on County Road 23 at the historical marker for the Holy Ground Battlefield, where on December 23, 1813, General F. L. Claiborne's army destroyed what was called the Holy Land Indian Village and essentially drove the Creek

Indians from southern Alabama. From there, they drove about four miles to the White Hall town hall, a sturdy twelve-year-old brick building. In White Hall the mayor was the former Black Panther John Jackson, the police chief was his brother, Horace Jackson, and the city proudly announced LOWNDES COUNTY COMMEMORATES THE THIRTIETH ANNIVERSARY OF THE VOTING RIGHTS STRUGGLE 1965–95.

Hobbs was so disgusted by the afternoon that he had stayed home, but most of the SNCC veterans from the afternoon were there: Bonner, Shaw, Mants, Scottie B, and Bettie Fikes, Matthew Jones, and Chico Neblett of the Freedom Singers. Two white veterans of the movement were among those on hand, a woman named Harriet Tanzman, who'd been active with the SCLC, and Strider Benson, a thin, shaggy-haired man known to all as "Arkansas," who radiated a manic glee at being back in Selma. The crowd included lots of Lowndes County folks plus dignitaries like John Lewis, who had been at the front of the line at the bridge and was now on the front lines in Congress, and James Forman, the former executive secretary of SNCC, who looked dignified but old and frail in a blue pinstripe suit and red tie, and carried a stack of copies of *Sammy Younge, Jr.,* a book he'd written in 1968 about the first black college student killed in the civil rights struggle.

Most people were so caught up in the warmth of the reunion that they had already forgotten about the afternoon, but Shaw was still brooding about it, and when I asked him about his own private calculus of progress versus stagnation, he said: "I always ask myself, 'Did we pull out of Selma too fast?' I think we laid a foundation, and then we didn't finish building the house. Because if we had done it right, no one would feel bad about a thirtieth-year anniversary. I think we left too quick, and we left Selma to people who weren't in the field to know what's going on. Everyone got a little bit and then moved on, which is why the mayor can go to the slummiest part of the city, come out, and eat catfish once a year, and get elected. It's sad, but that's the way it is."

People picked at the spread of potato chips, deviled eggs, chicken wings, franks and cheese squares on toothpicks, sliced ham, and pound cake until about seven, when we all sat down. We bowed our heads and the ceremony began with an invocation from Charles Smith, the first black elected to the Lowndes County Commission. "We thank you for the good sunshine that shined upon our booths today," he began. "We pray that you will bless this effort, bless this people that we may be strong and that they will never forget where they came from and that thou will give us the courage to fight on."

Mayor Jackson got up next and addressed the gathering: "If not for you, we would not be sitting in this building today," he said. "Bloody Lowndes welcomes you, because if it had not been for you and the 1965 Voting Rights Act, we would not be sitting in this building today and we would not be mayors, we would not be sheriffs, we would not be city council people. We need young people to start taking Scottie B's place, Jim Forman's place, John Lewis's place, Jimmy Rogers's place. But we've all been blessed to see some of these things change. It's a blessing to have you here. Enjoy yourself."

Things careened along, part reunion, part rally, part revival, full of confessions and testimony about what the movement meant to different individuals, homages to leaders past and present, and, most powerfully, the joyous music of the Freedom Singers, who led everyone in a version of "Keep Your Eyes on the Prize" that rumbled and moaned through the room, bouncing off the walls in a joyous clamor, half celebration, half admonition—"Keep your eyes on the prize, hold on, hold on." When each verse ended, you got the sense everyone had the same thought, that they hoped there'd be another verse, and the song would never end.

Finally it did, and things went on for a while until Mants, who was the emcee for the gathering, stood at the front of the room looking solemn. He had someone light a candle, and then we all stood and linked hands. "For those who've passed on, from SNCC, from other organizations, our brothers and comrades in the cause, I want you all to help me call the roll, for our brothers and sisters here in Lowndes County or who impacted what we did in Lowndes County."

And then, in the hushed silence of the room, one by one, they called the roll of the honored dead.

"Sammy Younge," called out a voice, remembering the hero of James Forman's book.

"Sammy Younge," Mants repeated respectfully.

"Jimmy Lytle," someone else called, remembering one of Lowndes County's SNCC stalwarts.

"Jimmy Lytle," Mants repeated.

The names rolled on, Mants repeating each one.

There were the giants of the movement and its most famous martyrs: Fannie Lou Hamer, Martin Luther King, Jr., Medgar Evers, Malcolm X, Andrew Goodman, James Chaney, Michael Schwerner, Emmett Till, Daddy King, Thurgood Marshall, and Bayard Rustin.

There were the martyrs of the Black Belt: Jonathan Daniels, Jimmie Lee Jackson, Viola Liuzzo, Reverend James Reeb, and names that only the locals were likely to know.

There were figures from history: Sojourner Truth, Nat Turner, Frederick Douglass, Harriet Tubman, Franz Fanon, W.E.B. DuBois. From Africa: Steve Biko, Patrice Lumumba, Kwame Nkrume, Sekou Touré.

Sometimes the names were introduced with a little flourish: "Bless his name, Ralph Abernathy," one woman called out. Sometimes they were surprises: "Karen Silkwood." "Cesar Chavez." "For those unknown." Some names got exclamation marks: "Yassuh!" "Yes!" "God bless!" Every now and then Mants would repeat a name with particular relish, caressing the syllables like a sax player bending notes–"ADAM ClayTON PoWELL!"–as if to say, "That's a good one. Now we cookin'." Whenever the names stopped for a moment, he would massage the silence with a dreamy "Call the roll. Call the roll" in a deep, incantatory voice, and the names would come again, more than a hundred of them in all, until the spirits of the dead filled the room and the links with the past were as real as the early-March chill in the swampland just over the tracks heading back to the highway.

Finally it wound down and everybody came back to earth, like meditators returning to what passes for reality. They finished the program with more songs and prayers and remembrances and in the end they had their wang dang doodle, dancing up a storm to old Motown and funk records until it was time to go home.

They all gathered the next morning at Brown Chapel Church in Selma, in a blinding rain, for one last go round. The women's heads sported leopardskin hats, African head wraps, grand straw boaters with red feathers coming out, hats with fluted frilly orange chiffon, black bolero hats, pink baseball caps, and a blocky gold hat that looked like a gold sandcastle on a tray. The men wore their Sunday suits or showed up in expensive Fila jogging wear carrying video cameras. High school kids showed up in suits or in their Starter jackets and oversized

Reeboks. On the dais dignitaries were packed shoulder to shoulder around the fourteen-member choir in white robes with red trim. The service began with the same hymn they sang at Mark Gibbs's church in Cobb County: "He is Lord. He is Lord. He has risen from the dead, and he is Lord."

"We come to Selma to sing the Lord's song, in the midst of strange contradictions," Reverend Joseph Lowery intoned in his sermon that rumbled and roared through the packed church, where people stood in the aisles and backed up into the vestibule. "It takes faith to sing the Lord's song these days. Those who interpret the last election as a mandate for malice we will resist with all our strength. We've come too far, marched too long, prayed too hard, been locked up too often, bled too profusely to turn back now. Don't let anybody turn back the clock on our journey home."

The stage was so jammed that there was barely a square foot unoccupied. Smitherman, the only white man on the podium, introduced Reverend Lowery and presented him with the key to the city. He spoke of his own childhood on welfare and criticized "those congressmen in their Brooks Brothers suits" who want to cut social spending while giving tax breaks to corporations. Who knows how much was real and how much was old slick Joe, but you couldn't watch and think nothing had changed in Selma, Alabama.

After Lowery came an endless parade of orators. John Lewis, who has kept the faith as much as anyone, bewailed the irony that thirty years after blacks won the right to vote at Selma, too few of them used it. "We need to get off our butts," he said. "If nineteen thousand of us had got off our butts rather than staying home on Election Day, Newt Gingrich would not be House speaker and Bob Dole would not be majority leader." Hosea Williams, once one of King's main lieutenants who became an increasingly eccentric Atlanta politician, said that he was sick of politics and that the answers lay elsewhere. James Bevel, now an indefinable mystic and right-winger wearing a white clerical collar, mouthed some mumbo jumbo about the need to learn the "science of government." Jesse Jackson declared the legal assault on the black electoral districts created under the Voting Rights Act to be akin to what happened a century earlier at the end of Reconstruction. "I will not so much challenge you as appeal to you on this one note. When

God gives you a rod and allows you to get to the Red Sea, if you have a fit of faithlessness and drop the rod as Moses did, it will turn into a snake and will go to Montgomery or Washington and bite you. We can't drop that mighty rod."

The procession continued. Representative Cynthia McKinney; Stewart Acuff, the white head of the AFL-CIO in Atlanta; Representative Eva Clayton; Ben Chavis; James Forman; some kid from the Atlanta University complex, who basically told his elders their day had come and gone and it was time for new leadership; Coretta Scott King. By the time they were finished the rain had stopped and they spilled out onto Dr. Martin Luther King Jr. Boulevard in front of the church. Then, in a ragged procession about fifteen hundred strong they meandered through the glistening, puddled streets to the bridge. I walked for part of the way with Bonner, tall and handsome in his neatly pressed blue jeans, expensive brown leather jacket, and blue shirt with a purple one layered underneath. Bonner was planning to march part of the way, come back to Selma to care for his ailing mother, meet up with his twenty-three-year-old daughter Bahati, and rejoin the marchers at the end when they returned once again to Montgomery.

Not reflecting the impassioned unity of the past, the speeches that morning splintered off in at least thirty directions. What had conveniently been cast as a distinctively Southern issue in 1965 was now clearly and unavoidably the racial agony of the nation. Still, when they stood at the base of the bridge, many of them had a feeling that went beyond déjà vu.

From the foot of the bridge the pitch was so steep that there was no way to know what was on the other side. In 1965 you had to take it on faith that the march was the right thing to do. In 1995, everyone knew there were no sheriff's posses on the other side, but beyond that you had to be willing to believe that there was a reason to march again. Older, slower, sadder, wiser, but still calling the roll, they marched up the bridge, over the crest, into the mist, and on, once again, to Montgomery.

Chapter 4

MONTGOMERY, ALABAMA
Wallace's Revenge

T HE OLD MAN LAY AT HOME IN HIS ELECTRIC THERAPULSE HOSPITAL bed under a brooding cloud of smoke from his Garcia y Vega cigars. He reached up with his right arm for the steel coat-hanger-shaped strap hanging above him so he could sit up and stare you down, eye to eye, as he talked.

Sometimes he'd choke and cough from the smoke. Sometimes he'd wince, his eyes closed and muscles tensed up in pain. Sometimes he lay silently with a dreamlike look on his face as if thinking of places and things far away. And sometimes he'd get a startled, panicked look, as if there was something he desperately needed to convey but there was no way to get it across. Mostly, though, he just stared at you with a fevered gaze as intense as a lantern beaming up from the bottom of a well.

"They all talking like me," said George Corley Wallace, pushing out his words in short hoarse breaths. "Nixon. Reagan. Clinton. Welfare reform. Crime. Big government. Taxes on the middle class. They all saying now what I was saying then."

Thirty years earlier, when twenty-five thousand demonstrators marching from Selma under the protection of a federal court order finally reached the grand, bone-white capitol in Montgomery on March 25, 1965, one of the protest songs they sang was the same one the Freedom Singers were singing that night in Lowndes County, "Keep Your Eyes on the Prize." But one verse that was sung with particular fervor in 1965 was among those omitted thirty years later. It went like this:

I've never been to heaven, but I think I'm right,
You won't find George Wallace anywhere in sight.
Oh, keep your eyes on the prize, hold on, hold on.

At the funeral of Jimmie Lee Jackson, who was fatally shot in Marion in 1965, SCLC leader James Bevel cited the Old Testament account of Esther's going to the king to plead for her people, a story that provided the impetus for the original Selma-to-Montgomery march. "We must go to Montgomery to see the king," he shouted, and the people, all of them inflamed at the mere thought of Governor George Wallace, the king of segregation, shouted the words back at him: "We must go to Montgomery to see the king." It was Wallace's bulldog determination not to appear to give in to the civil rights movement ("I'm not going to have a bunch of niggers walking along a highway in this state as long as I'm governor," he said at the time) that set in motion the bloody confrontation at the bridge.

Back then, only a fool or a white Southerner could fail to see that the marchers were on the side of history and that their tormentor in the state house in Montgomery was trying to uphold the doomed, dying empire of the segregated South. Almost everything was different thirty years later, but the most striking difference was this: in 1995, nothing seemed so dated or irrelevant, nothing seemed so to swim against the current political tides, as a bunch of aging black civil rights leaders marching fifty-four miles across the Alabama Black Belt from Selma to Montgomery. And in the year of the angry white male, the year of the Newt, the year the right took back both houses of Congress, few historical figures of our time seemed both so flamboyantly wrong and so blindingly prophetic as George Corley Wallace—wrong enough to lose the battle, but right enough to serve as a model for how to win the war.

Long before anyone talked of angry white males or Reagan Democrats or the forgotten middle class, long before Rush Limbaugh and a host of imitators turned hatred of liberals and elitists and government bureaucrats into the background noise of America, George Wallace tapped into the fears and resentments of white America in a way that has defined the political landscape and the critical voters ever since. And if his brand of right-wing populism was perhaps too razor-edged for prime time, you can say three things for sure about it. It was white.

It was angry. It was Southern. Now the nation's political center of gravity looks exactly the same way.

Nevertheless, an encounter with Wallace, at his modest brick house in Montgomery, had the feel of a trip back in time. At seventy-four, crippled and deaf, his shriveled legs lying motionless in rumpled blue slacks on the bed like those of a ventriloquist's dummy, Wallace could not hear a thing. Instead of conducting a conventional interview, I scrawled questions on pages torn out of a reporter's notebook. He stared at them as if trying to decipher hieroglyphics and then gasped out an answer.

You would think he wouldn't have cared. Wallace has spent much of his life trying to sell skeptical reporters his sanitized version of the World According to Wallace. Here was another reporter, probably as hopeless as the rest, but Wallace's watery eyes still had the wild glint of a salesman, preacher, or politician who figures he has a chance to close the sale.

"I never hated anyone," said Wallace. His once-taut features were flaccid and jowly, the coal-black brilliantined hair of his early days a lusterless ash gray. Behind him was a painting of a bald eagle poised for flight. "I don't hate the man who shot me. You find more hate in New York, Chicago, Washington, D.C., and Boston, than in all the Southern states put together. You'd find more hate in all those Northern cities in an hour than you'd find in the South in a year."

One by one he called in his two black attendants, Eddie Holcey and Jimmy Dallas, who had been sitting in the adjoining room eating sandwiches and watching *Gunsmoke* on TV, and a black state trooper, Benjamin Hamilton.

"Listen to me, Jimmy," he said, looking up at Jimmy Dallas. "Do you think I hate black people? Do I mistreat you? Am I as bad as they say I am?" he asked, and they all shook their heads and rolled their eyes, partly at the question and partly at the tableau, a quarter century out of date, in which they're asked to be actors. "Segregation was wrong," he said, as he has for much of his life since five bullets from Arthur Bremer's .38-caliber revolver in a Laurel, Maryland, parking lot left him a cripple and ended his career as a major national figure. "But I didn't bring segregation about. It was there when I got to the governor's office. It's gone, and I'm glad it's gone. It's so much better to see people together the way they are now."

He went on, quoting Scripture, professing his faith in God, asking out of the blue whether a former nemesis from *The New York Times* would marry a black woman. Like the good populist Democrat he began as, he was generally approving of Bill Clinton and quietly appalled by the billionaire bluster of Ross Perot. "He'd be nothing without his money," he said with a satisfied smile, as if sharing an obvious truth, one working man to another. Asked whom he admired in the world, he ran through a weird list that included Billy Graham and Bob Dole, Disraeli and Bismarck, Aldo Moro, John Major, and Nelson Rockefeller.

I wrote down a question about a picture at his office over at the Troy State University Montgomery campus that shows him with Elvis, like the South's version of a picture of Babe Ruth and Lou Gehrig. "You know he wanted to kill the man who shot me," Wallace said. "He was so upset, so distraught, he said he was going to go out and shoot him for me. 'Course I told him not to." I tried to get my mind around the image of Elvis in one of his sequined jumpsuits, his eyes moist and wild, his upper lip twitching in rage, a guitar in one hand, a pistol in the other, stalking the gray halls of some Maryland prison trying to hunt down Arthur Bremer.

Wallace went on, wincing in pain but eager to talk, spinning out fantasies of what might have been, saying, as he has in the past, that Hubert Humphrey felt him out as a possible running mate in 1972. "He had that bad heart, you know," he said. "He would have died in office, and I would have been president." He paused for a moment savoring the thought and then waited for the next question.

Finally he began to look tired, but before I left I asked him a favor. I'd been a journalist for twenty years, and I'd never even thought of trying to get an autograph from anyone I interviewed. But this one time I could not resist. I asked him to sign a recently published biography of him I'd brought with me, and he pulled himself up in his bed, picked up the black felt-tip pen sitting next to the Wild Turkey cigarette lighter by the side of his bed, and happily complied. "To my friend peter applebome," he wrote in a shaky but clear hand, my name in lower case. "Best wishes, George C. Wallace," he concluded, his name in capitals.

Lying in bed, talking about Elvis, Aldo Moro, and Hubert Humphrey, George Wallace seems as contemporary as a brass spittoon. But it's impossible to remember him in his cocky, strutting prime, to revisit his sneering taunts at "those pluperfect hypocrites in Washington," at "pointy-headed intellectuals," "loose-minded, high-living liberals," "intellectual morons," and "briefcase-totin' bureaucrats" and not see something so fresh it's startling.

With his genius for divining the gut of the electorate and his street fighter's compulsion to hit where the wound was most tender and raw, George Wallace did three things that changed American politics. He defined a constituency of angry, resentful whites, first in the South, then in the North, who felt alienated from the liberal social policies and snooty Ivy League mandarins of the Democratic party and who felt they were going to pay an undue price for an integrated society. He helped dynamite them out of what was left of their allegiance to the Democratic party. And he defined a newly demonized elite, the combination of liberals, bureaucrats, and intellectuals that came to replace the old Democratic bogeyman of cigar-smoking plutocrats as the real threat to ordinary working Americans.

Wallace did not start this process, and he certainly did not end it. In fact, his heyday came smack in the middle of the seismic shift in American politics that started in 1948 when Strom Thurmond's Dixiecrat revolt began the demise of the Democratic South and hit its high water mark in 1994 when Newt Gingrich engineered the Republican takeover of Congress. But to understand what has happened in American politics over the past thirty years it suffices to understand the constituency Wallace mobilized and defined and then to understand how that constituency moved from the Democratic party to the Republican.

The Wallace that endures is not the angry defender of segregation. Wallace backed off from that position by 1970, but his national ambitions were always limited by the hundred-proof racial poison he pumped into the body politic in his early days. It's not the post-bullet Wallace, reelected governor in 1974 and particularly in 1982 by a coalition of working-class whites and supportive blacks that held sway in much of the South until the Republican surge washed it away in 1994. And it's certainly not the all-but-forgotten figure lying in bed watching CNN with the sound turned off, or being wheeled by his black attendants into Morrison's Cafeteria or Martin's Cafeteria in Montgomery or Wilson's Barbecue in Troy, like a ghost of the South of old, coming back for some barbecue, Texas toast, slaw, and sweet tea for old times' sake.

Instead, it's the Wallace who before David Duke or Ross Perot or Jerry Brown or Newt Gingrich, before Howard Jarvis's tax revolt in California or Rush on the radio or Peter Finch in *Network* yelling "We're mad as hell and we're not going to take it anymore," before Pat Buchanan's angry, two-fisted campaign, before all the assorted tribunes of populist rage, left and right, real and fake, came roaring out of Clio, Alabama, like a bolt of white lightning that lit the stage for all the rest of them.

It was Wallace who first took on the road his send-them-a-message gumbo of right-wing populism and white racial resentment, lambasting big government and meddling federal judges, social engineers and liberal elitists, showing up on small-time radio and television talk shows to blast away at welfare, taxes, and liberals. It was Wallace, spreading out from the South like an ink stain on a white napkin, his shirt pocket full of cheap plastic-tip White Owl cigars, whose appeal to the white working class in Michigan and Wisconsin as well as Mississippi and Alabama first shot holes through the comfortable illusion of a racist South and an enlightened North.

And it was Wallace, preaching the gospel of pissed-off-ness decades before its time, who first attracted a national following based on the idea that neither national party was worth a damn. "You got a bayonet in yo' back with the national Democrats," he used to say, "and you got a bayonet in yo' back with the national Republicans." The Republicans got the message. The Democrats never did.

Wallace in the late sixties raised almost every issue–race, crime, federal power, taxes–that has defined U.S. politics over the past thirty years. "What are the people going to worry about in the nineteen-seventies?" he said in an interview with *The New York Times* near the end of 1969 in which he predicated a conservative backlash against liberal social policies, and a national tax revolt. "Why, about the things in our program–taxes, law and order, local control of government and other institutions." The phrases differ, but there's scarcely a thought in Wallace circa 1972 that can't be heard in Gingrich circa 1994 or Buchanan circa 1996.

George Wallace came from a relatively prosperous rural family. He is the grandson of a country physician in Barbour County at the edge of the Alabama Black Belt. But by the time he was born, on August 25, 1919, his father's farming business was already floundering and his

father's health was fading–Wallace Sr.'s sinus headaches were so severe
that he underwent an operation performed with only local anesthesia in
which part of his skull was removed. Perhaps to compensate, Wallace
developed the compulsive physicality of a force of nature–whether in
his youth as a bantamweight boxer who began by pummeling hapless
farmboys, black and white, in the chicken sheds behind his house or, as
an adult, as a compulsive campaigner and incessant womanizer.

Wallace's combination of acute political instincts and nervy, resentful
energy made him the perfect person to play the role of tribune of populist anger. "They say we gonna hurt 'em," he said of the national politicians, who condemned the political tornado he brought North. "And
I'll tell you sump'n: I wanta hurt 'em, 'cause they've hurt us long
enough, and I'm tired of it." With his compact boxer's build, his heavy
black eyebrows, and sharp black darting eyes, he was a man, the columnist James J. Kilpatrick once noted, who could "strut sitting down . . . full
of nervous stage business: standing up, sitting down, the horn-rimmed
glasses on, the glasses off, lighting his cigar, licking the cigar, spitting in
the wastebasket." He radiated such barbed energy that Senator Hugh
Scott of Pennsylvania once said, "He's a menace to the Democratic
and Republican parties. I think if he bit himself, he'd die of blood
poisoning."

I had encountered some of that energy from afar once in the past. It
was twenty-six years before our interview at his brick house on
Fitzgerald Road off of Zelda Avenue, named, of course, for Montgomery's beautiful, mad Zelda Sayre, who married Scott Fitzgerald. It
was 1968, and I was a student at Duke. Wallace had scheduled a rally in
downtown Durham during his 1968 presidential campaign. A bunch of
us snotty, privileged suburban college kids went, partly to listen, partly
to take in the spectacle, and partly to offer silent witness of our presumed moral superiority.

Unfortunately, several in our group made their witness quite vocal,
loudly heckling Wallace with the standard litany of "Sieg heil," and
"Fascist," in the process playing to perfection the arrogant, elitist foils
Wallace delighted in using to incite his crowds. "I heard some of them
four-letter words you hippies been using over there," he sneered in our
direction, waving his arms in disgust. "Too bad you don't know some
others like B-A-T-H and W-O-R-K." There were hollers of approval

from the Wallace people, more catcalls from our group. It felt more like an incipient rumble at a British soccer game than a political rally.

Suddenly, one of the Wallace supporters, his face red as a beet, wearing blue jeans and work boots caked in brown mud and a weathered Army-Navy store khaki shirt, charged into our group shouting, "Why don't y'all shut up and let the man speak." He shoved one kid to the ground and threatened to take on others. For a jagged moment, it looked like the parking lot would explode into a brawl, but the Wallace supporter backed off, we shut up, and the show went on. Still, there was an edgy chill that lingered, as if we'd picked up a bomb that hadn't gone off. Even liberal college kids in the sixties could figure out that if this one hadn't exploded, the next one might. What we were too dumb to realize, although it should have been obvious, was that there were a hell of a lot more of them than there were of us.

If Wallace had the right combination of brains and bile, he also came from the right place. It's impossible to imagine a non-Southerner striking the same national chords with the same ferocity as George Wallace did in the sixties and seventies. It was in the South that the resentment toward the federal government, wired into ancestral synapses from the Civil War, flared into hot flame during the civil rights movement. It was in the South that the theology of states' rights took hold from the time of John C. Calhoun and cropped up time after time like a sacred text. It was in the South, butt of a million jokes and gibes about dumb rednecks, hillbillies, grits, lintheads, and peckerwoods, that resentment had long smoldered against the smug elites at news networks in New York and Ivy League universities in New England. And of course it was in the South that race first became the defining poison of public life, where every issue from crime to government spending came to be filtered through the explicit or implicit filter of white fear and black menace. "Did Jack or Jock offer the more thrilling representation of the South in action against the Yankee and the black man?" offered W. J. Cash in his classic, *The Mind of the South,* the soundalike names satirizing the soundalike white Democrats all standing up for states' rights, white culture, and the sovereign South. "Here, and almost here alone, would there be a field of choice."

The result was a barbed, Manichaean politics of black and white, good and evil, whose tone veered between folksy bonhomie and raw

menace but where it never hurt to show you meant business in the way
that Gene Talmadge of Georgia used to boast, "I'm just as mean as cat
shit." In the one-party, no-ideology politics of the South, you didn't succeed through the best machine or the most enduring patronage or the
brightest ideas. The politicians who cut the broadest swath, like "Pitchfork Ben" Tillman, "Cotton Ed" Smith, Theodore Bilbo, or Gene Talmadge, were the ones who followed Cash's law by standing up most
dramatically for the right values against the wrong ones, for virtue
against sin, for white against black.

By most accounts, not just his own late-in-life mea culpas, Wallace
was never really animated by the purest form of racial hatred. Indeed,
he began in politics as a loyal follower of Big Jim Folsom, a 6-feet-8-
inch-tall, 275-pound populist maverick, who was elected governor in
1946 and 1954 in folksy campaigns during which he'd shake ragged old
mops at his campaign stops, promising to clean the corrupt big-money
interests out of state government. Folsom, whose heroes were Andrew
Jackson and Franklin Roosevelt, also promised to support equal rights–
including voting rights–for blacks. "As long as the Negroes are held
down by deprivation and lack of opportunity, all the other people will
be held down alongside them," he said in a remarkable 1949 Christmas
message to the state. "Let's start talking fellowship and brotherly love,
and doing unto others. And let's do more than talk about it; let's start
living it." An engaging but deeply flawed American original–his taste
for liquor and his record of small-time corruption in office became well
established–Folsom came to power at a time when Alabama probably
had the most vibrant liberal tradition in the South, although it played
out more in economics than in race. His goal was to establish a different
model for Southern politics than the cheap race-baiting that was the
norm. But he couldn't bring it off. When pressure for school integration
came after the *Brown* decision in 1954, he was run over by the tidal
wave of white reaction, and his drinking in the end scuttled any chances
of a comeback later on.

Wallace had not been in the Alabama Legislature long before he was
dubbed "the number one do-gooder in the legislature." It is often forgotten that along with their thinly coded racial bilge his national campaigns included calls for real tax reform that ended tax breaks for the
super-rich. "Now, George Wallace is not a racist. I am," John Kohn, a
Montgomery lawyer who fed Wallace some of his most overtly racist

rhetoric, told a Wallace biographer, Marshall Frady. "But he knows this state is the last stronghold of the Anglo-Saxon civilization. And he had enough practical sense to know that cussin' nigras was popular." After running Folsom's campaign in south Alabama in 1954, Wallace bolted as far from him as he could once the tide of white resistance became clear in 1955. Then, after running radio ads screaming "Vote right—vote white—vote for the fighting judge," Wallace was elected governor in 1962 in a race in which an apparently drunk Folsom ended his political career by babbling incoherently on statewide television the day before the Democratic primary. With the passions of race boiling as never before in the 1960s, no political journey is more predictable than the one from Folsom's words in 1949 to Wallace's most famous ones, written for him by the former Klansman Asa Carter, that the governor hissed into a bitter cold January day during his 1963 Inaugural address:

> Today I have stood where Jefferson Davis stood and taken an oath to my people. It is very appropriate then that from this cradle of the Confederacy, this very heart of the great Anglo-Saxon Southland, that today we sound the drum for freedom.... Let us rise to the call of freedom-loving blood that is in us and send our answer to the tyranny that clanks its chains upon the South. In the name of the greatest people that ever trod this earth, I draw the line in the dust and toss the gauntlet before the feet of tyranny, and I say: segregation now, segregation tomorrow, segregation forever.

After losing his 1958 governor's race Wallace had said famously, "John Patterson out-nigguhed me. And boys I'm not goin' to be out-nigguhed again." After his inauguration four years later he told a group of Alabama state senators, "I'm gonna make race the basis of politics in this state and the country." It seemed an idle boast at the time, but even in his inaugural speech, Wallace made it clear he wasn't just thinking about Alabama. "From this day," he declared, "we intend to take the offensive and carry our fight for freedom across the nation, wielding the balance of power we know we possess in the Southland."

Even in his defining political moment, there was far more than race at work. "Government has become our god," Wallace said in that inaugural address. "It is a system that is the very opposite of Christ." When Wallace took his campaigns national, race was usually the subtext while the pre-Limbaugh package of cultural grievances and bogeymen was always out front. Indeed, part of Wallace's legacy, one picked up over the years even more effectively by Southerners, native or transplanted, like Lee Atwater and Newt Gingrich, was his re-creation of the values-laden world of Southern politics on a national level with race implied in artful code rather than hurled out in angry epithets. Jack and Jock didn't need to hate all Yankees as long as they had the stand-ins of liberal elitists and a Democratic party that was, in Gingrich's resonant phrase, "the enemy of normal Americans." Early in the 1988 presidential campaign, as George Bush and Lee Atwater were just beginning to take a mallet to Michael Dukakis with one value-laden issue after another, Phil Gramm amiably drawled one day, "There's no one silver bullet, but you combine three or four of those issues and it induces Joe to say to Sarah across the kitchen table, 'Honey, that Dukakis guy is not our kind of person.'"

Wallace came on the national scene as busing was coming to Queens, King was marching through Cicero, Boston was erupting in violence over integration. Before the 1960s it was hard to imagine trying to use race, overtly or covertly, as a defining issue in elections outside the South. In 1940, only 24 percent of the nation's blacks lived outside the South, most of them invisible in Northern ghettos. But between 1940 and 1970, five million blacks left the South for the promise of a better life in the North or West. By 1970, only half the nation's blacks were in the South. In 1965, when Watts exploded, in 1967, when there were riots in 127 cities with damages of nearly a half billion dollars, when the face of black resistance changed from King's Christian forebearance in the South to Malcolm X and Rap Brown's angry urban defiance, it was clear that the racial fears of Southern whites were no longer much different than those of whites outside the South.

"You don't know what bad is," a woman working for Wallace in Jersey City during the 1968 campaign told a stunned reporter for the *Montgomery Advertiser.* "You folks down South have got it soft. Up here, we've really got a nigger problem." It didn't take Wallace long to see that a new national politics was evolving in which the politics of race and resentment that played in the South would play everywhere else as well. Douglas Kiker, a former NBC newsman and a native Southerner, explained in a 1968 article in *New York* magazine, it was as if Wallace came North and instantly had a vision: "They all hate black people, all of them. They're all afraid, all of them. Great God! That's it! They're all Southern! The whole United States is Southern!"

In his slapdash 1976 autobiography, *Stand Up for America,* Wallace recounted his first political forays into the North in 1964, including an appearance before a huge throng of Polish Americans and Serb Americans at the Serbian Memorial Hall in South Milwaukee. John F. Kennedy had received an enthusiastic welcome there during the Democratic primary in 1960, and it hardly seemed a likely place to warm to a Southern segregationist. But, in fact, by the time Wallace's rally began seven hundred people had jammed into the hall and another three hundred were milling around outside. As he charged into the room a polka band played "Way Down Upon the Swanee River" and then broke into a rousing version of "Dixie" as the assembled masses sang along in Polish. The gonzo journalist Hunter S. Thompson was stunned by the fervor of the event, which he compared to a Janis Joplin concert. Referring to Wallace, he wrote, "There was a sense that the bastard had somehow levitated himself and was hovering over us." In his speech, Wallace paid tribute to his audience's religious faith and called for prayer in school. He lambasted the 1964 civil rights bill, saying it would "destroy the union seniority system and impose racial quotas." He received thirty-four ovations for a forty-minute speech that concluded with "a vote for this little governor will let the people in Washington know that we want them to leave our homes, schools, jobs, businesses, and farms alone." As Wallace told it, in the standard, sanitized ain't-life-wonderful style of campaign biographies: "I remember that one fine-looking man grabbed me and said, 'Governor, I have never been south of South Milwaukee, but I am a Southerner.' Of course he was; the South is no longer geography—it's an attitude and a philosophy toward government."

Wallace's account inflated the crowd from seven hundred people to "thousands" but in retrospect, everything about that moment—from Wallace's themes to the urban blue-collar ethnics thought at the time to be solidly and eternally Democratic—feels like the beginning of a sea change few at the time could foresee.

It's likely that, even if fate had not intervened, Wallace himself never would have been able to overcome the toxic brew of his seg days. Race, like drugs or booze, works best when it's dispensed at something less than full strength. Still, it's amazing how far his high-test blend took him. In 1964, with national revulsion toward the South's institutional-ized apartheid allegedly at its peak, he entered the Wisconsin Demo-cratic primary "on a whim" with less than seven hundred dollars cash and no organization. He took nearly 34 percent of the vote, then got 30 percent in Indiana and nearly 45 percent in Maryland. In 1968, running as a third-party candidate, he got 10 million votes, 13 percent of the total, and won five states, the best third-party showing since Theodore Roosevelt in 1912. Only Strom Thurmond's all-out effort to save the South for Richard Nixon kept his showing from being even better.

In 1972, he won Democratic primaries in Florida, North Carolina, and Tennessee, and in Texas, a plurality of delegates elected in conven-tion. He finished second in Wisconsin, Pennsylvania, and Indiana and was running strong in the upcoming primaries in Maryland and Michigan when he left Alabama for Maryland on May 15, 1972. First came a boisterous rally in Wheaton, Maryland, then a quick lunch of hamburger steak doused in ketchup at a Howard Johnson's, then the rally in Laurel. After his speech, when he waded into the crowd, Arthur Bremer, a bland-looking twenty-one-year-old wearing a big Wallace button on his jacket lapel, was waiting for him. Bremer's five bullets didn't kill Wallace, but they killed him as a national force. The next day, while doctors labored to save Wallace's life, he won sweeping victories in Maryland, where he took 39 percent of the vote, and Michigan, where he won 51 percent.

The victories left him well ahead of his main Democratic rivals, Hubert Humphrey and George McGovern, in total votes—but not in the delegate count, where his appeal to the public hadn't translated into insider skill in Democratic party politics. Even if he had been healthy, he had little hope of picking up many delegates in the major primaries still to come. But his national political career was finished. He addressed the convention that nominated McGovern, calling for tax reform and tax relief for the middle class, prohibition of school busing, a constitutional amendment to bring back school prayer, a firm stance on law and order, and strong support for the military. Every item on his agenda was voted down by the convention and every one became part of the standard litany of the Republican revolution that has blown away Democratic candidates ever since.

The Wallace phenomenon didn't happen in a vacuum. Instead, he catalyzed two trends happening simultaneously: the shift of the South from Democratic to Republican, and the spread of racial politics and conservative ideology from the South to the rest of the nation. In their definitive book on modern Southern politics, *The Vital South,* Merle and Earl Black point out that during the New Deal era, once the Democrats cemented the solid South, they needed only 35 percent of the electoral vote outside the South to win. Now, with the continued flow of population to the South, if the Republicans sweep the South's 147 electoral votes, as they've done or almost done in four of the last five two-candidate presidential elections prior to 1996 (1972, 1980, 1984, 1988), they can win the presidency by capturing only 31 percent of the 391 electoral votes located outside the South. It's not much of a hurdle. No Democrat has ever lost the entire South and been elected president.

Like the Civil War, the realignment began in South Carolina, "too small to be a republic and too large to be an insane asylum," in the words of James Louis Petigru, a lonely Unionist, prior to the conflict. Back in 1936, when the idea of a Republican South was still an oxymoron, the state's venerable senator, "Cotton Ed" Smith, was stunned to walk into a Democratic National Convention and witness a black minister offering the invocation. "My God, he's as black as melted midnight!" Cotton Ed exclaimed. When a black Congressman came to the podium a little later, Cotton Ed stalked off and went home to South Carolina. Later, during his 1938 election campaign Cotton Ed retold his putative moment of triumph thus: "[When a] slew-footed, blue-gummed, kinky-headed Senegambian...started praying...I started walking, and as I...walked...it seemed to me that old John Calhoun leaned down from his mansion in the sky and whispered...you did right Ed."

It wasn't just race that had Southern Democrats worried. Much of the New Deal's pro-labor policies worried them even more, and it dawned on some that the suddenly dominant Democrats were becoming suspiciously urban, Northern, pro-labor, and liberal. Like his pre-secession South Carolina ancestors, Cotton Ed was before his time in sniffing out how radically the times were about to change. But when the old order first began to crack it was because of another South Carolinian, Strom Thurmond, who lit the match and then threw it on the bonfire, first by walking out on the Democrats and running for president as the candidate of the States' Rights Democratic or "Dixiecrat" party in 1948 and then, in 1964, by becoming the first leading Southern politician to switch from the Democratic to the Republican party.

George Wallace was like a cocked fist. Thurmond, with his young brides, his head stands and health food, his record twenty-four-hour, eighteen-minute Senate filibuster in 1957 to block jury trial provisions in a modest civil rights bill, was more in the Southern eccentric mode of Lester Maddox. Maddox, now Cobb County's elder statesman, made his name by brandishing an ax handle to keep blacks out of his Pickrick Restaurant, spent much of his life afterward selling ax handle souvenirs and Lester Maddox WAKE UP, AMERICA alarm clocks, and later dabbled in entertainment, appearing with his black aide, Bobby Lee Fears, in a vaudeville act called "The Governor and his Dishwasher."

By Southern standards, Thurmond, whose grandfather rode with Robert E. Lee, began in politics as something of a liberal; as a newly elected governor in 1947 he was willing to appoint a special prosecutor to investigate a particularly brutal racial murder near Greenville. But no ambitious Southern politician wanted to be on the wrong side of racial politics in the gathering storm of the period after World War II, and Thurmond was nothing if not ambitious. When Harry Truman signaled his commitment to civil rights by various measures, including desegregating the military, and when Hubert Humphrey at the Democratic National Convention in 1948 proclaimed, "It is time for the Democratic party to get out of the shadow of states' rights and walk forthrightly into the bright sunshine of human rights," the Mississippi delegation and half the Alabama delegation (but not George Wallace, who was with the half who stayed) walked forthrightly out of the convention hall. Before long, their successors walked forthrightly away from the party altogether.

Truman won in 1948 even with the Dixiecrat defections (Thurmond carried Mississippi, Alabama, South Carolina, and Louisiana), but a bigger crack came four years later when Dwight Eisenhower captured 50 percent of the Southern white vote, an almost unheard-of total for a Republican. In 1956, Eisenhower got more than half and easily won again.

With Lyndon Johnson as his running mate, John Kennedy managed to carry seven of eleven states of the old Confederacy in 1960, but even in the midst of Johnson's national landslide in 1964, the high-water mark of modern liberalism, L.B.J. lost Alabama, Georgia, Louisiana,

Mississippi, and South Carolina to Barry Goldwater. Amid the ashes of Goldwater's crushing defeat it was hard to see, but his strident conservative candidacy, his opposition to the 1964 Civil Rights Act, his appeals to states' rights and the antigovernment feelings of white Southerners ("Forced integration" he used to say, "is just as wrong as forced segregation"), created Southern Republicans in the Deep South like nothing else ever had. Goldwater closed his campaign in Columbia, South Carolina, standing on a lectern with Thurmond and a who's who of Southern segregationists, and ended up winning 70 percent of the white votes in South Carolina and almost 90 percent of the white votes in Mississippi.

That year Thurmond made his historic party switch. "The Democratic party has forsaken the people," Thurmond said. "It has become the party of minority groups, power-hungry union leaders, political bosses and big business men looking for government contracts and favors." He went on and on, sounding like one of today's radio–talk show hosts, tarring the Democrats with the brush of big government and high taxes, being soft on law and order, runaway spending, loose morals, weakness on defense. "The party of our fathers is dead," he thundered. "Those who took its name are engaged in another reconstruction, this time not only of the South, but of the entire nation."

When Goldwater was crushed it looked as though Thurmond had signed on for another lost cause. But Wallace, in one of his uglier, but more prescient moments, saw the Democratic train wreck to come.

> The Democrats have won with their new Negro friends. But this will be a lasting day in their memory. While they begin to force-feed welfare giveaway programs that reek of communism down the throats of the white South, the rest of the nation will look at us and it will know that the time will not be long coming before they too will face the same type of treatment. The time will come when all responsible Americans will want to join with the South in standing up against the tyranny of an unresponsive and overpowering federal government. They will at last realize that while on one hand you have a giveaway program, on the other hand you have a takeaway program.

Four years later, Thurmond's campaigning bore fruit. He held Southern delegates firm for Richard Nixon to win him the Republican nomination and then barnstormed through the South pleading with

Southerners to vote for Nixon, not Wallace. Wallace split enough votes
to allow Hubert Humphrey to win a paltry fifth of the Southern electoral vote, but between them Wallace and Nixon won 57 percent of the
national vote and 69 percent of the Southern vote. From that experience
came Nixon's obsessive dedication to pleasing the South, from his backtracking on civil rights to his ill-fated nominations of two unsuited
Southerners, G. Harrold Carswell and Clement Haynesworth, to the Supreme Court. "If Nixon gave more and more flamboyantly to the
South," wrote Gary Wills, "that was because the whole convention
hinged on the South. Others he could soothe or try to placate; those
delegates he had to serve."

When Nixon ran against George McGovern in 1972, using a political
game plan drawn largely by Thurmond's longtime political ally Harry
Dent, he swept the South; it was the first time in American history that
a Democratic presidential candidate would fail to win a single Southern
state. It would not be the last. "Democrats have spent all the years since
1948 trying to make the South join the rest of the country," Wills wrote
in 1974. "Maybe their only hope is to give in and join the South."
Watergate and Jimmy Carter's Southern candidacy allowed them to do
it one more time, when Carter resurrected the solid Democratic South
in 1976, winning every Southern state but Virginia. But Southern or not,
in 1980 Carter carried only his native Georgia. Walter Mondale in 1984
and Michael Dukakis in 1988 didn't win a single Southern state. In
1992, Arkansan Bill Clinton, running against two Texans, managed to
win North Carolina, Georgia, Arkansas, and Louisiana but still was
elected with only 42 percent of the popular vote nationally. With Bill
Clinton running as far to the right as any Democrat in memory and the
Republican primary fought out entirely on conservative turf, the 1996
election was an indicator of just how complete the Southern takeover of
presidential politics has been.

What is most remarkable about the tidal wave that ended four
decades of Democratic control of Congress in 1994 was not that it happened, but that it took so long to happen. Newt Gingrich has understood many aspects of American politics, from using the media to
raising money to turning GOPAC into a vast pool of cash to fund his
myriad activities. But central to his political strategy has been an understanding of geography. Like a kid trying to shake an apple from a tree,
he has always understood that if you shook the House hard enough, if

you held it up to enough ridicule and contempt, if you enunciated a stark moral grid of conservative purity and liberal depravity, you'd destroy the geographical anachronism at its heart: the white Southerner's ancestral ties to the Democratic party. And like a good demolition man placing his explosives one by one, he spent the decade from 1984 to 1994 bit by bit blowing up the old political foundation of Congress.

I first met Gingrich in 1985, the same way every reporter does, by turning on my tape recorder and letting him talk. I was covering the first stage of the G.O.P.'s rise in Texas, where in 1984 six freshman Republicans were elected to Congress for the first time—a notion then as strange and unnatural as dominoes without spots. They included Richard Armey, now the House majority leader and Newt's Number 2, and Tom DeLay, now the majority whip and the Number 3 Republican in the House.

Gingrich's cause célèbre at the time was a disputed election for the congressional seat in Indiana's Eighth District. Though both sides could point to recounts showing its man had won, the only vote that mattered was the one in the Democratic-controlled House that declared Democrat Frank McCloskey the winner over Republican Rick McIntyre—by all of four votes. When McCloskey was seated, Gingrich had buttons printed up proclaiming THOU SHALT NOT STEAL and orchestrated a walkout by House Republicans, the first such walkout this century. It included the Texas freshmen.

Gingrich then was exactly what he is now—a compulsively voluble quote machine and provocateur, sometimes brilliant, sometimes utterly out of control, speaking in a seamless barrage of sound bites like a computer programmed to provide good copy for reporters. When I asked him why Texas Republicans should be so agitated about the Indiana election, he paused for just a moment, and then began to speak in fully formed sentences like a man reading from a prepared text.

"The McIntyre case has convinced them more rapidly than any other experience would have that the Democrats they deal with on a regular basis are dishonest men," he began. "I think that when they went and heard Jim Wright at the Texas luncheon say, 'We're all in this together as Texans' and then they watched Jim Wright as the first motion of the year steal a seat from the people of Indiana, and when they tried to see Wright and reason with him and dealt with a cold, ruthless boss, that it radicalized them into understanding that the people on the Democratic side of the leadership in this House are not men of goodwill that you can deal with rationally and as reasonable people.

"Because of the nature of the modern Democratic party in the House, which is essentially an ostrich, ideological left-wing party combined with bossism, in order for people like Jim Wright to rise, they have to be willing to move to the left. So what you now have is a guy from Texas who represents the New York–California left-wing viewpoint but who brings enough pork barrel home to Texas to get reelected. I think that as people in Texas understand better the ideological cost, you're going to have more and more people faced with the choice, 'How much do I really want the next piece of pork barrel and how much am I willing to have my beliefs systematically betrayed?' And I think what they're going to say is they want a congressman who's effective in getting pork and is able to represent my viewpoint."

We shall see how much pork remains and how willing voters are to give up government perks for ideological purity. And, as with Gingrich's since-revised views of what sort of scrutiny a House speaker should be accorded, there's something hilariously Gingrichian in his depiction of Wright as a "cold, ruthless boss"–in distinction, one imagines, to Speaker Gingrich as a warm, accommodating, bipartisan statesman. But what happened in 1994 more than anything else reflected the breaks in the Democratic levees in the South. In 1990, Democrats in the eleven states of the Confederacy plus Oklahoma and Kentucky outnumbered Republicans in the House of Representatives by 83 to 46. After the Republican victories in 1994 and the subsequent switch of five Southern representatives from Democrats to Republicans, Republicans for the first time since Reconstruction outnumbered Democrats 78 to 59. During that time the Republicans overall gained 62 seats, meaning that more than half of the increase came from the South. Southerners in 1996 accounted for a third of all House Republicans and 30 percent of Senate Republicans.

Gingrich learned about more than geography during his years in Georgia politics. Gingrich may be an adopted Southerner, but he is too shrewd and analytical a pol not to learn pretty quickly how to make race work. In his first successful race for Congress in 1978, against a state legislator named Virginia Shepard, one of Gingrich's flyers showed a picture of Shepard with then state Senator Julian Bond, the black civil rights leader. "If you like welfare cheaters," it read, "you'll love Virginia Shepard."

There was a lot more than race at work in 1978, just as there was a lot more than race at work in 1994, but picturing your opponent with a black figure (it didn't hurt that it was a white woman and a black man) is the oldest trick in the South's racial deck. Similarly, when Gingrich in 1994 again and again hammered away at "the welfare state," it's safe to assume that he wasn't talking about doing away with Social Security or Medicaid. He was talking about welfare queens and welfare Cadillacs and the whole panoply of notions associated with them. Also, it's not too hard to figure out just which teenagers he was talking about in his famous comment, "It's impossible to maintain civilization with twelve-year-olds having babies, fifteen-year-olds killing each other, seventeen-year-olds dying of AIDS, and eighteen-year-olds getting diplomas they can't even read." It wasn't the kids in white suburbs, even if the ills he cited were not limited to black inner cities. Gingrich is way too smart to use the old vocabulary of race, but this is the sotto voce Wallaceism for the nineties, the language of Jack and Jock on the Internet and talk radio, that sells as well outside the South as inside.

Zillions of words have been spewed out about Gingrich over the years, but few have gotten it quite so right as that noted Yoknapatawphan Norman Mailer in these twenty-three:

> *Homage to Faulkner*
> *Newt Gingrich looks for angry votes;*
> *Ergo, he hammers welfare folks.*
> *There lie his Presidential hopes:*
> *Apotheosis of the Snopes.*

The power of the Republican South gives Southerners and Southern interests an ability to shape public perceptions and national politics to a degree they have not had since the Civil War. The result has been Lee Atwater and Newt Gingrich re-creating the good-against-evil moral universe of Southern politics on a national scale and the religious right holding something close to a veto over the Republican nominee. It means the nation's dominant party has Haley Barbour of Mississippi as the national chairman, Newt Gingrich of Georgia as the Speaker of the

House, Dick Armey of Texas as the House majority leader, Tom DeLay of Texas as the House majority whip, and Trent Lott of Mississippi as the Senate majority leader.

Nothing is forever. Racial politics, North and South, is a much more limited, risky game now than it used to be in the South when white politicians could play the race card with impunity. Now, both political sensibilities and social realities have changed to the point that even the Atwater-style racial politics of the eighties run into the obvious reality that racial division is a national cancer capable of dragging down the whole society. Similarly, the solid Republican South, in both the congressional and presidential elections, rests on far more shaky ground than the old Democratic version, which existed in a world where all the voters were whites. As long as blacks remain loyal Democrats, the party needs only about 40 percent of the white vote to be competitive in presidential politics in most Southern states. And the Republican congressional sweep of 1994 was helped immeasurably by the alliance of black Democrats and white Republicans, who under the prodding of the Bush Justice Department united to draw maps that packed blacks into serpentine districts across the South. Using the Voting Rights Act that came out of Selma as the underpinning, that alliance led to a historic increase in black representation but did so by making all the adjacent districts overwhelmingly white and Republican. A perfect example is Georgia, where prior to redistricting there were nine Democrats, one of them black, and one Republican, Newt Gingrich. After the postredistricting debacles of 1992 and 1994, the addition of one seat and the defection of the last white Democrat, Nathan Deal, to the Republicans in 1995, there were three black Democrats and eight white Republicans. The result, which Republicans had aimed for ever since the birth of the Southern Strategy in the Nixon years, made them look ever more like the party of the white South and the Democrats look like the party of the black South. A 1995 Supreme Court ruling saying states could not use race as the predominant factor in drawing districts led to changes in the districts in Georgia and other states. The ultimate effects on black representation and partisan politics remain unclear, but Democrats face a daunting challenge in trying to build a truly interracial majority party in the South.

One white Democrat who never made the shift over to the Republicans, it turns out, was George C. Wallace. Had he remained a figure with national aspirations, he probably would have decided that the only future he had was as a Republican. But Arthur Bremer's bullets changed everything. After being shot, Wallace went on to mount an extended white minstrel show of contrition, appointing record numbers of blacks to office when he came back as governor, appearing in black churches like a penitent seeking redemption. He made the case that the enemy was always the federal government, the meddling liberal judges, the arrogant Yankees, not the black people of Alabama. "The first people I saw when I opened my eyes when I came into the world and could see were black people," he once said. "I've lived among them all my life. I wouldn't know how to live where there were not black people. The country would be strange to me."

Toward the end of our interview, he started talking about going to heaven; he quoted from the Bible and held aloft fragments of Scripture he or his aides had written out on pieces of lined notebook paper. "I never hated anyone," he said again. "Never hated." He picked up one of the pieces of notebook paper and held it up. "Forgiven sins are not remembered by God," it said. He smiled a crooked, pleading smile as if this were all either of us needed to know.

On the day after our interview, Wallace made a rare public appearance at a book signing at a Montgomery mall. It was one of those moments when it was impossible not to see the South as a place eerily existing in two worlds at once, a place at once stuck in the past and halfway to Jordan. Hundreds of people, most of them white, but more than a few blacks as well, snaked through the mall, waiting on line until Wallace, after almost three hours of sitting upright and signing almost seven hundred books, slumped down in pain and was wheeled away.

Claude McClearen, known as Rooster, who used to give a defiant rooster crow at Mr. Wallace's campaign rallies and is still fighting the Civil War showed up. So did Sarah Norred, the Montgomery County tax collector, who, with the unerring Southern ability to gloss over minor unpleasantness, couldn't imagine race dimming Wallace's legacy. "Oh, I don't think people will hold that against him; it was a different time," she said blandly. "He's a good man, and he stood up for Alabama." Alva Lambert, a Montgomery county deputy district attorney, who does an absolutely perfect Wallace imitation and admired him as a shot of hundred-proof Bourbon in an age of Chablis politics, did his version of Wallace on the stump.

Ever attentive to his place in history, Wallace brought with him a written statement in which he apologized for segregation and called attention to the degree to which his agenda then was the nation's now. On race he sounded like a New Democrat: "I'm frankly concerned that much of this country is turning away from trying to overcome our differences and is retreating to resegregation. If it was wrong when I was supporting it, it's no less wrong now." On government spending he sounded like the populist he began as, calling for an economic stimulus program and spending on infrastructure and education. "These are the things that create hope–and it's a lot easier for people to get along when they are not hungry, they have a roof over their heads, and they have the self-respect that comes from having an honest productive job."

One old black woman, seventy-six-year-old Mattie Brinson, was bustling by when she looked up in amazement to see George Wallace in his wheelchair in front of her, like an apparition. "I have to shake his hand," she said excitedly. "I can't afford no book, but I have to shake his hand." I asked her whether she felt any ill will toward Mr. Wallace; she waved her arm, as if swatting the question away. "We're all human," she said. "The Lord made us all. We're born in this world alike, and we'll all go to sleep alike too."

In the South, where, after all, being born again is proof of redemption and not chicanery, Wallace as penitent rings true, and there's much that's comforting for both whites and blacks in the parable of the dark prince of segregation driven by pain and grief to become a model for racial healing. But the truth is, it's a lot easier to redeem one tortured soul than one troubled society. As an old man, wracked with pain and more concerned about the next life than this one, George Wallace could talk about hope and redemption, much as a dying Lee Atwater repented for the poisons he pumped into the body politic.

But everyone who knew Wallace when the racial text for our time began unfolding in the 1960s knew what he stood for then. "Oh, Wallace was always very supportive of everything we were doing," said Ed Fields, the neo-Nazi of Birmingham then and Cobb County now. "Our contact was Colonel Al Lingo, the head of the Alabama Highway Patrol. He'd ask us to hold demonstrations in front of schools that were to be integrated so Wallace had an excuse to shut them down. He'd ask us to collect petitions asking the governor to close the schools. There was a dinner down at the Jefferson Hotel where we were given a special table on the front row. He hired Klansmen like Asa Carter and arranged state business for Bobby Shelton, the Klan leader. Lester Maddox says something happened to Wallace when he was shot. I guess that has to be it."

Though Wallace says he was not motivated by hate, he must know that gives him more, not less, to atone for. What he taught the nation is what the South already knew: in U.S. politics, almost nothing plays quite like race. "I started talking about schools and highways and prisons and taxes—and I couldn't make them listen," he once told an Alabama newspaper editor. "Then I began talking about niggers—and they stomped the floor."

A year after he shook hands with Mrs. Brinson, Wallace ventured out in public once more. Thirty years before he had sent all the female state employees home early and otherwise done his best to ignore the twenty-five thousand marchers from Selma who came to Montgomery singing protest songs and predicting his eternal damnation. This time there were only two hundred marchers, but George Wallace, old, sick, hurting, and tired, wanted to greet them when they arrived in town. So when the marchers who had left Selma that drizzly, gray day after the services at Brown Chapel Church arrived at Saint Jude High School for the final ceremonies of the thirtieth-year anniversary events, there to greet them under a glorious, clear, early-spring sky was George Wallace. He sat on the podium in front of the old brick building along with Reverend Joseph Lowery and the other marchers and their supporters, and was one of the few white faces in an overwhelmingly black crowd. Stooped over in his chair in his dark blue pinstripe suit, his light blue tie hanging down in his lap, Wallace was too weak to make a speech but an aide read his words for him.

"My friends," the message began. "I have been watching your progress this week as you retrace your footsteps of thirty years ago and cannot help but reflect on those days that remain so vivid in my memory. Those were different days, and we all in our own ways were different people. We have learned hard and important lessons in the thirty years that have passed between us since the days surrounding your first walk along Highway Eighty. Those days were filled with passionate convictions and a magnified sense of purpose that imposed a feeling on us all that events of the day were bigger than any one individual. Much has transpired since those days. A great deal has been lost and a great deal has been gained, and here we are. My message to you is, 'Welcome to Montgomery.' May your message be heard. May your lessons never be forgotten. May our history be always remembered."

Standing in the crowd, Charles Bonner was among those deeply moved by the notion of Wallace redeemed and repentent. It's hard to overstate what that change said about the transformation in the opportunities Alabama offered to people like Bonner thirty years ago and what it could offer his daughter today. But, as more than a few others in the crowd noted, the greeting came only from a ghost of the South's past. The current governor, Fob James, a Democrat-turned-Republican who jumped on the Limbaugh-Gingrich bandwagon and spent his term bringing back chain gangs, ordering state prisoners to go to work breaking rocks, and calling for more corporal punishment in the schools, was nowhere to be seen. "Fob James did what George Wallace did thirty years ago," said John Lewis.

But in the South the blessings of the ghosts can mean as much as the blessings of the living. Shortly after his words were read for him, George Wallace looked up at Reverend Lowery and in his choked, hoarse voice, said, "I love you. Black and white people love you." He reached out with his right arm, Lowery took it and along with perhaps two hundred weary souls together they sang "We Shall Overcome." When it was over, Wallace was wheeled through the school and out the back. He gave a tired wave to the black woman eating ribs and selling souvenir SELMA TO MONTGOMERY 30TH ANNIVERSARY coffee mugs and then was lifted into his van and driven away.

Chapter 5

"ALOT OF OUR PEOPLE DON'T KNOW QUITE WHAT TO MAKE OF THE fact that the South is doing so well; they've had this premillennial view of things going to hell for so long, they're a little uncomfortable with prosperity," said Oran Smith, the editor of *Southern Partisan* magazine, the voice of the original "neo-Cons," the neo-Confederates, in Columbia, South Carolina. "There was a book published in 1981 called *Why the South Will Survive.* No one would think of publishing a book like that today. You might write one called *Why the South Is Surviving* or *How the South Has Won,* proclaiming victory. But even our pessimists are beginning to see that, after all these years, Southern values are renascent after all."

Smith, a ruddy, blond-haired, round-faced thirty-three-year-old graduate student in political science who was previously an aide to the former Republican governor, Carroll Campbell, has the easy bonhomie of a Southern fraternity boy a few years down the road. He was sitting in his crowded office surrounded by Confederate memorabilia and bric-a-brac. A huge print of Robert E. Lee was on the wall behind him, a portrait of Jefferson Davis on the wall to his right, and the third national flag of the Confederacy on the wall to the left. Next to Jefferson Davis was the front page of the *Charleston Mercury* of December 20, 1861, with the exultant headline: THE UNION IS DISSOLVED! The original stars and bars—(not the familiar Confederate Battle Flag, which was never the official flag of the Confederacy) hung from a flagpole. In other parts of the building, at the rear of the copy shop on East Gervais in downtown Columbia, were portraits or sketches of Confederate heroes like

Stonewall Jackson, Nathan Bedford Forrest, and John Mosby or other figures of the Confederate canon, like the *Book of the Confederate Dead,* a listing of all the South Carolina casualties in the war. The most recent issue of *Southern Partisan,* with a cover photo of a statue of Robert E. Lee, was sitting on Smith's desk along with an ad he was composing for the local paper in support of the continued flying of the Confederate Battle Flag over the state capitol just down the street.

Founded in 1979, *Southern Partisan* isn't *Time* or *Newsweek.* Its circulation is only about fifteen thousand, and even most Southerners are not familiar with its somewhat schizoid mix of Old South gun-and-musket lore, scholarly Burkean-Calhounian political philosophy, and contemporary hard-right politics. Not long ago its Confederate posturing would have seemed either utterly anachronistic or terminally silly, like the *Mad* magazine cartoons of old Confederate geezers wheezing, "Save your Confederate money, boys. The South will rise again." But instead of a mossy throwback, *Southern Partisan* these days is a window onto a world—the world of the Lost Cause—that now somehow turns out to be astonishingly robust, like a false ending in a Hitchcock film.

When George Wallace was wrapping himself in the holy mantle of Jefferson Davis, howling about the sanctity of states' rights and touring the country with country bands playing "Dixie," he and the other demagogues of his day, Lester Maddox, Mississippi's Governor Ross Barnett, et al. seemed to many like the Old South's last gasp. Indeed, they gave Southern culture such a bad name that for a quarter century afterward it was almost impossible to wrap yourself in the folds of the Old South without bringing the blood of Selma, Birmingham, and Philadelphia, Mississippi, along with you. When John Egerton was trying to balance the notions of the Americanization of Dixie versus the Southernization of America in the early 1970s, he wrote about the conferences he went to where earnest liberals sniffed around at various essences of the South with the assumption that they were the only ones doing the sniffing. "There aren't many meetings anymore to "preserve the Southern way of life," he noted. "So it is mostly Southerners with a particular perspective—for want of a better term, it is Southern liberals—who still gather to talk introspectively about their region, and where it has been, and where it is going."

But that was then. A quarter-century on, in hoary, century-old Confederate organizations and freshly minted, modern-day variations on the same theme, at conferences and Civil War reenactments, in cyber-space and the real world, the South is full of Lost Cause nostalgia, angry manifestos, secessionist verbiage, and assorted movements harking back to various elements of the Dixie of old.

The Internet is full of Old South activity. "Netscape, if we'd had it in 1861, we would have won the war," reads the home page of the 19th Alabama Infantry Regiment, C.S.A. Mailing lists include Heritage L, which tracks and exposes what it considers anti-Confederate and anti-Southern behavior, or the more protean Bubba List, which includes neo-Con issues and more diverse topics like Eastern North Carolina barbecue, sacred harp singing, Southern literature, or the best ways to make green tomato pickles or microwave your Moon Pies. Organiza-tions like the Southern League, the Sons of Confederate Veterans, and *Southern Partisan* magazine have homepages full of Old South lore and neo-Con politics.

"Is the Confederacy obsolete?" asks a typical *Southern Partisan* cover (Fall 1994), back in the nonvirtual world. The cover features a color photo of a putative Confederate widow in black and her young, blond-haired son clutching a Confederate flag in his hand. "The Confederacy is not obsolete," the article—actually a reprint of a speech given at the Museum of the Confederacy in Richmond—concludes, as if any *Southern Partisan* reader might possibly think otherwise. "This storm-cradled nation has much to teach us—as does the terrible war by which it lived and died."

The neo-Confederate groups are not a monolith. They range from hard-right and overtly racist politics to a relatively benign mix of monu-ment polishing, history, nostalgia, and agrarian conservatism suspicious of both big government and big business. *Southern Partisan* presents a mix of Confederate lore and hard-right politics. The Southern League was formed in June 1994 as "an activist organization of unreconstructed Southerners pursuing cultural, social, economic and political indepen-dence for Dixie." The Ludwig Von Mises Institute of Auburn, Alabama, dedicated to "Austrian economics" and minimalist government, gath-ered true believers and fringe scholars in Charleston in April 1995 for a conference on the hows and whys of secession, where cutting-edge scholarship was presented, such as the institute's own David Gordon on "The Fallacy of Anti-Secession," Scott Boykin's paper on "The Ethics of Secession," and James Ostrowski's paper on that old Dixie chestnut, still at issue after all these years, "Was the Invasion of the Confederate States a Lawful Act?"

Publications are sprouting all over the place: *Southern Heritage* magazine, with articles like "States Rights' Triumphant Return"; *The Journal of Confederate History, Confederate Underground, The Confederate Sentry,* plus *Counterattack,* published by a group called the Southern Defense Initiative Corporation. Groups, historical and political, include the Confederate Society of America, the Culture of the South Association, the Southern Heritage Association, the Heritage Preservation Society and the Military Order of the Stars and Bars. Not long ago, the Sons of Confederate Veterans, which is chartered as a nonpolitical organization open to the descendants of Confederate soldiers, was a moldy, moribound relic down to a few thousand graybeards. Now it's up to 25,000 and the group is adding 300 to 400 members a month as various fights over the Confederate flag and the vogue for states' rights have given it greater visibility than it's had for decades.

In the classified pages of *Southern Partisan,* the Southern Nationalist Party, which skirts the far right of the far right, announces it is now accepting applications for membership ("The time has come for our independence and sovereignty") and its Confederate States of America 2000 videotape explains "who and what the New World Order is and how it is trying to conquer our country, establish a one world government, enslave the people of the world, degenerate the White race, and why the South MUST Rise Again if our people are to survive." Michael Andrew Grissom's Confederate Nostalgia Trilogy of *Southern by the Grace of God, The Last Rebel Yell,* and *When the South was Southern* goes so far as to wax melancholic on some of the regalia of the Klan ("Stars, half-moons, circles, crosses, and diamonds of bright-colored cloth embellished the uniforms to give them a bizarre, supernatural look intended to frighten the superstitious negroes into mending their ways.") It goes on respectfully: "The world knows the story of the Ku Klux Klan. Riding in the dark of night, Southern men reclaimed the South from the black terror. Carpetbag rule was overthrown; civil law was reinstituted; and, negro rampage was summarily ended."

You can order Civil War Trading Cards ("Hallowed Ground," Series 1, Set 1, is only $7.95); Lost Cause music like the Rebelaires' *Carry the Memories On* goes for $10, and a Gettysburg Confederate Commemorative Collectors Edition Pro-Style Golf Cap ("The colors, the insignia, the Pride of the SOUTH") is $29.95. The Ruffin Flag Company of Crawfordville, Georgia, sells an assortment of Confederate T-shirts (Confederate Seal, N.B. Forrest, Robert E. Lee, Jeff Davis, Alex Stephens, Stonewall Jackson, Quantrill, Stone Mountain, Edmund Ruffin and Dixie's Pride), flags, and battle flags. Richards Gregory of Lancaster, South Carolina, offers his ARE YOU SCARED? T-shirts for $11.99 with the Confederate Battle Flag on the front and the eleven states of the old Confederacy on the back aside the acronym S.C.A.R.Y.– SOUTHERN CITIZENS ADVOCATING RELOCATION OF YANKEES. In the classified pages in *Southern Partisan* or *Confederate Veteran* you can get reading material like "Racial Separatism Defended–Why and How to Preserve the Traditional White Culture" or the 1995 Confederate Directory. You can order Confederate clip art on computer diskettes, "Wear Your Pride" T-shirts (SOUTHERN AND PROUD OF IT with Confederate Seal) or Confederate coins or passports.

It is not that thousands of Southerners have stockpiled their Enfield or Richmond armory muskets, their Harpers Ferry rifles or Sharps carbines, their Colt 1860 .44-caliber revolvers, their brass-handled rifle-sword bayonets and are getting ready to have at it again. Not even that the weird and growing collection of Lost Cause and Southern culture groups represents much more than an agitated, exotic fringe. Instead what's relevant here is that the spirit of the Lost Cause–the states' rights of Calhoun; the messianic religiosity of Stonewall Jackson; the paeans to tradition, history, faith, smaller government, and old-time values; the ubiquitous presence of race–tracks remarkably well with the ascendant conservative agenda of the 1990s. *Southern Partisan* turns out to be part of the arsenal of Richard Quinn, a savvy political consultant whose clients over the years have included Ronald Reagan and Strom Thurmond: it's hard to know these days where the Confederacy ends and the Republican party begins.

Take the Confederate Society of America. It may not be entirely mainstream, but its call to arms in *Southern Partisan* could come right out of any Republican consultant's playbook: "Worried about crime, high taxes, socialized medicine, gun control, runaway immigration, moral breakdown, sex education of your children, tyrannical government? We are too! Join Southerners working for constitutional government, morality and individual freedom."

Pat Buchanan is listed as one of three "senior advisors" to *Southern*

Partisan, which regularly ran his syndicated column until he stopped writing it to run for president. David Funderburk, a Republican congressman from North Carolina, is listed as one of the "advisors and contributors." Its pages are a vivid glimpse of the overlap between Confederate politics and conservative ones. In a long interview in *Southern Partisan*'s Fall 1984 issue, Senator Trent Lott of Mississippi, now the Majority Leader of the U.S. Senate, related Jefferson Davis to current political trends:

PARTISAN: At the Convention of the Sons of Confederate Veterans in Biloxi, Mississippi you made the statement that "the spirit of Jefferson Davis lives in the 1984 Republican platform." What did you mean by that?

LOTT: I think that a lot of the fundamental principles that Jefferson Davis believed in are very important today to people all across the country, and they apply to the Republican Party. It is the more conservative party. It is the party more concerned about not having government dominance. It is the party that believes the least government is the best government. . . . The platform we had in Dallas, the 1984 Republican platform, all the ideas we supported there—from tax policy to foreign policy, from individual rights to neighborhood security—are things that Jefferson Davis and his people believed in.

In the spring 1986 issue, Pat Buchanan previewed themes that became a part of his presidential campaign a decade later:

PARTISAN: How has being a Southerner by choice affected your world view and your political attitude?

BUCHANAN: My father was a tremendous partisan of the South. His grandfather was captured at Jonesboro at the Battle of Atlanta and spent the rest of the war in a federal prison. His great-grandfather died on the way to Vicksburg. He was very much a Southern partisan. . . . When you read all the books about the South and the Lost Cause, I think it goes through your system and somehow you become a partisan. . . . I think the Democratic party is going to come to realize that it simply can never again occupy the executive office of government unless it addresses the issues of concern to American Southerners. If it does not do that, it's going to reduce itself to an irrelevancy.

Other issues feature long, friendly interviews with Dick Armey, now the Number 2 man in the House, behind Newt Gingrich, and with the Texas senator and failed presidential aspirant, Phil Gramm. Though *Southern Partisan* often seems caught up in its lunatic Lost Cause world of refighting the war, debating the merits of slavery, and reviling Lincoln, Sherman, and Grant as "those who in modern times opened the Pandora's Box of genocide and the extermination of civilians," at times it has been much more in touch with a large chunk of America than the mainstream media has been. For example, the magazine published a long, anguished 1993 cover story on the disaster at Waco, "They Made a Desert and They Called It Peace—The Tragedy at Waco Revisited," that posed questions surrounding the government's ill-fated raid almost two years before the Congress and the mainstream media did.

Nowhere did the confluence of conservatives and Confederates come together so vividly as in Pat Buchanan's 1996 presidential bid. Buchanan's rise as a serious challenger caught the mainstream media entirely by surprise. But anyone looking at the Internet sites and newsletters of the neo-Cons could have seen that the most rabid conservatives in America—the shock troops of the Republican party's Southern base—were totally sold on Buchanan well before the race began.

Back in its August–September 1995 issue, *The Confederate Sentry*—the official newsletter of the Confederate Society of America—featured the endorsement by the organization's president, Wayne Powers, of Buchanan's nascent campaign. "No other presidential candidate from either party addresses essential issues like restoring State sovereignty, parental control of education, stopping illegal immigration, putting America first and restoring the Constitution," Powers said. "What other candidate proudly mentions Robert E. Lee and the Confederate battle flag in his campaign speeches? . . . A Buchanan victory will be a Confederate revolution at the ballot box—without one shot fired!"

Once his campaign began to take off—when it looked for a brief time as if a wealthy TV blabbermouth turned nineties' populist exhorting "peasants with pitchforks" might mount a serious challenge to Bob Dole—every neo-Con newsletter and web site was full of Buchanan fever, fervent endorsements, and the 1-800-GO-PAT-GO fund-raising number. But three things happened when the candidates came South for the crucial South Carolina primary. First, money and organization mattered in the mad dash of primaries in a way they didn't in New Hampshire and Iowa, where Dole had lost. Second, the South Carolina Republican establishment stood by Dole against Buchanan the way Strom Thurmond stood by Nixon against Wallace in 1968. Third, when all the Republicans paid homage to the Confederate flag, courted the religious right, and tried to outdo one another's conservative credentials, it was clear to most Southerners that pragmatism made more sense than a Pickett's Charge from the far right. Buchanan's white-hot candidacy—and particularly his dubious protectionism—proved too extreme even for Southern Republicans. But for many Southern conservatives the salient fact was not that the most Confederate candidate lost, but that the winner, Bob Dole, was a longtime fiscal conservative who earnestly courted Ralph Reed and the Christian Coalition and came into the campaign with a 100 percent rating on the Coalition's candidate's scorecard. The thing to remember about the Republican primaries in 1996 is not Buchanan's improbable campaign finally hitting an iceberg and sinking, but Barry Goldwater, who won only the Deep South in his "Extremism in the defense of liberty is no vice" 1964 campaign, in 1996 shaking his head in wonder and saying of Dole and himself, "We're the new liberals of the Republican party. Can you imagine that?"

Clearly, the more explicit the Republican party's link to the idea of the Confederacy, the less appealing all this is on the national (or even the regional) stage. Trent Lott may praise Jefferson Davis and the Confederacy to the S.C.V. in Biloxi and to *Southern Partisan,* but it's not the kind of thing likely to make him a major figure in the Senate. But that's not the point. What is important is the degree to which the traditional ideology of the South—stripped of its more purple cultural trappings, the hardest edge of race and the Sons of Confederate Veterans nostalgia—has gone mainstream.

There's a substantial school of thought among conservatives North and South that the Constitution of the Confederate States of America could be viewed as that era's Contract with America, or at least with the Confederate States of America—an attempt to subtly rework the U.S. Constitution and get it right this time by shifting power from the central government back to the states. Thus, its preamble was changed from the familiar "We, the People," which implied that the federal government was a proxy for all the people rather than of the individual sovereign states, to "We, the people of the Confederate States, each State acting in its sovereign and independent character...." It outlawed the slave trade (it didn't outlaw slavery). It required a balanced budget. It gave the states new abilities to impeach federal (that is, Confederate) officials working within their borders such as judges. It put new restrictions on the ability of the Confederate government to levy taxes and authorize spending. It acknowledged the sovereignty of God over the political order. It gave the president a line-item veto, and it offered its version of presidential term limits: one six-year term.

Whether such a union could have harnessed the power of the atom, put together a war effort to defeat Hitler, put a man on the moon, provided a measure of protection for the aged, the poor, and the sick, passed measures to protect the air and water from pollution, promoted the degree of economic interdependence that created the world's greatest economy, not to mention whether it would ever have dismantled the South's American apartheid, isn't something neo-Confederates worry about too much. But if the political rage of the nineties is to dismantle federal power and give it to the states, that's precisely what the Confederate Constitution was about.

As for the steps the South needed to get there, namely secession, the neo-Cons would have you believe secession is as contemporary as the Internet. "Secession!" the Ludwig Von Mises Institute proclaims. "From Staten Island to Quebec, Scotland to California, Chechnya to Texas, secession is in the air." Or, as Michael Hill, president of the Southern League, puts it in a typical mailing: "With little warning political devolution swept away the Soviet Union and its satellite Communist empire in eastern Europe. Secession presently is under serious discussion in Canada, Scotland, Brazil, and in our own western states.... With God's help we will deliver ourselves from a government that has deformed the intent of the Founding Fathers, usurped the states' sovereignty, and imperiled Western civilization."

In a less apocalyptic vein, the links between the South and the rise of contemporary conservatism go back to the man who essentially gave birth to the modern conservative movement, Russell Kirk. If modern conservatism has had a Bible–besides the original, of course–it was Kirk's 1953 book, *The Conservative Mind: From Burke to Santayana*. Published when the legacy of the New Deal seemed unassailable, Kirk's book maintained that the essence of the American experience was not liberalism but conservatism, and not just the hard-edged economic conservatism of the Republican party, but the values and traditions best represented by the South.

Kirk grew up in Michigan, but much of his intellectual inspiration came from the South, from John Randolph of Virginia, the subject of his master's thesis, from John Calhoun, and perhaps most of all from Donald Davidson, a poet and author. Davidson was one of the Vanderbilt Agrarians, twelve Southerners whose famous 1930 regional manifesto, "I'll Take My Stand," extolled the virtues of what Davidson described as a "traditional society . . . that is stable, religious, more rural than urban, and politically conservative," in which human needs were supplied by "family, bloodkinship, clanship, folkways, custom, community." In his *Attack on Leviathan,* Davidson portrayed the South as the last holdout against an industrial culture of big business, big government, and soulless modernism. Though neo-Cons don't dwell on it, he also remained a rabid segregationist until the end of his life.

Kirk lived in the South only as a graduate student at Duke. He later wrote about the time, using the third person: "Kirk had found in the South, a conservative society that had been struck a fearful blow 80 years before and still sometimes seemed dazed by that stroke; but he liked its life far better than the life of Detroit. In the South, then and later, he learned that some of the more oppressive 'problems' in life never are solved, unless by time and Providence."

The South, he decided, had the cultural and spiritual component of conservatism that the dominant philosophical strain, which was dominated largely by economic thought, seemed to lack, and he came to see a South that wasn't necessarily geographic at all but more totemic—an island of faith, tradition, and constancy in a world hostile to all three. He wrote in a 1958 issue of his journal, *Modern Age*, that was devoted entirely to the South:

> The South, then, has been the Permanence of America: the defender—
> sometimes consciously, sometimes blindly—of principles immensely
> ancient, of conventions that yet have meaning. . . . Without the South to
> act as its Permanence, the American Republic would be perilously out of
> joint. And the South need feel no shame for its defense of beliefs that
> were not concocted yesterday.

The self-conscious South he wrote about didn't develop overnight. In the beginning there was no North or South. There were thirteen colonies, some closer to the Equator and some closer to the North Pole, but in the nation's infancy, true sectional consciousness did not really exist. But there were significant cultural differences from the beginning between the largely non-Puritan South and the largely Puritan North, between the settlers of the South, sprawling over the lush hills and fertile valleys, and the Northern ones, drawn more to towns and cities. One of the favorite neo-Con books, *Cracker Culture,* by Grady McWhiney, a historian at Texas Christian University and a Southern League board member, goes so far as to assert that Northerners and Southerners were basically two different peoples. Southerners, he claims, came mostly from the "Celtic fringe" of the British Isles—the northern uplands of England, Wales, the Scottish Highlands, and Ireland—while Northerners came mostly from the lowlands of the southeastern half of Britain.

Even as early as the Constitutional Convention, the future of the slave trade—clearly on the wane in the North, where it had limited economic utility—was a divisive issue. Some, particularly in the South, saw right from the start that the marriage might not take. Pierce Butler, a delegate to the Constitutional Convention from—where else?—South Carolina said he considered "the interests of the [Southern] and Eastern states to be as different as the interests of Russia and Turkey."

But it wasn't until the sectional crises over slavery and tariffs arose in the 1840s that the South began to think of itself as a region, a development partly rooted in economic interest and the South's psychological circling of the wagons in defense of slavery, and partly a result of the brilliant, overheated propaganda of the Calhouns and the other South Carolinians.

Still, it wasn't until after the Civil War that the true myth of the South was born. Defeated in war, the myth of the Lost Cause became a Holy Grail, and the writing of history became, in the words of the great black historian John Hope Franklin, "an act of sectional allegiance and devotion." The tenets of the Lost Cause were familiar and inviolate: the nobility of the Southern planters and the romantic picture of the old plantation, the cult of the Confederacy—both the governmental entity and the men who died for it—and the evils of Reconstruction.

Given the fact that 360,000 Union soldiers and 258,000 Confederates died in battle or from disease during the war, one would think that misty romanticism would not have much appeal outside the South. And for a short time after the war, the abolitionist view of a malignant South held. But the view didn't outlive many of the men who fought the war. In fact, after the brief fitful experience of what one historian called "a Reconstruction that did not reconstruct," the South essentially recreated its old order while the rest of the nation yawned and looked away. Ultimately, the unreconstructed South soon gained a remarkable degree of sympathy from whites around the country.

Leading historians at the beginning of this century, William A. Dunning of Columbia University, and Walter L. Fleming, an Alabamian who studied under Dunning, were passionate defenders of the South and ardent proponents of the Southern view of the evils of Reconstruction. Claude Bowers, the best-read popular historian of his time and a major literary and political figure who delivered the keynote address to the Democratic National Convention in 1928, summed up the prevailing currents of the time in his work *The Tragic Era*, which offered up the most naked, unapologetic racism in its bleak depiction of Reconstruction. Though D. W. Griffith's classic *Birth of a Nation* may seem to us like an eccentric racist curio, Griffith, born in Kentucky the son of a Confederate cavalryman, was very much a self-conscious Southerner intent on winning through his art what had been lost on the battlefield, and he reflected as much as shaped the instincts of the nation. As Jack Temple Kirby put it in *Media-Made Dixie*, which meticulously tracks the trajectory of the South in the national imagination, Griffith "made movies which reflected popular understanding rather than instructed it. *Birth of a Nation* magnified convictions already there; it was a saga déjà vu: Dixie was glorious, fallen, raped-but-redeemed." Similarly, Thomas Dixon, the North Carolina–born preacher and author whose bestselling novel *The Clansman* provided the story line for the movie's second half, figured he was preaching to a sympathetic congregation. "Every man who comes out of one of our theatres," he said, "is a Southern partisan for life."

It's not hard to figure out why the North bought in to the myth. Slavery existed in the North for a hundred years until it died out for economic reasons after independence from England. Even Cotton

Mather, the voice of Puritan Massachusetts, upon receiving a slave as a gift in 1700, thanked the Lord for the comfort it would bring. A British geologist, Charles Lyell, traveling in the South prior to the Civil War, made a common observation: "It is notorious that the hardest task-masters to the slaves are those who come from the Northern free states." Simon Legree, the evil taskmaster of *Uncle Tom's Cabin,* was a Yankee. The abolitionists obviously had a moral vision that strongly shaped the politics of their time. But a fervent dedication to racial equality was almost as rare in the North as it was in the South. Indeed, when Alexis de Tocqueville made his famous voyage across America in 1831 and '32, he was struck by the depth of the racial bias he found in the North. "The prejudice of race," he wrote, "appears to be stronger in the states that have abolished slavery than in those where it still exists; and nowhere is it so intolerant as in those states where servitude has never been known." He also predicted "the abolition of slavery in the South will, in the common course of things, increase the repug-nance of the white population for the blacks."

Lincoln himself told a political rally in 1858, "I am not nor ever have been in favor of bringing about in any way the social and political equality of the white and black races . . . I am not nor ever have been in favor of making voters or jurors of negroes, nor of qualifying them to hold office, nor to intermarry." Among other historians, C. Vann Woodward, in *The Strange Career of Jim Crow,* has pointed out that Jim Crow began in the North, where laws were needed to define the rights of free blacks far sooner than in the South, where slavery defined all the codes of behavior. In *North of Slavery,* Leon F. Litwack wrote of free blacks in the North prior to the Civil War:

> In virtually every phase of existence, Negroes found themselves system-atically separated from whites. They were either excluded from railway cars, omnibuses, stagecoaches and steamboats or assigned to special "Jim Crow" sections; they sat, when permitted, in secluded and remote corners of theaters and lecture halls; they could not enter most hotels, restaurants and resorts, except as servants; they prayed in "Negro pews" in the white churches, and if partaking of the sacrament of the Lord's Supper, they waited until the whites had been served the bread and wine. Moreover, they were often educated in segregated schools, pun-ished in segregated prisons, nursed in segregated hospitals, and buried in segregated cemeteries.

When Frederick Douglass called together a convention of the nation's "free" Negroes in Rochester in 1853, they issued this proclamation at the end: "With the exception of the Jews, under the whole heavens, there is not to be found a people pursued with a more relentless prejudice and persecution than are the free colored people of the United States." Not for nothing does John Hope Franklin's epic history of blacks in America, *From Slavery to Freedom,* refer to blacks in the North as "quasi-free Negroes."

Blacks were allowed to vote in only five of the twenty-four Northern states after the end of the Civil War. Even after the heroic sacrifices of the war, eight Northern states turned down proposals to let blacks vote. Most states still had antimiscegenation laws on their books long after the war ended. Discrimination was common in housing and employment. "No group of Southern white men could get together and talk for sixty minutes without bringing up the 'race question,' the writer and leader James Weldon Johnson, later to become the longtime field secretary of the N.A.A.C.P., observed in 1912. "If a Northern white man happened to be in the group, the time could be safely cut to thirty minutes."

D. W. Griffith and Thomas Dixon or George Wallace and Lester Maddox are part of a long tradition of Southerners taking their view of race to the nation and getting a remarkably sympathetic response. Long before "Pitchfork Pat" Buchanan went from talk-show host to nativist/populist crusader, the most famous Southern partisan of his time was Benjamin Ryan ("Pitchfork Ben") Tillman, who took his virulently racist road show nationwide at the beginning of the century and whose statue still graces the state house grounds in Columbia.

An item of faith in the canon of the South-is-dead-folks is that when it comes to old-style Southern demagogues, they don't make 'em like they used to, and on this one they've got a point. Thank goodness.

Tillman was born in 1870 in Edgefield, South Carolina, which also gave the world such hotheads as James Bonham and William Travis, who died at the Alamo; Congressman Preston S. Brooks, who beat an abolitionist senator into unconsciousness on the Senate floor in 1856; Governor Francis B. Pickens, who led South Carolina out of the Union in 1860; and, later, Strom Thurmond.

Pitchfork Ben got his nickname from his fulminations against President Grover Cleveland, of whom he shouted one momentous July day in Lexington, South Carolina, in 1898: "When Judas betrayed Christ, his heart was not blacker than this scoundrel Cleveland.... He is an old bag of beef, and I am going to Washington with a pitchfork and prod him in his old fat ribs."

When the subject was race, Pitchfork Ben's favorite subject, it usually came out like this typical Tillman rant: "We of the South have never recognized the right of the negro to govern white men, and we never will. We have never believed him to be equal to the white men, and we will not submit to his gratifying his lust on our wives and daughters without lynching him. I would to God the last one of them was in Africa and that none of them had ever been brought to our shores."

In the first decade of the twentieth century Tillman mounted one of the most remarkable speaking campaigns in American history, a one-man crusade to sell the South's racial views to the rest of the country that brought him to more than three hundred audiences in thirty-eight states between 1901 and 1909. In one famous photo in the Library of Congress, Tillman stands against a black background, a chunky man with a round bulldog face in a long black coat, his index finger jabbing forward like a loaded .44 as he prepared to deliver yet another verbal fusillade at some ignorant Yankee or evil Lincoln Republican. His oratorical crusade had the same brawler's quality.

TILLMAN RANTS AT NEGRO RACE ... HEARD BY 1,400 ran a typical head-line in the *Spokane Spokesman Review* in Washington. The story de-scribed his speech as "fiery denunciations of the negro race, hurled almost in hisses through clenched teeth." His speech was an ex-planation of what he called "a universal racism" that was "planted there by God for some good purpose ... to keep the races from crossing." He denounced the horrors of Reconstruction, the depravity of Yankee do-gooders and abolitionists, and the notion that there could be any kind of equality between whites and blacks. "Negro equality in politics," he said, "means ... social equality, mongrelization, hell-fire and damnation."

Most striking about Tillman's crusade is not his words–which were standard post-Reconstruction rhetoric in the South–but the reception around the country. It's possible that part of the reaction he elicited was the product of his showmanship and oratorical fervor. But newspaper accounts at the time indicate again and again that his audiences–many of them in areas with hardly any blacks at all–were wildly enthusiastic. Tillman claimed that he found the people sympathetic to his views every place he went, and he was probably right. One study of his rhetoric concludes:

> His racist rhetoric came very close to being the mainstream of American thought at the beginning of the twentieth century. And though Tillman may have been somewhat intemperate in expressing his racism, he did not deviate sharply from what had become at the close of the gilded age the American position on black/white relations.

The message is not that the South or America remains a land of Pitchfork Ben Tillmans. Indeed, as bleak as race relations can seem now, no one could look at the racial norms of Tillman's day and those of the present and not see a remarkable degree of progress toward some measure of racial sanity. Instead, the message is that the notion that many of us grew up with of the South as a place apart when it comes to attitudes about race is hopelessly naive. Thus, though the cultural trappings of the neo-Confederates still strike many as a little dated or nutty, there's nothing all that extraordinary in the growing overlap between those who worship at the shrine of the Lost Cause and the rest of the nation.

And there's enough variety within the neo-Confederate world to give one pause about putting too simplistic a judgment on what it all adds up to. At the benign end of things you can look at my neighbor Leon McElveen. It's true that Leon—an architect, Georgia Tech graduate, whiz with any fossil fuel–powered yard-care implement, host supreme at his annual fall bonfire and barbecue, and a true prince of a person— has gone a little off the deep end since he ventured into the world of the neo-Cons a few years back. Not long afterward he joined the Sons of Confederate Veterans, and he now edits *The Rebel Yell,* the newsletter of the General John B. Gordon Camp 46 of the Sons of Confederate Veterans, with its monthly Confederate calendar, its history and genealogies, and its words of wisdom ("If at first you don't secede, try, try again"). He faithfully attends the meetings of the S.C.V. and of the Civil War Roundtable. He shows up regularly at Civil War reenactments at Georgia battle sites Resaca, Rome, Jonesboro, or Pickett's Mill, at Civil War memorabilia shows, at special events like the tour of Washington, Georgia, where the Confederate cabinet held its last meeting before the Confederacy was dissolved, and the annual S.C.V. march in Atlanta from the state capitol to the burial site in Oakland Cemetery of John B. Gordon, the Confederate general and Georgia governor for whom their chapter is named.

(It should also be noted that Gordon, a dramatic orator and passionate defender of "Dixie," "our soil," and "the spirit of Lee," was a former leader of the Georgia Klan. Neo-Cons argue, with some justification, that the Klan in its original incarnation attracted prominent men throughout the South, and Gordon's Klan involvement should not put him on the same plane as the violent thuggery of the current Klan. But terror was the Klan's modus operandi from the start and its aim was always to restore white rule and the values of the pre–Civil War South. The fundamental link between Old South history and white supremacism helps explain why many blacks, understandably, view almost any Confederate nostalgia with either suspicion or contempt.)

On McElveen's desk at home are a picture of Robert E. Lee and a couple of little Confederate Battle Flags. His computer mouse pad is a reproduction of a famous painting of the last meeting between Robert E. Lee and Stonewall Jackson. Downloaded in his computer are the Confederate Constitution, S.C.V. arcana, and Civil War diaries. In his library there are about 225 Civil War and Southern Heritage books, most purchased over the last few years. He backed off from his original threat to name his secondborn States' Rights McElveen. But when, to no one's surprise, she was born on Confederate Memorial Day, April 26, he did name her Erin Lee McElveen, after Robert E., of course. His wife, Linda, finally put her foot down, and he reluctantly agreed to remove the portrait of the great man from above the baby's crib.

And then there's the genealogy. One day in 1993, when McElveen was thirty-seven years old, he and his wife, Linda, were sitting at the old oak table in their kitchen, when they got to talking about how little they knew about their ancestors. They took a shopping bag, tore it open, and Leon began by writing down all the relatives he could think of, beginning with his daughter Sarah, and then tried to see how far back he could go. He came up with about forty-five. Two years later, thanks largely to a computer program called Family Tree Maker, he's up to about 2,200. He's turned up at least twenty-two Confederate soldiers on his side alone, four of whom died in the war, and at least one made-for-TV movie.

It's the tale of Leon's great-great-granduncle William Emanuel McElveen (1812–80). He took as his second wife his daughter-in-law, America Cone (it was her third marriage), in 1861, three years after she had married his son, John D. McElveen, a year after John D. died, and not long after William himself had been temporarily blinded in an explosion at the powderworks where he worked in Augusta, and after she nursed him back to health. I vote for Holly Hunter as America Cone and Kirk and Michael Douglas as McElveen père and fils.

Leon thinks the pro-secession, Southern nationalist types are out of touch with reality, but without reading *Southern Partisan* or Russell Kirk he instinctively buys into the states' rights, limited government, Southern heritage worldview of the mainstream neo-Cons. Still, he's into the Confederacy for the history—personal, regional, and national—not the dogma. It's hard to make the argument that there's something inherently suspect about Confederate history, as many people do who assume that others can celebrate their heritage, but white Southerners in groups like the S.C.V. are obviously bigots.

In fact, it's one of the routine ironies of Southern life that one of the best things that ever happened to the S.C.V. may have been *Roots*, Alex Haley's saga of black identity. As black Southerners started to dig through their past, so did white Southerners, and as blacks became more affirmative about staking a claim to their own vision and iconography of the South—one that didn't revolve around the Confederate flag and moonlight and magnolias—white Southerners started tugging back. The result has been an escalating war over the images that define the South fought on the level of symbols as vivid as blood.

There is a middle ground that the S.C.V. tries to peddle, based on their slogan "Heritage Not Hate." Some neo-Cons live up to it. Some don't. But it's insane for either side not to make a distinction between those whose version of Southern heritage is just white supremacy in disguise and those immersed in the defining episode in the nation's history. In April 1996, just as the first dogwood blossoms were finally heralding a late Southern spring, Leon rented a huge white Dodge van, signed up local Civil War historian Bill Scaife, and put together his own two-day tour of the Atlanta campaign, which played out from May 4 to September 2, 1864. The tour began with the site of the first near-skirmish at Snake Creek Gap about twenty miles south of the Tennessee line and ended up on the ridge across the Chattahoochee where Sherman first spied Atlanta.

We—eight middle-aged or older white guys—met at Leon's and exchanged appropriate greetings ("Is there a Major Rutherford Todd in your background?" Scaife asked Leon's friend Richard Todd). Then with Bobby Horton's *Songs of the C.S.A.* blaring out of the tape deck, we sped up I-75 toward Chattanooga, thumbing through the brochure Leon had put together with its battle maps and pictures of Union commander Sherman and Rebel Commander Joseph E. Johnston on the cover. If James Dickey were writing *Deliverance* today his suburban Atlantans wouldn't be rafting the Chattahoochee and fleeing hillbilly perverts. They'd be running Family Tree Maker on their PCs and exploring deserted Confederate wagon trails or railroad tunnels.

Scaife, who has written eleven books on the Civil War and was wearing a reproduction of the black hat with the C.S.A. pin his grandfather wore as a Confederate surgeon, led us from the granite dry-wall fortifications the Confederates built at Dug Gap, to the battlefields at Resaca and Kennesaw's Dead Angle, to the earthen Confederate fortifications called shoupades, built by slave labor, that now molder in anonymous repose at the edges of suburban homes or apartments with names like the Cannon Ridge Apartments.

Most of it's lost amid the exurban sprawl, but it's remarkable to think how the course of American history once hung in the balance here. Historians have been arguing over why the South lost the war and whether it ever had a chance to win ever since the publication in 1866 of *The Lost Cause* by Richmond journalist Edward Pollard, who blamed the defeat on Jefferson Davis. Some argue the North had such an advantage in population and industrial capacity that its victory was inevitable from the start. Others blame poor Southern strategy, sagging morale, superior Union leadership and generalship, or the limitations of the loose-knit Confederacy. It's clear that after the critical defeats at Gettysburg and Vicksburg in 1863, the Souths' offensive possibilities were shot. But by the summer of 1864, Northerners were becoming increasingly sick of what was looking like an endless war. The North's enthusiasm for the war was so strained that Lincoln, facing stiff opposition from General George B. McClellan running against him on a peace platform, seemed in grave danger of being voted out of office. Outnumbered in terms of troops and artillery, Johnston, the Confederate commander, didn't have to retake Tennessee in the Atlanta campaign. Instead, he only had to frustrate Sherman with a smart defensive battle plan, avoid a crushing defeat, hope for an attention-getting victory or two, and defend Atlanta through the November elections to have a realistic chance of achieving a peace that would have guaranteed Southern independence.

Jefferson Davis, however, wanted a bolder approach. Davis, often criticized for favoring generals skilled at flattery over generals skilled as commanders, had long feuded with Johnston (who, it must be said, seemed intent on hacking off Davis by refusing to let him know his battle plans). Fed up, Davis sacked Johnston on July 17 just before he was about to carry out the endgame of his battle plan. Davis replaced him with the hapless, thirty-three-year-old John Bell Hood, who had graduated forty-fourth in his class of forty-five at West Point in 1853, lost the use of his left arm at Gettysburg and his right leg at Chickamauga, and had the spaniel eyes and doleful look of an Edward Gorey character. Longer on guts than brains (his dispirited troops called him "Old Woodenhead"), Hood promptly staged a disastrous attack at precisely the wrong point in the Union lines and fought three other ill-fated battles soon afterward. Atlanta fell on September 2. Hood, ever astute, then left Sherman alone to make his march to the sea. Instead of harassing Sherman, he chose to mount a hopeless invasion of Union-held Tennessee, riding valiantly into battle strapped to his saddle and destroying what was left of his army in the process. The triumphant Lincoln was returned to office to finish winning the war and the Confederacy was dead.

At the end of our tour, after winding our way from Kennesaw past the cemetery in Marietta where Mary Phagan was buried, to Vinings, we clambered up a ridge to the Paces Family Cemetery, named for the family who gave their name to one of Atlanta's toniest addresses, West Paces Ferry Road. New office towers glistened to our right, the dense Piedmont forest spread over the hills in front of us, and the towers of Atlanta shimmered just beyond beneath a puffy halo of cloud. "Mine eyes have beheld the promised land!" Scaife read from the letters of one of the Union soldiers. "The domes and minarets and spires of Atlanta are glittering in the sunlight before us and only eight miles distant."

It was, in a word, thrilling, and if it takes S.C.V. types to fight for what's left of the battlefields and monuments and artifacts and memory of the nation's pivotal struggle, more power to them. In a nation of historical amnesiacs, there are worse sins than passionate remembrance.

Where the Confederate nostalgia does get suspect, however, is when white Southerners make the assumption that their South is *the* South—that it's somehow un-Southern, for example, to think the Battle Flag, a symbol as offensive to many blacks as the swastika is to Jews, doesn't belong at the heart of the Georgia state flag or flying above the state house in Columbia, South Carolina.

A lot of neo-Cons would say it's a low blow to identify them with the Klan, and they've got a point. Almost no one wants to be associated with the Klan, which is pretty much written off as a bunch of addled, out-of-it, snaggle-toothed trailer trash. Even David Duke eventually didn't want to be associated with Klan members.

But though they may be the poor relations, they fly the same flag and worship at the same shrines. You can see them at the Confederate memorabilia shows or the reenactments, figuring they're at home too. Once Leon and his daughter Sarah and my son Ben and I went to the reenactment of the battle of Resaca, where one of the celebrants was strutting around in a T-shirt showing an exhausted, caricatured pickaninny with his goo-goo eyes bulging and tongue hanging out at the end of a race and the wording, 6TH ANNUAL NORTH GEORGIA NIGGER NATIONALS.

It's true without question that you don't have to be a bigot to become immersed in Civil War history, but it's also true that neo-Cons can be amazingly tolerant of their brothers' excesses when it comes to race. So it's hard to be sure where to draw the line in the neo-Con canon. The "6th Annual North Georgia Nigger Nationals" obviously goes too far, but how about the stationery with the line I HAVE A DREAM and the Confederate Battle Flag flying over the U.S. Capitol? The T-shirt showing Lincoln's face and the words SIC SEMPER TYRANNUS, ("Thus always to tyrants") that John Wilkes Booth uttered as he pulled the trigger? The bumper stickers reading I'D RATHER BE SHOOTING YANKEES? The bottom line is that other than the occasional tributes to blacks who fought for the Confederacy—invariably trotted out as transcendent proof of the racial sensitivity of the Lost Cause world—the neo-Cons view history and the past through a totally white prism, as if the view of what constituted Southern culture in 1861 holds true in 1996 as well.

At least dealing with the Klan doesn't involve tough judgment calls. At a Klan rally one summer Saturday outside the courthouse in Cumming, Georgia, the featured speaker was the convicted church bomber J. B. Stoner. After some respectful introductions, Stoner kicked things off with a speech in the grand tradition of Pitchfork Ben, although he spent as much time ranting against Jews as blacks. "Every big and little nigger country in Africa has an immigrant quota given to them by the Jew-controlled Congress in 1965 and increased since then," he shouted to a group of perhaps thirty Klansmen and about seventy-five curious spectators watching from across the street. Most of the Klansmen wore their hoods and sheets, including one with a couple of Klan toddlers in their own little robes. Others had T-shirts showing hooded Klansmen and the words BOYS IN THE HOOD or the cheery message AIN'T RACIST. JUST NEVER MET A NIGGER I LIKED. Still others had a more mainstream T-shirt you see all the time, one showing the Battle Flag and carrying the in-your-face message, YOU WEAR YOUR X. I'LL WEAR MINE—an obvious reference to the Malcolm X one-letter message favored by blacks.

"They're still loyal to their fellow cannibals in Africa," Stoner ranted on. "The Jews want you to adopt a nigger baby if you can stand the odor and the smell, or a Korean baby, or a Chinese baby or a gook baby. I'm telling you the Jews and the Jew-controlled politicians hate our white race and they want to see our white race wiped off the face of the earth. That's what the illegal alien problem is all about. . . . Praise God for AIDS. Isn't it wonderful? They beat us down with integration; they forced us to send our children to schools with baboons, there's no education going on in the schools because you can't have education and niggers too. Same way you can't have quality products and niggers too. Why does your automobile have so many problems? Well, it's put together by monkeys."

He finally finished up and was followed by Ricky Draper, imperial wizard of America's Invisible Empire, who had driven over from Huntsville, Alabama, for the festivities. He had a beefy body and wore a white robe with gold trim. His long blond hair spilled raffishly out from under his hood, giving him the take-no-prisoners look of the professional wrestler Rick Flair. He was a little more contemporary than

Stoner: he emphasized that the Klan is opposed to violence. After the rally, he and his cohorts passed out literature replete with references to "America's Klan," as if a marketing man had come up with an approach for giving the Invisible Empire a more wholesome baseball, hot dogs, apple pie, and Chevrolet image.

Next up was Lewis Baxter, imperial wizard of the New Order White Knights of the Ku Klux Klan from Savannah, who was dressed in militia-style fatigues instead of the traditional robe and hood. "I get sick and tired of poor old nigger this and poor old nigger that," he shouted. "They're not good for anything other than lyin', thievin', stealin', and livin' off the white man." He was just moving onto illegal immigration, when suddenly a band of mariachis wearing studded black charro out-fits, strumming guitars, and singing at the top of their lungs like the paid annoyances at Mexican restaurants strolled in from stage right.

Baxter watched in dumbfounded rage for a moment, stunned by the validation of the world's ills unfolding right in the middle of his own rally. "How come they don't have a permit to have a demonstration?" he hollered to the cops. "They don't have a permit to be here. Tell me who's being discriminated against?" The mariachis piped down but before long a crowd of young girls who had come along with them started shouting, "One, two, three, four. We just want to love you more. Five, six, seven, eight. Even though you're filled with hate." It turned out to be a stunt put together by the TV show *TV Nation*, pretty suspect television, but a fairly accurate commentary on the marginalized nature of the Klan.

The rally went on, highlighted by still more Stoner and then a long harangue by Gordon Parks of Gainesville, Georgia, who was decked out in his Professional Security Services uniform and probably out-Tillmaned Stoner until things finally wound down. In an ignominious finale to the whole thing the *TV Nation* girls, one of them in a kissing booth, followed the Klansmen to their cars offering them red roses and kisses. "No, no. I'm already in love," Wizard Draper gallantly responded. The Klansmen took off their robes and walked off with their overweight wives and Klan toddlers, looking like ordinary, pinched working-class folks on their way to the Wal-Mart, still playing the South's dead-end game of venting their real frustrations of poverty and class on people who are the most victimized of all.

It would be a mistake to be too flippant about the Klan. It may be in decline–active membership is estimated at about 5,500, half of what it was in the early 1980s–but it still plays a role, in reality and as a grotesque example, in the universe of hate groups. Still, it's hard to make the case that the neo-Con resurgence has brought along a Klan resurgence as well. Even the Southern church fires, as alarming as they are, seem more the result of isolated racists, drunks, nuts and dirtballs, some motivated by race, some not, than a case of organized Klan-style terror. Indeed, by the summer of 1996, every credible investigation seemed to point out that church arsons are alarmingly common North and South, in white churches and black ones. There was without question a disturbing increase in arsons at black churches in the South in 1995 and 1996. That increase almost certainly reflected, at least in part, something grimly purposeful and racist, particularly given the role black churches have played, as one-pained observer put it, "as symbols of resistance and community and hope and refuge." But the vast majority were clearly not part of any Klan-style conspiracy and many of the arsons had nothing to do with race at all.

In fact, for all the horrors from the past, racist far-right activity is another case in which genes once thought to be Southern have pretty well mutated into the body politic. The varied groups of the extremist right fringe, from the armed militias to the white-supremacist right, have taken the worst elements of the South's past, its racism and blind hatred of the central government, tied them together with old and new strains of the frontier ethic and the antitax movement, and created new variations on old, dark American themes. But it would be hard to make the case that there's much distinctively Southern about it anymore. In fact, it's striking that the militia movement, while existing in the South, seems to have caught on more in the Midwest and Pacific Northwest than in the South. The South may have developed and refined the game, but these days you don't need to be Southern to play it.

Of course, it's worth remembering that the philosophical universe of the South is broader than the long winding road that runs from monument-polishing conservative neo-Cons to vulgar, snarling neo-Tillmans. Even while segregation seemed forever, there were liberal voices and groups expounding a different vision of the South, one based on neither misty Lost Cause nostalgia nor white supremacy. It wasn't an *entirely* different vision. Invariably, it came from the same distinctly Southern roots, from the church, from the land, from a broad sense of Southern community that included the ancient interconnections between blacks and whites. In fact, throughout this century, while the reign of segregation seemed immutable until the federal courts finally stepped in, there was a rich chorus of voices imagining a different kind of Southern partisanship. Organizations like the Commission on Interracial Cooperation, the Southern Conference for Human Welfare, and the Southern Regional Council were trying to build a truly interracial South.

Some experiments with interracial living and education were Myles Horton and Don West's Highlander Folk School, near Monteagle, Tennessee; the Providence Cooperative Farm, a farming cooperative organized by Christian socialists, black educators, and prairie populists near Tchula, Mississippi; Tom Alexander's Springdale School at Cruso in western North Carolina; and the Christian community called Koinonia established down the road from the Carter family farm in Plains, Georgia by a Georgia Baptist minister named Clarence Jordan that was designed to unite black and white farmers. Brave visionary journalists and academics like Ralph McGill of the *Atlanta Constitution,* Hodding Carter of the *Delta Democrat Times,* or Frank Porter Graham, W. T. Couch, and Howard Odum of the University of North Carolina have stood up for the right values when they weren't popular or easy. Dozens of literary voices, black and white, famous and forgotten, like James Weldon Johnson, Lillian Smith, Richard Wright, John Hope Franklin, Ralph Ellison, James McBride Dabbs, Langston Hughes, Zora Neale Hurston, James Agee, Erskine Caldwell, Carl Carmer, and Clarence Cason have captured the best instincts of the South and the nation. It's worth remembering that, conservative or not, the South was as staunch in its support of F.D.R. and the New Deal as any other region of the country—and probably gained more than any region from it.

The New Deal is the ultimate reminder that Southern politics need not all be cut from conservative cloth, but the fact is that it's in politics that the liberal train runs off the tracks in the South. There have been exceptions to the conservative dominance of Southern politics: liberal Texas populists like Ralph Yarborough and L.B.J.; Big Jim Folsom, Hugo Black, Lister Hill, and Carl Elliott in Alabama; Ellis Arnall in Georgia; LeRoy Collins in Florida; Albert Gore, Sr., and Estes Kefauver in Tennessee; Dale Bumpers and David Pryor in Arkansas; not to mention Bill Clinton and Al Gore and Jimmy Carter before them. But time and again in politics, the one-note cultural politics of Jack and Jock has meant more than all the earnest efforts to transcend race.

Typical of the triumph of race-baiting over substance was the infamous North Carolina Senate election in 1950, in which Frank Porter Graham, longtime president of the University of North Carolina, was defeated by Willis Smith in an election that provided the political baptism for a young aide named Jesse Helms. Smith used anything and everything, including a doctored photo showing Graham's wife dancing with a black man and a flyer that warned: "Race-mixing with all the worst sexual and social consequences is a Communist plot masterminded in Moscow and carried out through the seemingly innocent offices of sympathizers and dupes and traitors like Frank Porter Graham; for the sake of the sovereign South and its traditional way of life, these demons must be cast out and destroyed." It worked for Smith, who came from far behind to win. Similar tactics won all too often, which is why the Jesse Helmses of Southern politics almost invariably have longer tenures in office than the Frank Porter Grahams. The notion of "the sovereign South and its traditional way of life" has evolved over time, but conservatives still hold the patent on it, and because of that, they still control Southern politics.

The conservative and liberal traditions of the South have enough in common that plenty of nonconservatives continue to believe the abiding instincts of the South—respect for religion, love of the land, suspicion of the leviathans of big government or big corporations, fundamental human virtues of kindness and community, a healthy skepticism about what government can and can't do, and what individuals should do on their own—add up to a tradition of extraordinary value.

The least likely star in the Southern partisan constellation is the historian Eugene D. Genovese. A New Yorker who is usually associated with Marxist historians, Genovese has written landmark books on slavery and the South and in the process has become something of an unlikely Southern partisan himself. He writes in his 1994 book, *The Southern Tradition: The Achievement and Limitations of an American Conservatism,* "There are a great many reasons for my southern partisanship, the most important of which arose from my early recognition that the people of the South, across lines of race, class and sex, are as generous, gracious, courteous, decent—in a word, civilized—as any people it has ever been my privilege to get to know." He even sounds more partisan than the neo-Cons when he cites a "cultural and political atrocity–an increasingly successful campaign by the media and an academic elite to strip young white southerners and arguably black southerners as well of their heritage and therefore, their identity." But then he adds this thought: "If a political movement in defense of the best of the southern tradition does not include blacks as well as whites–if it is not deeply committed to racial equity and justice–it will degenerate into barbarism as fast as we can swallow our spit."

Which brings us back to today's neo-Cons. No, they're not closet Klansmen (not most of them, anyway), and they've got some very valid gripes about their place in the American cultural landscape. On January 14, 1995, a nineteen-year-old kid named Michael Westerman was shot through the heart as he drove with his wife between Guthrie, Kentucky, and Springfield, Tennessee. It turns out he was shot by a group of black youths who were angered by the sight of the Confederate flag flying from a metal post bolted to the tool box in the back of his new, red, jacked-up Chevy four-by-four pickup truck. The incident was shamelessly exploited by both Southern-heritage and far-right hate groups, who turned Westerman into the first neo-Con martyr, the first hero to die under the Battle Flag in 130 years. On the other hand, had a group of whites shot and killed a black man in the South because of, say, a Malcolm X flag decal, it would have been handled by my brothers and sisters in the media as a shocking racial atrocity and would have become a major national story. In this case, the shooting went virtually unnoticed by the national media and only got much regional coverage when a cross was burned by the road in front of the gunman's house. There is more than one way to descend into or to condone barbarism as fast as we can swallow our spit.

As for Genovese's notion, however, of a Southern movement that unites rather than divides whites and blacks, well, that ain't the neo-Cons. One gray day early in 1996 I drove from Atlanta to Tuscaloosa, Alabama, to meet Michael Hill, the founder of the Southern League. We got together at the Country Pride restaurant at a truckstop off Buttermilk Road in Cottondale, just outside Tuscaloosa. Hill is a big, soft-spoken man with piercing blue eyes, a full salt and pepper beard, and hair that's full on the sides and thin in the middle, giving him the look of a figure out of a Confederate tintype. He was wearing a white shirt and a red tie, and a white windbreaker, and he spoke with a soft, deferential Alabama drawl. He had taught history part time at the University of Alabama and has tenure at, of all places, historically black Stillman College in Tuscaloosa, an indication that being a neo-Con doesn't mean being a Stoner.

Hill grew up in northwestern Alabama, where his father had a small building supply business. He went to the University of Alabama, dropped out to drive a truck, went back, and eventually got a Ph.D. there in history. He studied under *Cracker Culture*'s author Grady McWhiney and became increasingly immersed in the political and cultural history of the South. Increasingly, Hill was convinced that Southern history—or at least the history of the white "Celtic" South—deserved better than what most historians taught. Like most neo-Cons, he concluded that the Civil War was about economics and different concepts of government more than about slavery, that the South had a right to secede, and that if slavery was wrong, the North was every bit as racist as the South ever was.

Eventually, he hooked up with a bunch of conservative Southern scholars and authors—most of them the usual suspects who write for *Southern Partisan* or whose books, like McWhiney's or Ron and Donnie Kennedy's *The South Was Right!*, provide the basic neo-Con texts—and formed the Southern League. According to an early mailing, the group intends to "foster and nourish the remnants of our all-but-discredited heritage," ranging from the political literature of Calhoun and Randolph to the folk culture of okra and shrimp festivals and rattlesnake rodeos to principles "that the establishment has done its best to ignore or discredit: confederalism, states' rights, nullification and self-determination [or secession]." The League still remains pretty obscure—even a Southern-heritage type like my neighbor Leon had never heard of it—but it already had chapters in twenty-six states, and Hill said he gets about five hundred requests a month for information.

"Two years ago, when we put this together, I had absolutely no idea how much interest there would be," he said when we sat down after getting our barbecue, fried okra, mashed potatos, and greens at the all-you-can-eat buffet. The restaurant was all bright tile and new Formica, more franchise McDonald's than dingy old truckstop, but with enough of the requisite Confederate bric-a-brac, Merle Haggard tapes, and John Wayne videos to still fill the bill. "But now I'm convinced there is a huge, huge group of folks out there who sympathize with us and think like we do. People used to think they were alone. When they see others who think like they do, they become emboldened enough to come out and say, "Hey, I'm not going to be quiet anymore.

"The South was not the evil society it was portrayed as by the abolitionists," he continued. "It was the most Bible-believing Christian part of the country. It had the most stable order. Our ancestors were not perfect. We don't defend everything they did. But the idea, the philosophy of secession was a correct philosophy. Was it the correct one at the time? It may not have been. The fact that we lost the war would suggest that maybe it wasn't the wisest thing. But whether one wishes to exercise it, our argument is that our Southern forebears had a right to secede or seek a political divorce. I don't regret what my ancestors did. I think they were honorable men, who did what they had to do at the time to protect their freedom."

I figured that Hill, an academic with an Internet home page that proclaims, "Hatemongers not welcome here," represented the respectable spectrum of the neo-Con world, and there's a mainstream thought at the heart of his pitch. "We adhere very much," he said, "to C. S. Lewis's quote that the most progressive man is the one, when he realizes he's on the wrong road, will turn around and go back and try to find the right way. We consider ourselves retrograde in the sense C. S. Lewis is talking about. We're looking for the way back to the right road." But his idea of the road back turns out to be the ruinous road his ancestors took toward disunion. Even if it's unlikely that even he really thinks the South will ever again try secession, it makes for a tantalizing thought in these days of devolution fever.

"The thing I always come back to," he said, "is that this continent's too big to be one nation, particularly when it has to be held together from Washington by the force it has to be held together with. So what you do is reinvoke the idea of states' rights, allow the people of the states to determine their own political future. We don't necessarily think that secession ought to be tried right now, but what we'd like is a return to true constitutional government where federal power is drastically cut back and states are allowed to run their affairs in most areas. If we can't within a reasonable time have a return to that then secession is the only answer to a continuing descent into centralized, perhaps even totalitarian government."

As often happens, we've veered from the neo-Confederate ideal as a Southern fantasy and gone to it as a node of right-wing paranoia. Soon Hill has veered all the way back from the Confederacy to the Holy Roman Empire, to a sixteenth-century German philosopher and neo-Con favorite named Johannes Althusius, who espoused the ultimate in the principle of devolution: power descended from a sovereign God to individual households. Only as a last resort, Althusius allowed, should power evolve upward from the household to the community or church, to the local parish government and finally to the centralized government. "I'd say that within the next few years, we're going to see some sort of crisis happen," Hill said, an edge of excitement in his soft, amiable drawl. "I have absolutely no idea what it is, but I think we're going to be faced with a situation whereby either the regions and individual states are going to go their separate ways or they're going to be held together by brute force by the central government. And I think if the latter happens, that you might see a Bosnia here. I really think that the only way we can avoid that kind of conflict is to give autonomy to states or regions or, if it devolves far enough, even to counties."

Even Hill concedes that the romance of devolution can get out of hand when the wrong element buys into it. Timothy McVeigh, alleged to be one of the men who blew up the Federal Building in Oklahoma City, wasn't exactly a neo-Confederate. But his favorite T-shirt is one you can order from the *Southern Partisan* General Store by calling 1-800-23Dixie. It bears a quote from Thomas Jefferson: THE TREE OF LIBERTY MUST BE REFRESHED FROM TIME TO TIME WITH THE BLOOD OF PATRIOTS AND TYRANTS. Asked about it, Hill enthused, "Oh, that's a wonderful quote. Jefferson could be a mild-mannered, scholarly fellow, but he wasn't averse to throwing around terms like blood and revolution and things like that. He was a gutsy fellow."

He follows with the ritual disclaimers that no movement can be held accountable for every excess some members might commit. "Whoever did it [the Oklahoma bombing] was stupid," he said. "Nothing good could ever come from it." As for the broader thought of smashing the leviathan state, well, that's not too stupid: "I'd like to see it bulldozed off into the Potomac and start over." He paused a moment. "Does smoke bother you?" he asked, all Southern courtesy. When I said it was O.K. he took out an eighty-cent Dominican Bances cigar (he prefers three-dollar Arturo Fuentes, but can only afford so many on a professor's

salary), lit it, and puffed contentedly while he drank his coffee underneath a smoky haze.

Who knows where all this leads. Repeated Southern League
endorsements didn't do Pat Buchanan much good in 1996. But Hill's
vision certainly doesn't lead to Genovese's notion of a political movement in defense of the best of the Southern tradition that includes
blacks as well as whites. Instead, it leads to its opposite, whether in the
form of constant battles over differing visions of the South or a new era
of separate but equal myths, symbols, and causes. I asked Hill about
Genovese's final thought about the necessity of a Southern movement
uniting blacks and whites. "I don't agree with that," Hill said. "We've
made it clear from the very beginning we don't want any trash. We
don't want any hate mongers. We feel we have an interest to protect
like other groups do. We don't stretch our principles to recruit blacks or
Yankees or anyone else. If people like the principles, then we welcome
them. But we're not an affirmative action recruiter. We don't mean
harm to anybody. But as long as we're honorable, principled men, if this
produces more polarization, we'll have to put up with it."

The week after I drove to Cottondale, I went with Leon to the
meeting of the Civil War Roundtable at the Ansley Country Club,
whose Men's Grill used to be the favorite hangout of the late Southern
humorist Lewis Grizzard, a neo-Con before there were neo-Cons. The
Roundtable is a national group of Civil War buffs that has chapters
around the country. It's about history, not politics, but given the
chapter's location, it's safe to assume the Atlanta group has more
Southern partisans than Northern ones. Leon was at the front table
wearing his Confederate tie. My across-the-street neighbor Bill was
across from me at my table, and the gathering had more the jovial,
clubby air of the Rotary or Kiwanis than anything seditious or conspira-
torial. We began by saluting the flag–American, not Confederate–
and ran through the announcements and Bill Scaife's monthly Civil
War trivia tests until it was time for the speaker. He was introduced as
Jack Bledsoe, an amateur historian, fifth-generation Atlantan, ninth-
generation Georgian, and thirteenth-generation Southerner, whose
ancestors landed at Jamestown and who was a member of such organizations as the Sons of Confederate Veterans, the Military Order of Stars
and Bars, and the Southern League and had traced his lineage back to
sixty-two men who fought in the American Revolution. He was a

rugged-looking, white-haired man of sixty-four in a blue blazer bearing the seal of the Old Guard of the Gate City Guard, founded in 1854 as Atlanta's first militia. His topic was, conveniently enough, "Looking Back on Secession."

It didn't take long to realize that his speech was going to be the standard Southern League "the South was right" neo-Con gospel. He argued that the Union was a compact of sovereign states who were free to join it and free to leave it. Secession as a doctrine first took hold in the North at the time of the War of 1812, not in the South. The Civil War was truly a war of Northern aggression, not a war over slavery. It was the Union, not the Confederacy, that betrayed the Constitution by pursuing war in 1861. Now secession and devolution were once again on the march, as people revolted against tyrannical centralized government from Russia to Canada to Yugoslavia, and states were increasingly resisting federal intrusions and mandates.

"Although the will to utilize it has long been missing, the Tenth Amendment was not repealed at Appomattox," he said in concluding his thirty-five-minute talk. "It is still in the Constitution and it still reads: 'The powers not delegated to the United States by the Constitution, nor prohibited by it to the states, are reserved to the states respectively or to the people.' Smaller, better, and closer to home is the kind of government most people want today, and there is reason to believe that we may be witnessing a general rethinking of the centralizing trend which has been in effect since the Civil War. A return to our original constitutional foundations may be underway. And as troubling as it might be to most Americans, if the expansion of government powers, which ever since 1861 centralizers have called progress, continues, we may see secession again become an important movement in American politics."

The room was as quiet as a tomb as he finished up. "In the last days of the war when an aide remarked to him that the cause seemed lost, Jefferson Davis replied: 'It appears so, but the principle for which we contend is bound to assert itself, though it may be at another time and in another form.' Although there is no record that this conversation went any further, the aide might have responded: 'Well, Mr. President, what you say makes me wonder, just how lost is our Lost Cause?'"

Chapter 6

CHARLOTTE, NORTH CAROLINA

Breakfast at Tiffany's, Jeb Stuart's Cavalry,
Dot Counts's Ordeal, and the Mind of the New South

LONG BEFORE THERE WERE NEO-CONFEDERATES, MANY SOUTHERNERS, even many proto-Confederates, realized that perhaps refighting the Civil War on the same old terms wasn't really a surefire way to rebuild their shattered lives. Thus, even before the ashes of the Old South were cold, many Southerners were trying to come up with a new one.

One of the first of them was Edwin DeLeon, a native South Carolinian, author, diplomat, and former Confederate propagandist who in 1870 published what may have been the first manifesto proclaiming that amorphous being that came to be known as the New South. "The Old South ... has gone 'down among the dead men,' and on its headstone we see not the word 'Resurgam,'" he wrote in "The New South: What It Is Doing and What It Wants," an essay in *Putnam's* magazine. "For that vanished form of society there can be no resurrection.... But the New South–its child and legitimate successor–sits in the seat of the dethroned king, exhibiting a lustier life, and the promise of greater growth and strength than did its predecessor."

Rather than harkening back to noble Virginia squires, grand cotton plantations, and the "Forget, Hell" reverberations from Appomattox, he envisioned a South of bustling new brick factories and mills, diversified agriculture, and cooperation with the North. Rather than John Egerton's contemporary vision of the North and South exchanging sins instead of virtues, DeLeon's New South vision blended the best of the two regions. "The Northerner will carry South his thrift, his caution, his restless activity, his love of new things; the Southerner will temper these with his reckless liberality, his careless confidence, his fiery energy and his old-time conservatism; and both will be benefited by the admixture."

Over time, the most celebrated promoter of this cheery, prosperous vision of "Sunshine everywhere and all the time" was Henry Grady (1850–89), the young editor of the Atlanta *Constitution* whose famous speech, "The New South," before the New England Society of New York in 1886 became the seminal New South manifesto. Grady declared the Old South dead, paid a friendly tribute to General William Tecumseh Sherman, who, he said, "is considered an able man in our parts, though some people think he is a kind of careless man about fire," and hailed a New South of industrial energy, civic virtue, and racial peace.

> We have sowed towns and cities in the place of theories and put business above politics.... We have established thrift in city and country. We have fallen in love with work. We have restored comfort to homes from which culture and elegance never departed.... Above all, we know that we have achieved in these "piping times of peace" a fuller independence for the South than that which our fathers sought to win in the forum by their eloquence or compel in the field by their swords. It is a rare privilege, sir, to have had part, however humble, in this work. Never was nobler duty confided to human hands than the uplifting and upbuilding of the prostrate and bleeding South—misguided, perhaps, but beautiful in her suffering and honest, brave and generous always. In the record of her social, industrial and political illustration we await with confidence the verdict of the world.

These caveats at the end—"misguided, perhaps, but beautiful in her suffering and honest, brave and generous always"—were a reminder that there was always going to be plenty of the Old South in the New. Indeed, on race, the idea was never for anything approaching equality, but instead for a new form of bondage for blacks who were still assumed to be as inferior outside of slavery as they were inside it. Above all, though, was the notion that what the South lost on the battlefield it could still win in the fields of politics and commerce.

To both the true-believing neo-Cons and some Southern liberals, the whole New South notion was suspect from the start—an attempt to create a bland, lifeless, corporate, faux South without either the rough edges or the ragged glory of the real thing. But even the neo-Cons know the unadulterated Old South canon remains a minority taste. One of the unmistakable truths of the South's current golden age is that it's not the grand old Southern cities like New Orleans, or Mobile, or Savannah, or Charleston, the most Southern cities in the South, that are leading the charge. Instead it's places like Atlanta, and Dallas, and Orlando, and Nashville, and Raleigh-Durham, and Charlotte—places animated more by the spirit of Henry Grady than Michael Hill—that as a group in the 1980s and '90s have been the most successful cities in America. What sort of New South they will in the end produce is not yet clear. One possibility is a bunch of black inner cities and white Cobb Counties without end. But another possibility is more intriguing: that the South, risen again, could turn out to be not the neo-Con version of the Old South renascent, but a blend of Yankee hustle and Southern charm with the potential to be not just the nation's economic heart, but its best hope for racial peace as well.

The phrase "New South" has been buried in such booster flotsam that no one knows what it means, but if there has to be something called the Museum of the New South, I'm kind of glad it's in Charlotte, where the town's most famous Chamber of Commerce executive was Booster Kuester, where the *Charlotte Observer* is forever running stories with headlines like CHARLOTTE HITS BIG TIME: WE NEED 2 PHONE BOOKS, where they threw together a whole fake nightclub district for the one weekend of the 1994 Final Four basketball tournament, lest anyone think Charlotte wasn't sufficiently world class. "When I came here in 1959, a cousin in Richmond told me Charlotte's a wonderful place," a bank executive, Thomas Storrs, reminisced while we were chatting in his office. "She said the best way to summarize Charlotte is to say that if the Russians bomb us and the first wave of bombs that comes over doesn't include one for Charlotte, people here would be very much disappointed." That's Charlotte, a place that would rather be incinerated than be small time.

No one asked me for my opinion, but my recommendation for the collection at the Museum of the New South would begin with the front page of the *Charlotte Observer* from October 27, 1993, the day after the National Football League picked Charlotte for its twenty-ninth franchise, the ultimate certification of big-city-dom for every up-and-coming Sun Belt striver.

The headline stripped across the top in Christ-returns-to-earth-size type reads, TOUCHDOWN! The line below it reads, CAROLINAS' NFL DREAM

COMES TRUE. Taking up three quarters of the page is a color photo of the downtown skyline, the holy letters NFL resplendent in the lighted windows of empty skyscrapers, pinwheels of fireworks exploding in the night.

On the left-hand side of the page, sports columnist Ron Green personally welcomes to Charlotte Joe Montana, Don Shula, Barry Sanders, Max McGee, Papa Bear Halas, Vince Lombardi, Joe Namath, and almost anyone alive or dead who has ever suffered, witnessed, or induced a concussion in a football game. He philosophized: "This is a wonderful thing you've done for us, a band-playing, street-dancing, can't-stop-grinning, hang-out-the-window screaming wonderful thing. . . . This is a sweet, proud moment in our lives, one of the grandest for this community." Over on the right-hand side, the staff writer Liz Clarke weighed in from Chicago, where Charlotte had been selected over such competitors as old has-beens St. Louis and Baltimore and fellow Dixie wannabees Jacksonville and Memphis. "And forevermore," she declaimed, "this single decision will likely change the way people across the country feel about what lies between Washington and Atlanta." Assorted economic experts from former governor Jim Martin to former Oakland Raider wide receiver Mike Siani are recruited to testify to the untold economic advantages that will accrue to the Queen City from having an NFL franchise. For good measure the only other story on the page, stripped across the bottom, is an up-close and personal view of the celebration back home, beginning with a heart-warming account of the tears of joy spilling down the cheeks of the town's most powerful fat cat, NationsBank Chairman Hugh McColl, Jr., at the magic moment of Charlotte's ascension to the big time (" 'My God,' McColl said, the rest of his words drowned out by the roar of the crowd and the boom of fireworks inside Founders Hall. . . .").

Sometimes a cigar is just a cigar, and even jaded old St. Louis and Baltimore no doubt got all hot and bothered a few years later when Charlotte managed to steal football teams from Los Angeles and Cleveland. But anyone who thinks this was just about football needs to go back and read Henry Grady's speech; the reflections of Charlotte's own version of Grady, D. A. Tompkins; or Charlotte's most important and least likely contribution to Southern letters, W. J. Cash's nutty, fevered, brilliant, utterly dated, absolutely up-to-the-minute snapshot of the Southern soul, *The Mind of the South*. The South is ascendant these days for many reasons—for cheap labor and warm weather, for government subsidies through defense contracts, most prosaically because air conditioning finally made the region habitable in the summer. But it is also ascendant because out of the ruins of the Civil War emerged a faith as intense as the one the preacher instilled each Sunday, that through commerce and hustle and promotion and entrepreneurial zeal the South would rise again stronger than ever before.

Back in 1941, Cash wrote: "In the feeling of the South, Progress stood quite accurately for a sort of new charge at Gettysburg, which should finally and incontestably win for it the right to be itself for which, in the last analysis, it had always fought." For decades that new charge produced more puffery than results, but today Charlotte, second perhaps only to Atlanta, stands for the degree to which the New South troops in pinstripes, starched white shirts, and spit-shined wing tips finally succeeded, producing along the way a remarkable turnabout in the nation's psychic balance of power.

C. Vann Woodward and others have noted time and again that one thing that always defined the South was the pain, pessimism, and sense of defeat that came from being the only part of the country to know the experience of losing a war and being occupied by the enemy. Now that has been turned on its head. Now, it's the North and even mighty California that are adrift and confused, fundamentally pessimistic about the future. But pessimism is about as much a part of the civic culture of Charlotte as communism. Indeed, a century after the first overheated drumbeaters of the New South started hailing the region as "the coming El Dorado of American adventure" and proclaiming "it is not only possible but it is also probable that this next century will belong to the South," reality is finally making the rhetoric credible.

I happen to love Charlotte, which may edge out Dallas and Atlanta as home to the purest strain ever discovered of the Southern booster gene. Charlotte has Dallas's hustle and go-go sense of civic unanimity without its meanness, and it has Atlanta's leafy geography and optimism without the worst of its big-city problems and insufferable sense of triumphalism. Like Montgomery, Alabama, Charlotte has some terrific plate-lunch places such as McDonald's Cafeteria and the Coffee Cup. In its NationsBank Corporate Center, with its massive, eerie triptych frescoes, it has the ultimate Sun Belt corporate building. Over the years it has produced the nation's first gold rush, Jim and Tammy Faye

Bakker's little exercise in entrepreneurial religion, and the world's bluntest Chamber of Commerce slogan, the lyrical mid-1970s corporate rallying cry, "Charlotte–A Good Place to Make Money."

I know that not everyone agrees. When George Washington rode through Charlotte in 1798, he pronounced it "a trifling place." A lot of people still think it is, a featureless blob of urban sprawl that grew up as the administrative hub for a vast Piedmont textile empire and that through sheer hustle turned itself into America's most anonymous urban area, the nation's third-largest banking center after New York and San Francisco, and the heart of a nondescript, posturban region of 1.2 million people. Yes, it's a place whose main contribution to American culture is merging the luxury-box ethos of football and base-ball with the six-pack world of NASCAR racing at the Charlotte Motor Speedway. Yes, they insist on referring to the mirrored-glass downtown by the far perkier appelation of "uptown," and pedestrians at night are about as plentiful there as Maoists at Sunday-morning services at the First Baptist Church. Yes, a *Washington Post* reporter dispatched there after Charlotte's historic ascension to NFL-dom observed that Char-lotte has "the vacant calm of a place where it's always 10:30 in the morning." As a nickname he suggested "White Shirt City" in honor of the look-alike, vaguely ominous platoons of eager young bankers out of Wake Forest and the University of South Carolina who pour through the downtown skyways at lunchtime looking like Mormon or Seventh Day Adventist missionaries. "New York may be the city that never sleeps," a local historian, David Goldfield, of the University of North Carolina at Charlotte once said. "This is a place that never wakes." And he's one of the boosters.

There's not much respite from the upbeat wonderfulness of it all. Doug Marlette once drew a cartoon suggesting the ultimate piece of Queen City civic sculpture, an empty suit carrying a briefcase with a dollar sign and standing on a pedestal with the inscription CHARLOTTE (BUBBUS-BOOBUS EMPTY SUITUS). Just about the only cynic in town is a sixty-eight-year-old radio commentator, Robert Raiford. "What I always say is that Charlotte's made up of a bunch of local yokels who've seen *Breakfast at Tiffany's* too many times, and they want to make Char-lotte a city like that, you know, this sterile sort of Manhattan," he says. "They get on these booster trips, and, oh, there's no stopping them.

They talk about world class. I mean if somebody farts louder than somebody else, it'll be a world-class fart.

"I mean the Babbitts here are always talking about the performing arts," he continued. "Hell, the performing arts here are stock-car races. They're always crowing; everything's the biggest in the Southeast. Well, you don't have to be very big to be the biggest in the Southeast. You can still put little uptown Charlotte in a pocket of a real city, and you wouldn't even notice it. Basically, Charlotte is ninety percent foam and ten percent beer."

And yet, it's also a place that in 1983 became the first Southern city with a white majority to choose a black mayor when it elected Harvey Gantt, a local architect who integrated Clemson University in 1963, and then reelected him two years later. It has had as much of a commitment to school integration as any city in America, so much so that when Ronald Reagan came to Charlotte to demagogue about busing in 1984, his all-white audience of suburban Charlotteans sat and watched in stony unappreciative silence. It turned out they were proud of the city's history of busing and school integration. It's a city that is as prosperous as any in America these days, with an unemployment rate usually hovering around 4 percent, and that has consistently vied with Atlanta in recent years for the nation's lead in job creation. It's a place where the black pastor of an all-white church in a neighborhood that was in the process of going from white to black could feel he had a reasonable chance of making his church a truly integrated one and not sound like a deluded dreamer, and where it's at least possible to believe that the South's compulsive religiosity can produce something truly redemptive rather than the cold pieties of the religious right.

God and Mammon—a desire to do good and a desire to do well—are knitted together in Charlotte like threads in an intricate pattern. The question now is whether the economic boom of the nineties is finally producing that idealized New South of prosperity and racial amity, or whether, in a cruel twist of history, interracial progress will hit a brick wall not because of the dissonant chords out of the South's past but because of the flood of Yankee transplants who have brought the casual, implicit, unreflective segregation of the North down South with them.

Charlotte sprawls across the dense green Piedmont forests of western

North Carolina just across from the South Carolina state line. Like Dallas, its evil twin to the west, Charlotte takes its central myth from the idea that it has no reason to exist—no great river, no port—except the indomitable will of its people to find new ways to make a buck. The idea may have as much to do with civic self-flattery as reality, but it does help explain the where-there's-a-tub-thumper-there's-a-way ethos of both cities.

Incorporated in 1768, the city was named for Queen Charlotte, the wife of King George III of England, which produced the civic moniker the Queen City. Given today's inevitable sexual connotations, the nickname over time has become a source of some unease in a conservative Southern city, but unless the *Post*'s "White Shirt City" catches on, Charlotte seems stuck with it.

Charlotte got its first big break in 1799, when a Cabarrus County farm boy named Conrad Reed found a sparkling seventeen-pound rock in a stream, which the family used as a doorstop until they figured out that it was full of gold. About twenty years later, the country's first gold rush was on. It turned Charlotte from a village to a town and lured fortune hunters from around the East Coast and Europe, including one Count Vincent de Rivafinoli, who claimed to have fought with Napoleon and sported a gold-headed cane. Had the *Observer* been around and the booster mentality fully formed, someone no doubt would have used the occasion to proclaim Charlotte a "truly international city," the mantra now of every second-tier city in the South.

The South's single biggest truly international coup was, of course, Atlanta's snaring of the 1996 Olympics, an event greeted in Atlanta with the delirious headline WORLD CLASS, as if that were all that needed to be said. Another seminal moment in the cult of "truly international-city-dom" came in 1984, when Dallas mounted one of the truly horrid sporting events in history, the Dallas Grand Prix. The event was held in the typical hundred-degree summer heat. People fainted left and right in the stands, cars overheated and broke down with such frequency that only eight of the twenty-five cars even finished the race, and one driver was treated for heat exhaustion after he collapsed while trying to push his car across the finish line. Nevertheless, the event had enough cosmopolitan panache for Mayor Starke Taylor to exult, "If there is any doubt in anyone's mind that we are truly an international city, we certainly have dispelled that."

Charlotte's gold rush petered out when it turned out that the ore did not come in rich nuggets as in California, whose own gold rush in 1849 eclipsed Charlotte's. But the mercenary and promotional instincts never faltered. Charlotte has a few neo-Cons, including Wayne Powers, the intrepid president of the Confederate Society of America, who was among the first on the Buchanan bandwagon. But even after the Civil War, when Southern partisans were churning out journals and manifestos extolling the Lost Cause, Charlotte's contribution was General D. H. Hill's journal, *The Land We Love,* which made a full confession of Southern sins and expressed the hope that the "everlasting twaddle about politics" would be replaced by attention to industry, thrift, and prosperity. Just after the turn of the century the *Observer*'s editor, Isaac Ervin Avery, gave a wry portrayal of Charlotte as a place where even the country mules had aspirations toward world classiness.

> Charlotte has passed through the transition stage and has become a sure-enough city. A strange woman wearing a Parisian gown, her body at a forward incline of forty-five degrees, and a poodle in evening dress, may parade the streets without causing a block in traffic or bringing all the shopkeepers to their windows.... You may dodge a creditor for days without remaining in hiding, the country mules do not shy at automobiles or silk hats walking around on weekdays ... and no one thinks about fainting when a Charlotte woman goes off to get a Ph.D. vocal degree and comes home singing in a high Dutch or broken Eye-talian.

Eventually, what gold began, cotton, the railroads, and most of all the textile mills fully developed, and Charlotte evolved into the administrative center for the whole region. A town of bankers and accountants, insurance salesmen and regional sales managers that grew from 18,000 people at the turn of the century to 100,000 by 1940, 200,000 by 1960, 315,000 by 1980, and 465,000 now—each round number greeted as a civic triumph rather than a mere demographic fact ("Let's Go Charlotte!" exhorted the January 30, 1941, Progress Section of the *Charlotte News*. "Now we have a population of 100,899 ... The only city between Richmond and Atlanta with a population over 100,000."). Charlotte's population now ranks thirty-third nationally among cities and forty-third among metropolitan areas; along with Atlanta and Nashville it has been one of the most prosperous American cities throughout the nineties. The resultant can-do mentality is so pervasive that even the ministers sound like Chamber of Commerce executives. "There is a kind of special sense that you have in Charlotte that you're in an unusual moment in history, that you're in a place where anything is doable," said Dr. William Wood, pastor of First Presbyterian Church, the oldest church in Charlotte. "There is a sense that there's almost a Camelot quality to the city today."

To understand this Piedmont, stock car, *Breakfast at Tiffany's* Camelot and its message about the South and the nation, it's worth thinking about two men. The first is the mogul and promoter Daniel Augustus Tompkins, whose go-go zeal and mercantile instincts made him the model Charlotte insider. The second is the writer, W. J. Cash, whose unhappy life and tormented view of Southern history relegated him to the status of Charlotte's ultimate visionary outsider.

W. J. "Sleepy" Cash was not, it must be said, the ultimate exemplar of the upbeat, go-go Charlotte lifestyle. He was born May 2, 1900, one of seven children of Nannie and John Cash, fundamentalist Baptists in the cotton mill town of Gaffney, South Carolina, and grew up in a world dominated by the strictures of religion, the rhythms of the mill, and the routine brutalities of race. When he was six years old, a large mob in a nearby county took an accused black rapist from the jail, tied him to a tree, and riddled his body with bullets; his head, a newspaper account put it, was "literally shot into pulp, his brains covering his hat and face."

Cash had brief stops at Wofford College in South Carolina and Valparaiso University in Indiana before enrolling at Wake Forest College (now University) in North Carolina, then a small Baptist college with a relatively liberal academic orientation. He wrote poetry, edited the school newspaper, *The Old Gold and Black,* played on the football team for exactly one day, and graduated in 1922. He considered the law, taught high school, and then drifted toward journalism. Soon he came under the sway of H. L. Mencken's acerbic view of the South and eventually caught on as a writer at the liberal-leaning *Charlotte News,* which at times delighted in throwing darts at Charlotte's big red balloon of unblemished virtue and prosperity. Back when Charlotte's motto was "After Edinburgh, the Greatest Church-going Town in the World," the *News* was billing Charlotte as "the murder capital of the United States," and Cash became one of the paper's most irreverent voices. Shy, withdrawn, a hypochondriac obsessed with a fear of impotence, Cash lived most of his life as a reclusive bookworm, owlish and balding in steel-rimmed glasses and three-piece suits. He had a history of manic-depression, melancholia, and alcoholism and was subject to weird spells in which he felt he was choking. He spent more than a decade pounding away on his Underwood typewriter writing *The Mind of the South,* and in 1940 he achieved two remarkable feats. He finished the book and he got married–to Mary Bagley Ross Northrop, a bright, vivacious divorcee.

A few months after the work was published, to largely glowing reviews, he became convinced that Nazi agents were threatening to assassinate him in Mexico City, where a John Simon Guggenheim Fellowship had enabled him and his wife to live while he worked on a novel. When his wife left him alone in their hotel room while she went for help, he made his way to another hotel nearby and hanged himself from a bathroom door with his own necktie. His wife had his body cremated and the ashes were brought back to North Carolina and given a proper Baptist burial in Shelby, near his parents' home. He was laid to rest under a small, flat stone reading in part, "He loved the South with intensity and was to all a friend. God's finger touched him and he slept." Not far away, a substantial monument honors one of his favorite boyhood authors, none other than Thomas Dixon, whose *The Clansman* had inspired *Birth of a Nation.*

The one book Cash left behind reads like a combination of history and hallucination, a richly romantic blend of analysis and reverie, classical allusions and masterful set pieces all grounded more in an abstract, imagined realm of a mythic South than in the conventional scholarship of footnotes and data. "This is writing that took the high style of nineteenth century Victorianism, hollowed it out, and turned it to other than entirely solemn purposes," Richard King, a professor of that Old South bastion, the University of Nottingham, England, allowed at a conference at Wake Forest marking the fiftieth anniversary of the book's publication, in 1991. "It is W.E.B. DuBois, unbuttoned and on a night out, Thomas Wolfe with a sense of the ridiculous serving to undermine his flowery rhetoric."

Like Cash himself, the book has had a complicated life. Published to flattering reviews, it initially had modest success and then received renewed attention when it was reissued in paperback in 1960 at the beginning of the civil rights era. For a time it enjoyed an enormous vogue. "The impact of Cash's book on me was about the same as if someone had rolled a hand grenade under my bed," John Egerton once wrote. "*The Mind of the South* echoed in my own mind like Jefferson's proverbial fire bell in the night. As a comatose person might emerge from deep unconsciousness, I slowly began to hear and understand." Over time, the book has received a far more jaundiced airing. Its patronizing or racist views of blacks are an embarrassment today. Critics say Cash knew nothing of the South beyond the Carolina Piedmont and that rather than being a book about the South or the Delta or the Black Belt or the Tidewater or the Gulf, it's really a book about the Carolina mill country. Clearly, the "mind" Cash plumbs is not that of the entire South but of the white males whom he took to be the only ones who really matter.

Worse, others say, is that in the end it's not about the mind of the South but about the overheated cauldron of insight, fever, and neurosis that was the mind of W. J. Cash. Others say that rather than focusing on the mind of the South—say, of Jefferson, Madison, Calhoun, or Randolph, or all the Virginians who are venerated in every issue of *Southern Partisan*—it focuses only on the instincts of the South. The historian C. Vann Woodward suggested the book be called, *The Temperament of the South, The Feelings of the South,* or *The Mindlessness of the South.* But that's just the point. Cash's book is indeed about the temperament of the South, presuming that temperament is what lives on from generation to generation, while fashions, ideas, politicians, and movements come and go. For all the book's limitations—and there are many—no one can read Cash today and not come away time and again with flashes of recognition so intense, it's as if Cash x-rayed something immutably imbedded in the Southern soul. If much of his book, like its endless disquisitions on mill culture and mores, is clearly a product of the North Carolina Piedmont, much of it reverberates with remarkable resonance through the region as a whole.

In Cash's South of a half century ago, whites are instinctively unified against blacks just as they were during the days of slavery, and politics revolves around those who can best capture and portray the resentments and fears of whites. The culture and mores that bind whites together count for far more than the lines of class and economics that might divide them; there is a wild, almost irrational hatred of government and a mania for individualism left behind from the days of the frontier. Perhaps this sounds familiar.

Cash's South is one driven by a passionate identification of the average white Southerner with the region as a whole and its leaders that he called the proto-Dorian bond and a sort of collective will to succeed as a region or a community particularly in distinction to the North. "There are strange notes–Yankee notes–in all this talk about the biggest factory, about bank clearings and car loadings and millions, but does anybody fail to detect the authentic Southern pitch and tone?... Progress was in many respects once more actually strengthening rather than weakening the hold of the Southern pattern."

Cash had the love-hate relationship with his region that resonates throughout most great Southern literature. When he writes about the region's mythic physicality, which he terms "a sort of cosmic conspiracy against reality in favor of romance," his prose is so purple, it could come from a romance novel. If his portrayal of blacks never rises much above the prejudices of his time, he was ahead of his time in focusing on the degree to which whites and blacks in the South were bound together by ties of culture, manners, religion, and history so intense that in the end, "Negro entered into white man as profoundly as white man entered into Negro–subtly influencing every gesture, every word, every emotion and idea, every attitude."

What he finds eighty years after Appomattox is a New South that looks exactly like a reconfigured version of the old one, of wonderful personal virtues of honor, courtesy, and generosity, yet a lingering suspicion of new ideas, a thralldom to individualism, a place suffering from "a too narrow concept of social responsibility, attachment to fictions and false values, above all too great attachment to racial values and a tendency to justify cruelty and injustice in the name of those values. The South," Cash concluded, "is a tree with many age rings, with its limbs and trunk bent and twisted by all the winds of the years, but with its tap root in the Old South."

There was no such ambivalence in the worldview of Daniel Augustus Tompkins. Born a year after Henry Grady, in 1851, Tompkins, the one-eyed son of a South Carolina planter, became one of the quintessential New South characters. One of his grandfathers was a first cousin of John C. Calhoun, and Tompkins became as fervent an advocate for his vision of the New South as Calhoun was for the Old. He built an empire of cottonseed mills across the South and a cotton mill in Charlotte, bought a newspaper that became the *Charlotte Observer,* founded the Southern Manufacturers Club as a powerful businessmen's group, wrote a two-volume history of Charlotte's Mecklenburg County, sold textile equipment and machinery, designed and equipped textile mills and power plants, and built North Carolina's first steel-frame skyscraper, the Independence Building, back when uptown Charlotte was plain old downtown. His overreaching passion was industrial development and the notion that the promise of the South could only be fulfilled by burying the agrarian economy of the Old South and replacing it with a can-do industrial base. Tompkins didn't disapprove of the spirit of the Old South, but he saw that it had reached an economic dead-end in slavery and one-crop agriculture. For the South to fulfill its destiny, he decided, it needed to retool both its economy and the worldview from which that economy developed.

When he bought the *Observer,* he said, "The only thing that I wanted the paper for was to preach the doctrines of industrial development." A hallmark of that effort was his "cotton mill campaign" to bring the cotton mills to the cotton fields, which succeeded so well that by 1903, one half of the South's looms and spindles were located within a hundred-mile radius of the city, most of them financed with indigenous capital.

It's hard to be sure whether Tompkins or Cash would be most taken with today's Charlotte; both would feel vindicated, if in entirely different ways. Back when the Independence Building was being constructed, it was reported that Charlotteans craned their necks to see "every morning whether or not it had climbed during the night, and every night how high it had climbed since morning." It was probably what Cash had in mind when he noted the South's first pallid attempts at building urban skylines in cities like Charlotte, which, he opined, "had little more use for them than a hog has for a morning coat."

Writing about this nascent New South, Cash was at his visionary best, by turns overwrought and romantic but right on the money.

> And the key to this atmosphere, if I do not altogether miss the fact, is that familiar word without which it would be impossible to tell the story of the Old South, that familiar word "extravagant." ... Softly, do you not hear behind that the gallop of Jeb Stuart's cavalrymen? Do you not recognize it for the native gesture of an incurably romantic people, enamoured before all else of the magnificent and the spectacular? A people at least as greatly moved by the histrionic urge to perform in splendor, and

by the patriotic will to testify to faith in their land and to vindicate it before the world's opinion, as by the hope of gain.

You can pick your favorite example of those same instincts at work in Charlotte today. The most obvious is the outsized NationsBank Corporate Center, built at the site of Charlotte's founding at Trade and Tryon streets downtown, whose sixty stories dwarf the rest of the downtown skyline. With its crown of 384 aluminum rods, adjacent mall with hundred-foot-high glass atrium, its lobby marble from Spain, Italy, France, Turkey, and the rest of the United States, it's the definitive Sun Belt office tower—the office building as a combination of Sistine Chapel and Ritz Carlton. Most arresting of all are its three monumental twenty-three by eighteen-foot frescoes by Ben Long, a native of Statesville, North Carolina, who studied art in New York, joined the Marines, and then learned the art of painting frescoes in Florence. The NationsBank triptych, his first secular fresco, depicts in rich shades of gold and red an oddly hellish earthly landscape of dronelike workers, tormented souls, stairways to nowhere, and cold-eyed corporate *Übermenschen*, all created in the style and colors of Renaissance religious frescoes—the ultimate ratification of the New South creed of redemption through commerce.

At least as astounding, and oddly similar in design, is the Calvary Church, which rises like an enormous spaceship in the form of a pink crown on Highway 51 in the middle of the endless suburban sprawl of South Charlotte. It's constructed in a gargantuan sort of suburban Gothic style, with curved mirrored glass and soaring stucco spires, a three-level green-carpeted sanctuary seating six thousand, and a $2.6 million organ with 11,499 pipes that's billed as the thirteenth-largest pipe organ on the planet—it's about the same size as the Mormon Tabernacle organ in Salt Lake City.

Inside is an utterly self-contained world, part church, part mall, part community center with day-care toddlers being ferried around in red plastic buggies or riding trikes through the halls of the child-care area. I sat one afternoon at dusk in the empty sanctuary watching the rush-hour traffic crawling by outside and reading the fourteen-point Doctrinal Statement (November 14: "We believe there is a personal devil of great cunning and power who is 'the prince of the power of the air,' 'The prince of this world,' 'The god of this age.' We believe that he can exert vast power but only so far as God suffers him to do so; that he shall ultimately be cast into the lake of fire and brimstone and shall be tormented day and night forever").

Everything felt so shiny and new, you could only imagine the cunning Prince of the Power of the Air in a new red Jaguar with a bumper sticker reading, IF GOD ISN'T A TAR HEEL, HOW COME THE SKY IS CAROLINA BLUE? If poor, tormented Cash were around today either he would buy himself a dozen white shirts, take a job at NationsBank, join Calvary's New Horizons Singles Ministry, and get with the program, or else his tender, overloaded synapses would never hold out long enough for him to make it to Mexico City.

Monuments aside, Tompkins's worldview lives on most vividly in Charlotte's current leadership caste, and it is redeemed by the way Charlotte's mania for being Number 1 has somehow become hooked up with virtues that go far beyond economics and dollars and cents. Charlotte's current version of Tompkins is Hugh McColl, a South Carolinian like Tompkins, who came to Charlotte in 1959 and has since helped turn what is now NationsBank from a scrappy regional bank into the nation's fourth largest bank with total assets of nearly $200 billion. Even in Charlotte, McColl, sixty-one years old, is sometimes viewed as a little too Charlottesque for comfort: "There's an element of parody about Hugh McColl—the glass hand grenade that sits on his desk, the stock certificates from a string of conquered banks that hang like mounted trophies on the wall," Frye Gaillard, Charlotte's most insightful journalist, wrote in the September 1996 issue of *Charlotte* magazine. In business, McColl is viewed as something of an SOB, a former Marine who views each deal like a mission into enemy territory.

But even many skeptics in Charlotte concede that McColl's competitive instincts go beyond buying banks. Corny as it sounds, it's clear he is committed to making Charlotte a great city—and not in the hollow sense of World Classiness without end—in much the way he is committed to making NationsBank a great bank. The bank, for example, has pledged to invest more than $10 billion across the South into low- and moderate-income neighborhoods and to spend 10 percent of its procurement dollars—spending on buildings, office furnishings, supplies, and the like—with minority-owned businesses. The bank has been intensely involved with inner-city development projects in Charlotte, and in his speeches McColl incessantly talks up the importance of public-sector investment—even taxes—and developing a shared vision of the common good.

NationsBank is a huge, hungry banking company, not a charity, and nobody doubts that McColl's highest priority is his company's performance. He does at times indeed border on parody—he has already voiced the inevitable nightmare scenario of Charlotte becoming the next Southern city to host the Olympics. But whether because it came naturally from his gut, because he's smart enough to know that a decaying inner city, racial division, and short-term thinking about urban needs is bad for business in the long run, or because he figured out quickly what the civic ground rules were in Charlotte and inevitably decided to play the game in a big way, he reflects a sense of public spirit that characterizes the upbeat New South ethic at its best.

Similarly, Susan Burgess came from someplace else—in her case, West Virginia via Princeton, New Jersey, via Birmingham, Alabama. She wears a dress-for-success Harris tweed suit with a monogram silver pin and spouts the party line about how much people in Charlotte care about their community. But her spiel has nothing to do with commerce; she's a mother of four who had just been elected president of the local school board in an election in which virtually all of the Christian right and hard-right candidates calling for an end to school desegregation were soundly defeated and Democrats took back control of the city council—this in the year after the great Republican sweep of the South.

"I was a flower child—organic gardens, babysitting co-ops, food co-ops," she said when we met on the fourth floor of the school district's building at the edge of downtown. "We left Princeton, where my husband was in graduate school, so he could go to medical school, and when he was finished I drew a circle around the part of the country I wanted to be in, made lists of climate and city size, went through city-county data books and ended up in Charlotte, where I'd never been before. I wanted to be in the South, I wanted a city but not too big a city, I wanted a good place to raise children where there was good public education. That's Charlotte. This is a young city. There are no old families who run things. Everyone is welcome to participate. In this community, the expectation in the corporate community is that you will contribute to the United Way, you will contribute to the arts, and you will somehow be involved in the religious community and it doesn't matter where. We're growing, and we're not always growing smart. But what I like about Charlotte is that people believe they can solve our problems, and some of them we are solving–the schools for example. We're making them work, and we're keeping them desegregated."

In fact, no place else–certainly no place in the enlightened North– has fought to keep its schools desegregated the way Charlotte has. It didn't come easily.

Charlotte's version of segregation wasn't quite as brutal as that in some locations in the South, and it was a place where a measure of dissent was never viewed as unpardonable apostasy. "We have said it before. We say it again today," the *Charlotte News* editorialized in 1950. "Segregation, as an abstract moral principle, cannot be defended by any intellectually or spiritually honest person." At the time the *Observer* was arguing for a true commitment to equal facilities for blacks coupled with a go-slow approach by the courts on dismantling segregation. This may sound tame, but there were many cities in the South where no one in power would dare raise a sliver of doubt about any facet of the South's American apartheid.

One of Charlotte's best-known figures of the 1950s was Harry Golden, whose *Only in America* became an unlikely bestseller in 1950. A rotund, cigar-smoking iconoclast, Golden was born on New York's Lower East Side in 1902, attended the New York City schools and the City College of New York, and later moved to Charlotte, where from 1942 until 1968 he edited *The Carolina Israelite,* an eccentric liberal voice from the South. *The Carolina Israelite* was a sixteen-page monthly newsletter, with fourteen thousand subscribers around the world, roughly half of them Jewish, who were as likely to find utterly off-the-wall esoterica ("How Dr. Samuel Johnson Prepared Oysters") or reminiscences about life in New York ("Sex Morals on the Lower East Side") as thoughtful, liberal essays on the great issues of the day. Charlotte never quite figured out what to make of Golden, who was probably more esteemed outside of town than in it, but nor was it scandalized by his consistently liberal views on race.

Golden's most famous essay was a proposal for what he called the Golden Vertical Negro Plan. He reasoned that blacks and whites seemed to be able to *stand* at the same grocery store and supermarket counters, deposit money at the same banks, pay taxes and bills to the same tellers, and *walk* through the same five and dimes. It was only when the blacks wanted to *sit* down, whether in lunch counters or school classrooms, that whites panicked. Golden suggested that the North Carolina legislature simply pass an amendment allowing only desks but no chairs in the state's schools. "Since no one in the South pays the slightest attention to a Vertical Negro, this would solve our problem completely," he wrote. "In every direction, the Golden Vertical Negro Plan will save millions of dollars, and forever eliminate any danger to our public education system, upon which rests the destiny, the hopes and the happiness of this society."

If that failed, he had other proposals. He noted that black school-teachers in Charlotte who wanted to attend *Hamlet* at a white movie theater were admitted when they escorted their friends' white children. Seeing broader potential here, he suggested blacks simply manufacture plastic white babies, which they could take with them to whatever all-white ball, concert, or theatrical performance they wanted to attend. As for the dread specter of integrated churches, he had a simple solution: "Here is the plan to solve this problem for all the members of the 'White Citizens Councils' throughout the South," he allowed. "BECOME JEWS! There is little likelihood of any appreciable number of Negroes ever going to shul. Every day when the sun goes down you'll have yourself a nice compact community. You'll never have to worry about Negroes again, and you'll even have yourselves your own country clubs, swimming pools, rummage sales and book reviews."

But if Charlotte wasn't Birmingham or Selma, it was still the South, and when integration finally came Charlotte didn't acquit itself at the start much better than anyplace else in the South. One of the most striking images from the civil rights era—not as famous as the police dogs and water hoses of Birmingham or the bloody melee at the bridge in Selma, but as compelling in its own way—is a picture from Charlotte of a young black girl taken in September 1957. The girl was a fifteen-year-old high school student named Dorothy Counts on her first day at all-white Harding High School. She is tall and slim in a prim checked dress with a long white bow cascading down from her collar almost to her knees. She is walking, her head erect, a look of stoic, defiant resolve on her face, her gaze completely inward, through a crowd of hundreds of leering, yelling, taunting white kids whose faces reveal either mind-

less anger or smug, arrogant amusement at the notion of this black girl
daring to enter their white world. She lasted four days, during which
teachers ignored her and students peppered her with racial slurs, threw
things at her in the hall, and dumped trash on her plate at lunch. Her
locker was ransacked and her brother's car windshield was shattered by
a hard piece of fruit when he came to pick her up for lunch.

Things were even worse after U.S. District Court Judge James
McMillan in 1969 and then the U.S. Supreme Court in the landmark
1971 *Swann v. Charlotte-Mecklenburg* ruling ordered widespread busing
in order to ensure desegregation. There were brawls in the schools,
bricks were thrown through the windows of school administrators' officers, and an arson attack destroyed the Charlotte offices of Julius
Chambers, the lead attorney for the black plaintiffs.

Over time, however, something remarkable happened. At first there
was reluctant acquiescence to the ruling, but then, as the years went by,
a fierce, abiding sense developed that busing wasn't easy but was right
and Charlotte should find a way to make it work. "This is the cross of
the day," a white steel company executive named Jim Postell said at one
mass meeting of residents and school board members in November of
1973, "that black and white people have got to learn to live together.
But it's a hard thing. Black and white is hard." As the years went by
Charlotte's commitment to busing became as much a part of the civic
mythos as the new glass towers sprouting on the streets of downtown.
When Boston was torn apart by resistance to busing in 1974, students
from Charlotte sent letters of encouragement to their Boston counter-
parts telling about their own positive experiences. A cartoon from a
Boston newspaper showing a battered Bostonian, his head bandaged
and arm in a sling, while two bright-eyed youths from Charlotte, one
black, one white, come by to offer support and encouragement, still
hangs in a conference room at West Charlotte High School.

In 1984, when on a campaign stop in Charlotte Reagan lambasted
busing, saying it's "a social experiment that nobody wants. And we've
found out that it failed," the *Observer* countered with an editorial
the next day headlined YOU WERE WRONG, MR. PRESIDENT. It began:
"Charlotte-Mecklenburg's proudest achievement of the past 20 years is
not the city's impressive new skyline or its strong, growing economy. Its
proudest achievement is its fully integrated school system."

Black and white is still hard, and maintaining desegregation for the long haul may be even harder than winning support for it at the start. As Charlotte sprawls willy nilly both north and south into instant new suburban subdivisions with names like St. George Place and Sardis Plantation, busing becomes less and less feasible–the trip is too long and the newcomers don't have the same zeal for it as the residents who remember the struggles of the seventies and eighties. Charlotte increasingly relies now on magnet schools–specialized schools designed to produce integration through parental choice rather than through involuntary busing–but the jury is still out on how successful they will be as desegregation tools.

Still, Charlotte's experience with desegregation provides an enduring model for a New South that's close to the ideal the term came to evoke during the civil rights era–a place not just of prosperity and racial peace, but where people genuinely believe you can't have one without the other. "Folks like the notion of integrated schools here," said Harvey Gantt, the former mayor, who was preparing for his second Senate race against Jesse Helms. "They don't like all of what's happening in them, but people don't want to go back to segregated schools."

We were sitting in royal-purple chairs in the conference room of his downtown architectural firm, where associates of both races in sweater vests and bow ties or starched shirts and suspenders bustled by. The office has the hip, tasteful feel of Elliot and Michael's ad agency in *Thirtysomething*, except that here, half the Elliots and Michaels are black. "What happened with busing in the nineteen-seventies," he continued, "is that the city got positive publicity out of it, I got elected mayor, people enjoyed the image. Who wants to be like Birmingham was in the sixties? We even got a little smug about the fact that we were showing Boston how to do it. Here was young, upstart Charlotte saying, 'Hey, down South, this is how we do it.' Charlotte's always been concerned with business and image and it turned out the image of integration was good for business. It's very interesting. You can live in any neighborhood you want in Charlotte. Now it's true there are basically white neighborhoods and black ones, but if one of the young black architects in this firm decided to buy a house in southeast Charlotte, there would be not one peep, not one word.

"Charlotte's a place where people are at least trying to find common ground. I like the notion that we're always contemplating our navel. I don't know whether we pick the city to come to or when we get here the water tastes a certain way, so you decide this is the smart thing to do, but there's an openness here you don't find in many other cities. James Baldwin was right about that years ago when he said, we're always on each other's minds down here, because we live so close together, so if there's ever going to be a resolution of the race problem in this country it's going to be in the South because everything is so intertwined."

Of course, now as then there are limits to creating racial common ground. The most consistent one played out in a remarkably succinct psychodrama between the summer of 1994 and the fall of 1995 at a little church northeast of downtown called Plaza United Methodist Church. The issue there was one that whites seldom have to confront but blacks confront every day: Must integration always be on white terms? Must it always be Dorothy Counts going to Harding High, Harvey Gantt going to Clemson or becoming mayor of a majority-white city, Charlotte fighting to maintain a racial balance in the schools close to the 60:40 white-to-black mix of the district with blacks bearing the biggest burden of being bused? Can't integration ever mean merging whites into predominantly black institutions? In this case the focus was a white church in what had become a black neighborhood.

Religion, as least as much as education, has been the other major backdrop for Charlotte's ongoing morality play over exactly what kind of a New South it wants to be. Charlotte's famous preachers—A. G. Garr, Carlyle Marney, James A. Jones, and Bishop C. M. "Daddy" Grace—are as much a part of Charlotte mythology as its business tub thumpers like Tompkins and Kuester. At times the result has been as much hokum as salvation, most notably when Jim and Tammy put together their ecclesiastical pyramid scheme just over the South Carolina state line in Fort Mill, which in 1989 netted Jim a forty-five-year sentence for mail fraud. But Charlotte's religion usually has tended more toward sober, Presbyterian rectitude than white-hot fundamentalist fervor, and religion has been more of a moderating, unifying force in Charlotte than in other parts of the South.

Charlotte's most famous contribution to world religion is Billy Graham; given the role religion plays in Charlotte it's appropriate that the first highway you come to when you leave the metro region's shiny, tidy new airport is Billy Graham Parkway. Graham, born on a Charlotte dairy farm, blended the city's entrepreneurial and evangelical qualities in a way very different from the Bakkers. When Charlotte was still an overgrown country town in the 1950s, he attracted 450,000 people and put together a 1,750-voice choir for his Crusade for Christ at the local coliseum. What the Gradys and Tompkinses did for the selling of the South, he did for the selling of Jesus nationwide and worldwide.

Many evangelists and preachers in the South helped fuel the fires of reaction, but not Graham, who was an early voice for integration; he personally pulled down the ropes separating the whites and blacks in the audience at a crusade in Chattanooga. Among the cards and letters of support Dorothy Counts got after her ordeal at Harding High School was one from Graham, an odd mix of Christian probity, can-do moralizing, and Cold War politics. Hand-written in pencil and dated September 6, 1957, it read:

> Dear Miss Counts,
> Democracy demands that you hold fast and carry on. The world of tomorrow is looking for leaders and you have been chosen. Those cowardly whites against you will never prosper because they are un-American and unfit to lead. Be of good faith. God is not dead. He will see you through. This is your one great chance to prove to Russia that democracy still prevails. Billy Graham, D.D.

It's quintessential Charlotte on race, at least as much from the head as the heart, but ending up at the right place.

The stakes were not quite as high as saving democracy from the Russians when Percy Reeves, a soft-spoken thirty-four-year-old former University of South Carolina running back with a shaved head and a warm, nonthreatening demeanor came to pastor at Plaza United Methodist Church in 1994. Reeves, the son of an African Methodist Episcopal preacher, had been drafted by the NFL's New York Giants but had opted for the ministry. Just as Dorothy Counts found herself on one era's racial frontier, he found himself at the same place for another time, a black man trying to build an integrated church at least as much on his own terms as on those of its white congregation.

Founded in 1961, Plaza United is a tidy, unprepossessing redbrick church located in what were once white suburbs that have since become a largely black area of neat, well-kept-up middle-class homes.

Over the years the church made efforts to minister to the neighborhood with a free lunch program and day care, but the congregation remained almost entirely white. When Reverend J. Matthew Burton, Jr., in February 1994 announced that he was leaving, there was some natural concern about who would come next, particularly in light of the obvious changes in the neighborhood and the fact that the church had slowly been losing members—about twenty a year—for more than a decade as old congregants moved away or died off and no new members from the neighborhood stepped in to replace them. Given the uncertainty, they were thrilled to learn that a well-regarded minister, a white man named Andy Sherrill, had been chosen to be the new pastor.

But before he arrived, the leaders of the Methodist district changed course. Shortly after Sherrill's name was floated by the congregation, the district leaders heard about Reeves, who had been at churches in Rochester, New York, and Louisville, Kentucky, and had been rated one of the six best black ministers in the denomination. The Methodist leadership, eager to increase their influence in a city with 169,000 blacks but only two black United Methodist churches, saw the opportunity as too good to pass up. "In our minds, he was something of a superstar," Dr. Donald Haynes, the superintendent of the Charlotte district, said later. "So I went back to the church and said we found someone we did not know existed, and I apologized for the shifting of candidates, but that Reeves was better suited."

It later became a common refrain among white members that it wasn't Reverend Reeves they had a problem with, but the way he was appointed, which is absurd, of course. The substitution of another white minister for Andy Sherrill would have barely caused a ripple. But it certainly did not help that many felt from the start that Dr. Haynes and the Bishop of the North Carolina Conference, L. Bevel Jones, had somehow pulled a fast one on them.

Still, only about eight families in a church of about four hundred people left immediately when Reeves was appointed. The rest held back to see what developed. Watching hardest perhaps was Charles Lamm, the church's fifty-three-year-old board chairman, who had been a member of the Plaza United Congregation for twenty-seven years. Lamm, who was the executive director of Lions' Services Inc., a social service agency for the blind, and was legally blind himself, had argued strenuously against Reeves's appointment, arguing that a white pastor with a black associate would be a better way to serve both the neighborhood and the congregation and move toward some measure of integration. When he talked about the situation at the church a few months after Reeves arrived, he seemed to focus on two points. The first was that the membership was willing to work with Reverend Reeves and hoped he would succeed. The other was that if he moved too fast, he was certain to fail.

"This is like anywhere [where there's] a dramatic change, whether it's a racial issue or when we first saw females in the pulpit or the I.R.S. called you for an audit," he said, not exactly brimming with enthusiasm. "People respond in different ways, but my opinion is that two thirds of the church is still attending on a regular basis. I think Percy Reeves is intelligent enough to see the necessity to walk a tightrope and not make radical changes very quickly. I haven't given any thought to changing churches in the last three, four, five months. I will not leave because Percy Reeves is the preacher and he's black. If I leave it will be because of dramatic changes in the style of worship that don't fit my style. I'll accept and learn to live with it a little at a time. If you try to drown me in it, I'm going to leave."

Soon Reeves and Lamm found themselves bound together in an odd symbiosis, each man knowing he needed the other to keep the church together, but never entirely seeing eye to eye on how to do it. Lamm soon became the keeper of the old virtues. If services went on past noon—common practice at most black churches, heresy at Plaza United and many white ones—Lamm would get up and walk to the rear and open the doors in an explicit signal that it was time to finish up. If the preacher's decibel level got too loud for the ears of the white parishioners accustomed to more sedate preaching, Lamm would hold his hand up to his ear as a signal to tone things down. "I've been here twenty-seven years," he said. "I like to say to the preachers, I was here when you came, and I'll be here when you're gone. We will debate our differences, and we'll reconcile those differences, and then we'll compromise."

Week by week the melodrama played out both inside and outside the gently vaulted, wood-paneled sanctuary. Sometimes when the church received local and national publicity, parishioners felt that Reeves was using them as a foil—the obligatory white bad guys—in a self-serving racial morality play. Another week it would be changes in the music or a passage in the sermon or the absence from the service of familiar elements like the Lord's Prayer or the Apostles' Creed. Events soon conspired to make things harder still. When I first attended services on a Sunday in October 1994, Lamm's wife, Becky, one of the bulwarks of the congregation, had just slipped into a coma after an extended bout with cancer. She died soon afterward, giving many members more reason to feel unsettled and uneasy.

Still, most of the regulars were still attending and, on the surface at least, were supportive of Reeves. His sermon that Sunday was a calm, elegant appeal for racial understanding that was at once disarming and challenging. He began with his own experience as a fourth-grader going to what had been a white school, moved on to the apostle Peter's experience of going beyond the hostility he had felt for Gentiles, and then brought the issue back, subtly, to the present. "So Peter had to have a change of heart. The bottom line is the truly great things that God will do through us, the truly wonderful things that God would accomplish in us, all require a change of heart. The Bible says, 'Be not conformed to the world, but be ye transformed by the renewal of your mind.' Transformed like a butterfly out of a cocoon. Transformed like a pearl from an oyster. A change of heart precedes all of God's work."

After it was over and he and the congregants had milled around outside the sanctuary under the watchful gaze of the framed photographs of his eight white predecessors, we went back to his office, which had three portraits on the wall of a very different type. One was of Nelson Mandela. One was of Malcolm X. The third was of Martin Luther King, Jr. We had talked on the phone, and I'd read some of his public statements, but as we talked it was clear that his vision of the church was nothing like Charles Lamm's vision. Lamm, like most congregants, felt Reeves's job was essentially to bring in some new black members to the church as it now existed. But Reeves, in a way he hadn't really enunciated publicly, didn't see it that way at all.

"I'll just say to you, you can't have everything on your terms," he said, doubling back to his sermon. "And I think that if we're going to genuinely integrate, we're going to have to share power, it's got to be a partnership. And that's not easy. That's why we have to have a change of heart, a genuine change of heart. Right now, musically, for instance, we're still Eurocentric. And the challenge is going to be turning it enough to where it reflects the tenor of the community, which is becoming more and more Afrocentric. This church still has some vitality in it, so it would be very insensitive to ignore some of the better things they have done. But I do think its future lies in appealing to the African-American community. That's why I'm here. But when people worry about it becoming a black church, well, it will never be a black church as long as they're here. So, see the burden is not on me; the burden is on them. That's what white folks do—they put the burden on us. This church will never be a black church if everybody stays."

He went on for a while, echoing almost exactly the words two decades ago of Jim Postell, the white steel executive who said, "Black and white is hard"—only this time it came from the black perspective, not the white one. "It's hard," he said, his voice suddenly as soft as a feather. "It's hard trying to make this work. You know, W.E.B. DuBois used to talk about the twoness. He was always talking about being black and an American. You always sense your twoness. You always do. But I'm never more conscious of that than when I'm here."

About a month after his wife died in October, Charles Lamm, Reeves, and the church's Bishop Jones met to consider the church's future. They gathered at 7:00 P.M. at a Red Lobster restaurant and met for two hours in a long, emotional airing of their differing visions of what the church would become. When they finished, Lamm was elated and Reeves was uneasy—the bishop had agreed with Lamm that it was important not to alienate the white members of the congregation by moving too fast. Reeves drove Lamm home to his house in the Shannon Park neighborhood near the church where they both lived. They sat in the car and talked for a few more minutes, and then Reeves walked Lamm inside and they talked a bit more. They still weren't on the same page, but they had come to respect each other as the process went on, and they agreed to talk some more after each had digested that night's session. They never did. Lamm, who had always told the preachers he was there when they came and he'd be there when they left, died that night in his sleep. As he had a month earlier for Becky, Percy Reeves presided over the funeral.

Members held a closed-door meeting a month or so later and ended up supporting, for the most part, the church's new direction. "It's really turned into an affirmation of Percy and his work here," said Ken Worthy, a white thirty-six-year-old Charlotte policeman who was the new board chairman. "People want him to stay and do God's work at

Plaza." Reeves, too, figured things just might work. "It's been frustrating at times, but this is the most exciting thing I've ever been involved in," he said when we talked in December 1994. "This is uncharted territory. You can't legislate it. You can't force it. It has to come from people's hearts. For now, it's coming."

But it only came so far. The next time I saw Reeves was when I picked up a copy of the local black newspaper, the *Charlotte Post,* almost a year later. He was on the front page wearing his black robe and its three black velvet stripes, holding a red Bible. "When the Rev. Reeves became pastor of Plaza United Methodist Church last year, the congregation was 99 percent white," the photo caption read. "Now it's 80 percent black. He said accepting differences is the biggest barrier to good race relations. 'The majority is not willing to cross over and try on your shoes,' Reeves said."

I drove out to see him that night, a Wednesday, which was youth night. Reeves was in the kitchen joking around with a bunch of black kids, who spilled out into the eating area, where they were leafing through mimeographed sheets explaining the history of the African festival called Kwanzaa, the meaning of African words and names, or the nature of the karamu, the main Kwanzaa celebration, usually held on the evening of December 31. Reeves greeted me warmly and we walked out to the church's creaky old gym, with its linoleum floor and steeply pitched roof with some of the ceiling tiles missing, where perhaps twenty black teenagers were playing basketball. With us were Willie Caldwell, a black man who helps out with the coaching, and Jim Burr, a white accountant—he had a Bible in his coat pocket—who lives in an integrated neighborhood five minutes from the church and is as committed as ever to seeing through the changes in the church.

Things had gone badly with the original congregation at the church. The past summer about forty members had had a secret meeting with the bishop in which they basically said, "Either he goes or we go." He stayed. They went. Soon afterward, on the second Sunday in August, a meeting was called of the Methodist Men's Group. Surprisingly, many of the men who had long since left the church—some of them even before Reeves arrived—showed up. Reeves knew something was up, and he soon realized what it was. The men had gathered before services at a big table in the middle of an open room at a nearby restaurant called the Tryon House, and the agenda turned out to be how to spend the

$5,000 remaining in the church charity fund. The departed members had come with a list prepared of favored charities. Their intent was to empty out the treasury, giving the money where they wanted it to go. Some of the others, including Burr, protested, saying it was wrong, and furthermore the church charter stipulates the need to keep at least $1,500 in the fund. But the old members knew what they wanted to do and they did it, leaving only $300 behind.

When the meeting was over, they left and never came back. Reeves got in his car, turned to a gospel station, broke out in tears and drove around aimlessly for forty-five minutes, feeling just about as low as he ever had in his life, until finally, the joyous, shouting clamor of the music and the empty ache of his tears evened one another out and he felt a sense of peace, calm, and resolution he hadn't felt since he'd come to Plaza United. "Well," he thought. "I don't have to fight that battle anymore." Then he drove to the church in time for Sunday School.

Three months later, watching Reeves with the kids in the gym, it all seemed to have traveled in an inevitable path. Wearing an applejack cap just like the one Bob Mants was wearing when he walked over the bridge at Selma on Bloody Sunday, gray slacks, a stylish patched jacket, black turtleneck, and black tassled Italian loafers, he joked with the kids and fooled around like the father most of them didn't have. "Gimme the ball," he yelled, caught a bounce pass, and threw up not one, but two impeccable three-pointers before launching an air ball to hoots and hollers. It was all part of the "elephant" club he was organizing for the neighborhood kids, one of the initiatives that had done him in with the old members, many of whom were willing to worship with blacks in church but didn't want the church to become a second home to a bunch of black teenagers in their baggy Carolina Tar Heels shorts and rap couture.

"I was sitting in my office, and I thought about this elephant club," he said, watching the game going on around him. "The idea is to get some big elephants. I don't know if elephants talk to other elephants or not, but certainly they model one another. So what we do with the kids, I start with the idea that there's nothing wrong with being big and bad, but I want you to look at the characteristics of an elephant. An elephant is big, powerful, intimidating, intelligent. It defends its turf. It protects its young. But it's not predatory. It's gentle, but it's tough. It has a thick skin, and all those characteristics are what it's going to take for you to make it. So what I wanted to do is to get big elephants together and let's model a two-part program, one spiritual, one social to help these kids make the transition from childhood to being young men and women. That's what I wanted to emphasize, a ministry to black youths, but even the liberals couldn't handle that.

"I'll tell you, a lot of those kids have been around the edge. They're right on the border of crime. There was one a few weeks ago. I told him, 'I ain't always been no preacher. I know the look of marijuana when I see it, and don't come back here with that on you. Anytime you want to talk to me that's fine. But you've got to respect this place and respect yourself.' I didn't want to run him off. The kid came back, his eyes were clear. Now, I don't know what he does away from here, but he's been fine here. They all are. You don't hear no cussin' out there. You got twenty young black guys and they're all respectful. All good kids. All I did was tell them that this is a friendly place. It can be a haven. And it should be."

Soon it was around nine, time to close up for the night. The kids filed out, leaving with a respectful "Bye, Rev" or a soul handshake, and we sat outside the gym in a commons area that had children's drawings and religious posters on the cinder-block walls. Reeves got very quiet again. He does have star quality, a combination of a natural gift for language and metaphor, imposing looks, and a preacher's gift for compelling, understated emoting. But it all makes him hard to read. Like dealing with a skilled actor, it's hard to be sure how much you're getting is from the heart and how much is put on for show. Still, it was difficult to listen to him in the empty, still room and not have a sense that his words captured, if not the truth, at least a truth, about race in the mid-nineties as indelibly as Dorothy Counts's fierce embattled gaze did in 1957.

"Ecclesiastes said there is a time and a season for everything under the sun," he said, sitting on the edge of a long table, his hands clasped in front of him. "We've missed our time for integration. We've missed it. Those kids that are in there, that generation of kids, you turn on BET [Black Entertainment Television] and listen to the radio stations they listen to, they ain't talking integration. They're talking black empowerment, they're talking self-reliance, they're talking we don't need no white man to do this and to do that and the other thing and they're right. They're not talking integration. You got the black elite talking integration. But that's it.

"I'm a very, very, moderate guy. I made some mistakes here. I could have been more candid. There were times when to spare feelings I didn't say what I should have. There were times when I no longer believed it was possible when I tried to make them believe it was possible. But this was always about power and control, and just as in every area of life, they're in the majority—in the schools, in the boardroom, in the malls, in the office—they wanted to be in control here. Religion is the retelling of a story. It doesn't matter if it's Jewish or Baptist or Catholic or Methodist, but what makes a church is that people with a shared experience come to celebrate that shared experience of Christ in our lives. But as long as the black experience in America is miles apart from the white experience, why would you think they could sit and worship together? It takes people willing to compromise to make it happen. And it's hard as hell. I think black people, on the whole, are willing to try to do it. I don't think white people, on the whole, are willing to try. We need to take steps toward reconciliation, but the next step has to be taken by whites, and they won't take it."

When he came to Plaza United, Sunday service attendance was about 130 people. At the end of 1995, it was down to about 40, and people were wondering if the church would survive. But soon it began to grow with black families and a few interracial couples from the neighborhood, and by the spring of 1996 attendance was back where it was when he began and the church was growing faster than it had in twenty years. In the process, it had gone from all white to perhaps 90 percent black.

If whites see integration as a one-way street, it's more a measure of how long and hard the road ahead is than of the progress along it in the thirty-eight years since Dorothy Counts walked through the angry mobs at Harding High. Indeed, what's most striking about Charlotte is that it's one of the few places where the kids in their mom's Plymouth Voyagers at the pink suburban palace of Calvary Church and the kids hanging out reading the Kwanzaa brochures in Percy Reeves's kitchen at Plaza United have a reasonable chance of going to the same school, a place where the push of history is more a groping toward reconciliation, however flawed, than acceptance of the status quo. Maybe it's human nature that doing well was destined to count for more than

doing good—at least about race—in the New South Gospel, but both
imperatives are still there. In the end, in the one reversal Cash would
never have imagined, the question for Charlotte is whether it will maintain enough of what it's had to make race relations work. Cash saw how
the South's drive for redemption could play out in commerce or religion, but Charlotte is clearly a place where, in a limited but real way, it's
played out in terms of race as well. The question many people are
asking now is whether Charlotte will stay Southern enough to keep the
faith.

Among the people pondering that question is Dorothy Counts. She's
stockier now than she was in the famous picture, her hair is cut stylishly
short, and her demeanor has a calm, sunny assurance rather than the
fierce resolve of that September day in 1957. Her story since that extraordinary time is a pretty ordinary one—marriage, divorce, two grown
kids, and a job as the supervisor of training at a nonprofit organization
called Child Care Resources Inc. We met at her office near downtown;
she bounded down the stairs and announced, "Hi, I'm Dot," and then
we drove to Frankie's, a popular luncheon spot where nonstop Sinatra
blared annoyingly out of the loudspeakers.

After leaving Harding, Dorothy Counts for a time attended an integrated school in Pennsylvania, then came home to attend Charlotte's
Johnson C. Smith University, the historically black school where her
father taught. She moved to New York for a few years and then came
home, living first in a largely white neighborhood in South Charlotte
and then, after her divorce, moving back to the black neighborhood
where she had lived when she briefly attended Harding.

It's so commonplace to think of race relations in America as a failure
that it's refreshing to ask whether the glass is half empty or half full and
get an unhesitating "half full" response—one you get from blacks in
Charlotte about as often as anywhere you can find. "Integration has
worked in Charlotte," Counts said. "I would hate for us to go back.
After what happened to me, and what happened in the late sixties and
early seventies, we integrated peacefully. People were determined to
make sure it worked. What I think is happening now is, you have a lot
of transplants, new people, that don't understand the history. They
want things to change, to become more like where they came from.
Once someone came to my door asking me to sign a petition against
busing, and I told them, "You just don't understand. All this got started

because my parents years ago felt this was something that had to happen." And it did.

"It hasn't all worked out. My daughter went to Davidson [College] here and it wasn't always a good experience. There's been backsliding over the last five or ten years, because a lot of the people who are part of the history are no longer here and the new people don't understand what we accomplished. It's true for blacks, too. Every year around February, for Black History Month, I go to the schools to talk about my experience and the kids look at me with their mouths open. They can't believe it happened. And some of them can't understand how you could let this happen and not fight back. So a lot's been forgotten. And that's what I worry most about. I don't want other people to come in from other places and make things change. I don't want people who don't know what we've gone through to try to make Charlotte a different kind of place."

Chapter 7

HONEA PATH, SOUTH CAROLINA
The Ghosts of the Chiquola Mill

Sue Cannon Hill was nine months old when her father, Claude Cannon, was shot to death, along with six other striking millworkers, in Honea Path, South Carolina. It happened on September 6, 1934, outside the old Chiquola Mill during the General Textile Strike that helped write the epitaph not just for seven millworkers, but for unions throughout the South.

She remembers that her mother, Iona, would never walk by the spot where her husband was killed because it was said that on rainy days the ground turned a bright red as his blood seeped up from the porous pavement. She remembers sitting in church with some of the men who fired the guns that killed the strikers and playing every day with their children, friends who wanted to know why she didn't have a daddy. She remembers how her mother, faced with raising six children alone, took an oath never to talk of the union again and went to work for the rest of her life in the mill where her husband had been killed. She remembers how her mother used to commune quietly with the bloody clothes in which her husband was killed, until Sue's older brother Marvin, in exasperation, took the blood-soaked, bullet-tattered rags and buried them in a vacant field.

Many of Sue's most vivid memories are the fondest ones–how her family would take tomatoes and Saltine crackers to an old poplar tree where they would spend the whole day picnicking and swimming in a creek called the Blue Hole, while her mama would hunt for ferns and flowers, which she would miraculously transplant in glorious profusion at their company-owned, bare-bones, three-room (kitchen and two bedrooms) frame house. They'd make turtle stews and chicken stews, have fish fries and laze in the sun, and at times like that she felt as if she were rich and there was no better place in the world to live than the mill hill of a South Carolina textile town—even one where the father she never got to know had been shot to death by the people for whom her mother now worked.

More than anything, though, she remembers the communal conspiracy of silence, how the most important event in her young life and in the life of everyone in the little mill village where they lived was never mentioned, as if the shots had never been fired, the men had never died, the union had never existed, the whole thing had never happened at all.

And then, on Memorial Day, 1995, something amazing happened in Honea Path, a three-stoplight town with a dusty, dog-eared main street of tired brick buildings where makeshift aerobics and weightlifting studios and the Honea Path Opry fill up otherwise vacant storefronts. About three hundred people, including about fifty members of Mrs. Hill's family, gathered in Dogwood Park under the shade of the green Pruitt Funeral Home awnings on a muggy May day, as the town's history was remembered anew, for a day at least.

First, Mayor Billy "Chicken Hawk" Gilmer spoke. He was a nervous-looking man in a shiny dark sport coat who said he had relatives on both sides of the shooting, and he hoped the memorial could be an occasion for healing. There were speeches by union supporters, by a representative from a workers' group, the Carolina Alliance for Fair Employment, and from Frank Beacham, the grandson of Dan Beacham, who had been the town mayor, the mill superintendent, and the man who armed the strike breakers and apparently gave the order to fire. Frank Beacham was a big man with long white hair and a gray beard dressed in a black jacket, the sweat soaking through his black T-shirt underneath. He had left town years ago to become a writer in New York but had returned for the memorial. "Memories are fragile," he said, "and we can see that here in Honea Path. But though memory is fragile, knowledge is power. That may explain why some people in South Carolina don't want us to know this story. I don't think we should let them win." When the service ended a few minutes later, he removed the cloth covering the 21-inch high, 2,000-pound, burgundy granite monument purchased from the Easley Marble Co. with

$1,598.30 in donated funds. "They died for the rights of the working man," it read. "These men were killed in Honea Path on September 6, 1934, in the General Textile Strike. This monument is dedicated to their memory, to their families and to all workers." Then it listed their names: "Claude Cannon, Lee Crawford, Ira Davis, E. M. Knight, Maxie Peterson, C. L. Rucker, Thomas Yarborough."

Honea Path's past was brought into the present largely because three documentary filmmakers, George Stoney, Judith Helfand, and Susanne Rostock, included parts of it in a remarkable documentary film, *The Uprising of '34,* on the all-but-forgotten Depression-era textile strikes in the South, that they made for the Public Broadcasting System. Their research helped many people in Honea Path to finally learn about the town's bitter labor history, and it led others to talk about the strike for the first time in decades. In the end, the process helped unearth so many stories that it was as if sixty years of history gushed to the surface.

Even more compelling than Honea Path's buried past was what its history had to say about the present. The South has been American labor's Waterloo, the nut that never cracked. The labor movement has had some organizing success in the South—in Appalachian coal hollows where the names of "scum-sucking scabs" are scrawled in bright colors on rickety pitched roofs, in gritty Alabama steel mills or big-city construction sites. But the region's core industries, particularly textiles, have remained among the least unionized in America. South Carolina boasts of having the lowest percentage of private-sector union workers of any state in America—2.4 percent in 1994 compared to a national average of 10.8 percent. Overall just 3.8 percent of all South Carolina workers belong to unions, compared to an average of 15.5 percent nationally. Other states with union membership below 8 percent include the Confederate states of Arkansas, Louisiana, Mississippi, North Carolina, Texas, and Virginia, plus Arizona, which might as well have been. North Carolina, the Southern state with the highest percentage of its workforce engaged in manufacturing, has the second-lowest (behind South Carolina) percentage of unionized private-sector workers: 3.5 percent. Just behind North Carolina in the percentage of the work force in manufacturing is Mississippi, which also pays the lowest wages in the nation.

The South isn't the only reason the unions have gone from representing 40 percent of the private employees in America to 10 percent. A shift in jobs from manufacturing to service, increased competition from overseas, and the degree to which many fat and happy unions ossified into lazy or corrupt guardians of the status quo are among many factors that have played a role. But by providing a safe haven for employers looking to move to a nonunion environment and by providing a hammer over the head of workers hoping to organize elsewhere, the South's resistance to unions is generally regarded as one of the major factors in the steep decline of union influence in America. By the same token, the South has traditionally sent to Congress the nation's most fiercely antiunion legislators, people like South Carolina's "Cotton Ed" Smith, who when he wasn't raving on about race was railing against efforts to establish minimum wages and maximum hours as attempts "by human legislation to overcome the splendid gifts of God to the South." In Washington, he and other Southern legislators have fought—and more often than not thwarted—most pro-labor initiatives since the New Deal and have been ardent supporters of antiunion legislation like the Taft-Hartley Act of 1947, which permitted states to pass "right-to-work" laws, which allow workers in unionized plants not to join the union. After its passage, Southern states were the first to enact the "right-to-work" provisions into law.

The South's fabled and endlessly trumpeted "favorable business climate"—read "no unions welcome"—has brought a mixed bounty. It has helped make the region, particularly the Interstate 85 corridor between Richmond and Atlanta, of which Honea Path is now one of the outer edges, the new manufacturing center of America. During the early 1990s, eight of the top ten states in terms of new manufacturing plants were in the South. With numbing regularity, in recent years the nation's most avidly sought-after industrial recruitment plums—most strikingly, high-employment, multi-million-dollar auto plants—have come to the South, among them the $1.2 billion, 6,000-job Nissan plant in Smyrna, Tennessee; the $3 billion, 5,900-job Saturn plant in Spring Hill, Tennessee; the $2 billion, 4,000-job BMW plant in Greer, South Carolina; and the $300 million, 1,500-job Mercedes-Benz plant in Vance, Alabama.

But along with the plums have come the lemons: the chicken- and catfish-processing plants and hog-processing factories and toxic waste dumps that define the floor of the low-wage, low-skill economy. Scattered throughout rural communities and tucked off the interstates on the poor side of small towns, they make the South the bad-job capital of

America. Years ago the South, poor and desperate for jobs, made a Faustian bargain with the nation's and the world's employers: ship us your jobs, any jobs, and we'll work for less than workers in the North would, and without unions.

Since then, two things have changed. The first is that a changing economy that isn't producing enough good jobs anyplace has made the bargaining position of workers across the country look like the traditional poor bargaining position of the South. The second is that the low-skill jobs that once came to the South can now go as easily to even lower-paid workers in Taiwan or Singapore or Honduras or Mexico. In short, everyone is playing the South's old game. That raises two questions: What has that game done for—and to—the South? And what are the odds that labor, suddenly full of bold talk about organizing the have-nots still living in the economic shadows in the trailer parks and ghettos and factory towns will reverse the long slow death spiral that began when the South held firm as a nonunion haven? You can get some ambiguous answers in towns like Honea Path.

Nothing in Honea Path's history would lead one to expect it to play much of a role in the nation's labor history. First settled around 1790, Honea Path barely existed until the Columbia and Greenville Railroad came through in 1852. To this day, the real piece of history people talk about is where its name comes from. Legend always had it that it came from a Cherokee Indian trail that had some of the South's best honey trees, but it's more likely it was named for William Honey, a trapper who was granted two hundred acres of land near the town on April 7, 1788, by William Pinckney, the governor of South Carolina. It was chartered in 1855 as Honey Path, but either because a clerk at the state capital in Columbia got it wrong or because people just decided to spell the town the way they pronounced it, it soon became Honea Path and the name stuck. Later, General Sherman came through "stealing and destroying everything that was available," as a local history puts it.

The town's symbol became the honey bee, the high school team became the Stingers, and the water tower still features a honey bee and the words HONEA PATH—THE LITTLE TOWN WITH THE BIG HEART. The big event each year is the annual Honey Soppin' festival in which contestants vie to see who can be the first to whistle after sopping up honey with a biscuit and eating it.

But what really made Honea Path was the mill. Honea Path's evolution from a little farming village to a real town began in 1902, when the Chiquola Mill was organized and a four-story, 83,200-square-foot cotton mill was built in the 160-by-130-foot redbrick building that still stands at the center of the mill village. The factory opened up with 15,360 spindles and 400 draper looms, and as happened in countless Southern villages like it, soon became a magnet for poor farmers, in this case those barely making a living across the Carolina Piedmont.

The era saw the beginning of industrialization in the South and almost everything about it made it a tough sell for the American labor movement. The South in spots played a significant part in the early history of labor unions in the United States. After the Civil War, the Knights of Labor, the nation's largest union, became the first national organization to launch a sustained unionization campaign in the South. The Knights eventually formed locals in every Southern state and in 1886 held their national convention in Richmond as a signal of their interest in the South. Influential unions that began in the South included the International Brotherhood of Boilermakers, Iron Shipbuilders and Helpers, and the International Association of Machinists.

But the South was always at the tail end of the labor movement's achievements. Segregation conflicted with the stated ideals, if not always the actual practice, of many unions and made organizing difficult. Mills were dispersed in distant, far-flung rural communities that formed a close-knit paternalistic world of company housing, company stories, and mill-owned churches where the pastors equated unions with the fires of Hades. The pervasive poverty of the South made the lure of a job, however modest, far more potent than a union's vague promise to fight for better pay and conditions. General poverty also ensured that there would be an eager supply of hungry workers off the farms who would be ready to take your job if you didn't seem to want it. And, just as it did with politics, culture trumped economics. There was always something foreign, menacing, un-Southern about unions, so that it was easy to tar the union movement with what the historian James C. Cobb called "the triple bugaboo of Yankeeism, race-mixing and communism."

Still, if ever there was a time when unions had a chance in the South it was in the early part of the century, especially during the Depression, when a new industrial South was being born and workers uprooted from the farms were thrust into the new, unsettling world of the mill villages. There were famous, bitter, usually unsuccessful strikes in Augusta, Georgia in 1898 and 1902; in Danville, Virginia, in 1901; in Atlanta in 1913; in Kannapolis and Concord City, North Carolina, in 1921; in Elizabethtown, Tennessee, in Gastonia and Marion, North Carolina, in 1929. Most significant was the general strike of 1934, when the combination of the Great Depression and a rising tide of union strength produced the second-largest industrial strike in American history. At its peak, some 400,000 workers, including 180,000 in the South, walked off their jobs.

To view the old photographs and footage showing thousands of white Southerners marching arm in arm under union banners past the tin awnings and brick shops of the small towns and cities of the South is to contemplate for a moment an utterly changed Southern history, where the cultural bonding that has always knitted Southerners together was binding them in an entirely different direction. It was the greatest show of labor power the South had ever seen, but when it was over, the union movement in the South was never the same again.

The issues in Honea Path were much the same as everywhere else: pay that was often below five dollars a week, twelve-hour days in hot, poorly insulated, lint-filled mills, and the speedup and stretch-out–the demand for more and more productivity, running looms and other equipment at ever faster speeds, and expecting weary bodies to stretch with them. The strike in Honea Path in 1934 began the way the strike unfolded in mill towns across the South. Workers formed ad hoc groups called flying squadrons that traveled from mill to mill trying to shut them down. National Guardsmen were called out to protect the mills in the textile center of Greenville, but there were no guardsmen thirty-five miles down the road in Honea Path when tensions came to a boil on Thursday morning, September 6.

By five A.M. that morning, strikers had gathered outside the gaunt redbrick factory in the heart of the mill hill, where the residents lived in identical houses: a worker once put a boot on top of his roof so he could tell which home was his own. Their intention was to form a picket line around the mill and thus keep nonunion workers out. But inside the mill, more than a hundred workers and police were already armed with shotguns, pistols, and .22 rifles; they had been deputized by Dan Beacham, acting in his dual capacity as mayor and mill superintendent.

As the morning went on things became more chaotic. Union supporters, nonunion workers, and the merely curious thronged around outside. Several nonunion workers made it inside the mill and others made it clear they wanted to enter the mill. In the confusion, strikers and nonunion workers started scuffling over picker-sticks, clublike hickory sticks used on the mill's looms. Suddenly a shot rang out, then a volley of shots from the armed workers inside the mill. Strikers and bystanders, many of them fleeing for their lives, started falling in the bedlam and panic that ensued. Most of the dead were shot in the back. Another thirteen men and women were wounded. It could have been far worse: witnesses said a World War I machine gun had been placed on the roof and that Beacham's men labored frantically but unsuccessfully to get it to work.

At the funeral two days later, ten thousand people turned out to pay their respects as six wooden coffins, painted gray, sat in a row under a brown tent before being mounted on hearses and carried past the mill to the burial ground nearby. (Rucker died a day later.) Labor leaders and clergymen from around the country flocked to Honea Path, convinced this was a historic moment in labor's long, hard, uphill effort to organize the South. Reverend James Myers from New York, the industrial secretary of the Federal Council of Churches, offered a special prayer for labor and called upon all workers to support the strikers "as a Christian duty": "These men need not have died if their employers had realized the right of the workers to organize, the right to which they are entitled as children of God. They died to make industry Christian."

But when the service ended and the labor leaders left, the reality of making a living in the Depression-era South counted for more than a nascent labor movement ever would. Life went on. Widows took their fallen mates' jobs in the mill. Staunch labor supporters either forgot they had ever heard the word "union" or they left the area and the blacklists that would keep them from working. The armed nonunion workers who had fired from inside the mill shared pine church pews with the people they had fired upon The strike became Honea Path's shared secret, the subject that no one in town could ever forget but that no one would ever discuss. Over the years, as old-timers died off and mothers kept it from children, it seemed to vanish altogether, like a message written in disappearing ink. All that remained was a bitter residue of antipathy for unions, handed down from generation to generation, with the narrative long gone but the conclusions still lingering: the unions caused the trouble and then couldn't protect their own people when the violence got out of hand.

What happened in Honea Path was an extreme case, but it wasn't that different from much of the routine violence employed against union organizers and supporters in the South. During the 1934 strike in Georgia, Governor Eugene Talmadge declared martial law and troops herded workers and their families to prison camps surrounded by barbed wire and guarded by armed troops. Afterward, more than twenty-five thousand strikers were blacklisted from ever working in the mills again, despite promises by management they would be able to return to their jobs. Thirty-six strikers were shot during a confrontation in Marion, North Carolina, in 1929. Sinclair Lewis went there and wrote a syndicated newspaper report entitled "Cheap and Contented Labor: The Picture of a Southern Mill Town." He concluded: "The workers, especially in Marion, have become discouraged. They are hungry, tired, bewildered. They are sick of being shot down. Unless the whole country encourages them (and there are few more delicate and tactful forms of encouragement than dollar bills), they will crawl back into the slavery I have sought to picture here." Before long, they did.

In Barnesville, Georgia, in 1938, an International Ladies' Garment Workers Union worker was kidnaped, taken sixty miles away, and ordered never to return by a mob led by businessmen who had guaranteed that the town would stay union free. When union organizers came to Greenville, South Carolina, in 1929, one minister called for organized public floggings as a means of proper punishment for "Northern reformers who think they are called upon to reform conditions in textile mill villages here." Touching upon two mob floggings of textile union organizers, the Reverend D. B. Hahn of Greenville's Pendleton Street Baptist Church said that there was no doubt the culprits got what they deserved but that public whipping posts were a better way of dispensing justice. The United Textile Workers Union had 80,000 Southern members during the summer of 1934. By early 1937, only 5,500 were left, leaving the textile industry in the South the largest nonunionized industry in the country.

The violence tended to subside after World War II, but companies like textile baron Roger Milliken's fiercely antiunion Milliken and Co., now the largest privately held textile firm in the world, with 13,500 employees worldwide and estimated 1994 sales of $2.7 billion, were willing to wield a bigger stick than random violence. Faced with workers who voted for a union, in Huntsville, Alabama, and Darlington, South Carolina, the company simply closed the plants, inviting years of litigation but sending workers the ultimate message: if you want a job, you don't want a union.

Clearly, the cultural factors slowed union organizing in the South. With hundreds of small mills producing the same products, unions almost had to organize them all at the same time to keep from pricing the union mills out of the market. But many historians argue that what really did the most damage to labor was that it was just beaten down—its strikes broken, its most committed members blacklisted. Even union victories often turned hollow when plants were shut down or battles to get a contract proved as protracted as battles to win representation. A Senate subcommittee looking at labor practices in the Southern textile industry concluded in 1951:

> In stopping a union organizing campaign, the employer will use some or all of the following methods: surveillance of organizers and union adherents; propaganda through rumors, letters, news stories, advertisements, speeches to the employees; denial of free speech and assembly to the union; organization of the whole community for antiunion activity; labor espionage; discharges of union sympathizers; violence and gun play; injunctions; the closing or moving of the mill; endless litigation before the NLRB and the courts, etc. If all this fails, the employer will try to stall in slow succession, first the election, then the certification of the union and finally, the negotiation of a contract. Few organizing campaigns survive this type of onslaught.

More than forty years later, the story was pretty much the same. After investigating union complaints against Fieldcrest Cannon, Inc., in North Carolina, stemming from a 1991 organizing campaign, the National Labor Relations Board found that the company engaged in unfair labor practices that were "numerous, pervasive and outrageous"—including many of those cited in the 1951 report. To this day, the religion of antiunionism flourishes as it always has throughout the South. The historian James C. Cobb calls it "the South's most respectable prejudice" and quotes a labor leader as saying of Strom Thurmond:

"He'll accept blacks now, but you still don't see Strom shaking hands with union people."

Sixty-one years after the shootings at Honea Path, South Carolina's public television station refused to show the *Uprising of '34* documentary, and it finally aired on a commercial network at 11:30 P.M. on a Sunday night a half year after the rest of the country got to see it. When Simon Greer, an organizer with the Carolina Alliance for Fair Employment, tried to show the film as part of a noncredit course at nearby Spartanburg Technical College in Roger Milliken's hometown in the heart of the I-85 manufacturing belt, he was told that the course was being canceled because it was too controversial and the major manufacturers in the area like Milliken and Michelin tires didn't want it shown.

Many in Honea Path felt the same way. Fred Moore ran the town newspaper, then called the *Honea Path Chronicle*, from 1945 to 1981 and served for twenty-two years in the state legislature. At seventy-five, he still runs a profitable and sophisticated printing business whose main customers are the textile and apparel mills in the area. We were sitting in the airy vaulted living room of his white brick house, which has four white pillars out front and a trailer full of treasured junk out back, bearing a sign that reads *Col. Fred T. Moore, S.C. Lic. Auctioneer 101. Honea Path, S.C.* Inside the living room were porcelain dolls and bric-a-brac all around, his wife's Bible open to Isaiah 29, and mix-and-match upholstered chairs of all shapes and sizes. Jerry Springer was on the TV, interviewing folks who slept with their wife's sister or their husband's brother or brother or sister's mate. An infidelity scorecard flashed on the screen (MARRIED TO TONYA—HAVING AFFAIR WITH HER SISTER JAMIE) for those who couldn't keep up. It was around noon, and Moore, a big affable man with snow-white hair, was sitting in a wing chair in sky-blue pajamas wearing white slip-on sneakers.

Fred Moore talked about a lot of things, from a long description of Fritz Hollings's legislative style as governor to an intricate description of how a loom works, using two envelopes and the weave in his pajamas as props. But for the life of him he couldn't see why anyone would want to dredge up Honea Path's labor history.

"I didn't make a single mention of it in all the years I ran the paper, and I don't see why anyone would mention it now. There are too many bad memories, too many people it could hurt. And there's not a lot of unions around here and there's not gonna be. The union movement never did catch on here. They came in with some of those wildcat strikes, but they never did do their homework and they never understood the people around here. They moved too fast and people got scared. Now you have people making higher wages than they ever made and there's plants everywhere. We've got Dixie Container making boxes and Chiquola and we got a shirt plant and the Maxxim Medical glove plant, there's Coleman Machine that makes parts for corrugated box companies all around the world, there's Owens Corning, we got beaucoups of industry. Why would anyone want to mess it up by bringing in a union? Fact is, people don't want a union, they feel like we're all the same. We don't have rich people or poor people–well, maybe some dopeheads that don't want to work. But otherwise we're pretty much the same, not greedy people, not capitalists, not peasants. We don't have any upper class, and we don't have any lower class."

To underscore his populist credentials–in the way that well-to-do whites in the South have been able to affect a folksy, "plain-folks" proletarianism that seldom worked in the industrial North–Moore walked across the room and picked up a red, white, and blue Grammer guitar with thirteen white stars on it. He strummed it once and started to tell a story he'd heard at the legislature about a fellow who staggered home on Monday morning to find his mobile home gone, his clothes hanging in a Chinaberry tree, and his shoes in the sand, where a dog was playing with them. "It was sad, so sad, I decided to write this little song about it," he said, and then, sitting there in his pajamas and slippers, he started singing:

> Last night, I let temptation lead me on.
> I got home this morning, Lord, home was gone.
> Now I'm standing on the very spot where my home used to be.
> She left me and took my home sweet mobile home.
>
> Home sweet mobile home; home sweet home to me.
> Now it's rolling down the highway, where it stops where will it be?
> She took the patio. Lord the concrete slab is gone.
> She left me and took my home sweet mobile home.
>
> Well I staggered in at daybreak feeling funky.
> While I'd been out a-drinking, Lord, my wife had hauled her donkey.
> I don't know how she hitched it up or put them damn wheels on.
> She left me and took my home sweet mobile home.

Home sweet mobile home; home sweet home to me.
Now it's rolling down the interstate somewheres in Tennessee.
A thousand-gallon butane tank, Lord the storage building's gone.
She left me and took my home sweet mobile home.

He laughed a big satisfied laugh, escorted me out for a tour of the treasured junk in his trailer by the Cadillacs out back, and padded back inside.

There was a little more class consciousness at the trailers across town in the mill village. "This here's the Shit Creek Gang," said Brooks Townsend, better known as Peanut. "To the uptown people on the other end of Main Street we're lower than whale shit, but we have a good time and these are good people." It was six P.M. on a Friday evening, and Peanut, Tommy Creel, and James Tripp were drinking beers in a grove of South Carolina white oaks around a huge empty wooden spool for industrial cable they call the round table. The trailers were decorated with Confederate flags, busty pinups, and Harley-Davidson and beer company paraphernalia, like the poster reading TO HELL WITH THE MOUNTAINS, SHOW ME YOUR BUSCH. Peanut and Creel were bare-chested, their tanned arms and chests marked with tattoos. Tripp was wearing a blue cotton shirt that looked like a doctor's scrubs. He had thick glasses and a round friendly face that brought to mind the writer and Southern savant Roy Blount Jr. On his cap was the Confederate Battle Flag and the words THESE COLORS DON'T RUN. NEVER HAVE. NEVER WILL.

Before long, old, rusted-out Cutlasses and battered pickups full of mill hill folks were driving up, almost all of them children and grandchildren of people who worked at Chiquola, which is now operated by Springs Industries. First to arrive was Jimmy Gambrell, who had curly hair and olive-colored skin and who pulled up with a twenty-four pack of Budweiser he seemed intent on killing by himself. He staggered over toward the round table carrying a plastic bag that was two thirds ice and one third water; apropos of nothing he started pounding himself on the forehead with it, all the while flashing a dopey grin.

There was an old pair of pliers sitting on the cable spool and not a full set of teeth in the bunch, and before long they launched into good-natured anecdotes about the virtues of do-it-yourself dentistry. I figured it was all beery hyperbole for the benefit of the credulous visitor from

Atlanta, until Tripp casually picked up the pliers and attached them to a yellowed tooth hanging tenuously from Gambrell's upper jaw. Tripp studied the tooth with a practiced eye, shimmied the pliers back and forth back and forth with an authoritative hand like an expert carpenter, gave a firm yank, and, presto, instant oral surgery. Gambrell hopped around in pleasant, drunken agony for a few moments like a man who had jumped into an icy pool and wasn't sure whether it was torture or bliss, then stuffed a pink towel into his mouth and chomped down on it to stanch the bleeding.

On the utility of unions, opinions were split. Peanut and Larry Fields, another late arrival, seemed to think that employers were such sorry assholes that unions were good. Fields had a staunch union man in Atlanta for an uncle, who was always telling him how much the unions can do in terms of protecting workers' rights and fighting for better benefits. Still, that didn't mean Fields was optimistic about seeing much union activity in their neck of the woods anytime soon. "This whole state is run by the Baptists," said Fields, behind his blue-tinted designer shades. "If the Baptists don't want it, it don't happen, and they don't want no unions, I can tell you that."

Some of the others couldn't see much value to unions. Ernest Yarborough, the most sober fellow in the bunch, was the grandson of Thomas Yarborough and the nephew of Maxie Peterson, two of the seven names on the monument. But the idea of unions left him cold. "The way I look at it is that if a man hires me, and pays me his money, he didn't hire you to referee," he said. "And if I got to work and he says he's paying six dollars, where do I get off turning around and having some union tell him to pay me eight dollars? If he don't treat me right, well, I can go work for someone else, but it's my decision to go to work for him and it's my decision if I want to leave. He don't need no union looking over his shoulder over everything he's doing."

We talked awhile, but it was clear the issue was too ancillary and philosophical to have much interest—sort of like sweating in the South Carolina heat and discussing whether the Arctic is colder than the Antarctic. "I don't care if they have unions or don't have unions as long as they keep the fucking niggers off the mill hill," one of the more agitated ones said. The mill village had always been white and the recent arrival of a few blacks was not popular. "I have a son who's mildly mentally retarded. I take him over to the food-stamp office in Anderson, and I can probably get a few dollars, but that's all. Niggers walk in there, and they get hundreds of dollars in food stamps. They get the light bill paid. They get the water bill paid. They get the fucking rent paid. If I get there, and I'm the first one there and five niggers come in behind me, you can bet the nigger clerk is going to call her nigger brothers and sisters before they take me. Just keep the niggers off the mill hill. That's what I care about. I got no use for the thick-lipped, blue-gummed sons of bitches whatsoever."

We talked for a while longer, until Gambrell draped his arm around my shoulder, offered to give me his bloody, yellowed pulled tooth as a souvenir, and asked how my teeth were doing. I figured it was time to leave.

The memorial and observance of the Honea Path confrontation were the work of Kathy Lamb from Belton, the next town up Highway 76 toward Greenville. At forty-one, Kathy Lamb had a face from the mill hill—round and pinched at the same time, with two missing lower teeth—and a frosted patch of short auburn hair. Her pear shape rolled and swayed under her blue and white cotton dress; her knotty hands, distended by tendonitis and carpal tunnel syndrome, were the product of sixteen years in the sewing rooms of South Carolina apparel plants.

She tended to rattle on and on amiably in her thick Piedmont drawl, but there was a bite to her words and enough ice in her blue eyes to give the overall effect of someone not to be messed with. That was probably why Honea Path Police Chief Steve Hanks just backed off when she made it clear she was going ahead with the memorial service no matter what he thought about it.

Kathy had been a member of what was then called the Amalgamated Clothing and Textile Workers Union (A.C.T.W.U.) at the plant she worked at in Belton, until the plant closed and took its work to Mexico and Costa Rica. She didn't miss the work, which required sitting bent over a machine, sometimes from six A.M. to nine at night, not getting up except to go to the bathroom, while your legs swelled up and your shoulders ached, and your fingers and joints throbbed from making six thousand scissor cuts a day in order to meet production quotas. But it was clear that she did miss the give and take of the workplace, the ability to stand her ground when pushed around. "It takes a brave person to organize around here, because you put so much on the line, but I think I could organize the hell out of these mills. If people know you, they'll trust you. You got good unions and bad unions, but if you work in these plants, you need someone who can stand up to management. You got the same crap all over the South, and sooner or later people are not going to put up with it."

Sometimes, in large and small ways, Southerners have put up with it until it was too late. The worst-case scenario on a large scale occurred the day after Labor Day, 1991, when a hydraulic line on a deep-fat fryer ruptured at the Imperial Food Products chicken-processing plant, just across the South Carolina border in Hamlet, North Carolina. It ignited a fire that spread toxic smoke throughout the plant, killing twenty-five people and injuring fifty-six, many of them trapped behind improperly locked exit doors that were blocked off so workers wouldn't steal chickens. The plant had never had a fire drill, and in its eleven years of operation it had never been inspected for fire code or safety violations by any local, state, or federal agency.

The most striking thing about Imperial's story was not what was extraordinary about it, but what was routine. Its owner, Emmett Roe, began in the chicken-processing business in Moosic, Pennsylvania, near Scranton, but, tired of the unions and fussy state regulators in the North, he closed the Moosic plant and headed for more hospitable environs in the South, opening plants in Hamlet, Birmingham, and Cumming, Georgia. He piled up a long litany of health and safety violations at other plants before the Hamlet fire, which broke out when maintenance workers, under intense pressure to keep up production, tried to repair a hydraulic line without shutting down the nearby fryer it controlled.

Four years after the blaze the site sat vacant amid ivy and kudzu, broken glass, and rubble. It was on a narrow street just across from the Leroy Hubbard Homes, a black housing project run by the Hamlet Housing Authority, whose residents provided many of the workers. Hamlet is a small town of 4,700 people, about one quarter of them black, but it was easy to drive through the picture-book small-town streets with their grand oaks, ample front porches, and American flags and never see the poor black areas tucked away at the edge of abandoned rail yards or industrial areas. It was once a railroad hub, where the trains provided good, well-paying jobs, where jazz saxophonist John Coltrane and journalist Tom Wicker were born in the same year–1926.

But when the railroads faded away by the 1950s it was just another small town hustling up whatever jobs it could get and unfortunately some of the ones it got were the ones at Imperial. As I poked around out front, two black kids rode their bicycles by, and one of them said he had an uncle who died in the fire. "You can't do nothing if you don't have no job," he said, when I asked him about the plant. "If it opened back up, people would probably go right back."

But if horrific tragedies like the Hamlet fire focus attention on working conditions, often the smaller, quieter horror stories say as much. Take the case of Margaret Gail Rogers and the Kunja Knitting Mills of Mullins, South Carolina. Kunja, a Korean-owned firm, was lured to South Carolina by Governor Carroll Campbell in 1988 by ample tax breaks, state-funded employee training, and, of course, a friendly regulatory climate. Rogers went to work there in 1988, keying in data on a high-tech knitting machine that made sweaters. Part of the job consisted of oiling the machine with one of two kinds of low-grade motor oils they were cleared to use. But before long the supervisors were handing out a third kind of yellow-colored oil, which stung and burned like acid whenever she used it, turning her fingernails black and leaving scars like cigarette burns on her hands. Working while pregnant, she got sicker and sicker over time; she became weak and her vision became blurred. Others in the plant, which was staffed mostly with Korean supervisors and black South Carolinians, developed less-severe health problems as well. Once there was a chemical leak and the plant had to be evacuated as workers left bleeding from their noses, mouths, and ears. Before long the International Ladies Garment Workers Union began an organizing campaign, but it went nowhere because union supporters were soon summarily fired. The National Labor Relations Board in 1990 cited the plant for numerous labor law violations, including unlawfully firing union supporters, threatening to close the mill if a union was formed, and soliciting employees to inform on other employees' union activities. In his report on the hearings, Administrative Law Judge Lowell Goerlich concluded: "The record, as noted above, is replete with evidence of the Respondent's antiunion animus, of its commission of unfair labor practices, and its determination to bar the Union from its plant.... Such circumstances teach a lesson which the dullest employee would not fail to comprehend." The state Department of Labor, Licensing, and Regulation in 1989 cited the plant for failing to label and identify hazardous materials and to properly instruct employees in their safe use.

As the labor issue heated up, Rogers's health got worse. She suffered from dizziness, nausea, and numbness in her hands. She almost miscarried three times, until she finally delivered in May 1989. Six days after delivering, while on maternity leave, she testified for the union at a grievance hearing. When she tried to come back to work she was told she had been fired. The union filed suit to get her her job back, but instead of her old knitter's job she was put to work dabbing the yellow oil on machines from a bucket, wringing out the wet, oil-soaked rags with her bare hands. She felt worse than ever. Then, on what was to become her last night of work, she for the first time got a look at the container from which the oil was dispensed. She was stunned to find out it was supposed to be kept off human skin and handled with extreme caution. Complaining of dizziness and being so weak she could hardly walk, she went the next day to her doctor who placed her in a hospital where, at age thirty-five, she underwent an emergency hysterectomy. When she tried to return to work, she was told she had been terminated again. At the NLRB hearings, company supervisors said Rogers was terminated because of excessive medical leaves but Judge Goerlich ruled she was really fired because she testified against the company at the grievance hearing.

In a deposition, her doctor, Dr. Allan Lieberman of Charleston, a specialist in occupational and environmental medicine, said she suffered from "acute and chronic toxic injury to corrosive and solvent chemicals which resulted in injury to multiple organs, including her nervous system, her musculoskeletal system, her immune system, her skin, and her ear, nose, and throat." But doctors for the company have found no serious health problems due to chemical exposure, and attorneys for the two companies that insure the plant argue that the oil she used most likely caused no injuries other than skin irritation and the workman's compensation system has heard and rejected her claims. However it's resolved, her case is a reminder that the new American workplace can offer more subtle hazards than the old one. Rogers didn't face the mangling of the old industrial world (although clearly much of the new Southern workplace like the chicken and catfish plants can pose more traditional health risks). Instead, she found herself in a high-tech environment of industrial chemicals that can affect different individuals in very different ways, so much so that it may be difficult to prove in a definitive way what caused her ailments.

Meanwhile the $20 million plant, which employed five hundred workers, is long gone. Facing unfair labor practices complaints and immigration and customs investigations, it was suddenly shut down by the company after two years of operation in March 1991. Only a lawsuit filed by the union forced the company to comply with a federal law requiring sixty-day notice for plant closures and back pay for employees unlawfully discharged.

And, whatever the result of the protracted proceedings, Margaret Rogers will always believe she was poisoned at the Kunja work site. When she started work in 1988, she had been a smart, tough, striking woman, five feet, nine inches tall, with a regal bearing. Now, at thirty-nine, she takes thirty pills a day, has headaches and joint pain all the time, her immune system is shot, and her face is scarred. She lives on disability payments and is still pursuing workmen's compensation claims, despite rulings that she erred in not filing her claims earlier.

"South Carolina is a place where a company can do almost anything and get away with it," Rogers said. "We should have been given data sheets telling us about the chemicals we were using. We should have had some protection, but we didn't have anything. The fact was I was using a hundred-thousand-dollar machine and they thought the hundred-thousand-dollar machine was worth more than a black person was. I didn't believe something like this could go on, but it did."

Or take a more prosaic case, that of Wilhemina Green, who leaves her home on St. Helena Island each day around one P.M. to ride what they call the slave ships, the L.R.T.A. buses that serve the burgeoning seaside resort plantations on Hilton Head Island. She rides for three hours on a bus full of other black cooks, dishwashers, maids, waitresses, bellhops, and gardeners, dozing fitfully as the bus stops and starts. She gets to Hilton Head at about four P.M. and works in one of the giant resort plantation restaurants until midnight. With less traffic on the ride back, she gets home around two A.M. She makes $6.50 an hour with benefits in an environment where talk of unionization almost always means firings, and where it's a commonplace observation that the black people who once picked cotton on the old agricultural plantations now cut grass, trim azaleas, and scrape crabcakes off dirty plates at the resort plantations.

Countless stories like these lead Bruce Raynor, the Southeast Coordinator for UNITE, formed in 1995 from the merger of the Amalgamated Clothing and Textile Workers Union and the International Ladies Garment Workers Union, to believe that you can unionize the South. He is even having quite a bit of success doing it. To the Southern powers that be Raynor is an Antichrist from Central Casting, a union organizer from Brooklyn who had been a member of Students for a Democratic Society at Cornell in the sixties and was married to a black woman. His office is dominated by a big poster of the 1955 champion Brooklyn Dodgers and a map of the Southeast.

Raynor was an intense, driven man wearing an olive-colored suit with a bright, Peter Max–like tie that featured a worker with a lunch pail under a bright sky of shining stars. He had become something of a legend in labor for his record of success in organizing in the South, but even he kept his expectations reasonable and his time-frame long.

"You can't organize Southern workers in a serious way in any short-term way," he said over Chinese food at a restaurant down the way from the UNITE headquarters in Union City, south of Atlanta. "It's all long-term battles. You've got to win the battle to change the region, to change the power relationships over a long period of time. It's not one fight. You have to keep winning. If you win the union election, then you have to win the first contract. If you win that, you have to win the second contract. It's like being on a treadmill. It takes incredible focus. You can't let up for a fucking second. The barbarians are at the gates at every moment.

"But Southern workers aren't antiunion. There's a tremendous anti-union culture built up in these towns; you have to fight the whole town, the politicians, the preachers, the funeral home director, the grocery store owner. Sure, there's an element of conservatism among white workers in particular about unions, but not that much. Basically, a lot of Southern workers have drawn the conclusion that the union can't win, not that it's not a good thing. I've never seen a case where management was neutral where we didn't win."

Richard Bensinger of the Organizing Institute in Washington, D.C., spent years in futile organizing drives in Virginia and the Carolinas, but he too was not at all convinced that the lesson of the South was that conservative workers don't want unions. Instead, he harkens back to one of the signal, if often forgotten, political moments of our time, the 1968 presidential campaign, when poll results showed a startling degree of overlap in the support for Robert Kennedy and George Wallace. Kennedy was reaching the frustration of white working people from the left and Wallace was reaching it from the right. Kennedy did not live long enough to test his appeal, and Wallace's version was the one that won out, but Bensinger makes the case that it doesn't have to be the one that wins out in the end.

"Here's a really interesting thing about the South," Bensinger said. "A.C.T.W.U. recently won a big campaign in Martinsville, Virginia, at the Tultex plant. They signed up three thousand new members. Now, that town was one of Ollie North's real strongholds in his Senate race, and the workers who signed for the union were about seventy percent white; they were basically Ollie North's supporters. I think that's important. Lee Atwater said it best—he said you won by tapping into people's anger, and that's what we're trying to do. We train our organizers to tap into anger and self-interest. Atwater did it by blaming welfare mothers. We're blaming greedy bosses, and I have to believe that there are a lot of angry white males and even angrier blacks and women who are willing to respond to their real self-interest, not the social issues the Republicans and Atwater came up with. If you want to return to a high-wage economy, how do you do it without pressure on employers, and where will the pressure come from but unions? It's ironic that Republicans have succeeded with a social agenda that gets people to vote against their economic self-interest, while the Democrats are so elitist, they can't tap into the anger that's real. They just say people are stupid, and they should feel happier than they do. I think unions grow again when we tap into that anger, and I think the place you have to start is in the South, if only because that's where all the opportunities are."

This isn't an arcane issue about an increasingly marginalized union movement. It gets to the heart of the pervasive fears about job security and income inequality eating at the nation's social fabric. Unions in many ways dug their own graves by becoming the defenders of yesterday's jobs and work rules. But, in fact, as unions have declined, the wages of American workers and any sense of job security have declined with them. While corporate profits in the summer of 1995 were at a forty-five-year peak, workers were getting an ever-smaller piece of the pie, sinking to levels last seen thirty years earlier. In 1972, chief executives at major corporations brought home forty times what the average worker made. Since then, the ratio had grown to more than 140 to one. Since 1980, total CEO pay has increased by 360 percent while factory wages have risen by 75 percent—less than the inflation rate.

In the 1980s, the amount spent on salaries over $1 million grew by 2,200 percent, fifty times the growth of salaries between $20,000 and $50,000. Between 1980 and 1989, the income of the top 1 percent of American families grew by 62.9 percent. That added up to 53.2 percent of all families' income growth in that period. During the same period the income of the bottom 60 percent of all families declined.

From 1983 to 1989, the wealthiest 1 percent of the population received 62 percent of the increase in total wealth, the value of total household assets, primarily financial assets like stocks, bonds, and real estate investments. The next 19 percent received 37 percent, leaving the bottom 80 percent with 1 percent of the gain. The same trend held true in the early 1990s. The United States now has the most unequal distribution of wealth in the industrialized world. The wealthiest 1 percent has 39 percent of all household wealth, compared to 26 percent in France, 25 percent in Canada, 18 percent in Great Britain, and 16 percent in Sweden. The top 20 percent of households now get half the nation's total income and control 85 percent of all wealth.

The disparities reflected the dog-eat-dog economics of the global marketplace, Wall Street's infatuation with corporate downsizing, and technological change. But they also clearly reflected the diminished clout of labor around the country. At the end of the nineteenth century and during the Depression, the same kind of galloping disparities helped create the labor movement as a major force in American life. Many people in the labor movement saw the same potential at the end of the twentieth century. In fact, in 1996 labor, including unions like UNITE and the AFL-CIO under its new President John J. Sweeney was making bigger, bolder, louder noises about organizing in a concerted way—particularly in the South—than at any time in decades. The AFL-CIO, for example, planned to increase its budget for organizing in 1997 to $15 million from just $2 million in 1995, with the biggest focus on the South. The logic is clear: just as labor's long, slow decline began in the South, any major resurgence would have to begin there as well.

How far it comes will depend a lot on people like Anthony Romano, a 1990 Harvard graduate from Atlanta who is one of hundreds of young union organizers at the heart of labor's new organizing push. We met one summer afternoon in Rock Hill, where he was working on an organizing campaign at Conco Medical Company, a medical bandage manufacturer that moved from Bridgeport, Connecticut, to South Carolina in 1994. Romano was tall and slim with thick black hair and a goatee that made him look like a late-fifties beatnik. He wore a black and white short-sleeve shirt and had a ring of keys tied to his tan shorts. "In the South, it's kind of like you're climbing an ice-covered mountain without a pick," he said, his inflections an odd mix of black street talk and working-class bravado, almost a mirror of the coalition labor must put together to succeed in the South. "The companies will scare the hell out of workers, tell them the plant will close, fire union activists, hire the nastiest, most vicious antiunion law firms in the world. But for all that–playing with a straightjacket on, blindfolded, wearing a muzzle–we're adding thousands of workers. Can you imagine what would happen if we had a level playing field?"

As things turned out, however, management eventually turned the tide at Conco, defeating the union drive despite initial enthusiasm for it. Everyone in the union movement was well aware that attempting to crack the South was nothing new. From the textile strikes of the thirties to labor's Operation Dixie in the forties, to an all-out Southern strategy initiated in the seventies to a major push in Texas in the eighties, organizing the South in a big way has been one of the recurring themes of American union lore with few great achievements to show from it. Many of the old problems–particularly the tendency of blacks and whites to focus on their racial differences rather than their class commonalities–were as significant now as in the past. Only now, the fault line that had always divided workers in the South was increasingly likely to divide them outside the South as well.

The other problem was in persuading Southerners to see their self-interest in banding together against the economic powers that be. The Southern states, particularly its bottom dwellers like Mississippi, had invented the game of luring industry with sweetheart deals and promises of a nonunion environment. Now everyone–including the resurgent smokestack states of the Midwest–was joining the bidding war. In an increasingly Darwinian economic world of winners and

losers, made all the more perilous by feared job losses resulting from
NAFTA and new technology that replaced workers with machines, it
was a hard time to get people to stand up and fight for a union.

It was particularly hard because, by the diminished ground rules for
workers in the nineties, the new economic game was working in some
ways–though not for the workers at the bottom in the chicken plants or
low-tech apparel mills, and for whites far more than blacks, which was
why blacks in the South were far more receptive to unions than whites
were. But Greenville and Spartanburg had more direct foreign investment per capita than any other metropolitan area in American. In 1995
South Carolina announced $5.4 billion in new capital investment, 40
percent higher than the previous record. Unemployment was around 5
percent. And unlike so many of the forlorn factory towns or shuttered
mill villages of the Northeast, Honea Path had the unmistakable feel of
a place where life had gotten better, not worse, over the years.

Walking around Honea Path reminded me of a piece that appeared
in *Esquire* a few years ago on Levittown, Long Island, that monument
to the supposed killing blandness of suburban conformity. Instead of the
suburban sameness, the writer was struck by how all the cookie-cutter
look-alike homes had metamorphosed over the years into distinctive
places animated more by the people who lived there than some
implacable dynamic of industrial conformity. You get the same sense
from the mill hill now. There are rickety trailers and ramshackle frame
houses where a telephone is a luxury that's out of reach. But there are
also homes with new plastic swimming pools and fancy new siding,
bricked-up mill homes, ranch-style mill homes, houses with big old
Harleys and gleaming new Toyotas, with great golden rows of corn
growing outside, with neat gardens and green planters hanging from
every inch of screened-in front porches.

And if class in the South can at times seem as immutable as family,
the people who returned for the memorial at Honea Path generally
reflected how far workers had come economically since the uprising
of '34. Sue Cannon Hill now lived in a soaring cypress house on a
hilltop near Belton overlooking the seventy-five-acre spread where her
husband used to raise paint horses. There was a huge satellite dish to
the side of the house and a Jacuzzi out back on the deck where the
family sat in their rockers each night to watch the sunsets. In front of

them was a fishpond stocked with catfish, crappy, and bream and on the other side of the jacuzzi were the day lilies and red flowers called flags that she grew as successfully as her mother did back on the mill hill. They sold the five-thousand-square-foot home where she raised her kids to buy this one, with its knotty pine high-vaulted ceiling, grandfather clocks, antique quilts, and tony copies of *Southern Horseman* magazine.

She was exceptional. Most workers lived closer to the trailers of the Shit Creek Gang than to Hill's impeccable *Country Living* magazine version of down-home chic. But in Honea Path, even those with the most emotional stake in the meaning of the past were more likely now to view the bloody battle of '34 as personal history, not as an object lesson about labor or economics or class. W. A. Smith was the last living person who was shot that day. "I never was no union man," Smith said after viewing the film. "I never did get my card. I started off working for ten cents an hour and I went from that to twelve dollars a week. I've got two places, three automobiles, and three trucks. I've kept cows, hogs, I've earned a living. I always figured I was doing pretty good and if I didn't want my job, someone else did so I was better off getting along with the bossman than fighting with him."

He was an old man from another age. Yet now, when a pinched national mood has labor on its heels, when everyone seems to be worried about his job moving away or having to scale back or being phased out, the edgy, unequal alliance between workers and their bosses in Honea Path looks like the state of labor nationally.

"The strikers were fighting for better wages and better working conditions," said Lucille Hammett, who was seven when the shootings took place, and whose grandfather was one of the ones shooting from the second-floor windows. "The nonstrikers were fighting to keep a roof over their families' heads and food on their tables. Now, which side was right and which side was wrong?" We were talking in her kitchen as she first calmly, then with a bit of exasperation, thought back on the calculus workers had assessed over the years between supporting the union and sticking with their bosses. "Back then everybody had it bad. I go back to what some of the French girls said after World War Two, the ones who shacked up with the Germans and then had their heads shaved. People asked them why they did it, and they said, 'I had my children to care for. My husband had been killed, or he was out fighting. I needed money to feed my children with.' People will do anything when they have to. So I ask you, 'Which side was right and which was wrong?' No one can give you an answer. All I know is we're not going to have unions here. They'll just close those plants down if the unions come."

Maybe. There are so many voices like her's that the brave talk of labor rebirth has an inherently quixotic quality. But there's at least one thunderous voice from the South's past that gives reason to think otherwise. It is usually forgotten in the soft-focus memories of the Dreamer and the Dream, but few Southerners this century believed more deeply in the importance of unions as tools for economic justice and racial healing than did Dr. Martin Luther King, Jr., who, after all, died in Memphis rallying support for striking sanitation workers. King, particularly in his later years, had come to realize the movement for civil rights in the South was a beginning, not an end, and the next step had to be a focus on economics and working conditions—North and South, black and white. From the '50s until his death, he hailed labor as "the principal force that transformed misery and despair into hope and progress." He said, "Negroes in the United States read the history of labor, and it mirrors their own experience." He said, "The two most dynamic and cohesive liberal forces in the country are the labor movement and the Negro freedom movement." In his famous "I've Been to the Mountaintop" speech the night before he was assassinated on April 4, 1968, he said: "You may not be on strike. But either we go up together or we go down together."

In a very different way than W. A. Smith, he's a voice from another time too, and whether unions still have the potential to be the vehicle he envisioned is unclear. Still, to remember his words, like these spoken in Memphis seventeen days before his death, is to be reminded that history flows in many directions and no one can know for sure where it will flow next:

> We are tired of smothering in an air-tight cage of poverty in the midst of an affluent society. We are tired of walking the streets in search for jobs that do not exist. We are tired of working our hands off and laboring every day and not even making a wage adequate with the daily basic necessities of life . . . So in Memphis we have begun. We are saying,

'Now is the time.' Get the word across to everybody in power in this town that now is the time to make real the promises of democracy.... Now is the time for justice to roll down like water, and righteousness like a mighty stream. Now is the time.... If we believe this, we will do this; we will win this struggle and many other struggles. I close by saying, 'Walk together, children.'

Chapter 8

WILMINGTON, NORTH CAROLINA
Back to the Future at Williston High

H ISTORY COULD NOT HAVE THROWN A MORE VEXING CURVEBALL TO the black people of the seaport city of Wilmington, in southeastern North Carolina, than what played out in May 1954. It happened on the joyous occasion of the dedication of the new black Williston High School, which was the result of a bitter legal battle waged by blacks to force Wilmington to make good on the South's ever-empty promise of separate but equal education.

As exuberant crowds of blacks and a few whites filed into the new redbrick building in the heart of Wilmington's black community and filled the folding chairs on the main floor and the seats in the upstairs balcony, the speaker for the day, Dr. Rufus E. Clement, president of Atlanta University, was called away to take an urgent phone call. When he returned he leaned over to Dr. Hubert Eaton, the black Wilmington physician whose lawsuit had forced the bond election that led to the school's construction. "The Supreme Court has just issued a ruling overturning *Plessy v. Ferguson* and has ordered the desegregation of the public schools in four states and in Washington, D.C.," Dr. Clement whispered in Dr. Eaton's ear. He was referring to the historic *Brown v. Board of Education* ruling announced May 17, 1954. So the two men sat, their heads swimming with the possibilities of a new era about to dawn, while Wilmington dedicated a segregated high school just as the Supreme Court had ruled segregation illegal.

The *Brown* decision was so momentous that it is likely no one then would have been surprised that people still talk about it almost a half century later. It would amaze them, however, that as the century nears its end, the issues of *Brown* and what it means for Williston and Wilmington are not just matters of history but of contemporary politics and that questions about separate but equal education raised then are still compelling, alive, and up for grabs. Indeed, when black people in Wilmington today talk about education, the conversation almost invariably leads to Williston High School, the segregated black high school that was dedicated that day, was closed when the schools integrated fourteen years later, and is mourned, eulogized, and pined for still. More often than not, the message, offered with a combination of pride, anger, and regret, is this: no school has educated blacks in an integrated world as well as Williston did in a segregated one. Where that leads is a subject of endless debate, one that is taking place across the South and, increasingly, across the country as support for busing ebbs and school districts contemplate the pros and cons of what amounts to resegregation.

For a school that was closed in 1968, Williston High School, known to all Wilmington blacks by its nickname, "the greatest school under the sun," seems amazingly alive today. Though the building reopened as a junior high and then a middle school after integration, when people pine for Williston, they mean the original. There's a Williston Alumni Association, which meets regularly to address educational and civic issues. There's the thirty-eight member Williston Alumni Chorale Ensemble, which regularly performs programs that range from Bach to Negro spirituals to *Fiddler on the Roof, South Pacific,* and *My Fair Lady* and in December 1994 even performed at the White House. Every July Fourth alumni reunions take place on the lawn in front of the school and there are periodic tributes to the men and women who taught there. A 1993 exhibit at Wilmington's Cape Fear Museum, "More Than an Education: The Black Learning Experience in New Hanover County," revolved around Williston's legacy.

As the years have passed the school has taken on the status of a shrine. The most respected black man in Wilmington may be Joe McQueen, Williston '65, who is serving his fourth term as sheriff. He's the ultimate straight-arrow whose biggest indulgences are listening to New Age music like Zamfir or *The Magic Music of the Andes* on the portable tape machine in his office (when we met the music playing was "The Shadow of Your Smile" on what sounded like bagpipes) and staying up until two in the morning tinkering with car engines at home.

To whites, he's Wilmington's answer to Colin Powell, an exemplar of how much race relations have improved. If some blacks are slightly exasperated by the degree to which he fits all the white requirements for admired blacks, most see him as a success story who hasn't let his triumphs go to his head. Plus, he has always had the rare ability, even during segregation, to live in both white and black worlds, fitting in at Williston but also hanging out with white kids who built or raced cars and hung out at the white drive-ins like the Chic Chic or Carol's.

Sheriff McQueen has done well enough in the present not to have a great need to pine for the past, but whenever he feels stressed out, he has a little ritual. He gets into his old gray 1984 Lincoln Mark VII, turns the police radio, car radio, and police scanner on, and cruises slowly past Williston, thinking of old times and old friends, the auto shop and football field that used to be across the street, the time when he was first dating the high school sweetheart who became his wife, favorite teachers, good times. It's long ago but it seems like yesterday and invariably by the time he passes the school, he feels better.

Williston may evoke nostalgia but more often when it's evoked it's with a sense of purpose, mission, and grievance. "The closing of Williston High School contributed to further disruption of the lives of hundreds of teachers, students and citizens within the community," Kenneth McLaurin, a Williston alumnus who is now principal of the new Williston Middle School, wrote in an anniversary yearbook published in 1993 to commemorate the twenty-fifth anniversary of the school's closing in 1968. "Sent into an unknown world by the powers who had made decisions behind closed doors, teachers and students were precisely misplaced without benefit of preparation. Being snatched from the comfort of our own environment was unreal. It was like a nightmare ... unwarranted and unjust. We lost the bond between school, parents and teachers. We lost the ability to love and live together in the way to which we were accustomed. ... It still hurts!" As Linda Pearce, another Williston alumna, put it: "Twenty-five years ago, a death occurred in our family. Why? Why close our school?"

Sitting in the Huddle House restaurant on Market Street one summer morning, she didn't have a good answer. A large, energetic, naturally assertive woman who speaks in quick, crisp, decisive bursts, Pearce would have made a good general. She's forty-nine years old, the daughter of a minister and a nurse, who left town to go to North Carolina College (now North Carolina Central University) in Durham and then took the "chicken-bone express," the local term for the buses north, to Washington, D.C., where she worked for thirteen years at the Library of Congress. She came home in 1980 and now runs Elderhaus Inc., a nonprofit agency that provides day care for the elderly at two sites in Wilmington. She was wearing a floral print dress, a yellow beaded necklace and gold cross, and a Mickey Mouse watch. When I first talked with her, around the time the museum exhibit was being put together, I was struck by how passionate and eloquent she was about Williston and what it represented. "We were in a cocoon bathed in a warm fluid, where we were expected to excel," she said. "And then something called desegregation punctured it. We went from our own land to being tourists in someone else's. It never did come together, and I think it's on the verge of falling apart altogether now."

As we sat in the Huddle House, with its array of clocks helpfully showing the exact time in all the different Wilmingtons in the United States, a white teenager got out of a pickup truck wearing the YOU WEAR YOUR X. I'LL WEAR MINE Confederate Battle Flag T-shirt. Pearce grimaced and then shrugged. "Oh well. I don't like it, but I can understand it. I try not to sweat the small stuff."

The large stuff in many ways revolves around Williston and the widespread current belief that the black institutions of segregation supported blacks in a way the integrated world has not. "We lived in a world that was nurturing," she said, eyeing the kid with the rebel flag T-shirt as he ambled into the restaurant. "We were made to excel, to be the best in everything. Typing tests. My girlfriend Sandra Yates, now in D.C., she still types about a hundred thirty words a minute with no mistakes. Glee Club. You have to talk to B. Constance O'Dell. We took all the awards everywhere. Cooking classes, bricklayers, tailors. We always won the awards. We excelled in debate. I went to North Carolina College and anyone from Williston was exempt from all the requirements for the band, because they knew how good we were. We all learned the prologue to *The Canterbury Tales* in Old English. Anyone in Wilmington over fifty can recite it for you.

"It's reached the point now where so many in our community are beginning to wonder if we would not be better off educating our own kids because they're not getting the education now that they should. Back then the teachers knew the parents who knew the neighbors and they were going to make sure those children succeeded no matter what it took. If one didn't get you, the others would. Now these children are out there adrift. I can't see anyone who's there for them. It's gotten so that there's now a movement to get black schools and black kids and black teachers back in the black community. I'm not saying that's the way to go. But this town has never been right on race, and now it's a powder keg."

Just a few days earlier, Jerry Spivey, the good-ol'-boy district attorney, had gotten sloppy drunk at Clarence Foster's bar, on swanky Wrightsville Beach, called a 258-pound Denver Broncos linebacker named Ray Jacobs a "nigger," and tried to duke it out with him, a date with disaster he was mercifully spared when he was summarily escorted to the door. The next day Spivey said he got himself "a snort full of liquor and made a fool of myself," apologized to one and all in the black community, and promised to get help with his alcoholism. It wasn't enough for most outraged blacks in Wilmington, who were demanding that he resign or be forced from office.

Despite the many Spiveys that remain, the notion that Southern blacks could pine for any remnant of the segregation era seems perverse, but it's a common theme across the South. You can hear the same feelings from graduates of the old black R. B. Hudson High School in Selma or Eureka High School in Hattiesburg, Mississippi, or Booker T. Washington High School in Rocky Mount, North Carolina. I first became aware how pervasive those sentiments were back in June of 1982, when I attended the reunion of the Annie E. Colbert High School in Dayton, Texas, built a year after Williston and also closed in 1968. About six hundred people showed up, some from as far away as Seattle, an astonishing figure for a school whose graduating classes averaged fewer than twenty-five people.

In some ways it was like any reunion, full of nostalgia, reminiscence, and remembrance. People joked about receding hairlines and advancing bellies. They showed pictures of spouses, ex-spouses, kids, and grand-kids. They delighted in the former principal T. C. Tyson's rendition of the hymn "In the Garden," hooted and cackled at the slide show Diane Paul had put together from old yearbooks and family albums, and recalled the glory days before the purple and gold of the Colbert Tigers was traded in for the purple and white of the Dayton Broncos, three quarters white after integration.

But along with the usual nostalgia, there was also an extraordinary undercurrent of regret, as if they were regaining for an afternoon a lost world that should not have perished, of black teachers who cared about and understood black kids and expected them to succeed, as opposed to white teachers who too often expected them to fail. Lois Pruitt was one of nine graduates of Colbert's class of 1949, taught there for two years, and then went on to teach in the nearby town of Cleveland. She picked up an old snapshot that showed the 1955 Colbert football team and pointed to a sturdily built man in the back row. "You take this man," she said. "That's Mr. Beasley. He's deceased now. But back then he had tremendous influence on these boys. It was a beautiful relationship, in school and after school. Those kids all counted on him and treated him with respect. Where are they going to find someone like that now? Integration has its advantages. But it has more disadvantages where the students are concerned. Here our kids had an identity. At Dayton they don't."

All reunions are exercises in selective memory and this was no different, but if the memories were edited the joy and regret were real. Not many people in Wilmington or Dayton really think going back is the answer or that you can separate the evils and routine indignities of Jim Crow from the feelings of unity blacks had in those times. To take the most obvious example, Wilmington has produced two famous basketball players. The one who went to Williston, Meadowlark Lemon, went on to relative fame in the basketball minstrel show that is the Harlem Globetrotters. The one who graduated from the integrated Laney High School in 1981 and then went on to the University of North Carolina was Michael Jordan, whose life and times are the subject of two different displays at Wilmington's Cape Fear Museum. Anyone who thinks Meadowlark Lemon had better options than Michael Jordan has yet to make his case.

To some blacks the nostalgia for the past is an insidious form of historical amnesia that cheapens the hard-fought gains of the civil rights era by glossing over the horrors of the past. Nelson Rivers is the former N.A.A.C.P. head in South Carolina who became southeast regional director in 1994. He's a blunt, intense man who seems to burn forever at a slow boil over the racial history of the South. When I once asked him about the schools like Williston and Colbert, his eyes glazed into a frosty look that said, "Oh, Lord, not that again," and then he responded with irritation—not so much with the question as with the fact that so many blacks are asking it.

"What gets me now is that so many people are asking, 'Was integration the right thing to do? Was it worth it? Was *Brown* a good decision? It's asinine. To this day, I can remember bus drivers pulling off and blowing smoke in my mother's face. I can remember the back of the bus, colored water fountains. I can go home to Charleston, and I can remember the police cussing you out when you tried to cross Calhoun Street, which was the invisible line of demarcation saying this is as far as black folk can go. I can hear a cop telling me, 'Take your black butt back to nigger town.' What makes it so real and dramatic now is that forty years from now if you were to ask people in South Africa was it worth it to end apartheid forty years ago, their answer would have to be 'Hell, yes.' What I tell folk in my speeches all the time is that there are a lot of romanticists now who want to take this trip down Memory Lane, and they want to go back, and I tell the young people that anybody who wants to take you back to segregation, make sure you get a round-trip ticket because you won't stay. Like Michael J. Fox in *Back to the Future*, the minute you get back [to the past], you will say, 'Take me back to the future.' "

If going all the way back is not much of an option, just how to go forward is at least as prickly an issue now as it ever has been. Given Wilmington's racial history that's a pretty depressing thought.

Located on a sandy bluff at the confluence of the Northeast and Northwest Cape Fear rivers, Wilmington's modern history dates back to the 1730s, when it was settled first as New Liverpool, then dubbed Carthage, then Newton, then Wilmington—for Spencer Compton, the earl of Wilmington. It soon became North Carolina's leading port, and because of its strategic position and the vast forests of longleaf pine in the hinterland, which were used for making tar, pitch, turpentine, and other resinous products (called naval stores) used in shipbuilding, it soon became North Carolina's largest city, a position it held until the beginning of this century.

Wilmington hasn't gone all out in the relentlessly marketed Old South, pralines-and-cobblestone, historic-preservation sweepstakes like its coastal neighbors Charleston and Savannah. But it's one of those places where history is everywhere, even if residents of the instant suburbs and retirement communities popping up between downtown and the coast sometimes think the town's history began when they arrived. The heart of the past is downtown, near the river, where giant magnolias and live oaks shade the two hundred–block Wilmington historic district, which has structures in every major architectural style used in the United States in the eighteenth and nineteenth centuries.

In fact, there's a touch of history run amuck, expressed in historical markers to anything and everything: from Mary Baker Glover Eddy, founder of the Christian Science church, who spent part of 1844 at the Hanover House hotel, to Rose Greenhow, the Confederate spy and Washington society woman drowned near Fort Fisher in 1864, to George Washington's Southern tour, when he was a guest at the Quince House April 24–25, 1791, to Whistler's mother, Anna McNeill Whistler, who was born in Wilmington, to the Temple of Israel, erected in 1875 as the first Jewish house of worship in North Carolina, to Woodrow Wilson, whose boyhood home from 1874 to 1882 was the Presbyterian Manse, to the Cape Fear Club, the oldest gentlemen's club in continuous existence in the South.

But mostly, in the old historic homes and mansions in Tudor, Italianate, Federal, Georgian, and Greek Revival styles with their flower gardens and celebration flags, their wide front porches with swings and Brumby rockers, their tales of hauntings and ghosts, their elaborate genealogies of visits by Henry Clay, Daniel Webster, or William Tecumseh Sherman, life ambles on with an agreeable sense of history as something with a presence in the real world as opposed to a museum.

There's much the same sense of history across the bridges in the booming beachfront communities, most notably Wrightsville Beach, its gorgeous marina of yachts and pleasure boats from around the East Coast. It doesn't have the wall-to-wall historical markers, but people still recount tales of buried treasure, Civil War blockade running, and the early days when vacationers rode the Sea Coast Railroad and then the electrified trolleys to the beach for moonlight turtle egg hunts to the sounds of strolling musicians.

Wrightsville's most famous attraction was the Lumina, a two-story beachfront resort built in 1905. Its first story had bowling alleys, snack bars, a ladies' parlor, slot machines, and other attractions. A broad stairway led to the second-floor dance hall, which measured fifty by seventy feet, where the likes of Tommy Dorsey, Guy Lombardo, Cab Calloway, Louis Armstrong, Kay Kyser, Woody Herman, and Lionel

Hampton played amid the sea breezes and rustle of the ocean. Outside on the beach were bleachers where people could sit and gaze at the ocean during the day and at night watch movies projected on a huge screen that rose on stilts from the ocean. The Lumina's thousands of incandescent lights, spelling out LUMINA in enormous letters, allowed it to serve as a lighthouse for ships miles out at sea. Its glory days didn't stretch much past the end of World War II, but to this day, people take their kids down to South Lumina Avenue to gaze out at the sea and reminisce about the magic days before the wrecking ball took the Lumina apart in May 1973.

Another Wilmington is easy for visitors to overlook: the rickety old black neighborhoods of neat frame homes and dilapidated projects. Here the sagging old businesses on Castle and Dawson streets reflect the world of pre-franchise America and the old barber shops and beauty salons and corner stores are mostly aging versions of their forebears from segregation. Black Wilmington has quite a history, too. West African and Caribbean slaves were imported during the eighteenth century to work the rice and pine plantations in the area. When the planters went to town, many of them traveled in barges manned by crews of slaves instead of in carriages. Some of the slaves eventually gained their freedom and moved to town, but they were free in name only. Lest any rambunctious young blacks get out of line, Wilmington town commissioners in 1853 passed an ordinance that "negro boys found in the street ... pitching cents ... playing marbles, rolling hoops, playing ball or any other kind of game shall receive 20 lashes."

Following the Civil War, in the brave new uncharted waters of Reconstruction, it looked as if everything might change. In the state that had the most vital black political organizations and most diverse, competitive politics in the region, Wilmington gained a reputation as one of the most racially tolerant cities in the South. Blacks owned restaurants and shops and a feisty newspaper, *The Wilmington Record.* There were several black lawyers, and the collector of customs at the Port of Wilmington was black, as were one of the city auditors, the coroner, and 30 percent of the aldermen, clerks, firemen, policemen, and justices of the peace. A black voting majority produced biracial governance, particularly after the state legislature in 1897 revised the city charter to help ensure black representation.

But events within and outside Wilmington were conspiring to make the era a short one. Despite its reputation for moderation, North Carolina in the 1890s was the site of one of the most brutal collisions between the politics of race and the politics of economics. Race won and the ultimate example of its victory was the experience of Wilmington.

After Reconstruction ended and white Democrats regained power, they faced challenges from Populists and Republicans in many Southern states, but only in North Carolina did they lose control of the state. Populists and Republicans succeeded in portraying the Democrats as tools of big-money interests such as the railroads, and in 1894, they formed a "Fusion" ticket of farmers, former Union sympathizers, and blacks. In 1894 and 1896 they took control of the state legislature and the congressional delegation, elected a Republican senator in 1894 and in 1897, and in 1896 they elected a Republican governor.

The suddenly embattled Democratic party came under the control of one Furnifold M. Simmons, a lawyer who was sort of the Lee Atwater of his time; he possessed an instinctive sense of racial politics as blood sport and had been elected to Congress in 1886 and was then defeated by a black Republican in 1890. He would go on to become a U.S. senator who dominated the Democratic party for three decades. He helped organize a "white supremacy crusade," which attempted to cut through the clutter of economic and social issues with a simple choice: white or black? Simmons sent speakers across the state who warned of the "evils of Negro domination" and appealed to men of "Anglo-Saxon blood"; they churned out broadsides against the "corruption and arrogance of the Republican-Negro rule" and invocations of the need to assert white supremacy. To achieve it, there was the Democratic party, "washed, purged, and made white as snow." North Carolina for the first time saw the rise of "Red Shirts," armed vigilantes who already flourished across the border, in South Carolina–then, as ever, ahead of the game when it came to racial politics. Mill owners and businessmen, encouraged by the Democrats' commitment to low taxes and racial correctness, joined the Red Shirts so that, as one said, the "white property owners of North Carolina" should not "be ruled by a parcel of ignorant Negroes."

The appeals to race, the support of white businessmen, and a low black turnout–depressed by intimidation by the Red Shirts and others who broke up political rallies, disrupted black church meetings, and drove black voters from the polls–produced a massive Democratic victory in the state legislature in 1898 and ushered in the one-party, one-race politics to come that saw blacks disenfranchised in 1901. It was a political climate so ugly that even some Democrats, intent as they were on reasserting white rule, shuddered about the potential for antiblack violence. "I do pray for their deliverance from destruction or further degradation," one party member wrote to the speaker of the North Carolina house, "and hope that enough good strong men may be found to protect them from the vile ambitions and low instincts of men of our race."

In Wilmington the same currents were swirling and were made all the more volatile by the degree to which local blacks' relative success had emboldened them into thinking that the strictures and prejudices of the past no longer applied. After Democrats were ousted from office in 1897, a group called the Secret Nine began plotting what amounted to an angry-white-male coup. Their aim was to hook into the white-supremacist tempest being stirred up by Simmons and his followers. Before long, they found the perfect pretext for doing just that: an explosive editorial that ran in the August 18, 1898, edition of *The Wilmington Record*. Written by the paper's editor, Alex Manley, the mulatto son of a former governor of the state, the editorial said poor white men were careless about protecting their women and "our experience among poor white people in the country teaches us that the women of that race are not any more particular in the matter of clandestine meetings with colored men, than are the white men with colored women." He refuted claims that there had been rapes of white women by black men and stated instead that black men "were sufficiently attractive for white girls of culture and refinement to fall in love with them."

As wedge issues went, this was off the charts. Printed out of context and repeated daily in the local and state papers, Manley's comments were enough to whip the town into a frenzy. "If it does not make every decent man's blood boil, then the manhood is gone, and with it Anglo-Saxon loyalty to the pure and noble white women of our land," responded the white *Wilmington Messenger*. "We hope the white men will read again and again that brutal attack . . . and swear upon the altar of their country to wipe out negro rule for all time in this noble old commonwealth." At a meeting at a local theater, one of the town's leading citizens gave a Tillmanesque oration in which he said that whites now faced "intolerable conditions" and that "we are resolved to change them if we have to choke the current of the Cape Fear with carcasses."

It didn't take long for words to turn to actions. On the morning of November 10, two days after the Democrats' massive victories across the state, an armed mob of about five hundred white men gathered in front of the headquarters of the Wilmington Light Infantry, which had just returned from serving in the Spanish-American War. An attempt had been made to forestall violence by getting Manley to leave town. As it turned out he had agreed, but owing to a communications mix-up the aggrieved whites never got the word.

Instead, led by many of Wilmington's most respected businessmen and professionals—the kind of folks who strung up Leo Frank in Cobb County—they marched in military order to the *Record* office, forced the door open, and after destroying what they could, burned the building down. Manley had already fled town, but before long gunshots were fired from a group of blacks witnessing the scene and a white man was injured. At that point the mob turned furious and began firing on whatever blacks they could find.

The exact toll isn't certain, but estimates are that twelve blacks were killed and twenty-five wounded in one of the most infamous race riots in American history. State newspapers said that three whites were injured. Blacks, particularly prominent or affluent ones, fled the town en masse, including Silas Wright, who had been elected mayor. Other Republicans, black and white, were dragged to the train station and sent out of town. The blacks who stayed crawled out of the pine forests a few days later to find that their property, jobs, and businesses had been taken over by the group that had staged the coup. NEGRO RULE IS AT END IN NORTH CAROLINA FOREVER, commented the *Raleigh News and Observer*.

For the next sixty years or so, blacks in the city had no political or economic power to speak of, but they had two institutions that became the community glue. First was the church. Second was the school. The first school built for blacks in Wilmington was completed in 1866, and within a year had two hundred students and three teachers. Like many such schools in the South, it was built and staffed by whites from the American Missionary Association. One of its prime benefactors was a Mr. Williston, thought to be a white philanthropist from Massachusetts.

Different schools in Wilmington named for him came and went over the years, but the name Williston today means two massive brick build-ings that sit next to each other on the block bounded by Tenth, Thir-teenth, Ann, and Castle streets. The first school was built in 1931 as Williston Industrial High School and was rebuilt to the same exact specifications after being destroyed by fire in 1936. The second was built in 1953 and dedicated a year later.

Almost everyone seems to share the same memories. Only seniors were allowed to enter through the front door, and almost everyone can recall the thrill of finally stepping proudly over that threshold for the first time. The Picture Man, James H. Harris, Jr., the assistant principal from 1954 to 1968, lived three blocks from the school and his house became the community photo studio where everyone went for their class picture, their baby picture, their wedding picture, or a picture with their ninth-grade sweetheart.

Teachers lived in the neighborhood and you were likely to see them at church or tending their yards or fanning themselves on their front porches. The most famous ones—like Ida Mae McMillan or Lucille Simon Williams or the imposing, godlike principal Booker T. Wash-ington, who always bustled around with the long end of his tie thrown over his shoulder—were figures of such power and authority that one would no more cross them than pursue a career in Sumo wrestling. At some black schools, teachers could not get their first paycheck until they had visited the homes of all their students.

Over the years, Williston became a true community center, not just a school. There were fish fries and raffles to raise funds for books or supplies. Sometimes famous black celebrities like the educator Mary McLeod Bethune or performers like Leontyne Price or Marian Anderson or Mahalia Jackson would speak or perform at the Williston Auditorium, and everyone in the black community—plus plenty of white folks, too—would show up. Sometimes the attraction was the Harlem Globetrotters with Williston's own Meadowlark Lemon in the starring role. No doubt, Willistonians view the past through a rosy lens. In addi-tion to making do with second-rate resources in terms of salaries and supplies and living with the demeaning indignities of Jim Crow, Willis-ton reflected the black caste system in which light-skinned blacks tended be favored over darker-skinned ones, as whites were favored over blacks in the society as a whole.

But to watch the parade of teachers sharing their remembrances in the 1992 teachers appreciation video–to watch Ezell Juliette Johnson say she gave "every fiber of my being to help the children to learn" or William D. Bryant talk about the "sense of urgency and the sense of belonging and the sense of obligation between the students and the teachers in the segregated situation"–is to get an indelible sense of how deep and lasting and intense a commitment they had to the kids who came under their care and how hard it would be ever to replicate that commitment in an integrated setting.

"I just don't feel like the teachers in the schools today feel as close to those kids as we did in a segregated school," said John C. Newkirk on the video. "You can't feel it unless they have had the experience that blacks have had. Schools now are trying to provide the things they feel kids need to be successful, but there's a difference between providing and implementing. You can put all the tools before the teachers that you want to do the job, but if you don't have teachers who use those tools in a proper way, the tools will just be a waste of time."

Still, for all the seemingly intractable and eternal verities of segregation in the South, some blacks never forgot that Williston, for all its virtues, was a black school in a world where almost everything was owned and run by whites. Williston students often got the old school books after whites got the new ones. Their labs, libraries, gyms, and buildings couldn't compare to the ones in the white schools. But while the broad currents of the civil rights movement were a little slow in coming to Wilmington, Wilmington didn't really need a movement. It had Dr. Hubert A. Eaton.

Hubert Eaton, who died in 1991, stares out with no expression from the Carolina-blue cover of his book, *Every Man Should Try,* a remarkable locally published account of what it took to take on Jim Crow. He's a copper-colored man wearing wire-rimmed glasses, a white lab coat, a white shirt, and a jacquard-weave silk tie; his hands rest on what looks like a medical file. There is a crest of gray in his thick, combed-back hair, and his lips are slightly pursed as if he were holding something in.

The same stoic, controlled, impassive visage Eaton had before the camera was the one he chose in life. In his book he describes a disastrous encounter when, at the Woolworth's in Winston-Salem, where he worked as a boy of fourteen in 1931, he accidentally touched a white woman while trying to check the time on her watch. "Nigger! Don't touch me, you nigger!" she screamed. He ran out in terror, and after his father, also a doctor, calmly took him back to repair the damage he drew the following lesson:

> I concluded that it was dangerous to act on impulse around white people. I learned to be deliberate and controlled so that I would not provoke a similar situation again.... Always, I was measured and careful. As a colored boy in a white-dominated society, I felt I could not afford to be otherwise.

Eaton became a championship tennis player who played a controlled, cautious, steady game, based on always trying to win the first point of every game and waiting for his opponent to make mistakes. When he began his medical practice a colleague told him his patients would be more comfortable if he could find a way to smile a bit, so he practiced smiling until his face hurt. He had to place a towel over his face and hold his head under warm water to soothe the muscles strained by doing what they had never done before. "In time," he reported, "my facial muscles became stronger and I could smile with no residual discomfort."

As he tells it, just about the only incident that broke his composure came in 1947; he had to testify in court when an accident victim he had treated was involved in a lawsuit over liability and expenses. He walked to the bench, raised his right hand, and reached with his left for the Bible, only to see there were two, each wrapped shut with a strip of dirty adhesive tape. One was labeled COLORED, the other, WHITE. "Segregated Bibles!" he wrote. "I was stunned. It was like a TIA–a little stroke. My eyes fogged, my ears hummed and a quiver ran down my spine. I almost gasped.... The charge built up in me by years of racial prejudice had finally exploded."

Exactly why that indignity registered with such force in a world of routine indignities is hard to say. Probably because it was one of the few unexpected interractions Eaton had with the grim strictures of Jim Crow outside the familiar, barely noticed, daily rituals of segregated life or the warm cocoon of black institutions like Williston, which provided the illusion that they were the world that really mattered. Whatever the case, he said the incident galvanized him into a life of challenging all the indignities of segregation–"measly black schools, segregated hospitals, segregated tennis courts, all-white government, segregated libraries, and segregated Bibles."

Dr. Eaton was a man accustomed to success. The year before, he and his family had taken in a talented young tennis player from Harlem who needed nurturing and teaching. Her name was Althea Gibson. She lived with his family, attended Williston, played each day on the court at his house, and eventually became the first black to break the color line at the National Championship at Forest Hills, the first black to win at Wimbledon, and the greatest black woman player in history.

He took on Jim Crow with the same focus and precision he approached everything else. First he sued the local school board, demanding to make the black schools equal to the white ones. Then, after acquiring a court order, he visited every school in the district with photographers who documented comparable buildings, classrooms, gyms, and cafeterias to assess their relative resources. His study found that white schools, which had two thirds of the students, were valued at $3.6 million, while the black ones were worth $714,438. Beyond that, the school board was spending only $65.72 per month each on its black students compared to $168.73 on the whites.

The suit led to the new Williston High. In 1964, Eaton sued again, this time to force the schools to desegregate as ordered in *Brown v. Board of Education*. In his customary unflappable style, he fought one legal battle after another for integrating hospitals and medical societies, golf courses and the local Y. He appealed to federal agencies to cut off financial support for North Carolina medical programs until blacks were better represented on the boards of state agencies. He ran unsuccessfully for the school board. The effect of the book is numbing–you wonder how he had the time and the mental stamina to fight so many dispiriting battles, while also managing to keep up a medical practice, hone his tennis game, and saw away on his father's old violin–which, when he took it to Smith's House of Violins in Florence, South Carolina, for restoration, he learned was a Stradivarius.

When school integration finally came it was a disaster. After dodging, delaying, and looking for ways to get around desegregation for fourteen years, the school board in 1968 was finally forced to throw together a desegregation plan in a matter of months. Several years of legal wrangling, racial turmoil, and changing plans ensued, until 1971 when things flared out of control. Fights or mini-riots flared up almost daily at the by-now integrated local high school. Black students called for a boycott to protest the closing of Williston two and a half years earlier. "What desegregation did was destroy the black institutions," charged Ben Chavis, then a young United Church of Christ minister, later the ill-fated head of the National Association for the Advancement of Colored People, who had come to Wilmington to help organize the students. Before tempers cooled a spree of arson incidents and shootings erupted in the spring of 1972 that left two dead and several businesses and a church gutted by fire.

A year later, Chavis and nine other defendants, seven of them teenagers, were charged with arson in connection with the firebombing of a white-owned store. After the prosecutor described them as "dangerous animals who should be put away for the rest of their lives," all were convicted and sentenced to a total of 282 years in prison. The convictions earned them civil rights martyrdom as the Wilmington Ten, and all charges were eventually dropped when it became clear that every one of the prosecution witnesses, most of whom recanted their testimony, was hopelessly tainted.

A year later there was another series of bombings, this time against black targets, including the current black newspaper, *The Wilmington Journal.* An eighteen-year-old former marine named Lawrence R. Little, who identified himself as the propaganda minister of a group called Rights of White People, was convicted and sentenced to life in prison.

Oddly enough, after leading the fight for so long, Dr. Eaton found himself in a somewhat ambiguous position among some local blacks by the early seventies, when most of the battles had been won. His cool, imperious style and the divisions of class and color in the black community had always made him seem a little too full of himself for some blacks. Similarly, his methodical, unemotional approach seemed out of touch with the red-hot passions of the time. And with his apparent sense that widespread integration was more important than keeping open Williston, a school he had never attended, some wondered whether his crusade for integration was the right one after all.

The *Wilmington Morning Star* in March 1971 contrasted his views with those of Golden Frinks of the Southern Christian Leadership Conference, who called the closing of Williston "an act of destruction against the black community." Frinks said, "We've come to the view that we've got to turn back before we can go forward in education," while Eaton held firm to the goal of integration, saying, "It has been my belief that black people should continue to make efforts to move into the mainstream of American life, and Williston School is not a prime issue in the controversy." Oddly, after being vilified for most of his life by resentful whites, he ended up as something of a widely respected elder statesman in the white community, who in 1981 was elected chairman of the board of the University of North Carolina at Wilmington, one of the dominant institutions in town.

A quarter century later, the same issues are raging again, ratcheted up in intensity by the takeover in 1994 of the school board by Republicans who are once again raising the venerable rallying cry of "neighborhood schools" as the ultimate goal. No one knows for sure what "neighborhood schools" means, but it sure doesn't mean that integration is much of a priority.

For some blacks, that's a tough onion to slice. Peter Grear is a black attorney and proud Willistonian who has his office in a modest hundred-year-old Italianate frame house on Princess Street downtown. The day of our interview, in July 1995, *The Wilmington Morning Star* reported the settlement of one of two racial discrimination complaints filed by blacks against the school district. The settlement's main feature was an agreement that no school will have a minority enrollment of more than 50 percent by the 1997–98 school year. There was nothing about a minimal figure, presumably leaving open the possibility of virtually all-white suburban schools.

Grear, a fifty-one-year-old graduate of Williston, class of 1962, wasn't impressed. "I'm not high on the educational system as it exists," he said. "I don't think integrated education is the answer for all black children so I'm a little bit dubious about that quota, if you will. Some kids aren't necessarily able to function to their highest level in an integrated educational system. They may need to be somewhere where's there's a lot more culture dominating the educational system, just the way cultural factors played such a role at Williston. I wouldn't stress integration over education. Integration has its place, but if a child is not being educated properly in an integrated setting, then you have to have some other option that will work."

In fact, there are widespread concerns that the schools just don't work for many black kids, that blacks are routinely tracked into slow-learning classes, that they're the first to be disciplined, that white teachers' expectations all too often are the precise opposite of black teachers', which are that each child can learn and succeed. Grear said his priorities would be hiring and promoting more black teachers and administrators, early remediation programs for black students, and all-black schools, where needed. He certainly was not an admirer of the Republicans on the school board, but he figured that if his agenda and theirs overlap in some small ways, it's like two trains passing on parallel tracks. "They want what's good for white kids and that's understandable. I think any concerns they have for blacks kids are incidental at best. I don't think what's bad about black education can be fixed by the games they're playing on the school board. I think it will be fixed when black folks decide to educate black kids."

There's both a degree of logic and something truly spooky about hearing him talk, because the Willistonians today can sound much like many of the white segregationists of the 1960s. Perhaps Wilmington's most ardent segregationist was Herrick M. Roland, Wilmington's school superintendent from 1936 to 1960, a talkative, endlessly opinionated man from the North Carolina mountains, who is viewed to this day as a visionary by some in town and as a crank by others. Roland was obsessed with the idea that segregated schools were best for both blacks and whites and was extraordinarily proud of Williston, notions he expressed in humorous doggerel and serious essays he relentlessly circulated around town. "Williston was a crowning example of what the Negro can do for himself," he wrote. "The memory of Williston will be the 'high water mark' of Negro progress in public education."

Dr. Eaton, ever astute and ever optimistic about the prospects for integration, made the persuasive argument that opposition to integration became a self-fulfilling prophecy, that whites who stalled and resisted integration almost ensured it would not go well. And, unlike Roland, he never forgot for a moment that "separate but equal" had always been a false promise and that it made no sense to prepare for an integrated world by going to segregated schools.

Still, looking at the problems of schools South and North, it doesn't seem remotely odd that blacks would still pine for the days when their kids were automatically going to be the valedictorians and cheerleaders at their own schools, when you wouldn't create a firestorm by trying to wear at Kinte cloth at graduation, as happened in Wilmington a few years back, when the old social clubs like the Uniques and the Gaylords and the Glee Club reflected a black sensibility. And how many Hubert Eatons are there willing to fight battle after battle, risk indignity after indignity, for the dubious victories and gains of an integrated world?

But there is mere nostalgia, too. Heywood Bellamy served as superintendent from 1968 to 1981, presided over the desegregation of the schools, and is widely respected by whites and blacks. He lives downtown in a Georgian-style cottage on Church Street just off the Cape Fear River, whose main section dates to the 1770s and which was built by his wife's ancestors who were colonial shipbuilders. He thinks it would be disastrous to give up on integration and doubts that many blacks, if really given the opportunity, would choose to go in that direction. "I get the same nostalgia bit from the whites I taught at New Hanover High School," he said. He was a handsome, aristocratic-looking, white-haired man wearing a blue-and-white-striped sport shirt, white slacks, and sandals over black socks. "They'll ask you, 'What happened to happy days? It was literally happy days, and they go into all the nostalgia the way the Williston people do. Now, I know there are some different issues at Williston, but there's a lot of the same happy-days view of things as well. I'd like to know if people think all the opportunities available now would have just automatically taken place if someone had not broken the ice and declared that separating people just because of their skin color is wrong."

Some blacks see the same thing. Billy Fewell, the son of two Williston teachers, was one of the first blacks to go to the University of North Carolina at Chapel Hill. He left the state to practice civil rights law in Pittsburgh but came back home a few years ago when his parents were in ill health. Since their deaths he has lived in their old white frame house two doors up from a service station, in the heart of the black communities near downtown.

He looks like a hip college professor in his blue Oxford shirt and chinos, his hair prematurely gray, his expression the blend of irony and frustration that comes from reaching fifty and finding not enough has changed and knowing not enough is going to. His frustration is palpable. Here he is, back in Wilmington, which is prospering like never before, and everyone around him is pining for Williston, the district attorney was in trouble for using the N-word in public, the town had been taken over by white fundamentalist Republicans, and the school board was all in a lather over neighborhood schools.

"People have fond remembrances of being in a small community, and that's fine, but you can't forget that segregation shrouded our entire existence," he said as we sat in a spare room at Elderhaus. "I analogize it to a prison. You can form relationships in prison. The fact that you share mutual stresses and mutual conditions of hostility kind of bonds you together. They foster feelings of closeness just as any group of people faced with oppression are going to bond. But that's not the kind of situation you want to go back to. There's nothing, well, very little, that was better then than it is now."

Which, some would say, is one of the two great flaws in the Adoration of Williston. In the first place, if the game is happy days, it's the whites who are the winners. They go back to the Lumina and to the magnolias and live oaks in the historic district and to Dr. Bellamy's gorgeous old house by the river. The blacks go back to Williston, to the desultory black neighborhoods near downtown where they lived then and live now, where old men and women sit on the porches the way the old teachers did, fanning themselves in the summer heat. The other problem is even more elementary: most of those wonderful black teachers and the world that created them are gone, never to be duplicated. One reason Williston succeeded so well was because teaching, along with the church and the mortuary, was about the only option open to ambitious blacks. Back then Linda Pearce and Joe McQueen and Peter Grear and Billy Fewell would most likely have ended up on the revered faculty of Williston. Now they have other options, and they're taking them. In a completely different way than the neo-Cons, the Willistonians would like to find the future in the past. But you can't get there from here, and in their heart of hearts most of them know it.

Still, there is one crushing, unavoidable truth in the fondness for Williston that mirrors what Percy Reeves confronted in Charlotte and what blacks grapple with around the country as they try to fashion an ethic that goes beyond the civil rights era. It's that integration has meant "instead of the passage from all things wrong to all things right, the passage from all things black to all things white," as Dr. Joseph Lowery of the Southern Christian Leadership Council likes to put it. It's always on white terms. When I asked Dr. Bellamy whether it would have made sense to keep Williston open as one of the integrated high schools, he talked about practical considerations like building size and conditions and then said, "Basically we had to show people that the sun would come up the next morning if we desegregated the schools. I just don't think at that point we would have had a lot of success opening up that building as a desegregated facility. People would have resisted."

It's a measure of progress that both of the old Williston buildings are integrated now, one as a middle school that's roughly half black and half white, the other as a sought-after science and technology magnet school.

But residentially, Wilmington is more segregated now than it was in 1954. Then, most everyone lived near downtown in a ragged grid in which white and black streets, even white and black homes, sat cheek by jowl with each other and where black and white children played in the streets before being sorted into the racial caste system. These days Wilmington is a boom town, with its tourism, manufacturing, and port businesses all going great guns and Yankee retirees arriving in unprecedented numbers.

There are a number of black streets and even little subdivisions scattered out in the 'burbs and near the beaches. But almost all the growth is in the burgeoning retirement communities and new beachfront subdivisions where people haven't the slightest interest in dealing with a legacy of race they figure is either old news or someone else's problem.

In fact, like the old adage about being careful what you wish for because you just might get it, Wilmington's real problem may not be losing Williston but regaining it. The least predictable man in Wilmington may be Fred McRee. The son of a West Indian woman who ran a boarding house for a white family and an American father who was a leather worker, McRee is a smart, garrulous, cranky Africanist who went to Catholic schools in Wilmington before taking one course at Williston to graduate in 1942.

He left town the next day, expecting never to come back. Subsequently he earned degrees from Fordham University in New York, worked at the Port Authority of New York, got a double master's in urban planning and human resources management, went to Europe, and eventually earned a doctorate in African studies at the Sorbonne. After taking early retirement from the Port Authority fifteen years ago, he moved back to Wilmington, where he now runs an African history program, the Heritage House Center for Afrikana Studies, an AIDS counseling program, and a program called Saving Our Sons and Daughters, which he describes as a youth program working to steer kids away from "drugs, premarital sex, and all that."

He finds the pining for Williston understandable and valuable to the degree that it resurrects history and focuses attention on the ways blacks have always supported other blacks. Everyone needs their history—particularly those whose past has so often been trampled on and denigrated. But beyond that, he can't see how history teaches that there's much future in Williston nostalgia.

"Doc was a pragmatist," he said, referring to Dr. Eaton. "He was about inclusion because he saw that as the only way to advance. I'm not against nostalgia. Anything that gets you from can't see to can't see—from daybreak to sundown—is okay. People did remarkable things at Williston. I don't want to denigrate it. And it's natural that people now are looking to the past. People were not prepared for the high price they paid for something which has never happened, which is integration.

"But the reason we fought for inclusion, why Doc believed in it, is that the system takes care of whites. It always has. I always figured that if you're near where lightning strikes, some of it might fall on you. What's happening now is that with the way housing is, you're going to go back to all-black schools. It's interesting. With the influx of people from the North, the lines have hardened. The North has never had integration. The South at least at times made some efforts. [The Northerners] have brought some of the Northern attitudes toward race, which is many times a more brittle, much more exclusionary kind of thing. That's the way we seem to be going. Anyone who doesn't see us going to all-black schools is either incredibly naive or in need of a good therapist."

It was summer and school was out, so I never made it to Williston, but I made sure to drop by when I came back six months later in January. The morning was cold, rainy and gray, the color of the battleship U.S.S. *North Carolina*, which was berthed outside my hotel window looking as if it were prepared to empty its 16-inch guns on downtown.

But the sky had turned clear with brisk, gusty winter winds by the time I met Linda Pearce for lunch at Elijah's, a seafood place on the river featuring ceiling fans and nautical watercolors and a model of a Confederate blockade runner, the C.S.S. *Colonel Lamb*. Pearce was wearing a cool blue blouse, jacket and skirt along with a silver cross and her incongruous Mickey Mouse watch. She'd lost thirty pounds, and she seemed more of a go-getter than ever, pointing out local bigwigs as they walked in and spinning out one tale of local political intrigue and racial politics after another. A court order had forced the drunken district attorney, Jerry Spivey, from office, but he was pursuing appeals and trying to get his job back. Pearce was part of a group trying to recruit a second black to run for the school board to augment the one black Republican who was there at the time. The big question was whether the Christian Coalition types would be able to take over the board, which had become all Republican in 1994, its members ranging from far-right Christian coalition types to moderate/conservative Republicans. "Most of it now is this in-your-face, I-don't-care, if-you're-not-able-to-keep-up-get-off-the-track mean-spiritedness," she said with a matter-of-fact grimace, as if commenting on another shift in the weather. "At least the slave masters had a reason to take care of their slaves. Sometimes I think these days we've got to burn their land and poison their food to get noticed."

After lunch we drove over to Williston, Pearce punching in phone calls and scribbling phone numbers on her palm as she drove her 1989 cranberry Buick Le Sabre. On the front was a WILLISTON ALUMNI souvenir license plate. On the back was her North Carolina license plate reading I LUV OLD and a DON'T BLAME ME, I VOTED FOR GANTT bumper sticker, hearkening back to the 1990 Senate race between Harvey Gantt and Jesse Helms. Kenny G's Christmas album was in the cassette deck. When we got there, she said she had to make a few more calls. "God-dog it," she said. "My school-board candidate just said he wasn't going to run. I can't believe it." She sat in the car for about ten or fifteen minutes, locked in animated conversation, and then we walked toward the former Williston High, a low-slung, two-story brick building with a sign out front reading WILLISTON MIDDLE SCHOOL–HOME OF THE MIGHTY TIGERS.

We walked in the front door, which used to be limited to the Williston seniors, and dropped in to see Ken McLaurin, Williston '61, the current principal, who had provided one of the more eloquent tributes in the Williston Anniversary Yearbook in 1993. Now he sits every day–with no small amount of pride–at the old oak desk from which the longtime Williston principal Booker T. Washington ruled the old black school. It was a teacher-training day, so he was casually dressed in a blue and white sweater-shirt, neatly pressed blue jeans, and penny loafers. He had tortoise-shell glasses and a mustache and a calm, understated reassuring presence that seemed yin to Pearce's brisk, edgy hyperbolic yang. But after thirty years as a teacher or principal in Wilmington, including being principal when Michael Jordan was at Laney High, he was on the "neighborhood schools" bandwagon too, even if he didn't feel much in common with the white and black conservatives most aggressively ringing the bell.

"I hate to agree with Clarence Thomas on anything, but the one thing I agree with him on was when he said black kids don't necessarily have to sit next to white kids to learn," he said. "I was at a meeting the other day, and I said when Williston closed, we had one and a half full-time teachers teaching chemistry. Now we can't get thirty-five black kids at the three schools taking chemistry. You can't tell me it didn't work. People have different spins and different definitions of neighborhoods, but basically I think a kid is better off going to school in his neighborhood. Black folks don't want their kids bused all over the world just for the sake of integration."

We walked around the school, which now has 725 students, 60 percent white, 40 percent black, and he and Pearce indulged in more Williston nostalgia—what a difficult decision it was to remove the old screen door that remained from the days of Williston's home ec classes, what to do with the old yearbooks and memorabilia they both had, when the alumni choir would next perform.

"I played the alma mater this morning," she said as we sat in the armchairs in the school's lobby. In the old days it was full of glass display cases jammed with trophies and awards, but it now had the informal feel of the school's living room, which is furnished with old sofas and armchairs. "The '59 yearbook has Williston music in it, and I've Xeroxed it and play it every morning."

"I've got all the old yearbooks, now," he replied. "They're Mr. Washington's. I got them from the building next door."

"I've got so much Williston stuff now, I don't know what the hell I'm going to do with it. The majorette's uniform. My cat sleeps on it every night. All that stuff."

"You know, a band came here a few years back from Washington, and the man with them talked about strutting. Not the way they do it now," he said, moving his arms in a lackadaisical fashion. "The way we did it back then."

His eyes lit up as they swept the hall, a sly smile played across his lips, and for a moment he seemed almost transported back to Williston's glory days.

"Lord, back then we *strutted*."

Chapter 9

NASHVILLE, TENNESSEE
How Bud, Garth, Tim, and the Renfro Valley
Home Folks Took Over America

T HIS IS HOW BUD WENDELL BECAME ONE OF THE MOST INFLUENTIAL men in American entertainment, even if no one in New York or Los Angeles knows his name.

Raised in Akron, Ohio, he went to work selling insurance door to door in 1950, as soon as he graduated from Wooster College in Wooster, Ohio. He began in Hamilton, Ohio, and then was sent to the coal fields outside Charleston and Logan, West Virginia, before being transferred to the home office of the National Life & Accident Insurance Company in Nashville, Tennessee, in 1962.

When an administrative assistant in the company's broadcast division died of a sudden heart attack in 1964, Wendell was shuffled over to WSM ("We Shield Millions") radio, where the main product was the hillbilly singers who played down at the Grand Ole Opry at the Ryman Auditorium. In 1970, he was named manager of the Opry. Back in those days singers would come in off the road with a paper sack full of the proceeds from their last job and would have him stash it in the Opry's safe while they performed.

Though a prudent insurance man–he still likes low-rise rather than high-rise buildings because they cut down your fire risk–he soon saw that there was incredible potential in the Opry, which had long since outgrown the beloved but outdated Ryman. In the 1960s he starting thinking big–maybe instead of just music, there could be a theme park, a new enlarged Opry House with air conditioning, maybe a little two hundred–room tourist motel in the pastureland northeast of town. In 1972 the Opryland theme park opened; in 1974, the Opry moved from downtown; in 1977 the six hundred–room Opryland Hotel opened; and by the time the Opryland Properties were sold to the Gaylord Broadcasting Company of Dallas in 1983, the Opry and indeed country music had long since gone from a ragged, regional music business to a two billion–dollar national phenomenon.

"When I was managing the Grand Ole Opry in the late sixties, my memory is that there were less than two hundred full-time country music stations in the United States. It was just a handful!" Wendell said over his corn tortilla soup in a private dining room at Rhett's restaurant at the Opryland Hotel. It's an astonishing mixture of cascading waterfalls, verdant foliage, and country kitsch that has become the biggest hotel and convention center complex under one roof in the world. An affable, square-faced man with close-cropped hair, in his red tie, blue shirt, and houndstooth jacket he looked like a Buckeye on his way to his class reunion at Ohio State. Wendell now serves as president of Gaylord Entertainment Company, with $700 million in annual revenues, whose annual report proclaims "Country's gone mainstream . . . and we're bringing it home."

"We used to do a disc jockey convention," he said. "We tried to get every disc jockey that played country music in here, and we didn't get five hundred of them. Today we've got over twenty-four hundred radio stations that play this music. Dramatic growth! It's the biggest radio format in the country! One of the big pieces in all this is, when we got the ability to give national exposure on television to the good-looking young people that are in the business, because it changed people's mind-set about who and what is country music. You see them on television and you think, 'Golly, Vince Gill is a good-looking young 'un and so's Reba' and all these hat groups that we call them, the Garths and so on."

For the uninitiated, he was talking about Vince Gill, who has an arresting tenor, an aw-shucks manner, and boy-next-door good looks; Reba McEntire, the buoyant redhead who, like Gill, is a staple of MCA Records/Nashville; and Garth Brooks, whose astonishing run of success in the early 1990s catapulted country music to a whole new level. "They're in their thirties, they have all their teeth, they don't all wear pigtails, and the boys wear shoes," he continued. "They all don't have a plug of tobacco in their cheek. You know, that was the impression the world had of country music. Hillbillies! Down South! Southern thing!

"And other forms of music have had an impact on country music. Heavy metal drove away as many people as it attracted. Rap drove away people. You had to listen to something. And here we are! I mean, you didn't have Perry Como out there in the middle of the road, and you didn't have Frank Sinatra, but you did have the Rebas and the Vinces and the Randy Travises, and once we've got 'em here, well, we hope we've got 'em hooked. Sure, we're selling apple pie, Mom, good things. No question. But we've switched from being that rural dirt road, backroad, to almost suburban, don't you think?"

Bud Wendell had a lot of reasons to be excited. His Opryland Hotel–with its Holiday Inn–meets–Colonial Williamsburg architecture, its four-story indoor waterfall cascading into a 12,500-square-foot lake, its Victorian-style gazebo with Greek columns and beveled glass panels, and its Dancing Waters light show shooting 22 feet into the air–was in the process of expanding even more. A new $175 million addition then under construction, which eventually opened in June 1996, added a thousand rooms, bringing the number to almost three thousand; included in the same project was a quarter-mile indoor waterway traversed by flat-bottomed boats holding thirty people, which floated around a 4.5-acre covered atrium. The 300,000 square feet of new meeting and convention facilities made Opryland the largest hotel and convention center under one roof in the world.

A year earlier he had reopened the Opry's former home, the venerable Ryman Auditorium downtown and built the $7.5 million Wildhorse Saloon, a nightclub where country hunks and hunkettes in Garth Brooks merchandise and overweight geezer couples in matching fringed denim shirts, white Stetsons, and Tony Lama boots line-danced for the cameras of Gaylord's Nashville Network. Opryland, which sprawls over 120 acres, was drawing two million visitors each year. Its General Jackson showboat, the largest in the world, was prowling the murky waters of the Cumberland, as were the water taxis shooting visitors from Opryland to the Ryman and Wildhorse downtown. The Nashville Network and Country Music Television, country's answer to MTV, were going great guns. Wendell's broadcast incursions into NASCAR road racing and his purchase of Bass Pro Shops, the fishing gear empire that distributes thirty million catalogues a year, were prospering as well.

More than a few people groused that Bud Wendell and Gaylord had too much power to shape everything, from downtown development to people's careers. But in the giddy boom world of mid-nineties Nashville and country music, Bud Wendell's story was sort of Nashville's own in caricature. Nashville was growing so fast and workers were in such short supply—unemployment was below 3 percent—that Gaylord had to recruit employees from as far away as Puerto Rico and then buy a 150-room Quality Inn where they could live for up to ten months at $50 a week while they searched for a place to live.

And the country music industry, whose size had quadrupled in just six years from a $500 million business in 1989 to $2 billion in 1995, was prospering like never before. With 2,400 radio stations, country is on 1,600 more stations than the next most popular format, news talk. Each week, 70 million Americans listen to country radio, leading its nearest rival, adult contemporary, by almost 19 million listeners. In 1985 only ten new country albums went gold, with sales of 500,000 units, and seven went platinum, with sales of one million. By 1994, country artists had seventy-six gold albums, thirty-six platinum ones, and thirty-one multiplatinum. By the middle of 1996 Garth Brooks had sold 60 million albums, or about $725 million worth, in only seven years, making him second only to the Beatles in total U.S. album sales. Reba McEntire ranked third behind Barbra Streisand and Linda Ronstadt on the list of the most gold albums for a female singer. Dolly Parton was fourth. Increasingly, in a way no one could have imagined even twenty years earlier, country had become white America's music of choice and country radio the current version of the Top 40.

Its performers are young, attractive, and accessible in an inoffensive Main Street way. Its lyrics, churned out by the most talented song-writing colony in America—Nashville is truly the Tin Pan Alley of the nineties—speak to the concerns of what Newt Gingrich calls "normal Americans," sometimes coming out sounding like schlock or bubble-gum country, often being marvels of wit and compression. Country's sound has taken the mainstream rock of groups like the Eagles and pop like James Taylor's and has repackaged it into an easy-on-the-ears blend of country, rock, and folk that appeals to almost everyone, from high school kids to their grandparents.

As remarkable as the sales growth is the new image of country. Only ten years earlier, country was synonymous with the rednecks, white socks, and Pabst Blue Ribbon beer image of the rural South, the music of the truckstop and the Dew Drop Inn. Now, when Rhett Akins sings "That Ain't My Truck," it isn't some Bubba on his CB looking for his eighteen-wheeler, but suburban date music about a kid who found someone else's Chevy pickup in his girlfriend's driveway. The award shows on TV, like the Country Music Association Awards, with their endless parade of young, attractive, all-white performers combining suburban sensibilities and rural styles, make it hard to miss what a reassuring environment contemporary country is for selling McDonald's, Wranglers, and Chevrolet—as safe and clean as the neighborhood mall. In fact, if you were looking for heroic, straight-shooter all-American types in popular culture these days, the contemporary versions of Gary Cooper and John Wayne, you couldn't do better than a country icon like George Strait, another MCA Records/Nashville heartthrob who has been cranking out country hits for a decade. A lot of the performers are "country" more as a marketing category than as a musical identity, so that "country" acts include made-for-video hot bodies like Shania Twain from Windsor, Ontario, or feminist folkies like Mary Chapin Carpenter from Princeton, New Jersey, via Brown University, or roots rockers like the Tractors. Just as it made sense in 1995 for almost any white politician in the South to be a Republican, it made sense for almost any astute young white performer to find a niche in Nashville.

On the surface, it is a startling transformation. After all, no music other than polka, and perhaps disco, has been subjected to more disdain and ridicule than the despised music of the white South—the music of Uncle Dave Macon and Grandpa Jones of *Hee Haw* and Webb Pierce's customized Pontiac Bonneville with silver rifles mounted on the fenders, a silver pistol on the hood, and horseshoes on the gas and brake pedals; the cornpone music associated with Minnie Pearl's hat, Roy Acuff's twang, and Dolly Parton's boobs.

Even today, there's no tacky like Nashville tacky. To cruise the souvenir shops and pseudo-museums just off Music Row—with their Black Sambo and Aunt Jemima figurines; their hats with an unsightly lump of brown plastic on the bill under the single word SHITHEAD; their T-shirts reading ASHES 2 ASHES, DUST 2 DUST, IF IT WASN'T FOR WOMEN YOUR DING DONG WOULD RUST or I'LL TELL YOU WHY I CAME HOME HALF DRUNK—I RAN OUT OF MONEY; their $39.95 Hank Williams, Sr., decanters that play "Your Cheatin' Heart"; their NASCAR souvenir plates and shot glasses; their Elvis Presley "Love Me Tender" moisturizing lotion and swivel-hipped Elvis clocks—is to know the King did not die in vain.

Still, country's transformation made sense. America's music—from rock 'n' roll to blues to jazz to folk to country—is essentially Southern music, perhaps the most enduring flower of the region's rich minglings of black and white cultures. Rock's deepest roots may well be black—the percussive, participatory music the slaves brought from Africa, back-country blues and gospel, "rocking and reeling" spirituals. But along with Little Richard from Macon, Georgia, Fats Domino from New Orleans, and all the other black rock pioneers whose roots were in the South, virtually all the whites who gave birth to rock 'n' roll were Southerners who took a left turn off the country highway into a music that melded black rhythm and blues with country honky-tonk and Western swing music. The first white rock 'n' roll star, Bill Haley, grew up in the North but began his recording career playing country songs by the likes of Red Foley and Hank Williams. Elvis's first recording was "Blue Moon of Kentucky," by Bill Monroe and his Blue Grass Boys. His first records were all listed on the country charts; *Billboard* hailed him as "the youngster with the hillbilly blues beat," and the April 1995 issue of *Country and Western Jamboree* called him "one of the bright new-comers in the country fields." Virtually all of the white performers who invented rock 'n' roll were Southerners who began with one or both feet in the world of country music—Carl Perkins from Tiptonville, Tennessee; Gene Vincent from Norfolk, Virginia; Buddy Holly from Lubbock, Texas; Jerry Lee Lewis from Hell via Ferriday, Louisiana.

Much of country has been sound-alike schlock, but at its best the music has been as rich, evocative, and distinctly American as any the country has ever produced. In fact, just as American culture has always had a layered, schizophrenic take on most things Southern, country—especially with its Western trappings—has always spoken to something that goes well beyond its regional roots. Rather than being a pure product of the Tennessee hills, country, the musicologist Bill Malone has written, "was called into existence in the early 1920s by those powerful urban forces of technology, radio, and recording." To start with, country evolved as a sort of slaphappy amalgam of all sorts of American musics. The Anglo-Celtic folk and fiddle music that grew and metamorphosed in the hollows of Appalachia and the villages of the South formed its core, but the hymns and devotional songs of the church, sharp slivers of rags, blues, and gospel, the slick songwriting of Tin Pan Alley, and the American minstrel and American cowboy traditions enriched its soul.

Just as George Wallace slammed his way into the gut of the white working class, country formed a visceral bond with lower- and lower-middle-class whites like no other music of our time. It was no accident that the recent Republican presidents with the least instinctive appeal to the white working class—Richard Nixon and George Bush—were the ones who took the most pains to show up at the Opry, invite country stars to the White House, and, whenever possible, use their affection for country music as evidence that they were just plain folks too.

In its earliest days, the sound of country may have been too rough-hewn for Yankee eyes and ears, but even then, its basic sources of imagery, the two dominant strains of cowboys and mountaineers, cut to the heart of the American myth. As Malone put it, in a passage in his book *Singing Cowboys and Musical Mountaineers,* with resonance for both the current cultural environment and that of country's early days:

> Mountaineers and cowboys were not simply colorful and exotic; they were vivid reminders of frontier America and of the allegedly individual-istic traits that once characterized American life. Unlike most of the other local color characters, mountaineers and cowboys had the addi-tional advantage of being "Anglo-Saxon," a deeply satisfying attribute to many people who viewed with regret the inundation of the nation by "new" and perhaps unassimilable immigrants. Furthermore, moun-taineers and cowboys valued, and presumably embodied, freedom and independence; both were heroic and fearless; both preserved those manly traits that had ensured survival on the frontier and that were dis-tinctive and defining ingredients of American life. Cowboys and moutaineers, in short, were profoundly American.

The imagery isn't much different today. In fact, the shotgun wedding of "country" and "Western" (who in South Carolina or Mississippi walks around in cowboy hats like all the young hunks of Nashville do?) could be viewed as the cultural version of John Calhoun's political vision of South and West uniting to dominate American politics. Just as the political vision now seems ascendant, so does the cultural. If any-thing, the imagery has more appeal than ever, a result of the changing perceptions of what it means to be country and urban.

In the office of Bruce Hinton, the chairman of MCA Records/ Nashville, are two framed posters that perfectly capture the traditional imagery of urban and rural, North and South. One is MCA's 1936 roster of artists when the company was the big-band powerhouse, as it is the country hit machine today. Against a glittering urban skyline and a green background were arrayed a list of "America's Greatest Radio Dance Orchestras." There were perhaps thirty-five of them: Tommy Tucker, Guy Lombardo, Kay Kyser, Horace Zito, Ted Weems–the hunks of their day in slicked back hair and tuxedos–and they were trotted out the way Nashville record labels today take out full-page ads featuring their bulging rosters of country studs. It was the heyday of urban America when urban meant sophistication, class, and affluence, and the city was the place where small-town strivers escaped from the narrow, hayseed dead-ends of rural life.

The other poster, for a film called *Renfro Valley Barn Dance,* offers an image exactly opposite of that on the MCA poster: a cavalcade of bizarre rustics like Red Brigham, Ole Joe Clark, Aunt Mandy, and Ginger Callahan and their exotic customs and rites, billed as "the biggest singin' dancin' fiddlin' show that ever dropped out of Renfro Valley." It gushed: "See for the first time on film! A fiddlin' contest! The Sunday morning gathering! Renfro Valley on film! The exchange of instruments!" It comes across as something between a weekend in Dogpatch and a Satanic rite. This was the land of America's nitwits that Mencken labeled the "Sahara of the Bozart," populated by "the poor white trash" in whose veins flowed "the worst blood of Western Europe."

Country is prospering for all the reasons cited by Bud Wendell. But it–and the South–are also prospering because the popular images on Bruce Hinton's walls have flipped. Unless you are a rich investment banker or a hip kid just out of school, to whites urban is likely to mean crime and noise and traffic and angry minorities, a place to get mugged or have your car broken into rather than a glittering Mecca of sophistication and class. And country–at least the booming midsized towns, cities, and suburbs of the South and West–is more likely to mean the place where you can afford a house, get to work in fifteen minutes and get home in time to coach Little League, send your kids to the local schools, and buy a condo at Hilton Head or Destin that you could never afford in a million years on Martha's Vineyard or in East Hampton.

The people running this music business are headquartered in a roy-
ally nondescript stretch of Nashville called Music Row. People in town
talk nostalgically of the old days, when all the companies were headquartered in old frame houses and modest cottages and Music Row was
like a small town full of village eccentrics where you could walk in off
the street with your guitar and try out your songs for some of the labels
or music publishers. Two toothless brothers walked around with their
guitars playing their songs in Russian fur hats and coats like country-
and-western Cossacks, and a woman named Miss Kimberly stood on a
streetcorner singing to the accompaniment of her tape recorder in an
effort to catch the attention of one of the labels. Some of the cottages
remain, but the record companies and big publishing firms tend to be in
blocky low-rise brick buildings that look like parking garages, and the
days are long gone—if they ever really existed—when you could walk
in on Bruce Hinton or Tony Brown at MCA, Jim Ed Norman at
Warner/Reprise, Joe Galante at RCA, or Tim DuBois at Arista and try
out a few songs for him.

But Music Row still has the appealing feel of a small town where the
only industry is music. The streets have names like Roy Acuff Place and
Chet Atkins Place. Successes are marked with banners hung from windows, for example, CONGRATULATIONS #1 MADELINE STONE "I'M A
BELIEVER" SONY MUSIC PUBLISHING or FALCON MANAGEMENT CONGRATU-
LATES #1 R&R; #1 CMT (2 WEEKS); #1 TNW TRAVIS TRITT "TELL ME I WAS
DREAMING" in just the way the old Acme Farm Supply store across the
street from the new Hard Rock Café downtown had an inviting banner
outside reading FREE DOG DIP EVERY SATURDAY. On the other hand,
every country star has his own web sites and home pages (like Tritt's
http://www.he.net/luberia/tritt or http://www/wbr.com/travistritt/)
not to mention Internet concert schedules, song clips, biographies and
links to the whole cyber-country world of Absolutely Country from
the UK, Robbert's Country Music Page from Holland, Wild Willie's
Country Music Page and the like. These days Nashville is a lot more
than bedsheets hung outside Music Row buildings.

If the ethic at the top of the business in Los Angeles or New York is
the edgy overdrive of Doberman-style gatekeepers and power lunches
at Spago or the Four Seasons, the ethic of the movers and shakers in
Nashville is, well, country. No one wears a tie. Executives and stars take
Nashville's version of a power breakfast at the Pancake Pantry or hang

out over greasy burgers at Brown's Diner. The boss's gatekeeper chats with you about her favorites on the label's roster, and the pictures next to the gold and platinum albums on the boss's walls usually reflect the artists and sessions he likes best, not necessarily the biggest sellers.

Capitol has Garth Brooks, which all by itself means it is one of the biggest labels in town. Warner/Reprise has the most diverse lineup, ranging from mainstream hit makers like Faith Hill and Randy Travis to the fiddle virtuoso Mark O'Connor and the black singing cowboy music of Herb Jeffries. RCA is reviewed as the label to watch because of the return of Joe Galante, a New Yorker, who made RCA into the hottest label in town with Willie Nelson, Dolly Parton, and Waylon Jennings in the eighties and had come back from New York to try to do it again.

But to take the temperature of Nashville the two men to go to were Tony Brown, president of MCA/Nashville and Tim DuBois, president of Arista/Nashville. Like most of the people at the top of the anthill in Nashville, both are Southerners, both come from the "creative" end of things–Brown is a piano player and producer, DuBois is a producer and songwriter–both have a seductive sort of country-boy charm that makes you think of the quiet guy at the poker table who ends up with all the chips, and both have put together an amazing string of successes. After that the similarities end.

MCA was the outgrowth of Decca Records, which has been a major force in Nashville since 1934, when it signed Jimmie Davis, who rode his success with songs such as "You Are My Sunshine" all the way to the governorship of Louisiana. Over the years, Decca had such legendary country artists as Ernest Tubb, Bill Monroe, Kitty Wells, and Webb Pierce. MCA, which acquired Decca in 1962, now has the deepest roster in Nashville, a well-oiled machine that relentlessly cranks out winners by the likes of Vince Gill, George Strait, Reba McEntire, Wynonna Judd, the Mavericks, Trisha Yearwood, Marty Stuart, and Tracy Byrd. It has gone from $40 million in annual sales in 1984 to more than triple that now.

Brown, the man who has come to personify MCA's success, as a producer has a reputation for working with some of the hippest, edgiest people in country music and its environs, people like Steve Earle, Joe Ely, Nanci Griffith, and Lyle Lovett, as well as with mainstream hit makers like George Strait, Vince Gill, and Wynonna Judd. *Billboard* named him country's top producer four years in a row and *Entertainment Weekly* put him on its list of the one hundred most powerful people in the entertainment industry.

Brown, the son of an evangelist, grew up traveling the South as part of his family gospel group, the Brown Family. He is a short, compactly built man with a neatly cropped beard and the sly, feral quality of the class wiseguy who has hit it big while all the kids who got A's are out selling insurance or doing small-town real estate law.

His father was a nondenominational evangelist, so the family sang at everything from Salvation Army shelters to Quaker meetings to Pentecostal churches where the congregants spoke in tongues, threw babies in the air, and passed out in rapture. Brown, who taught himself to play the piano, came to savor the different musical styles, and the diversity gave him a sense of the infinite variations music could have even if it came from the same stream.

He started off professionally playing gospel piano and played with Elvis from 1975 until his death three years later. Before that he was also associated with the King, albeit under slightly weirder circumstances. He was part of a quartet called Voice, and their entire job was to be on call twenty-four hours a day in case Elvis wanted someone around to sing with him—not for spur-of-the-moment recording, just for recreational singing.

"We'd get these phone calls," Brown said in his office, which was filled with folk and original art that he collects and music industry memorabilia. Behind him were six black-and-white pictures from the recording sessions for *Rhythm Country & Blues,* a memorable MCA record of 1994 that brought together black R&B and white country artists and that produced one true masterpiece, Sam Moore (of Sam and Dave) and Conway Twitty's transcendent rendition of "Rainy Night in Georgia," recorded two weeks before Twitty died.

"They'd [Elvis's people] say, 'We're sending a plane for you,' or 'Catch a plane and go to Hollywood, check in at the Holiday Inn. We'll call you.' We'd check in, they'd say, 'Go to the house at eight P.M. Elvis will be up.' We'd sit around and watch TV and play pool, and if Elvis started going 'Oooooooohhhhhh,' starting to sing, I was to find what key he was in, and we'd join in singing. We were like court jesters. Sometimes they'd say, 'Fly to L.A. Check in at the Holiday Inn. We'll call you.' We'd check in and they'd say, 'Go to the house in Beverly Hills.'

We'd get there. They'd say, 'He just left. He went to the house in Palm Springs. He drove.' We'd check out, go to Palm Springs, check in at the Hilton. They'd say, 'Elvis got to the house. The air conditioning's broke. He's pissed. He went to Memphis. Wait here a couple of days. He might be back.' That kind of stuff. We were Elvis's pets, so everyone hated our guts.

"Eventually the group sort of disbanded, and I took the job playing piano with Elvis because I knew Glen D. Hardin was leaving Elvis to play with Emmylou Harris, and me being the opportunist that I am, I wanted to play with Elvis. He never rehearsed. I remember Felton Jarvis saying, 'The second song he does is "Teddy Bear," da da dada dada dada dada da, you gotta get that and you have to get "I Can't Help Falling in Love." If you can do that, you've got it made.' I'll never forget that first night. Kansas City, Kemper Arena, twenty thousand people. Elvis looked over at me and, man, my butthole was real tight."

A skeptic might say there was a little bit of opportunism in MCA as well. After its meteoric rise in the early eighties, country had begun to flatten out by 1995. Even the moguls admitted that the craze for look-alike hunks in hats ran the risk of turning country radio into a land of bland, sound-alike clones in which no one could tell John Michael Montgomery from Tracy Byrd from Kenny Chesney from Wade Hayes from Clay Walker from Doug Stone from Ty England from Jeff Carson. MCA is the ultimate country hit machine, but aside from the Mavericks, who are sort of hip retro-country-pop with a great Cuban-American singer, Raul Malo, who sounds like Roy Orbison, and Todd Snider, a Dylanesque, grunge-country iconoclast whose career hasn't yet taken off, it wasn't exactly awash in cutting-edge music.

Still, a Nashville powerhouse playing it safe was not exactly a startling development. The music business in Nashville had always gravitated, however clumsily, toward the mainstream, like the days in the 1960s when Owen Bradley at Decca/MCA helped invent the slick, overproduced "Nashville sound" of heavenly choirs and glistening strings. Nashville has always wanted to be mainstream music; whether it now has finally hit the mainstream or the mainstream has finally hit it, country as the new American pop music has an impeccable logic.

"The boundaries of what country music will allow expand ever so slightly," Brown said. "Certain guitar sounds, drum sounds, lyrics that are acceptable. I always try to push the envelope ever so slightly.

What's changed is the exposure. In country music we always thought small. We always said we were the stepchild of popular music. As we started thinking bigger we were actually more accessible than the music industry gave us credit for. I agree that the male artists all sound alike. But if they say in L.A. that we're a formula here, hell, they're a formula there. They're machines. There aren't any human beings playing on most of those records out there. At least we have human beings playing. They may be copying each other, but at least they're playing. Basically country has been a thorn in [L.A.'s] flesh since we went mainstream. Me, I'm glad to see the South get its due."

Brown's rival for the status of the hottest man in Nashville is Tim DuBois. If Brown seems like the class bad boy who's made good, DuBois seems like the avuncular teacher who has saved him from a life of sin. In fact, DuBois, the son of two schoolteachers from Oklahoma, is a former educator who sports one of the all-time great mix-and-match résumés. It includes an M.B.A. degree and C.P.A. certificate, a stint as a senior financial analyst with the Federal Reserve Bank in Dallas, a successful songwriting career that includes the classic country song title "She Got the Gold Mine (I Got the Shaft)," and stints as an accounting professor at the University of Tulsa and Vanderbilt University. The current résumé line is president, Arista/Nashville. DuBois is the most talked-about success story in Nashville.

MCA is like country's version of Bloomingdale's at its peak: it offers the best full-service merchandise around. Arista is like the classiest boutique on Madison Avenue: you are never sure what you will find, but you know someone really smart is stocking the shelves. Clive Davis, president of Arista/Nashville's parent label, hired DuBois in 1990 to start the label from scratch. Since then, almost half of its acts have gone platinum, the best success rate by far for any label in Nashville, which makes getting signed by Arista Nashville's version of getting the fat envelope from Harvard.

Arista's acts range from the Georgia laid-back honky-tonk of Alan Jackson to the slick, country rock of Brooks and Dunn to the blue-eyed country soul of Lee Roy Parnell to classy mainstream country acts like Pam Tillis, Steve Wariner, and Radney Foster. Best of all—and furthest from the country radio mainstream—is the off-the-wall geezer boogie of the Tractors, who are a bunch of over-the-hill (average age forty-seven), overweight curmudgeons at a time when you almost have to be young and pretty to get played on the radio. Their debut album in 1995 was a woozy amalgam of rock, country, Cajun, and swing music that perfectly caught the pinched, weary truculence of working-class America and turned it into something ragged and sublime at the same time. It was what The Band might have sounded like if they had spent their formative years playing at roadhouses in Lubbock, Tulsa, Odessa, and Amarillo.

Not only did DuBois start the label, he also created some of its biggest acts. For example, he took two struggling solo artists named Kix Brooks and Ronnie Dunn to lunch and told them, "You guys don't know one another, but I think you're an act. Why don't you hang out and see if you like one another." Their first record, released in 1992, went quintuple platinum, and by the summer of 1995 they had sold more than 10 million albums. Arista was no hotbed of exotica. The really exotic acts don't get signed by any of the big labels in Nashville, and Warners has more out-in-left-field acts than Arista does—it just doesn't have big hits with any of them. For now, at least, Arista seems to have the magic touch for churning out hits while sniffing around at, and sometimes going a little beyond, the outer edges of the country mainstream.

DuBois has brown hair that has pretty much gone gray and is combed straight back, a salt and pepper beard that is mostly salt, an Oklahoma twang, and a genial teddy-bear quality that masks what he calls "the recovering accountant" inside. If the ethic of Nashville is the regular-guy, plain-folks persona of the most successful artists like Vince Gill or Alan Jackson, DuBois is the executive who has it down best.

"Part of country's success is generational," said DuBois, who was wearing a gray print shirt with no tie, olive slacks, and brown loafers. "I'm forty-seven, and I think most baby boomers are alienated from urban dance, rap. All that left these people cold. It didn't translate with their value system, and it didn't translate with their musical taste. When they began to search around they found that some of the music that was coming out of Nashville in the early nineties was more like the rock 'n' roll they were comfortable with than anything else out there. How much oldies rock can you listen to without getting tired of hearing 'Brown Sugar' eighteen thousand times? I grew up playing in rock 'n' roll bands and writing rock 'n' roll music, and it wasn't until I moved to Texas in the early seventies and started listening to people like Jerry Jeff

Walker, Willie, Waylon, Rusty Weir, a guy named Willis Alan Ramsey, that I made the crossover. Very few of us grew up listening to the Grand Ole Opry. Most of us grew up listening to the Beatles and the Eagles. And when people started listening to country, they found something that wasn't all about truck drivers and cheating; it was about life, a lot of baby-boomer issues, and there were still stories there, and there were still great harmonies, and it was just a comfortable place to be."

The most adventurous people in town felt that Nashville's version of Manifest Destiny is to truly become America's Music City, the place that cranks out a broad range of American music—country, pop, rock, gospel. New York and L.A. can have the urban stuff. Nashville will produce the rest. Without thinking that big, DuBois had in 1995 just begun a new Arista Texas label, which would mostly produce Tejano music, and had bought Reunion Records, a major Christian music label.

But Nashville's imperial visions have never really happened and though country may have become the music of white America, the entertainment business is still run by the gorillas on both coasts. In fact, the record companies in Nashville can't even really control their own business. They pump out music, but its success depends almost entirely on whether it gets played by the 2,400-hundred-station monster of country radio, which rewards only the artists who play by its rules.

"Radio is not in the business of making new artists," DuBois said. "They're not in the business of being on the cutting edge musically, they're in the business of selling advertising and the way they sell advertising is to keep you listening for as long a period of time as possible. The way to do that is not to offend you. It's not not to bore you. It's not to offend you. If they play something you're uncomfortable with, that's when you push the button and go to the next station. Granted, the call letters and the way they position themselves in the market makes them seem like the music people, but they're not the music people. They're the advertising people. The music is dead space to them. They only make money when they quit playing music and start playing advertising. In pop music, there's a bunch of little places you can go to start a record. You can go to Triple A, you can go to alternative rock, there's a lot of formats. We've got one thing. If you can't make it narrow enough to fit through what the gatekeepers are letting in, then you've got problems."

He said it more as the accountant sizing up the business than the musician complaining about the rules of the game. When I was getting ready to leave, he fished out some "product," as the tapes and CDs are always called in the music business, from the gold-inlaid maple cabinets behind him. One was a Merle Haggard tribute album that featured Nashville's best covering Haggard songs. Another was Arista's five-year anniversary sampler, four discs using as a title Arista's somewhat irritating, self-congratulatory fifth-anniversary promotional theme, *Hey, This Thing Just Might Work.* The third was the Tractors, a group I knew of but had not heard at the time. He put their CD in the player, and Steve Ripley's gravelly voice accompanied only by spare noodlings of piano and guitar boomed out of cranked-up speakers:

> *All across the South*
> *They've got the boogie bands that sound so fine*
> *And on both coasts they've got the record company machines*
> *Turnin' out hits on an assembly line*
> *But in the heart of America, we've got the beat*
> *That's guaranteed to tap your toes*
> *Oklahoma's got the Tulsa shuffle*
> *And this am the way it goes. Two, three, four . . .*

At which point guitars, horns, drums, and what sounds like half of New Orleans hit you right between the eyes. DuBois listened with the contented smile of a guy who had played by the rules and broken them at the same time. You had to think this beat the Federal Reserve any day of the week.

Nashville has so many people as appealing as Tim DuBois that it is easy to get seduced. But the city, founded on Christmas Day, 1779, has more claims to fame than just country music. It gave the world Dinah Shore, Pat Boone, Maxwell House Coffee, the neo-Con's beloved Old South agrarian manifesto *I'll Take My Stand,* and the world's best-named candy, Goo Goo Clusters. It is home to various command posts of the Methodists and Southern Baptists, much of the nation's health-care management and religious publishing industries, and a slew of universities—historically white ones like Vanderbilt and historically black ones like Fisk—as well as the giant Nissan and Saturn plants outside town. Oprah Winfrey and John Tesh used to do the news there, Pat Sajak did the weather, President James K. Polk is buried at the State Capitol, and President Andrew Jackson is buried at the Hermitage out-

side town. It has one of the South's quintessential rich folks' neighborhoods, Belle Meade, where the old-money folks until recently would
rather have bathed in grits than have anything to do with the hillbillies
at the Opry. By any standard, Nashville's famous replica of the Par-
thenon featured in Robert Altman's brilliantly defamatory movie of the
1970s is one of the oddest civic monuments sprouting in the middle of
an American city.

Nashville is a lot like Charlotte, only ten times as much fun, the difference between a place whose signature industry is banking and one
whose signature business is music. Like Charlotte, Nashville has been
on a roll economically and growing like a weed with a population that
had increased by over a quarter in the last fifteen years and metro-area
employment by 65 percent in the same period. Both cities have the
same leafy green topography and relatively relaxed race relations, the
latter a function largely of the degree to which blacks are a distinct
minority rather than a dominant part of the cultural and political mix
the way they are in the Deep South. But if Nashville's leadership has the
same lust for the big time–particularly when, like Charlotte, it comes to
luring a professional sports team–its residents have a refreshing degree
of skepticism about the Truly International City disease. Citizens in the
end supported a referendum in May 1996 to build a $150 million sta-
dium to lure the Houston Oilers, but at least the opponents forced a
vote and gave it a good shot, which reflected an unusual degree of skepticism about the alleged blessings of World Classiness. If the neo-Cons
have both feet in the mythic past and Charlotte has both feet in the
commercial present, Nashville comes as close as anywhere in the South
to striking a felicitous balance between the two.

Certainly the music business is benefiting from the degree to which
Nashville is such an attractive alternative to New York and Los
Angeles. A few years earlier I had talked to one Charles Sandford, who
had just packed twenty-nine thousand pounds of recording gear into a
U-Haul and had left Los Angeles for Nashville. "Between crime, riots,
gangs, earthquakes, and fires, it's like *Blade Runner* out there," he said.
"I'd say twenty-five percent of the people I know have moved and a lot
of them have come to Nashville, where you don't see graffiti every time
you open your eyes, and you don't hear helicopters over your house all
the time." Since then the exodus has only increased. At the Bluebird
Café, the wonderful, intimate showcase in the Green Hills area south of

downtown, I sat down next to a hulking kid with long dark hair and a UCLA Bruins T-shirt. He turned out to be Mark Islam, a twenty-seven-year-old aspiring songwriter who kept popping up to go from table to table to greet all his friends from L.A. who had already moved to Nashville.

Increasingly, the city is home to a unlikely army of old rockers–turned–Nashville songwriters or producers trying to get away from the L.A. and New York rat race. They include Steve Winwood, Peter Frampton, Leon Russell, Bernie Leadon of the Eagles, John Kay of Steppenwolf, Felix Cavalieri of The Rascals, Al Anderson of NRBQ, Kim Carnes, Mark Farner of Grand Funk Railroad, the legendary Memphis guitarist Steve Cropper, Bob Welch of Fleetwood Mac, twangy guitar pioneer Duane Eddy, and Al Kooper, the great keyboard man on all of Dylan's greatest late-sixties albums. Neil Diamond was spending the summer there while working on an album, and Donna Summer, of all people, was house-hunting.

One morning I ventured over to an old frame house down the road from Music Row that had been turned into a latte and cappuccino joint called Bongo Java to meet that archetypal hillbilly, Janis Ian. She first became known in the sixties for her interracial love song, "Society's Child," and had a big hit a decade later with her lovely rumination on teenage ugly ducklinghood, "At Seventeen." With her anguished, Yankee liberal sensibilities she seemed as Nashville as Luciano Pavarroti. But, as things turned out, she had been living there for ten years as a happily gay woman, recording and performing some but mostly making a living as a songwriter. She, too, sounded like a Nashville chauvinist.

She was sitting at a corner table, under a kid's painting in wild, throbbing colors, entitled *Squids Shoot Poison.* She was a tiny woman wearing a red T-shirt, white slacks, and black high-top sneakers; she had frizzy black hair that one of her songwriting mentors in Nashville said gave her the look of a rat terrier with a perm.

"When I first moved here I had a friend, a journalist from L.A., who stayed with me for two weeks in 1988, and she just got more and more depressed," she said. "I finally said, 'What's wrong?' and she said, 'I thought I knew this country, and I don't know what's going on at all.' She suddenly realized the country was not New York and L.A. It's a cliché, but there's a lot of truth to it. When I moved here the exodus hadn't started yet. But I walked off the plane in 1986 and thought, I'm home. I didn't want to be in L.A. and write dance music. I didn't want to put up with New York and L.A. I liked the fact that writers are respected here. I liked the unpretentiousness of this place. I still follow people around the supermarkets to listen to what they say. The other day I was behind these people who said, 'Well, you got a dog-eyed woman, and you got a dog-eyed man. That marriage won't last.' I love that. I took such shit when I moved here. I remember I went to New York with some people here for a radio seminar, and there was this guy taking our picture who said in a big broad accent, 'Why don't y'all put on your grins now. Where's your hat?' The Central Park jogger had just happened, and I said, 'Well, why don't we just go take a walk in the park and get mugged?'

"In New York or L.A. you can have a hit record and suddenly every maitre d' knows your name, every valet parking person knows your name. Everything changes. Here, nothing changes. The bagel's still late. Your car gets serviced the same as everyone else. They don't care because at the end of the day life goes on. That's why it's okay to be gay here. I haven't had one problem being gay here. My only complaint is that Nashville's grown so much since I got here, it's beginning to wear me out."

In fact, for all its redneck connotations and family values posturing, country at times these days feels vaguely, well, liberal. Not in a big way, mind you. But the in-your-face rebel flag waving of Hank Williams, Jr., musing about how swell life would have been if the Confederates had won the Civil War in "If the South Woulda Won . . ." is largely a thing of the past. A more contemporary lyric is Collin Raye singing about his kind of girl who quotes William Faulkner and Martin Luther King; Garth Brooks singing in "We Shall Be Free" that the world would be a better place when people could love anyone they chose, a line he said refers to homosexual love; or Martin McBride singing in "Independence Day" about an abused wife who burns down her husband's house. Hillary Clinton, with her tin ear for the nation's soul, might have derisively cited Tammy Wynette's "Stand By Your Man," as if country were merely for honky-tonk angels in bouffants and polyester, but there weren't too many feminist anthems in the nineties that got the details better than Mary Chapin Carpenter's portrait of suburban disillusionment in "He Thinks He'll Keep Her." On MCA's blending of country and soul, *Rhythm Country and Blues,* the music was more white boys and white girls from Nashville trying to sing "black" then black musicians trying to sound like they belonged in Nashville. From the clear-eyed heartland feminism of Reba McEntire to the AIDS ribbons everyone wore to the ubiquitous awards ceremonies to every label's multicultural quest for the first big Tejano/country crossover artist, you could see Nashville as a reminder that the country—and the South—was a hell of a lot more complicated than the new ayatollahs of the right would have you believe.

"Perhaps the problem is that just as in the Great Struggle of 1861–65, there are more of Them than there are of Us," *Southern Partisan,* ever vigilant, groused in lamenting what it saw as the country's drift toward creeping Yankee liberalism. "When a thing becomes lucrative, the Yankees smell profits and inevitably take it over. A leftward shift soon follows. . . . But then there's a brighter side. With the strength of country music, there are enough radio stations playing it that for now we can still escape political correctness with just a turn of the dial."

On the other hand, the message is still the narrow individualism that Cash wrote about in *The Mind of the South.* If you are abused at work, you don't form a union, you tell the boss to take this job and shove it.

And though the musicians and many of the people at the labels and music-publishing firms can be vaguely liberal—a far cry from the days when Minnie Pearl campaigned for George Wallace and the Opry stars could be counted on as reliable right wingers—the music business still seems in some ways like the last preserve of the old days. One reason Music Row has such an amiable, small-town feel is that no one has to worry about messy issues like affirmative action because virtually everyone is white. Despite its roots in the interracial culture of the South, the music is whiter than it has ever been, now that Cleve Francis and Charlie Pride, the only two major black country acts, are no longer big factors. As for women, there are plenty of sexy young stars (a woman almost has to be young and sexy to be a country star these days), and women increasingly are succeeding as songwriters and hold a fair number of important jobs in the music business. But the person at the top—particularly at the labels—invariably is a man, often one with grown kids and a hot young wife or girlfriend. Of the seventy-seven movers and shakers on the board of the Country Music Association, the industry's main trade organization, only five are women. *Southern Partisan* really doesn't have that much to worry about.

All that is too ingrained in Nashville's culture to be much of an issue, and country's record on women may not be much different than any other business. What is an issue is that so much of the music is being churned out by the big labels is so safe and predictable at a time when the range of music around town has never been richer.

One morning I drove out to a neighborhood of new subdivisions and old cottages not far from Opryland along the Cumberland River to see Marty Stuart. If Garth Brooks is Nashville's Michael Jordan, Marty Stuart is sort of Horace Grant with great hair—not the biggest star in town, but a talent, a team player, and a big part of what is left of Nashville's institutional memory. His house was full of country artifacts and Western art, a signed photo of Hank Williams, Sr., a majestic tin-type of Geronimo, Roy Acuff posters, Navajo rugs, a hand-tooled saddle, Western prints with titles like *An Oasis in the Bad Lands,* and a classic photo he had taken showing Johnny Cash and Elvis together at the Ryman.

At thirty-seven, Stuart has a modified Keith Richards rooster cut already flecked with gray, and is partial to rhinestone-studded, elaborately embroidered jackets by Nudie and artfully torn jeans like those worn by Dwight Yoakam, the reigning king of hillbilly music. Stuart was a little bleary-eyed in shorts and a blue denim shirt when I got there at nine on a morning when he had to hit the road for Florida early in the afternoon. He offered me iced tea and some banana nut bread his mom had baked, and we headed out to talk on his back porch overlooking the Cumberland, where you could hit Bud Wendell's General Jackson showboat with a water balloon launcher if you were in the mood.

Unlike most of the country yuppies of the new Nashville, Stuart is a combination performer-hobbyist-historian who believes country isn't just a business but a true window onto the nation's soul. He grew up in Philadelphia, Mississippi, and first went on the road at the age of twelve, playing mandolin during the summer with a gospel and blue-grass band called the Sullivan Family Gospel Singers. He met the blue-grass legends Lester Flatt and Earl Scruggs the same summer. When they offered him a job in their band at the age of thirteen, he talked his parents into letting him sign on; he went to live with Flatt, who became his legal guardian, and took correspondence courses to continue his schooling.

He became a solo act in 1986, and while not a huge hit maker, he plays at the Opry, has a loyal following and respectable record sales, and plays the dual role of being sort of a hip ambassador for the new Nashville and one of the few people in town willing to say the emperor often has no clothes on. In fact, he often says both in the same sentence, as if Marty the Nashville pitchman and Marty the kid bluegrasser are fighting it out for his soul.

"The best quote I ever heard about country music these days is that the reason Long John Silver's outsells Uncle Bud's Catfish Cabin on the edge of town is because they've made fish succeed in not tasting like fish," he said. "And I think it's the same thing with country music. There's only a measure of the heart and soul of country music left on the radio and on the concert trail these days, and the real thing, the Bill Monroe, Hank Williams thing, is that far from being long gone. Country is such a huge industry now, that there are people coming to work in it every day who don't have a clue who Porter Waggoner is, the accomplishments of Bill Monroe. Even the executives are starting to say, we're making cookie-cutter music, the soul's leaving. But then with all the money rolling in, it's understandable, and I'd say country has done a good job of not completely whoring out. We're in pretty good shape these days. The quality of songwriting is impeccable, the musicians are impeccable, and the greed factor is impeccable too."

Most impeccable of all, everyone agrees, is Garth Brooks, who roared out of Oklahoma, home of the Tractors, where the South, Midwest, and West collide like a three-way train wreck, and single-handedly brought country into a new era. Garth, a graduate of Oklahoma State University with a degree in advertising, is an odd revolutionary. It is impossible to listen to his records and hear any startling breaks with the past. As country hunks go, he is kind of a dud— balding, a little paunchy, by no means the biggest heartthrob in Nashville.

But what Garth has done is bring a whole new level of marketing savvy and stagecraft to country music, along with an unerring instinct for the gut of a nation that has become a whole lot more like Tulsa or Oklahoma City than Boston or New York. His songs shrewdly play to both the "hard-hat, gun-rack, achin' back, overtaxed, fun-loving crowd" down at the honky-tonk and the suburban boomers coming to grips with middle age. One critic got it right in comparing him to a "franchise honky-tonk in a suburban strip mall," churning out user-friendly barroom anthems for high school kids and their boomer parents, none of whom has ever been in a honky-tonk. He pioneered a whole new genre of country extravaganzas staged in arenas, with elaborate fireworks displays, in which he shattered guitars as Pete Townsend of the Who used to do, or flew around on ropes and harnesses like a country Peter Pan. The signature geometric-pattern shirts he wore turned into instantly recognizable, eminently marketable Garth-wear clothes, and he affected an insufferable "Yes ma'am, no sir" public persona that was half the just-folks ethos of NASCAR and half a throwback to an idealized vision of middle-American celebrity. No fool, Garth summed up his greatest talent by remarking, "I believe that the one gift I have been granted is that I am the common dude." It took forever for the mainstream media to figure out that Garth Brooks, not Michael Jackson, was the real king of pop.

In Nashville, people talk about him all the time as a force of nature that needs to be explained. There are stories of Good Garth, the plain Joe who still orders from Taco Bell on the road and goes out to pick up his own takeout pizzas at Lion's Head Mall in Nashville, or Supernatural Garth, hanging his own lights before a concert to make sure they are just right. Marty Stuart was trying to figure it out too.

"Garth Brooks is one of the smartest people country music's ever had," he said, not quite sure whether to be Marty the booster or Marty the cynic. "I think when he got through with college, he could have said, 'Well, I'm going to run for president, I'm going to run for governor, I'm going to be an actor, I think I'll be a country singer,' but he had the same sort of expectations whichever he did. He's a marketing genius. Where some of us came from the Roy Acuff–Bill Monroe–Johnny Cash school, Garth comes from the school of James Taylor and the Eagles. Now they call it country music. So be it. Whatever it is, he's got it down from a marketing point of view. Any cowboy in America or any kid in America can look like Garth Brooks for three hundred dollars. Between the hat, the off-the-rack shirt, the Wranglers, and the Ropers, you look like Garth Brooks. To look like me or Dwight Yoakam, it's stupid. You have to mortgage the house. Then when you're through, you still come out looking like a ridiculous rhinestone comet.

"But the thing about country is, it always swings between innovation and imitation, and I think we're heading back to some innovation. You've got some great music all over town now, more than there's been for years, and it would be a sin for Nashville not to expose that culture that's trying to manufacture itself. And I think it's going to happen because, to me, the culture of America really is what comes out of the backroads of the South. When you come down to it, the only things in America that really qualify as hard-core American culture are the American Indians, the black people, and the hard-core Southern white folks. That's what America's about."

Still, even if you bought the premise, that didn't mean you knew what came out of it. If country music until recently has flown almost completely under the radar of the media giants on the coast, there is another side of Nashville that is still just as invisible and potentially just as revealing about where the nation is headed. The most concentrated glimpse of that world can be found in a shiny new suburban office building at 101 Winners Circle in suburban Brentwood, not far from Granny White Pike, where Mark Gibbs's wife had the seizure that changed his life. To wander around the gleaming new offices with their polished Scandinavian wood, track lighting, and earnest, well-scrubbed staffers is like encountering an entire parallel universe. Just like at Arista and MCA on Music Row, the walls were full of gold and platinum albums, the receptionists' areas were stocked with trade publications, and there were glossy photos and posters and life-sized cutouts every-where of fresh-faced young stars. But the music magazine wasn't *New Country* or *Music Row*, it was something called *Release*, which was sitting next to a Bible open to the Revelation of John. All the people in the photos were utter ciphers. They could have been advertisements for the Hair Club of America or part of a bizarre fantasy some incredibly rich man was playing out for fun—a whole fake company putting out fake CDs by made-up artists with names like Out of the Gray, Charlie Pea-cock, the Walter Eugenes, and Margaret Becker.

"What kind of story are you doing?" demanded Steve Griffin, the president of the EMI Christian Music Group's Chordant distribution division. He is an intense Arkansas native and Baylor graduate with the smooth good looks and confident manner of a photocopier salesman. "*The New York Times* wrote something awhile back that was terrible. You here to do the same thing?" I told him I wasn't writing this for the

Times, and I wasn't planning to do anything terrible, and after a while he relaxed a little and went into his spiel.

Griffin graduated from Baylor back when it, not David Koresh, was the best-known thing about Waco, Texas, and after graduation started out with IBM. He got into the entertainment business about six years ago with a company that made Disney-style Bible videos and went from no sales to sales of $58 million in thirty-seven months. Then he joined EMI's Chordant division, the Nashville subsidiary of the international entertainment giant and the world's biggest Christian music company, with about a third of the $700 million Christian music industry. He figured he had one of the great marketing opportunities in American music.

"There are a hundred and forty-eight million adults that say they're religious," he said, throwing out numbers like the emcee at a church bingo game. "About eighty or ninety million Americans go to church every Sunday. A hundred and five million go at least once a month. Well, that's the largest niche market in America today. This industry exists predominantly by selling through Christian bookstores and that's where eighty percent of the revenue comes from–from five to seven thousand Christian bookstores. We know demographically that over eighty million people go to church every Sunday but only fifteen million ever darken the door of a Christian bookstore. So if only fifteen million people are driving a seven hundred million–dollar industry of Christian music, then I would have to say that we have a potentially huge upside."

Griffin's job was to find a way to get Christian music a broader airing and distribution. The feeling was that if country was right for the times, Christian music was even more so, and the middle-of-the-road people who went to church, bought William Bennett's *Book of Virtues,* or worried about what was influencing their kids–which meant most people– would buy into a family-values alternative to pop, rock, and even country if its musical content was comparable. "We're a safe alternative," he said. "That doesn't make it bland. People say they need an alternative to some of the entertainment that's out there. Well, there is one, it's just not publicized."

The people at EMI Chordant's major label, Sparrow Records, gave me a bunch of CDs to take home, and a lot of it, like the slick L.A. pop of Steven Curtis Chapman or the melodic rock of the Newsboys, turned out to be tuneful and well produced but a little preachy for my tastes. Most memorable was Carman, Christian music's answer to Garth, whose scary, unsmiling face posed against a blue flag with a bloodred cross evoked images of guys who took AK-47s to abortion clinics. Carman had sold over six million albums and five bestselling videos, including *Revival in the Land* and *Addicted to Jesus.* I listened to Carman's *The Standard.* The first song on it was sort of a Caribbean-conga-rap number in which Carman repeatedly bopped out, "Tell me who's in the house?" and the audience was supposed to respond by yelling back: "J.C., " as in Jesus Christ. Here's a typical lyric from the last song, "America Again":

> *We eliminated God from the equation of American life.*
> *Thus eliminating the reason this nation first began.*
> *From beyond the grave I hear the voices*
> *of our Founding Fathers plead*
> *You need God in America Again*

I figured I'd stick with the Tractors.

Before leaving I met Billy Ray Hearn, another good Baylor Baptist, who was kind of the godfather of big-time Christian music and the chairman of the EMI Christian Music Group. Hearn, now sixty-seven, had started out as the music minister at a church in Thomasville, Georgia. In 1968 he joined Word records, a little Christian record company in Waco, where he started a contemporary Christian label called Myrrh in 1972. He moved to California, started Sparrow in 1976, moved his company to Nashville, where everyone else in Christian music was, in 1991, and then sold out to EMI for untold millions. "This music is everywhere," he said happily. "Everywhere but New York City. They're so inward and self-contained that they never think there's anything in the world they don't know about. Well, New York doesn't know about a lot of things."

New York also didn't know about the group BR5-49, the kings of Lower Broadway, but everyone in Nashville did. They were fresh enough to make you believe that despite all the saccharine country fatheads on the radio and the creeping Carmanization of America there was still hope.

If the South has one foot in the past and one in the present, downtown Nashville is metaphor turned to flesh. Just a few years ago it was a seedy, atmospheric losers' lounge of old brick warehouses, cheap pawn-shops, cheesy clubs frequented by winos and tourists, along with glorious fading Nashville institutions like Gruhn Guitars, the Ernest Tubb Record Shop, and Tootsie's Orchid Lounge, the most famous of the ancient downtown clubs.

But as country took off, so finally did downtown Nashville. First came a few yupped-up restaurants and galleries. Then the Ryman Auditorium reopened. At the same time Gaylord invested $7.5 million in the Wildhorse Saloon, which immediately became a country version of the Roseland Ballroom crossed with American Bandstand. Before long, the old Phillips and Quarles Hardware Store was a Hard Rock Café and the old Alamo Furniture was a Planet Hollywood. In 1994, I had wandered into Toby Carr's Music, next to Tootsie's, where Carr sold his fringed white boots, oversized beaverskin hats, banjos, and guitars. "Nashville hates the old *Hee Haw* hillbilly image," he said with a scowl. "When they talk about history, they don't care about the music that made Nashville, all they want to preserve down here is the bricks. It could be wall-to-wall sushi bars for all they care."

Two years later there were two sushi bars, two microbreweries, and an upscale country-and-western transvestite cabaret called Cowboys LaCage. But there was no longer a Toby Carr's Music. The old winos were mixing with German tourists and families from Topeka, and a local historian named Jim Summerville was arguing that Second Avenue, the heart of downtown, should be removed from the National Register of Historic Places because developers were demolishing or defacing beyond recognition all the old buildings that the designation was based on. It had all the makings of yet another Central Tourist District of old bricks and new neon, and you had to figure that, particularly once Nashville's new $100-million sports arena was completed around the corner from the dingiest of the remaining dives, most of the gritty raunch was pretty much doomed.

But–amazingly–amid the neon and glitz, ragged, raunchy flowers were blooming. Tootsie's–where the decor was thousands of old, faded eight-by-ten glossy publicity photos of every star and never-was who ever toted a guitar along Broadway or sang an off-key version of "I Walk the Line"–had been going downhill for years. Over time it had become a caricature of itself where British tourists in Confederate flag

T-shirts and Billy Ray Cyrus baseball caps listened to faceless pickers wheezing out old Willie Nelson songs. But as the new downtown germinated, somehow the old one did too.

Tootsie's backroom in the fifties and sixties was like a private club for Nashville's songwriters and the country stars who played at the Ryman, which backed up to it. They'd walk across the alley from the Ryman to Tootsie's and hang out in a dingy backroom where Tootsie plied them with homemade stew and drinks. Now, the backroom had been reopened as a dive within a dive, sort of Nashville meets Berlin. There was a filthy linoleum floor that probably still had Lefty Frizzell's stew stains, a ceiling with a quarter of the old dingy tiles missing, and pictures on the walls that tended more toward T. O. Hogan, Rich Muth, and Slim Chance and the Convicts than Vince Gill or Garth Brooks. Holding court on stage was a singer named Greg Garing, a tall, gaunt figure with stringy blond hair who had become a cult figure locally with his mix of blues, bluegrass, and rockabilly, half overheated retro-country, half brooding rootsy hybrid.

Even better was Robert's Western World, which had somehow metamorphosed into the hippest thing in town. Also known as Three Doors Down, because it was three doors down from Tootsie's, Robert's back in the 1950s housed the Show-Bud steel guitar factory. In the recent past it had been and still was a Western-wear store where dusty old boxes of Justin boots, fancy Stetsons, and $12.95 Arlop straw hats lined the walls.

But its owner, Robert Moore, a few years back had put up a rickety little stage with a ratty blue rug at the front, installed a bar festooned with laminated pictures of country stars and assorted low lifes, and begun selling beer, one-dollar hot dogs, two-fifty chili dog plates, beef jerky, Bayer Aspirin, and Goody's Headache Powder. Behind the stage was a painted mural of Patsy Cline, Ernest Tubb, Marty Stuart, Dolly Parton, Hank Williams, Jr., and Roy Acuff. Ancient fans drooping from the black molded-copper ceiling swept the moist air. Neon beer signs and assorted goofy pictures, like the one of four fat golfers from Wisconsin in shorts, adorned the walls. Ancient bar stools with sunflower patterns, mix-and-match Formica tables and metal chairs, glorious turquoise booths, assorted old trophies, and enough smoke to leave you coughing for weeks fleshed out the decorative theme. In the attic above, although almost no one knew it, sweaty fighters managed by Robert jumped rope, shadow-boxed, and pounded punching bags amid old kitchen fixtures, plastic pipe, and stacks of wood in a makeshift boxing gym.

The main attraction was BR5-49, whose name came from a constantly flubbed phone number in a famous *Hee Haw* skit the rotund comic Junior Samples used to do about an inept car dealer who'd be hawking his wares while the bumpers were falling off or the tires were going flat. The members of the group were five guys ranging in age from twenty-five to thirty-five who dressed in Salvation Army Western wear or hillbilly overalls, played four-hour sets for tips without a break every night from Wednesday through Saturday, and just sang and played holy hell out of a mix of old country, Western swing, and rockabilly songs by assorted legends and geezers, most of them from the forties and fifties, like Johnny Horton, Webb Pierce, Ferlin Huskey, Hank Williams, Bob Wills, Lefty Frizzell, and Jimmie Rogers.

I sat at the door a few nights and watched people walk in. They invariably gave a dazed smile and their jaws dropped to the floor as if they'd walked into a turbocharged time warp of an imagined Nashville from forty years ago. The boys would be wailing out Hank Williams's "Setting the Woods on Fire," Carl Perkins's "Lend Me Your Comb," Bob Wills's "Time Changes Everything," Johnny Horton's "Ole Slew Foot," or Webb Pierce's "I Ain't Never" with the energy of punk rockers who'd decided to fish in another musical pond. The place would be full of Vanderbilt fraternity boys and their dates; old truckers and street veterans like Buddy Shupe, a retired coal miner who came by his Virginia Black Lung Association baseball cap honestly; and Music Row bigwigs and musicians like Marty Stuart, Chet Atkins, or Trisha Yearwood. Some of them grew up on this stuff, and some of them wouldn't know Hank Williams from Hank Aaron, but they all seemed equally entranced. For most of my life, I would have been as interested in hearing cats screeching at night as listening to Ferlin Huskey or Webb Pierce, but it struck me as just about the coolest place I'd ever been.

It wasn't the marketing geniuses on Music Row trying to thread country radio's needle or the slick country pageant at Opryland, but the real deal, the most American music on earth played with berserk, merry abandon. BR5-49 had a repertoire of four hundred songs, famous, original, or utterly obscure, but they pretty much could and did play anything. If someone called for "El Paso," Marty Robbins's endless, forlorn chestnut, they'd shake the tip jar and finally start singing when they got a few contributions. If someone called for cowboy yodeling, Chuck Mead, one of the two guitarists and lead singers, would deadpan "Okay, it's your funeral," and oblige.

One evening I went next door with them to eat at Jack's Bar-B-Que. They turned out to be five heartland boys who gravitated to Nashville as naturally as a hog to a mud wallow. The two guitarists and lead singers were Mead, from Lawrence, Kansas, who had a quick wit and the square-faced good looks of the big-timers over at Opryland, and Gary Bennett from Cougar, Washington, who had more of a Depression-era dust bowl quality. The one in the overalls was Don Heron, a whiz on fiddle, dobro, lap steel guitar, and mandolin, from Moundsville, West Virginia, via South Plains College in Levelland, Texas; he was small, blond, and thin with an endearingly ingenuous starstruck quality. The drummer, Shaw Wilson from Topeka, Kansas, had slicked-back black hair, a pencil-thin mustache, and the dark, vaguely ominous, smoky good looks of a 1940s matinee idol. Smilin' Jay McDowell from Lafayette, Indiana, who was tall and thin with long gangly arms covered with tattoos and who had previously played guitar for a band called Hellbilly, played stand-up bass.

For now they were basically workaday stiffs having the time of their lives playing for tips at Robert's and making enough to pay the rent and afford food and gas for their old clunkers but not enough to buy a new set of tires. But every record label in Nashville was looking at them, and everyone knew they were the hottest thing in town. Two years from now they could be millionaires or they could still be working stiffs at Robert's. All the Music Row folks sniffing around asked themselves the same questions. First, how much would this stuff translate outside the atmospheric time capsule at Robert's? Second, if country radio would never play this stuff, how were they going to sell records? The BR5s knew all that but were having too much fun to worry about it.

"I'm not the greatest player in the world, but I sure like what I'm doing," said Chuck. We were sitting upstairs at Jack's while a bluegrass band played at the other end of the room. "We didn't come here because we wanted to become big hillbilly stars. I just came down here because the music drew me here. I wanted to be near the spirit of it. I wanted to get the feel of this street. There are so many jaded people in this town. I mean unbelievably jaded people because of what people come here for and what they expect to happen. Well, we never had any expectations except to get to play and have a good time. We're not a contrived act putting on goofy suits because some manager is trying to market us. We love this stuff, and we really hope the grittiness that's around now is going to survive. When we first got here it was a shit-hole, but, man, was it cool. We just hope some of the real honky-tonks can exist with the sushi bars that are coming in. They're already talking of tearing down the stuff across the street, tearing down the Ernest Tubb Record Shop. What would they do that for? It's sacred. They even tried to tear down the Ryman, which is the most incredible thing in the world. They would all burn in hell forever if they did that. And they should. They should burn in hell for even thinking about it."

We talked until it was almost time for their show, and then hung out in the alley behind the Ryman, hoping to catch a few breaths of an early evening breeze. "People ask me what we'll be doing in ten years if this doesn't work out," said Gary from underneath his moth-eaten Hank Williams–style hat. "And I say, 'We'll be doing just what we're doing right now.' Why wouldn't we? This is like being in a really great movie, and it never goes off."

The last night I was in town they were doing a showcase–an invitation-only performance–for none other than Tim DuBois and the folks at Arista. In true Lower Broadway fashion, the invitation-only business was pretty much waived, and the room soon filled up with the Arista crowd and whoever walked in off the street. Most of the Arista types looked to be in their thirties and forties, with the hip, breezy, confident, hey-this-thing-just-might-work air of folks who knew they were playing on the A team in a hot league. Tim sat at the first table in front of the stage, wearing a short-sleeved knit shirt in a diamond pattern, his usual loafers and dark socks, sipping a Miller Lite. Next to him a guy stood videotaping the proceedings for further review.

For a while, Tim sat watching with a half smile and furrowed brow, sometimes stroking his chin as if pondering a really enticing riddle. But as the show went on, you could see he was just enjoying himself, smiling at the dumb patter ("Ladies and gentlemen, it's been a business doing pleasure with you . . .") and then grinning from ear to ear as they ripped through a hells bells version of "Red Hot," originally recorded by Billy Riley on Sun Records, with its immortal lyric, "My gal is red hot; your gal ain't doodly squat." When it was over, after Chuck did his seriocomic begging for tips, Tim walked up to Chuck, shook his hand, and handed him two twenties. I couldn't tell if it meant, "I really love what you guys do, but I don't think I can make this work," or "I really love what you guys do. Let's talk."

Even though they were completely wrong for country radio, I should have realized it was the latter. Clearly, the BR5s had it: great music, a funny, retro-hip stage presence, and a concept so wrong it was utterly right for the times. They had metamorphosed into exactly the kind of corny Nashville success story that never comes true, only this time it did. I called Tim a few weeks later, and he said he was going to try to sign them. "There's a uniqueness there that you can't deny, like the Tractors," he said. "I try really hard never to pigeonhole anything, and I'd be lying if I said I honestly know how to do this, but the passion's there within my staff and within me for what these guys are doing." As things turned out, either the group were so good or the country-hunk zeitgeist was so stale that almost everyone in Nashville—but not Tony Brown at MCA—tried to sign them. No fools, they signed with Arista.

I came back about six weeks later for their signing party at Robert's. The place was packed with a crowd that included Chuck Mead's mom and dad from Kansas, who recorded the scene on their camcorder; the Arista crowd; minor luminaries like Manuel, Clothier to the Stars, Nashville's wizard of rhinestone-studded, outrageous country couture; and assorted Robert's regulars, Nashville press types, Lower Broadway veterans, and downtown musicians.

Even in the short time I'd been gone, a lot had changed. There was a new McDonald's on Second Avenue, the ratty T-shirt shop down from Tootsie's had closed, and the new half-finished sports arena had progressed to become a huge steel giant looming over the pygmy brick buildings on Broadway. At Robert's, Robert had painted the walls, had begun selling liquor as well as beer, and had replaced the cruddy old photographs with assorted ephemera, including a big framed picture of himself in front of a truck. And he was already touting BR5-49's anointed successor, a group called Brasilbilly. Its lead singer, named Jesse Lee Jones, had grown up in São Paulo speaking Portuguese and listening to Hank Williams and Marty Robbins. They weren't half bad, either.

The BR5s seemed a little different, too. Jay wore a natty tweed jacket instead of his old T-shirts, Don and Shaw had on crisp new shirts, and most of them, even ol' Don, the starstruck kid from West Virginia, waltzed in with hot, young, rail-thin dames on their arms. They climbed on chairs outside to pose under the big ROBERT'S WESTERN WORLD BR5-49 sign out front, exchanged Robert's boots and Arista baseball caps with Tim for the cameras, and then ripped through a truncated but fabulous little set highlighted by a rousing rendition of Johnny Horton's "Cherokee Boogie" and a hilariously deadpan version of the Farmer Boys' "Humdinger," the least erotic love song ever written.

Given the prevailing winds downtown, it had the bittersweet air of something ending more than something beginning. But out on the street the old electric sign was still spinning around in front of the Ernest Tubb Record Shop, the winos were out in force in front of the Turf Club, Heilig Meyers Furniture was aglow under the street-lights, and on this night at least, the grimy, ancestral rhythms of the old Nashville were holding their own against the slick big-bucks hum of the new Music City machine. You hoped it would stay that way forever.

Chapter 10

MISSISSIPPI I
Highway 61 Revisited

T HERE'S ANOTHER STREAM OF SOUTHERN MUSIC THAT HAS ALL BUT dried up, the radical-populist protest songs personified by Woody Guthrie's spare, gritty Okie odes to the working people of another time. One of his last, fervent disciples was Phil Ochs, a Yankee who grew up on Southern music. Ochs rose to prominence in the early sixties, paid homage to Guthrie on his deathbed in New York City, and went on to develop a memorable voice of his own, inspired in equal parts by the Southern spirits of Guthrie, Hank Williams, and Faron Young and the anti-Southern currents of the protest music of the civil rights era. Ochs had some significant success for a few years and then saw his career go downhill; his health broke down, his idealism corroded into cynicism, and he turned to alcohol. He never fully recovered his voice after his vocal chords were damaged when he was attacked while traveling in Africa; he hanged himself in 1976 at the age of thirty-five.

In 1964 he was part of a caravan of liberal musicians who traveled through Mississippi, scanning the audiences for potential assassins as they sang. That was back when the face of the South was Ross Barnett and George Wallace, not Garth Brooks and Reba McEntire, and no place was more Southern than Mississippi. One product of that period was a bleak, bitter rant he wrote called "Here's to the State of Mississippi." A typical verse went like this:

> For underneath her borders the Devil draws no line
> If you drag her muddy rivers nameless bodies you will find
> And the fat trees of the forest have hid a thousand crimes

And the calendar is lying when it reads the present time,
Here's to the land you've torn out the heart of
Mississippi find yourself another country to be part of.

I've been to Mississippi dozens of times, to Jackson and Jonestown, Mendenhall and McComb, Biloxi and Belzoni, and invariably that song pops into my head, not as a reflection of what is but as a memory of how the South was perceived not so long ago. I can't help but wonder what Ochs would think if he were around today and realized that instead of finding another country to be part of, Mississippi and its neighbors had instead managed to dominate this one. Maybe he saw it coming.

In the summer of 1995, the summer of OJ, I decided I'd drive across Mississippi, beginning in the great Delta, which William Faulkner's Issac McCasklin describes as a region

> where white men rent farms and live like niggers, and niggers crop on shares and live like animals, where cotton is planted and grows man-tall in the very cracks of the sidewalks, and usury and mortgage and bank-ruptcy and measureless wealth, Chinese and African and Aryan and Jew, all breed and spawn together until no man has time to say which one is which and no one cares.

The Delta of the blues greats Son House, Robert Johnson, Muddy Waters, and B.B. King; of Early Wright on WROX in Clarksdale playing the blues, plugging the Meat House or Dip's Drive-in Laundromat and reporting on who is about to be funeralized at the True Bibleway Church of Jesus Christ on Dr. Martin Luther King Boulevard. The Delta, where Dr. King, who had seen everything the South had to offer, wept bitter tears in 1966 when he saw the soul-crushing poverty in Marks, which was no different than the poverty in Tchula or Falcon, Ruleville, Choctaw, Glendora, Arcola, or a hundred other Delta towns. The Delta of Bruno Fava's all-Bruno shopping plaza—Bruno's Coin-Op, Bruno's Quick-Mart, and Bruno's Package Store—in Alligator, where every young stud who goes on to play football at Ole Miss is, of course, automatically dubbed "Gator." The Delta, where fifteen thousand years of flooding by the Mississippi and Yazoo rivers have deposited layer upon layer of moist, black soil, a planter's paradise of 7,110 square miles of the richest farmland on earth, where most of the inhabitants are the poorest people in America. The Delta of what the writer Ellen Gilchrist called "million volt a minute sunlight," of endless, tabletop-flat vistas of cotton, of sibilant bayous still as death in the early evening heat, and of cedar swamps covered in a green, still, primordial ooze. The Delta whose physicality led Eudora Welty to write: "In the Delta, most of the world seemed sky, but it shimmered like the wing of a lighted dragonfly." The Delta that's still such a presence that people always talk of going "into the Delta" as if the place should have border guards and crossing gates.

If Mississippi is the South's South, the Delta is Mississippi's Mississippi. There the gap between the gleaming white plantation homes of the planters and the cinder-block hovels and tar-paper shacks of the poor seem starker, the currents of life denser and muddier, the burden of race heavier than anywhere else in America. Described once as "cotton obsessed, Negro obsessed and flood ridden...the deepest South," the Delta is a place where even the names of the cities, counties, and streams–Tallahatchie and Hushpuckeena; Issaqueena, Itta Bena, and Yazoo; Rattlesnake Bayou and Quiver River–hang in the moist, hot air like tantalizing, dark riddles.

Still, even during the darkest days of the sixties it dawned on a few people that maybe even Mississippi wasn't entirely a place apart. Once, when Ochs finished his bitter salute to Mississippi, Dave Van Ronk, another prominent folksinger of the time, spread his arms, drink in hand, and shouted at him, "Philly, I'm trying to tell you. Why single out Mississippi from the other forty-nine? It's just as bad down the block as it is across the river." I'm not sure that many black people would have made quite that case in 1964. James C. Cobb gets it right in the title of his 1992 book on the Delta, *The Most Southern Place on Earth,* but he takes pains to point out in the end that it's a pretty American one as well. "Behind the seductive and disarming Old South facade of the Delta," he wrote, "the American Dream had been not so much perverted as simply pursued to its ultimate realization in a setting where human and natural resources could be exploited to the fullest with but little regard for social or institutional restraint."

My plan was to drive through the Delta, to Jackson, and then circuitously down to the Gulf Coast to see what I'd see. I flew to Memphis, rented a big white Buick, and headed south on Highway 61, past the used-car lots, check-cashing stores, pawnshops and flea markets, past the convenience stores selling minnows, bait, and crickets and the ragged strip shopping centers south of town. I was headed toward Mississippi, but the Delta jumped up like an overeager blue tick hound before I even left Tennessee. It wasn't quite Yoknapatawpha redux.

JUMBO SIZE CASINO THRILLS—CIRCUS CIRCUS CASINO CENTER, read the first billboard I saw. Others followed in dizzying profusion. COMING SOON, *THE NEW BALLY'S*. SHERATON CASINO—FOR THE THRILL OF IT. 3 BUCKS + 3 DUCKS EQUALS MISSISSIPPI'S NEXT MILLIONAIRE. THE DUCK STOPS HERE—FITZGERALD'S. This profusion of gambling come-ons was not utterly unexpected. For the past three years, Mississippi had been in the midst of a mad dash toward legalized gambling that had made the state, for once, something of an economic pacesetter. It had sprouted twenty-seven casinos, which generated $128 million in state tax revenues and had turned Mississippi into the third-largest gambling center in the United States, behind Las Vegas and Atlantic City. Tunica County alone, the location of all the establishments touted on the billboards, had almost half the casino floor space of Atlantic City, and boosters hoped it was just the start of yet another Southern resort heaven, like Branson or Myrtle Beach, but built around gambling and golf instead of country music and golf (Branson) or the beach, country music, and golf (Myrtle Beach).

It will take a lot more than a few years of gambling to magically transform Mississippi, which still has the second-lowest median income in the nation, behind only West Virginia. It remains a place where one in three children lives in poverty, where the percentage of households without telephones or indoor plumbing is twice the national average, and where more than one in five babies are born to teenaged mothers. But, for once, Mississippi was leading in some more positive economic indices as well. One study a year earlier had found its economy growing faster than any state in the nation. Per capita income in the nineties had risen three times as fast as the national average. Given Mississippi's bottom-of-the-barrel history, these were findings roughly as predictable as ones proclaiming New York City to be the most polite city in the country, and the cleanest to boot.

Still, only the most perverse and fanciful blending of the sensibilities of William Faulkner and Quentin Tarantino could have dreamed up the notion of the Mississippi Delta as a sun-baked Dixie Vegas. Tunica County, the northernmost outpost of Mississippi's emerging republic of

family values, conservative politics, Caribbean stud poker, and slots
without end, for decades had ranked at the very bottom of the poorest
counties in the country; when Jesse Jackson came to Tunica's infamous
"Sugar Ditch," named for the open sewer that ran through it, and
dubbed it "America's Ethiopia," no one argued. When the Lower Mississippi Development Commission surveyed the 214 counties in its
study area in 1990, Tunica was the poorest of all, with 53 percent of the
population living below the poverty level, the highest percentage in the
country. In the mid-1980s, one in four families were still living without
indoor plumbing, 70 percent of residents over the age of twenty-five
had no high school diploma, the county had the nation's eighth-highest
infant mortality rate and fourth-highest percentage of births to teenage
mothers. Though periodic stabs of damning publicity produced fitful
progress like the new federal housing replacing the infamous slums
along Sugar Ditch, most of the Delta slumbered as ever in a surreal sort
of hyperpoverty of tin-roof shacks with rats as big as possums chewing
through the ancient linoleum floors, and ghostlike towns, their main
streets as quiet as an empty funeral parlor, slouching and stooping their
way toward a long, slow death.

Periodically, politicians would make loud noises about reviving the
Delta, like the time the young, mediagenic, up-and-coming, Ivy League
Democratic governors of Louisiana, Mississippi, and Arkansas met on a
barge on the river in 1988 to warble sweet nothings to the television
cameras about economic redevelopment. Since then Buddy Roemer of
Louisiana had become a New Age Republican knocked out of office by
Klansman David Duke and wheeler-dealer Edwin Edwards; Ray Mabus
of Mississippi had been bounced out of office by Kirk Fordice, a neo-
Dixiecrat at a time when Southern dinosaurs could run honestly as
Republicans; and Bill Clinton of Arkansas had moved to Washington,
where he was last seen at the center of his ongoing presidential soap
opera.

And yet, no thanks to the "Barge Compact," here in the summer of
1995 you could tool down Highway 61 past Lynchburg, Walls, and
Glover, hang a right on the spanking new four-lane access road, and,
boom, there like a mirage in front of you was a gleaming slice of Vegas.
Side by side by side, baking in the sun in a treeless field, were Circus
Circus, with its festive pink, white, yellow, and tan big top design; the
Horseshoe Casino Hotel, with its exploding horseshoe decorative motif;

and the sophisticated continental decor of the Sheraton Casino, with its European chalet design of stone facing, spiked turquoise spires, and Renaissance-style murals of fair damsels cavorting with bears, squirrels, and deer. I parked next to a red Dodge pickup with Tennessee plates, one bumper sticker reading GOLD PROSPECTORS ASSOCIATION OF AMERICA, and another, in camouflage style, reading MARINES. I headed straight for the Sheraton chalet.

There is no such thing as an empty casino in America, and sure enough, early on an August Wednesday afternoon in the middle of the Mississippi Delta, with the temperature climbing toward 100, the Sheraton was a madcap vision of American prosperity run amuck punctuated by the lunatic *clank-clank-clank* of coins plopping from slot machines into metal pans and an electronic calliope symphony of bonks, blips, and doodles.

A tour group of senior citizens from St. Louis and Owensboro, Kentucky, trooped off the bus, grabbed their plastic cups, and bolted toward the slots. College boys from Memphis State in Tennessee and Delta State in Mississippi shared blackjack tables with high rollers who had just driven in from Little Rock or Dallas or had flown in private planes to the tiny Twinkletown Airport just north of the casinos. Memphis suburbanites in J. Crew chinos and pastel knit shirts stood shoulder-to-shoulder at the slots next to rheumy-eyed old men in blue jumpsuits and dusty Braves caps. Bored teenagers in Malcolm X T-shirts pushed old black ladies in wheelchairs. Busty cocktail waitresses in sexy paisley outfits with ID tags reading KIMBERLY—OAKLAND, TN. or DEEDRA—MEMPHIS hustled past bored-looking blackjack dealers from Reno who looked as if they had woken up with a hangover and found themselves playing AA casino ball in rural Mississippi. "Ain't nothing to do in Tutweiler," said W. C. Willis, a seventy-seven-year-old black man who had lived his whole life in the Delta. He was feeding nickels into the slots and plotting strategy with his fellow Tutweileran Lucinda Buchanan, who was moving from machine to machine looking for the one with the right feel. "We come here twice a week, spend a little money, have a good time. Sometimes you win. Sometimes you don't, but it gives some people jobs, and some people something to do, so I can't see no harm in it."

Maybe. The censorious liberal in me was more likely to see gambling as money being taken from the Willises and Buchanans of the world, sucking the life out of local businesses, and providing a quick fix almost certain to collapse of its own weight as every town in America tried to get rich on casinos. Indeed, the first wave of casinos in Tunica County had already closed, beaten out by the new crop closer to Memphis.

I figured the least I could do would be to try to beat the lords of casinoland in a penny ante way by defying the first rule of gambling: the house always wins because most suckers play until they lose. I bought ten dollars' worth of quarters and set up shop at a quarter machine next to Buchanan. I hit a few quarters here or there, moved to another machine on the next row, and before long hit a big ten-dollar jackpot. I played five more quarters, and then, sneering in the face of temptation, took my $8.75 in winnings and strode triumphantly out of the casino and into the sun.

It doesn't take long to go from casinoland to the real Delta. A half mile down old Highway 61, the new highway's semideserted precursor, is the town of Robinsonville, which sits like an abandoned movie set, its streets empty, its stores boarded up, new graffiti the only sign that life in some form still goes on. Down the street a dozen or so black men, women, and children sat on the stoops of frame houses that listed to the side like drunks in the rain and gray cinder-block boxes that looked more like chicken coops than homes. One woman wearing a green bathrobe with pink curlers in her hair sat cleaning okra and shelling peas. Shirtless men sat sipping on malt liquor, kids drank Cokes, and wary-faced teenage mothers leaned against the door frames from which hung forlorn shreds of tattered screens. The Delta is approximately two-hundred miles long and, at its widest point, seventy miles across, and you can find a scene like this in almost any town you come to, as if an ancient civilization had died out, leaving behind only a desultory colony of black survivors and ramshackle houses and ghost towns baking under the Mississippi sun.

Still, if the casinos had the feel of spaceships full of money that had landed in the midst of the Delta poverty, they also felt weirdly familiar. There has always been plenty of money in the Delta. It's just that none of it has ever belonged to the black people who lived there. Before the Civil War, Bolivar, Coahoma, Issaquena, and Tunica counties were among the thirty-six wealthiest counties in the United States, most of the wealth accounted for in the form of slaves. After Reconstruction, when sharecropping replaced slavery, the old system simply reconstituted itself, the planters becoming richer than ever before and the sharecroppers living pretty much the way they always had. Even now, Tunica County is said to have at least thirty millionaires, and the incorporated town of Tunica, which is 74 percent white, is full of handsome homes and estates owned by prosperous whites. The casinos had the feel of the most baroque of post–civil rights plantations, where people got to work inside and where everyone from the most regal planter to the lowliest field hand was equally welcome to do his bit for the balance sheet of whatever giant corporation was running the show.

In truth, many of the local blacks were too poorly educated or too poorly motivated to get jobs at the casinos and there was an ongoing battle over the county board of supervisors' original reluctance to give any of their casino revenues to the local schools, which ranked 152nd out of 153 on a statewide literacy exam in a state with perhaps the worst schools in America. But if some of the local preachers and do-gooders looked askance, most people seemed to see the casinos as the greatest thing to hit in years. Just outside Tunica, in a neighborhood of new trailers and ancient shacks down the street from an equipment depot for farm machinery, I found Michael Williams, Sandy McGee, and Tony Dixon drinking Busch beers in the midday sun. Michael and Tony were sitting outside, and Sandy was in the backseat of a big gold-colored Oldsmobile. Michael and Tony were eighteen and made $6.75 an hour as dishwashers at the casinos. Sandy was twenty-eight and made a princely $9.50 as a casino security guard. "It's a hell of a lot better than sitting on top of a John Deere tractor in the middle of August in Tunica, Mississippi," he said contentedly.

Even without the gambling, the Delta had the hallucinatory sense of being exotic and familiar at the same time. As rising economic inequality separated the haves from the have-nots nationwide, the Delta was America's most grandiose laboratory for a world of rich and poor and nothing in between. At a time when racial division was becoming increasingly ingrained in the nation's fabric, the Delta had become a place where the ghettos were not just neighborhoods, but whole towns. One geographer at the University of Tennessee described them as rural ghettos–virtually all-black poverty enclaves like urban ghettos characterized by the same sort of economic disinvestment, white flight, and an economy based on government transfer payments.

In fact, if the small towns of the Delta looked like the remains of a

vanished civilization, it's because it was true. The whites who had all
the Delta's wealth had been leaving ever since the schools integrated,
taking most of the resources with them and leaving only the black poor
behind. Glendora was 50 percent black in 1950, 90 percent black in
1990; Alligator, 54 percent in 1950, 75 percent in 1990; Jonestown, 66
percent in 1950, 95 percent in 1990; Benoit, 47 percent in 1950, 77 percent in 1990; Sledge, 19 percent in 1950, 56 percent in 1990; Crenshaw,
50 percent in 1950, 77 percent in 1990; Arcola, 57 percent in 1950, 84
percent in 1990, Friars Point, 66 percent in 1950, 90 percent in 1990.

In Jonestown, where a gin and a cotton seed mill outside the old
business district were prospering because of cotton's resurgence over
the past decade, the town still had the same neutron-bomb look of the
rest of the Delta. On Main Street were a bank with an all-white staff,
city hall, two dog-eared eateries, and a food market, but much of downtown was either boarded up or reduced to rubble. Around the corner
was the most visible link with the old order, Q&B Used Furniture,
where Quincy Bryant and his half brother Ray Bryant were helping to
load an old yellow sofa into the back of Bertha Eades's creaky white
Buick station wagon before returning to their dusty recliners to watch
Elvis Presley in *Shiloh*. "It's Elvis Presley Week in this part of the
country," Quincy, the Boss Hogg at Q&B, announced. Back up
Highway 61, in Memphis, the faithful were gathering at Graceland by
the tens of thousands to pray, mourn, commune, and bear witness to
the memory of the once and future King on the anniversary of his
death, on August 16, 1977.

Q&B was painted a faded Indian red with a brown wood awning, a
heavy burglar-proof steel door, and a sign out front reading ELECT
SCOTTY MEREDITH CORONER. An ancient high chair sat by the front door
like the perch of some baby who had vaporized in the sun forty years
ago which no one had gotten around to bringing back inside. Inside
was a great gaggle of random merchandise that had not so much accumulated as accreted over the years. By the register were jars and displays of Milky Way and Snickers candy bars, Jujy Fruits, jaw breakers
and Big League Chew gum that attracted a random trickle of black kids
who browsed attentively and then paid politely after chatting amiably
with Quincy. Throughout the rest of the store were scattered Marx
Brothers, John Wayne, and Mighty Morphin Power Rangers posters;
pantyhose, styling gel, and yellow cling sliced peaches; toy Humvee

military vehicles, butter churns, and super maxi pads. Q&B specials included the plastic floral arrangements Quincy's wife had made by hand and a grand array of baseball caps from the West Point Auto Mart in West Point, Kentucky, and RC Drywall in Frankfort, Kentucky, not to mention the used sofas, recliners, and bedding in the adjacent furniture shop.

Quincy was wearing a white shirt, dark slacks, white socks, and black loafers and was smoking his Marlboros in a calm, meditative way. He had thick dark hair, gray at the roots, and his wife Nell's name tattooed onto his right forearm. He had been in business at the same location since 1958, back when Jonestown bustled with four grocery stores, a drug store, two dry goods stores, and three car lots. One by one all the whites and a handful of Chinese-Americans had left, but he was still there spending his days rattling on about the heat or an aunt's recent illness with his steady trickle of black customers in the compulsive sort of Southern amity that doesn't so much transcend race as ignore it.

Quincy had been saved right there at the store in 1972, not long after reading the pamphlet *Second Judas*. As a Christian, he didn't have much use for the casinos and had never set foot in one, but like a lot of people in the Delta, he found it hard to totally dump on something that was providing hundreds of jobs in a region with nothing else. "They're taking food out of the mouths of children," he said. "People go and gamble their paycheck and they've got nothing left. I can see in my store people who suddenly can't make their payments and I know the money's gone to the boats. But then I also know at least five people who got off welfare and are working on the boats. Now, I could eat free, but I've never been in one. Just not interested. But I've got a brother who goes and him and his wife won twenty-seven hundred at Lady Luck. Now, how much he lost, I don't know."

Some more black kids came in and he chatted with them about their lawnmowing business and the beginning of school that week. "They're good kids, mostly," he said, turning his attention back to Elvis Week, "but no one who wasn't here already would open a business like this. My kids don't want it. When I'm gone, it's gone too."

On Main Street I stopped by Donal Barnett's Jonestown Service Station. He was a forty-five-year-old black man whose cinder-block office was another hopeless jumble of tools, books, Delta necessities like Black Flag Flying Insect Killer and accumulated junk. But he was one of those wonders who had made the worst of the Delta work. He and his wife, Lavorn, came to work every morning at 5:30 and began the day by cleaning up candy wrappers, cigarette butts, liquor bottles, dead snakes, and any other debris on Main Street. His five kids were either serving as sergeants in the army, studying computers at college, finishing up high school, or working successfully out of state. We talked politics a little—he'd probably hold his nose and vote for Clinton. But, like a lot of thoughtful people, he was looking for a post–civil rights ethic somewhere between Republican social Darwinism and Democratic paternalism. When I had first met him a few years earlier, he had been pretty pessimistic. "People have to take responsibility for the community they live in," he said then. "I don't see that here. If businesses came here and people aren't responsible enough to work, you're not going to get anywhere. You have too many people waiting for the welfare checks. If you were lying in bed, and someone kept bringing you food, so you never had to get up, what would you do? You'd probably just lie there too."

This time he was a little more optimistic. The liquor store where kids had hung out on Main Street had closed, there was a bit more sense of parental concern. "It's maybe a little better. My big thing now is trying to get this softball field built for the kids. It's probably gonna take another year before we get it leveled off, and I just got a new leg, so I've been a little slow lately." He'd gone out three or four times to pump gas, and I'd never noticed his limp, which he took as a compliment. On the casinos he was agnostic too. "A lot of the people gambling there were gambling at home before. The difference is they can gamble in a cleaner and nicer place where they probably won't get shot and killed when they go out the door."

For three days I wandered around the Delta taking in the elegant swoops and dives of the crop dusters, the impeccable geometry of the cotton fields, the dada sculpture of the kudzu—here a dragon that's eaten most of a barn, there a giant bunny growing out of what was left of a grove of oaks. At night, I'd faithfully tune in the famous blues and gospel show—two hours of each—that Early Wright had been broadcasting from Clarksdale for the past forty-seven years. Punctuating the blues of Bobby Rush, Buddy Guy, Robert Cray, and B.B. King would be his improvised soliloquies on the virtues of his advertisers, all wondrous places with aisles so wide two people could shop at the same time, female meat cutters who were A's instead of B's, or friendly help who were nice from the cash register to the meat box. Just as on Tony Brown's *Rhythm Country and Blues* album, it was hard to miss how much the music of the blacks of the Delta and the whites of Nashville had in common, and after a while I found myself listening to some of the blues lyrics ("Drop that zero, get yourself a hero") and imagining them as country songs.

It was 100 degrees every day and unusually humid, so hot even by Mississippi standards that they were talking of power outages in Jackson and the corn had already shriveled up into a sickly witch's gold color in the fields. It was the kind of heat that William Styron described when he attended William Faulkner's funeral after Faulkner's death near Oxford on July 6, 1962, heat "like a small mean death itself, as if one were being smothered to extinction in a damp woolen overcoat." I had always thought of the vogue for bottled water as a yuppie affectation—like women wearing their tennis shoes to walk from their car to their office in Atlanta. But you could feel the heat even in your air-conditioned car, so I drove around buying bottled water—Abite Springs, Evian, Pure American, Kentwood, Naya, White Rock, Meridian, Grayson, Ozarka, Avalon—like a pilgrim in a desert, and then tossed the plastic bottles into a heap on the floor of the backseat.

I stopped by the all-black town of Mound Bayou. It was founded in 1887 by the freed slaves from the Hurricane Plantation owned by Jefferson Davis's older brother, Joseph. Joseph Davis had been influenced by the utopian theories of Robert Owen and was one of the few slave owners to educate his slaves. The massive redbrick city hall with an elaborate woodcarving of African-American heroes was probably the most impressive small-town public building in the Delta, but most of it was dark and empty, a victim of a financial crisis a few years back that left the city more than a million dollars in the red. The last census had shown the city's population dropping from 2,715 in 1980 to 2,222 in 1990. City officials claimed the magnitude of decline reflected an undercount, but the old boarded-up hospital, ragged shops, and Delta languor left it clear that the argument was over the numbers, not the general tenor of Mound Bayou's economic life.

I drove through Sledge, home of the black country singer Charlie Pride, and skirted the edges of Parchman, Mississippi's infamous state prison that launched a thousand bluesmen and where Elvis's father,

Vernon, was consigned when Elvis was three for altering a four-dollar check from the sale of the family pig to read fourteen dollars. In Darling, on the sides of ramshackle markets like the Shameie and Shashanta Food Mart, named by Leon Phipps for his two daughters, were six-pointed stars with various arcane markings, apparently local gang insignia. My most expressive host, a black teenager wearing black shorts and no shirt, was in Falcon, where I stopped outside Phannies Dresses & Things and the Snappy Sack Grocery to take some notes. He scowled at the white tourist in his big white car venturing into his bruised and battered black world, gave me the finger, and then glared at me and repeatedly humped his pelvis to mimick the sex act as I drove on.

Sometimes, race was so integrated into the fabric of life that it seemed either invisible or benign. In Bobo, just down from a white-columned mansion with two concrete lions guarding the gates, I wandered into a rickety market and beer joint with the standard WE ACCEPT FOOD STAMPS sign out front. There was video poker, a pool table, and an old black-and-white TV on which some lucky contestant had just solved the puzzle, "Black Inverted Heart Playing Card," on *Wheel of Fortune*. A handful of black and white men and women sat almost immobile sipping beers, and the late-afternoon light, filtered through grimy, almost opaque, windows, bathed the place in a soothing yellow-brown haze so that the scene looked like a Delta still life painted by a redneck Rembrandt. It seemed like the most peaceful place on earth.

In Indianola white and black workers got out of their trucks to pick up their lunch at a little stand bearing the sign BARBECUE EXPRESS—IF YOU'RE STARVIN' SEE MARVIN. In Tunica, I ran into the county judge, a white man named Ted Emanuel who was having coffee with the chief sheriff's investigator, another white man named Jesse Powell. I asked Emanuel about the Delta's black congressman, Bennie Thompson, who was reviled as too militant by most whites, who much preferred his predecessor, Mike Espy. Although Emanuel had to get along with blacks to stay in office, he could easily have badmouthed Thompson to me— one white boy to another. Instead, he simply said: "Bennie's doing a good job. He's a fair man working hard for the Delta. A lot of people try to paint him as a racist just because he's black."

But mostly, the scars and jagged edges were still unmistakable. The towns with enough white people to support them all had cafés or restaurants like David's Diner in Shelby (a town the diner owner, David Favi, described as composed of "two hundred whites and twenty-four hundred welfare recipients"), or the Ranchero in Clarksdale, that were designated by custom as white enclaves where a few blacks might filter in, but not many. At Campbell's Famous Bar-B-Q in Tunica, the school picture on the wall showed the white seg academy, the Tunica Institute of Learning, and its eighteen seniors in glittering prom gowns and tuxes. At the Ranchero, one of the classic eateries of the Delta, the walls were jammed with old memorabilia of class photos and football teams, but the world seemed to have ended with integration in the 1970s, and the school photos ended when the schools went black.

In Alligator, about thirty young blacks were milling around at a rest stop on Highway 61, drinking beer and sitting on cars in the early-evening heat. Inside Bruno's Quik Mart were perhaps ten blacks and one sour-faced old white man watching them like a hawk. "I'm eighty years old, and I've been in business sixty-one years," said Bruno Fava. "I used to be over there where all those niggers are now, but the government took the land, so I moved over here. I've been around these lazy, no-good black people for too long. This one over here is deaf and dumb. I 'bout raised him. He's better than most. He can't talk, but least he don't steal. This used to be a nice town, but it's not coming back, and I'll tell you why. They're building that low-income housing, and people in low-income housing are not gonna amount to a damn thing in life. They loaf, live off the fat of the land, don't produce anything. It's a waste of time to try to educate them. They got no goddamn sense."

In Shelby, LaJeune Fullilove was holding down the fort at the local library, housed in the old Yazoo & Mississippi Valley Railroad Station depot. She had a sweeter disposition than Mr. Fava, but the same worldview. She fished out a history of the town's grander days. "To name the 'best' town in the Mississippi Delta would very likely bring on a discussion," it began. "But the writer can say . . . that he has never visited a more prosperous community or one containing a more hospitable and happy people than at Shelby, Bolivar County, Mississippi, the banner cotton center of Bolivar County, and about the wealthiest town in the State for its population." But the prosperity was long gone, and when whites talked about the town, they tended to do it in the past tense. "This town has been going downhill since the schools inte-grated," Mrs. Fullilove said. "Would you send your daughter to school with blacks? It's not something I could do. I just wasn't raised that way."

After only a few days, the Delta felt like a wholly self-contained world, like a fishbowl filled with heat and light instead of water. One morning I drove east from the Delta to Oxford, home of the University of Mississippi. Vast squadrons of dragonflies filled the air and wafted onto my windshield as I sped by. I stopped midway for gas and bottled water at Sunny's Country Store near Batesville, which was a cinder-block building painted in camouflage colors with a big sign out front on a piece of plywood reading HAPPY HOLIDAYS. I asked Ollie Grant, who owned the place, about the sign. "We have a holiday every two months or so, so we just keep the sign up," she said. "It's almost Labor Day, ain't it?"

When I was growing up the University of Mississippi immediately evoked one thing: the riot of September 30, 1962, precipitated by the defiant segregationist rhetoric of Governor Ross Barnett, Mississippi's buffoonish, third-rate version of George Wallace. *The Citizen,* the publi-cation of the segregationist Citizens' Councils of America, hailed the riots brought on by the school's integration as the South's first stand in a new Civil War over states' rights. Of the Kennedys in particular and the national Democrats in general, *The Citizen* thundered: "They have gained no negro votes, for they had them all in the bag already. But they have alienated the South beyond all hope of recovery!... When the histories of our time are written, one fact will stand forth as clear as the warm Southern sunshine on that bright autumn day: The South won at Oxford! And we have just begun to fight."

Since then, Oxford had metamorphosed into one of the last great college towns, with its busy downtown courthouse square, William Faulkner's ghosts at Rowan Oak and a fair-sized writers colony sniffing after them, its fabulous Square Books bookstore and the plantationlike Ole Miss campus with its broad green lawns and old Confederate statu-ary. Most of all, Oxford and Ole Miss had become sort of Bubba Cen-tral during the current golden age of the vogue for studying all things Southern. Just the week before I arrived Oxford had hosted the epochal first-ever, six-day International Conference on Elvis Presley. The modest title of the gathering was "In Search of Elvis: Music, Race, Religion, Art, Performance," and the modest view of Elvis was that he was, as various experts opined, "the most important popular figure of this century."

While opinions varied on the high point, almost everyone seemed taken with the Reverend Howard Finster, folk artist and Elvis acolyte, who delivered his "Sermon on Elvis," in which he told of seeing Elvis while tending the flowers recently at his Paradise Garden Sculpture Park in Summerville, Georgia. "I turned around and looked up and saw his face," Reverend Finster told the faithful. "I said to him the only thing I could think of to say. I said, 'Elvis, can you stay awhile with me?' And he said, 'Howard, I'm on a tight schedule.' "

The conference was organized by an English professor, Vernon Chadwick, who, it turns out, was a second cousin to Ross Barnett. In addition to his archsegregationist views, Barnett, the last of a Civil War veteran's ten children, was best known for his genius for malapropisms, like a combination of the worst of George Wallace and Dan Quayle rolled into one folksy package. Addressing the centennial of a Jackson synagogue in 1961, he repeatedly extolled "this fine Christian gathering." Meaning to pay tribute to Olympic Gold Medalist Ralph Boston, he instead hailed Ralph Bunche, also black, who happened to be a former State Department official and the first black to win the Nobel Peace Prize. Once a convicted murderer and prison trusty was inexplicably dispatched alone, from Parchman to Arkansas to bring back livestock and failed to return. When reporters asked Governor Barnett how that could happen, he shook his head sadly and allowed, "If you can't trust a trusty, who can you trust?"

Things change. Chadwick was best known on campus for a course, fondly called "Melvis," that compared Herman Melville's Polynesian trilogy with three Elvis films, *Blue Hawaii, Paradise, Hawaiian Style,* and *Girls! Girls! Girls!* and saw both oeuvres as carrying a similar multicultural, taboo-shattering, anti-imperialist message of transcultural social and sexual intercourse. He was also teaching a graduate-level course on the metaphorical content of the swastika and the Confederate Flag.

We met at the natural foods Harvest Café on the square. He said he hoped the conference would resurrect the early and enduring reality of Elvis as a subversive, biracial, working-class, rebellious, hunka-hunka burning Elvis rather than the fat, sequined, Las Vegas pill popper of tabloid lore who died on his toilet while reading *The Scientific Search for the Face of Jesus* or the sanitized Saint Elvis of the Elvis adoration industry. "In twenty years they may be talking about our conference like Woodstock–'Were You There for the First Conference?'" he said hopefully. He was forty-one years old, in his fifth year teaching at Ole Miss, with degrees from Dartmouth, Oxford, and Yale and the vaguely emaciated look of a compulsive runner. He was wearing shorts and black tennis sneakers and a T-shirt he had designed featuring what he described as the green funky flag of the South–the cross of the Confederate Battle Flag on a postmodern green field of the eco-South with black and white stars, all hanging vertically rather than horizontally. He had long brown hair and a ragged beard and blue eyes that were on fire with the endless metaphorical possibilities of Elvisdom.

"Like bad wine, the Bad South travels more easily than the Good South," he said. "But what's most transportable about the positive side of the South is Elvis. Culturally, he's everywhere and in everything. People want to make him out to be a conservative icon but that's too neat. In the Third Conference I want to do one on Elvis and Nixon and put all those questions on the front burner. Was Elvis the poster boy for the right or the left? Liberal or conservative? There's the famous picture of him and Wallace, but Muhammad Ali was one of his closest friends. It's not as simple as people want to make it."

The same thought had occurred to, of all people, Phil Ochs. Near the end of the 1960s, Ochs decided that what the left, and his own fading career, needed was a way to fuse the youthful anger of the sixties counterculture with the working-class, Confederate flag, black-velvet, six-pack Elvis constituency most of his own fans looked down on. Like Chadwick a quarter century later, Ochs wanted to take back Elvis and the South for the left.

In fact, Ochs became obsessed with Elvis as his own life and career began to fall apart. He attended the King's famous comeback concert in Las Vegas and couldn't stop talking about it. He had Nudie Cohen, Elvis's famous L.A. tailor, make him an exact copy of the famous gold suit Elvis used to wear. He put together a concert of his own protest and confessional songs, Southern honky-tonk, and Merle Haggard and Elvis music at Carnegie Hall in New York in 1970. Unfortunately, his fans, expecting angst, not Elvis, booed, hooted, and demanded their money back. As the debacle wound down, Ochs–drunk, woozy, and bulging out of his ridiculous gold Elvis suit—proclaimed, "If there's any hope for America, it lies in a revolution, and if there's any hope for a revolution in America, it lies in getting Elvis Presley to be Che Guevara. If you don't do that you're just beating your head against the wall, or the cop down the street will be beating your head against the wall." With that he launched into an Elvis medley that had the remaining fans cheering and dancing in the aisles, before the Carnegie Hall management cut off the power to the stage and banned him for life from performing there again.

The left never took back Elvis or the South, but thanks to the wonders of technology, the Elvis cult now offers salvation and balm as never before. Back up Highway 61 at Graceland, the graffiti proclaimed, "There have been only two people upon their departure who have moved the world so much, Jesus Christ Our Lord, and Elvis the king." Even casual Elvisians can recite dozens of eerie parallels between the Lord and the King, beginning with their birth to sainted women and ending with their death, resurrection, and adoration. Both were Capricorns. Jesus was a carpenter. Elvis's favorite high school class was wood shop. Jesus said, "Love thy neighbor" (Matthew 22:39). Elvis said, "Don't be cruel" (RCA, 1956). Jesus walked on water. Elvis surfed. Mary had an immaculate conception. Priscilla went to Immaculate Conception High School. Jesus' "countenance was like lightning, and his raiment white as snow." Elvis wore snow-white jumpsuits with lightning bolts. But we digress.

Elvis is a perfect example of why the South-is-dead theory is such a crock. One need only surf the Internet—the least intrinsically Southern medium imaginable—to see how it has become yet another cultural vehicle used to spread the gospel, whether it's the neo-Confederates on the Southern League home page, the Bubba chauvinists, or the Elvis cultists. Thus, one can spend a day—and Vernon Chadwick no doubt has many times—surfing from the Elvis Home Page to Disgraceland to the First Presleyterian Church of Elvis the Divine, Elvis and Jesus, Jesus and Elvis, the Lesser Elvis Banishing Ritual of the Sequined Pentagram, the First Church of Jesus Christ—Elvis, the 24-Hour Church of Elvis, and other Elvis sites without end, where the faithful can partake of such wisdom as "The King's Prayer," at the Greater Las Vegas Church of Elvis. With solemn cyber-reverence, it pays homage to the King and castigates false prophets like Billy Ray Cyrus's "Achy Breaky Heart," the quintessence of faux country, nouveau Nashville at its most heretical:

> *Our King, who art in heaven*
> *Hallowed by thy hips.*
> *Thy Graceland come,*
> *Thy song be sung.*
> *In Reno as it is in Vegas.*
> *Give us this day our fried chicken.*
> *And forgive us our Achy Breaky*
> *As we forgive those who step*
> *on our blue suede shoes.*
> *And lead us not into line dancing,*
> *But deliver us from Billy Ray.*
> *For thine is the Graceland,*
> *and the rhinestones,*
> *and the rock 'n' roll,*
> *Forever and ever.*
> *Viva Las Vegas.*

The Elvis conference was fairly controversial in academia, where some stuffed shirts felt the academy should have better things to do than to trot out the likes of the acclaimed Mexican faux Elvis, El Vez. But it was wholly in keeping with the liberal takeover of Southern studies on college campuses that had taken them from the misty-eyed Old South hagiography the neo-Cons were belatedly trying to revive to a celebration of the pop culture of the South, with the clear subtext that the pop culture of the South had largely become the mainstream culture of America.

I stopped by to see Charles Reagan Wilson, who along with William Ferris was one of the two guiding spirits for Ole Miss's Center for the Study of Southern Culture. On his shelves and outside his office was a display of Southern ephemera–tiny vials of what is alleged to be Elvis's sweat (PRAYERS ANSWERED: THE KING LIVES!); Diddy Wah Diddy Beer; a leather wallet with stitching reading *Attend Church;* a Bear Bryant Coke bottle; a tin of Old South Jack Mackerel; an old red metal RC Cola thermometer with markings going as high as 120 degrees but only as low as 30; Li'l Reb fireworks; the picture of Elvis and Wallace.

It was great trivia, but more than that it was an expression of a regional identity far stronger than anything you could find elsewhere in

the United States. Whoever heard of a Northern studies program? To
the degree that regionalism exists in, say, New England, as it undeniably
does, it is regional in the narrowest sense, inward-looking and quaint. It
bore no resemblance to the expansive, proselytizing world of Elvis conferences, Dixie journals, and encyclopedias of all things Southern–like
the mammoth *Encyclopedia of Southern Culture* edited by Wilson and
Ferris–emanating out of Ole Miss and its competitors at the University
of North Carolina, the University of South Carolina, and other
Southern universities.

"Southerners in the past always talked about being the most
American of Americans from the early national period to Thomas Jefferson, when they were so involved with creating the nation," said
Wilson, who was sitting behind a plaque reading THE DIDEROT OF DIXIE.
"Then came the late troubles of the late-nineteenth century to sidetrack
that." He was talking about the Civil War. "But a major theme of the
twentieth century is Southerners as Americans, and it's come to fruition
since World War Two. The country has always had an ambivalent attitude toward that. At times when race relations in the South were the
most turbulent, the country didn't want to see itself in the South and
didn't want to listen to Southerners make that claim. But since the sixties the nation has been able to accept those Southern claims again.

"We swing between seeing the Savage South and the Sunny South
and neither of them ever goes away. Even in the sixties, when race relations were at their worst, you still had *The Andy Griffith Show,* this wonderful homespun ideal. What's different now is that when the South
had bad race relations the country always wanted to distance itself from
the South. Now there's bad race relations everywhere and we're elect-
ing all these Southern conservatives, and you have all these Southern
preachers running around playing a big role in national politics the way
they always did in the South. Maybe we're in the post-Reconstruction
era again, seeing the same rapprochement, only this time maybe the
country is letting itself be defined by the South, which would be something new."

We talked a little about the strength of Southern identity, why
Southerners seemed to take so much more of their identity with them
when they moved to, say, Chicago, than Chicagoans took with
them when they moved to Birmingham.

"There's always been that intensity because issues of identity have always been so bound up with the South," Wilson said. "The migration out of the South—of both blacks and whites—came at a time when the region had defined itself so thoroughly, so dramatically, after the eighteen-nineties with the hardening of race relations. Issues of identity are so tied up with the South in the twentieth century, more so even than in the nineteenth century, I think. People were told there were definite things about being a Southerner and those were enforced very rigidly, and they left with those very powerful sentiments they had learned. One of my favorite books is Katharine Du Pre Lumpkin's *The Making of a Southerner* because it talks about that very process, how she learned to be a Southerner, how intense it was, and what it was like to break away from racial orthodoxy. Or at the end of Richard Wright's *Black Boy,* there's a wonderful passage where he talks about leaving the South, but he knows he can never get rid of the South. The best he could hope for was to take some aspect of Southern culture and make it bloom, make something good come out of it. That same intensity is common to blacks and whites. They never lose that sense of identity, no matter where they go."

In the same way, the sense of identity went a long way toward explaining how much continuity there was amid change throughout the South. Take the case of Ole Miss. Sure, you had Ross Barnett's second cousin running around like a wild man comparing the Confederate Battle Flag to the swastika and trying to make Elvis out to be closer to Richard Pryor than Richard Nixon. But downtown at Smitty's, Oxford's plate-lunch version of the Ranchero in Clarksdale, and at Neilson's Department Store, where generations of Ole Miss sorority girls had bought their Villager blouses and khaki Bermudas, in the banners on campus blaring WELCOME TO OLE MISS—what was most striking was how much the university and Oxford, long revered as a musty Old South white man's paradise, now felt like a hip, literary New South white man's paradise.

It wasn't that it was a hotbed of racism. Over the years Ole Miss had played out various psychodramas of racial redemption, the most recent one being the remarkable outpouring of affection the university showed for a black football player named Chuckie Mullins who was crippled and who later died, after making a ferocious hit in a game against Vanderbilt on October 28, 1989. Perhaps more significantly, in a state where politicians once routinely vowed defiance of federal law, the dean of the

University of Mississippi Law School was now a Mississippi-born black man, Louis Westerfield. (He died of a heart attack a year later at age 47.) All the racial issues of the nineties, like the self-segregation of blacks and whites and bitter arguments over affirmative action, played out at Ole Miss, but it was hard to make the case that the issues were any more volatile than they were at the University of Michigan or at Yale. It's just that in the iconography of the South there are few institutions that are truly neutral turf when it comes to race, and Ole Miss, indelibly linked by history and family ties to the state's past, wasn't one of them.

Students and alumni still waved the rebel flag at the football games. Even the cheeky Center for the Study of Southern Culture was overwhelmingly white. The university now had 748 blacks among its 7,946 undergraduates and eagerly sought more, but the catch was, they had to come to Ole Miss in almost the same way the blacks at Williston came to New Hanover High School in Wilmington, North Carolina. I saw one black kid walking around with a T-shirt that featured a wanted poster for a runaway slave and wondered why he had come in the first place.

Before leaving I wandered around and stopped to read the inscription on the Confederate monument at the base of the tree-lined circle leading up to the white-columned administration building, the Lyceum. Under the statue of a Confederate soldier, his musket held upright in his right hand, his left hand on his hat as he peered into the distance in a "Look away, Dixieland" pose, was the inscription:

> They fell devoted but undying; the very gale their names seem'd sighing. The waters murmur'd of their name: the woods were peopled with their fame; the silent pillar, lone and gray; claim'd kindred with their sacred clay; their spirits wrapp'd the dusky mountain, their memory sparkled o'er the fountain; the meanest rill, the mightiest river; roll'd mingling with their fame forever!–Byron

After Oxford, I headed South toward Jackson, zigzagging back into the Delta on backroads toward Tchula, once a busy little railroad town, now as dismal a sliver of Delta poverty as you can find. From 1938 to 1955 it was the scene of one of those brave, improbable interracial experiments, the cooperative farming community called Providence Farm, which was shut down by its fearful neighbors in 1955. In Tchula, I had hoped to visit Dr. Ronald Myers, a massive, gospel-singing, piano-playing black physician from Chicago who had gained a lot of publicity a few years ago for his fight to open a clinic in one of the Delta's poorest towns. But he wasn't there, and folks in town said he seldom was that summer. When he called me on the phone a week later he said that he had put together a foundation for rural health, was giving jazz concerts to raise money, and planned to resume regular office hours and add a nurse practitioner soon in Tchula. But either he was spread way too thin or he was just another reason to be cynical about the possibility that anything much would ever change for the poor in the Delta because people black and white tended to roll their eyes or express utter ignorance of what, if anything, he was doing in Tchula these days.

In Belzoni—pronounced "Belzona"—in Humphreys County, I visited the catfish museum in what's known as "Catfish Capital of the World"— yet another parable of the triumph of the stealth South. All the cotton farmers laughed in 1965 when J. B. Williams dug his first muddy pond, walked in his rubber waders out into waist-deep water, and started raising catfish. Now Humphreys County has 35,000 acres of ponds, in which 400 million catfish a year are raised, and instead of endless fields of cotton, you drive past endless ponds with hoses spraying fresh water into the air to keep the oxygen levels just right.

The museum was in the old Itta Bena and Belzoni Railroad depot in Belzoni. To the side of the low-slung wood-frame building in a dried-up pond was the forty-foot-long, half-ton *King Cat* sculpture. In front was a sculpture called *Catfish's Flowering* by Greely Myatt of Amory, Mississippi. It looked like a clunky windmill made out of 110-pound howitzer ammunition containers and was supposed to symbolize the way catfish lay their eggs in dark holes like those provided by the ammunition cans. Inside the museum was Gene Luster; he had set the sprinkler so that it was watering the roof and had turned the lights off to provide some relief—any relief—from the heat. He was thrilled to have a visitor and jumped at the bait when I asked him the same dumb question every ignorant visitor asks: Is there any difference in taste between farm-raised catfish and plain old river catfish?

"There's a big difference between farm and mud-raised or river-raised catfish," he said, emphasizing the word "mud" to make it clear how far the once-lowly catfish has come. "There's no comparison between what farmers produce and scavenger or river cats. What we've done is teach them table manners. In the wild, they're bottom-feeding scavengers. Farm-raised catfish are taught to come to the surface to feed on floating feed pellets—corn- and soybean-based high-protein rations—so they're light, white, flaky, almost meat-tasting with none of the putrid odor like the mudcats." Not only that, they were ecologically correct, he added, showing me a chart that indicated that while it took eight pounds of feed to raise a pound of beef, and four pounds to a pound of pork, and three pounds to raise a pound of chicken, it only took two pounds of feed to raise a pound of catfish.

Catfish may have undergone a sea change, but one thing that hasn't changed is that the jobs produced in the Delta continue to be among the worst in America, where hands that once picked cotton now debone catfish. Like the chicken plants throughout the South, the burgeoning catfish plants are notorious for numbing, painful, dangerous, subsistence-wage work where black men and women—mostly women—in hairnets slice and dice fish on hot, wet, bloody, noisy, assembly lines like something out of Upton Sinclair transplanted to the South and updated for the nineties.

A 1988 internal memo at Delta Pride, the nation's largest catfish producer, said head-saw operators were expected to cut off sixty catfish heads a minute—as many as *43,000* a day. A typical worker on the "kill line" would gut and rip fish as they sped by on a conveyer belt at a rate of 33 a minute, 1,980 an hour, as many as 20,000 a day. As in the chicken plants, carpal tunnel syndrome was epidemic from the painful, repetitive work. In 1990 the Occupational Safety and Health Administration cited Delta Pride for exposing employees to dangerous working conditions and for failing to report injuries as required by law.

There had already been union-organizing drives at Delta. When I asked Luster whether the casinos made it harder to get workers, he seemed unconcerned. Belzoni was too far from the casinos for most people to drive there, and anyway, he said with the blithe, blind paternalism Delta planters always voiced for their slaves or sharecroppers, "They're treated so well, they've got it made as long as they perform." No wonder the casinos looked so good.

At Ole Miss, Dr. Wilson and I had talked about how the South had to approach the cultural mainstream to be really effective in selling its ideological wares, like a magnet that only locks onto its opposite when it gets close enough. Too exotic and unfiltered–like vintage George Wallace–the message may work but the messenger doesn't. Toned down a bit–the South Lite of Newt Gingrich, Trent Lott, and Haley Barbour–a similar message gives better mileage.

In the same way, here was Gene Luster selling his mud-averse, ecologically aware, New South yuppie catfish to the Germans and the Japanese as fast as the Delta could raise them. I took two catfish pins for my kids, a catfish key chain, and the Catfish Institute's helpful cookbook, which contains such recipes as Catfish and Goat Cheese Pastries, Catfish Pasta Primavera, Catfish Meunière, Catfish Brie Soufflé, and Catfish Nuggets with Champagne Mustard Sauce, and got in my car and drove until I reached Clancy's High Altitude Food on Jerry Clower Boulevard in Yazoo City near the southern edge of the Delta. I ordered the fried catfish platter and tried to envision the yuppie catfish of the Delta tooling around Humphreys County in little catfish Beemers with OLE MISS, ELECT FORDICE, and EARTH FIRST! bumper stickers.

It wasn't exactly the Delta of myth and fable. But it was still the Delta.

Chapter 11

THIS MEMORIAL IS PRAYERFULLY
AND PROUDLY DEDICATED
TO THE MEMORY OF
JAMES CHANEY
ANDREW GOODMAN
MICHAEL SCHWERNER
WHO GAVE THEIR LIVES IN THE
STRUGGLE TO OBTAIN HUMAN
RIGHTS FOR ALL PEOPLE.

MISSISSIPPI II
In the Electric Casinos with the Confederate Dead

AROUND YAZOO CITY, THE FLAT DELTA FARMLAND GAVE WAY TO THE gentle rolling terrain around Jackson; eventually the endless vistas of sky broken only by tiny towns, random country stores, and hulking cotton gins or cottonseed mills gave way to the outskirts of the city. Since I'd just left Yazoo City it made sense to hook up with Yazoo's most famous celebrator, Willie Morris, whose *North Toward Home* was one of the classic coming-of-age-in-the-South books. Morris, the former editor of *Harper's Magazine,* had moved back to Mississippi from New York in 1980, lived in Oxford for a while, and now lives in a two-story white house in a lovely northeast Jackson neighborhood full of giant oaks and magnolias and pink and purple crape myrtles. His neighbors include William Winter, the legendary liberal governor of the early eighties; Ray Mabus, the failed liberal governor of the late eighties; James Meredith, whose enrollment as the first black at Ole Miss set off the riots in 1962 and who later turned into a right-wing nut who worked for Jesse Helms and lent support to David Duke; and Roy McMillan, Jackson's most rabid antiabortion activist, who drove around in a maroon Mercury Sable station wagon with a bumper sticker reading, IF THEY TAKE AWAY OUR GUNS, HOW WILL WE SHOOT THE LIBERALS?

I went out with Morris and his wife, JoAnne Prichard, the executive editor of the University Press of Mississippi, to Bill's Greek Tavern, a friendly, modest joint that is Eudora Welty's favorite restaurant. The owner, Bill Matheos, once hired a belly dancer for one of Miss Eudora's birthdays who had EUDORA WELTY, I LOVE YOU, written on her undulating belly. We got to talking about the persistence of Southern identity and what it was that made Southernness the dominant gene in the nation's cultural soup, a longtime Morris theme. He drew himself up like Stonewall Jackson at Chancellorsville, took a dramatic drag on his cigarette, put down his glass of red wine, and orated: "I can answer in one word. Remembrance. Eudora Welty said we only have one thing as human beings and that is memory. The South today with all of its horrendous, damn near existentialist failings, with Nazis like Fordice running this state and Jim Meredith five doors down from us who worked for David Duke, has one thing that distinguishes us as a culture within the great American commonwealth, and that is remembrance, memory and everything that is implied by it. The South never forgets, which is a blessing and a curse."

He ripped off a piece of the blue-and-white menu with GOD BLESS AMERICA! printed at the bottom and on the other side sketched a map of his childhood neighborhood in Yazoo City. A block from his home on Grand Avenue between Fourth and Fifth streets lived Mike Espy, who became Mississippi's first black congressman since Reconstruction and then Bill Clinton's ill-fated Secretary of Agriculture, and Haley Barbour, who became the national chairman of the Republican party. A few blocks over on the west side of the railroad tracks lived Zig Ziglar, the amazingly successful motivational speaker and secular evangelist, and on the east side of the tracks lived Willie Brown, who went on to become perhaps the best defensive back in the history of the National Football League. All of these men took assorted Southern passions and brought them to the nation.

"Haley was about ten years younger than me. We used him as our tackling dummy," he said. "He was a tough kid. Zig Ziglar, his real name is Hillary, was a little older. They were very poor and lived right next to to the Illinois Central Railroad track in a little old shack that's not there anymore. But they were so close to the railroad track that when the freight train from Memphis to New Orleans came through every midnight, the word around Yazoo City was that they would have to open the kitchen door every night to let the freight train through."

On our way to Morris's house, he asked me a great Southern trivia question, courtesy, it turned out, of Charles Reagan Wilson at Ole Miss (it's a pretty small world in Mississippi): What were the five best-attended Southern funerals? Elvis was easy. Jefferson Davis. I guessed wrong on Hank Williams, then recovered with Huey P. Long. Given the hint "A sports figure," I got Bear Bryant. Given the hint "A black person," I got Martin Luther King, Jr. Back home we watched the O.J. news on *Nightline,* and before I left Morris picked up a felt-tip pen and scrawled something on a three-by-five card and handed it to me. It read: "The contemporary South from my perspective: It's the juxtapositions, emotional and in remembrance, that drive you crazy."

I got up the next morning and went to see Dick Molpus, Mississippi's secretary of state and the Democratic candidate for governor, running against the ferocious Kirk Fordice. Fordice, a Vicksburg construction company owner who had never held public office before being elected governor in 1991, was the exemplar of the meaner-than-cat-shit, tough-nosed-businessman-turned-politician school of Southern Republicans. Near the end of his race against Ray Mabus, he breezily introduced my *New York Times* colleague Ronald Smothers, who is black, around his campaign headquarters as "the spook from *The New York Times.*" He made a name for himself nationally by insisting at a Republican governors' meeting a year later, in 1992, that "America is a Christian nation"; shortly after taking office he said he would call out the National Guard to fight any court-ordered equalization of funds for Mississippi's black and white universities.

Molpus was the darling of Mississippi liberals and moderates, a famously decent native of Philadelphia, in Neshoba County, a place synonymous still with the murders of James Earl Chaney, Andrew Goodman, and Michael Schwerner. The three civil rights workers were arrested on a traffic violation on June 21, 1964, taken to jail in Philadelphia, and then released and chased through the Mississippi countryside by sheriff's deputies and armed Klansmen. Once caught, they were executed one by one at point-blank range and their bodies buried under an earthen dam.

Molpus was fourteen at the time of the "unpleasantness," as it's commonly known, and thus couldn't be blamed for any of it. But on the twenty-fifth anniversary of the killings, June 21, 1989, a day almost as hot as the ones this summer, Molpus appeared at an ecumenical service at Mount Zion Church, whose firebombing in 1964 had brought the three to Neshoba County, and gave a speech people still talk about— a stark, lucid, plainspoken plea for remembrance and for healing that evoked the best of the South in language as simple as the Lord's

Prayer. Addressing directly the families of the victims, under a burning Mississippi sun, he said:

> We deeply regret what happened here twenty-five years ago. We wish we could undo it. We are profoundly sorry that they are gone. We wish we could bring them back. Every decent person in Philadelphia and Neshoba County and Mississippi feels that way.... Today we pay tribute to those who died. We acknowledge that dark corner of our past. But we also take pride in the present, and we are hopeful about the future.... My heart is full today because I know that if James Chaney, Andy Goodman, and Mickey Schwerner were to return today, they would see a Philadelphia and a Mississippi that, while far from perfect, are closer to being the kind of place the God who put us here wants them to be. And they would find—perhaps to their surprise—that our trials and difficulties have given Mississippi a special understanding of the need for redemption and reconciliation and have empowered us to serve as a beacon for the nation.... Fear has waned—fear of the unknown, fear of each other—and hope abides. That is our story. And you and yours are part of it. God bless each of you. We are genuinely glad to have you here.

Six years later, the speech had become something of a millstone, as Fordice courted white votes by making it clear he wasn't interested in dwelling on the past and didn't think Mississippi had anything much to apologize for. I met Molpus at his home in Belhaven, a lovely old neighborhood of stately homes and modest middle-class cottages near downtown. Like Marty Stuart in Nashville, his friend from Philadelphia and political supporter, he offered me banana nut bread when we sat down to talk.

Molpus had doughy, blond good looks and a soothing, earnest demeanor. In an earlier time he would have been poised to climb the Democratic ranks to become governor. He had helped form a group called Parents for Public Schools, which had chapters in thirty-five cities, whose aim was to build a critical mass of parents—like himself—committed to sending their children to public schools and drawing other parents they knew in the same direction. Without being a showy liberal, he could be said to have lived up to the best ideals of the post-segregation South, only to see the political tides shift in Mississippi and the nation so that a throwback to the South's past like Fordice seemed right for the times, while Molpus seemed like yesterday's model, an easy target for the liberal-bedwetter, bleeding-heart jibes of the knee-jerk Rush Limbaugh Dittoheads of the world. Polls showed him well behind Fordice at a time when the gambling-based economy was healthy and being a Democrat was like the mark of Cain for a white candidate in the South. Even many of his supporters saw him as the right man running in the wrong year. I asked him about that and he shrugged.

"There are enough centrist men and women, not radicals on the left or the right but simply people with good hearts and good minds who want to join together to make Mississippi a beacon for the rest of the country," he said, echoing part of his speech six years earlier. "There are more of us than there are of them. I'm no left-wing nut. I'm a cen-trist moderate businessman who reflects mainstream Mississippi values, running with a twelve-year record of accomplishment. But I do believe we have to end this racial bitterness and work together, and that mes-sage ought to be a powerful one across Mississippi and across the country."

I described my theories of the Southernization of America, and he listened intently, as if hearing a song he knew in a different key. "It's frightening to think what our future holds if we allow demagogues to continue to play the race card," he said. "It may be effective, but it's evil and dangerous. But one of my pet peeves is the Northeastern white lib-eral stuff. For them it's all very much in the abstract, but they wouldn't consider sending their children to the public schools because they might be around someone from the lower class. That type of hypocrisy to me is worse than anything I've seen in Mississippi. Watch this race. It's more than one governor's race in one small state."

As it turned out, however, the election didn't add up to much more than a political cat-and-mouse game revolving around race. Molpus, who seemed hopelessly behind as the race got underway, made it close and even had a late surge when Fordice committed one of the cardinal sins of Southern politics by insulting Molpus's wife. But in the end Molpus slipped up by running ads on black radio stations accusing Fordice of sending blacks back to the back of the bus. Given a perfect opening, Fordice shot back with ads thundering, "I don't do race," which conveniently allowed him to remind white voters just who the blacks were backing. In the end, Fordice won 55 percent of the vote to Molpus's 45, a reminder that though moderates may not be doomed in the South these days, they don't have much margin for error.

Later the same day, I drove out to the campus of Jackson State University, one of the three historically black public universities in Mississippi. Located at the edges of a poor, black neighborhood west of downtown, it has an enrollment of 6,313 students, 98 percent of them black. Here were none of the baronial columns, grand rhetorical flourishes, or great green groves of Ole Miss. Instead there were blocky, functional brick buildings painted in drab institutional colors. Cars cruised by with stereos blasting the thumping bass notes of rap and funk. In the middle of the campus was a squat centennial monument marking the school's first hundred years, but instead of Ole Miss's Confederate soldier and Byron's dusky mountains, meanest rills, and mightiest rivers, there was just the alma mater and the centennial theme:

> TO SURVIVE AND THRIVE
> FROM A CENTURY OF
> SERVICE
> WE GO FORWARD

If Jackson State looked like the poor relation, it was: blacks in Mississippi had always made do with less. But Jackson State, like many black schools in the South, was undergoing something of a renaissance; a T-shirt reads, THE BLACKER THE COLLEGE, THE SWEETER THE KNOWLEDGE. The state of Mississippi was slogging through decades-long litigation aimed at desegregating or equalizing resources for white and black universities. While many whites saw black institutions as throwbacks to the past, most blacks saw them as sources of power, unity, and pride every bit as relevant to today as the sacred groves of Ole Miss. The time was long gone when integration could simply mean merging blacks into white institutions, as happened in Wilmington. The question was whether Mississippi was going to create truly integrated institutions—shaped by black and white sensibilities—or whether it was going to find a way to provide something closer to equity between black institutions and white ones. For now, it wasn't making great progress on either front.

It was registration day, and I wandered into the gymnasium with its rows of red, mustard, and blue seats. Near me a handful of male students were eyeing the women and greeting friends. They seemed breezily self-confident, like a black version of the Sigma Chis over at Ole Miss. I asked a few of them whether a school like Ole Miss had much appeal for them and most of them said they'd much rather be at Jackson State.

"I'm from Grand Rapids, Michigan. It's a big Christian Reform city–Dutch. There's not even a black radio station that's on all day," said Suriya Davenport, a twenty-year-old wearing Madras shorts and a pink Ralph Lauren Polo shirt. "I came here just once to see what it feels like to be in the majority, and it just feels better. I'm not a racist. I'm not against white people. But you have a sense of belonging here. The teachers care about you, it's not like walking into a class at Ole Miss with four or five black people and everybody looking at you like they're wondering why you're there. I'll tell you, blacks in the South don't know how good they have it. I like Mississippi. I love Mississippi. My dad's generation moved north from the Delta for jobs in the North and now their kids are coming back. He can't understand it."

I felt like I was back in Wilmington with the Williston crowd. Davenport started pointing to his friends. "He's from Michigan, he's from Michigan, he's from Michigan. They're all down here. I mean, you go out to North Jackson and see all these big houses owned by black people, and you think, wow, I never saw this in Michigan. You live here and you think, I can succeed."

I'd been to Jackson often, but I'd spent most of my time at places like the capitol talking to legislators. I didn't know residential Jackson at all. Willie Morris and Dick Molpus lived on the northeast side of town, so I figured the area that Suriya was talking about must be on the northwest. I drove in that direction past shady white neigbhorhoods that felt like the ones I knew in Birmingham or Charlotte or where I lived in Atlanta: leafy patches of middle-class homes near upscale strip shopping centers or fancy malls, where a person could buy a nice house for a third of what it would cost in New York, Washington, Boston, or L.A. Eventually, most of the faces in the cars or on the street became black, and I figured I was in the right place. I turned right into a neighborhood of condos on streets with names like Wimbledon Court, Dickens Court, and Copperfield Court. Neat condominiums gave way to streets of unprepossessing brick houses on new cul-de-sacs with an occasional estatelike house sprinkled in.

It seemed nice enough, but, as usual, as a model of black prosperity it seemed pretty modest—not quite the difference between Jackson State and Ole Miss, but the same principle. But as I drove around more, I saw that there were prosperous black neighborhoods everywhere, ranging from rambling ranch houses to huge new brick Tudor and colonial style homes with tennis courts and swimming pools and lawns like putting greens on streets where the signs hung from black metal horses. (There were a few white holdovers from the time the neighborhood was white but all the huge new houses were being built for blacks.) This was a world I knew in Atlanta but hadn't expected on this scale in Jackson, and I cruised around soaking it all in just as I had the battered towns of the Delta.

At North Jackson Baptist Church a bunch of black kids were playing volleyball, observed by a handful of black men and women and one heavy-set white man with bad teeth whom I took to be the janitor or caretaker—a nice enough role reversal. The event was a party for kids from a low-income apartment complex who had been adopted by the church, whose members included L. C. Farris, a retiree from the Delta, and Herman Mannery, the postmaster of Vicksburg. But the white man turned out to be Bill Patrick, the fifty-seven-year-old pastor. I don't know why the black preachers at the white churches seemed more likely than a white preacher at a black church, but they did.

Patrick said North Jackson began as a white-flight church back when whites were fleeing downtown neighborhoods to North Jackson. "In the bylaws it said no colored person could be a member," he said. "God has a sense of humor." His goal was to have the first truly integrated Southern Baptist church in Jackson, and though it hasn't happened yet— the church is now all black—he's still hopeful. "I think the Lord sent me here to prove it can work," he said. "I feel my mission is to help people overcome denominational barriers, gender barriers, and racial barriers. I used to think it was just the South until I was on my way back from Korea in fifty-nine and stopped at the house of one of my buddies from the army. All of a sudden, his father came in saying, 'We've gotta move! There are niggers moving in down the street!' I thought, 'Whoooaa. This is Chicago. What's going on here?' There's still a lot of hate everywhere, but I think this is a place where things are getting better, and I'd like to think I can do a little bit toward making it a little bit more inhabitable." I watched the men load the kids into vans to send them home and then drove off myself.

Like most things in the South these days, it was all like a Rorschach test for viewing race in America. What mattered more, that there was this sprawling grove of affluent blacks in Ozzie and Harriet neighborhoods in the middle of a state that not too far back was the hellhole of hellholes for black people in America, or that the reason it existed was that all the whites who used to live there had moved out past the city limits into all-white suburbs? I voted half full rather than half empty on this one, but I also realized the question missed the point in a way Southerners tend to know instinctively and Yankees have never figured out. Race is so powerful that we usually can only see it in searing vivid colors—"I Have a Dream" or *Mississippi Burning*. O.J. framed by racist cops or O.J. as vicious murderer who gets off by playing the race card. But there are moments when you remember that the shades of gray are so infinite and subtle, the lessons so elusive, that the bright colors are more likely to blind than to guide. As Willie Morris said, "It's the juxtapositions, emotional and in remembrance, that drive you crazy."

My plan was to follow the casinos down to the coast, so I left Jackson and headed west for Vicksburg, the hilly river town where the Confederate surrender on July 4, 1863, after fourteen months of naval shelling, seven months of land assault, and forty-seven days of total siege, left the Confederacy cut in half. I went straight to Harrah's on the river.

There was not a soul on the renovated streets of downtown, where half the storefronts were empty, but Harrah's was jammed to the gills with a crowd much like the one at Tunica. Jackson country-club types in Cancún T-shirts and weary-faced blacks in overalls sat in antique armchairs like honored guests at some planters' mansion or browsed at Faulkner's gift shop, where the clerks said they weren't sure how the shop got its name, but, no, there were no books by William Faulkner.

Just in front of the casino entrance was an exhibit of antique gambling machines: the 1938 Jennings Triplex Chief; the 1934 Mills QT; a 1900 Watling Draw Poker Machine that was the rage in San Francisco's cigar stores and saloons; the 1898 Caille Puck, "The Cadillac of the coin machine industry." Outside on the patio, people sat on metal lawn chairs around metal tables under brightly colored umbrellas, sweating in the sun and looking at the murky waters of the Mississippi just upstream from a clunky industrial plant. Monte Carlo it was not, but I was ready for Round Two.

I quickly won a few dollars at the slots and then ventured over to the five-dollar blackjack table, where I sat down next to a white man in a baseball cap from the National Civil Rights Museum in Memphis and a black man wearing a T-shirt that said I LOVE BLUEGRASS. Maybe they woke up in each other's clothes. I paid twenty dollars for four chips, lost a hand, won a hand, lost a hand, won a hand, and then won two hands. I was up a big ten dollars plus the three or four bucks I had won at the slots. Keeping to my battle plan of leaving with my paltry earnings rather than playing until I lost, I said adios to the dealer and cashed in my chips.

Vicksburg was truly dismal—the casinos may be pumping money into the local treasury, but they seemed to be sucking the life out of everything else. But, like most other things, the gambling mania wasn't as new as it seemed. The South has always been in love with gambling—with dice and cards, on dogs and horses, in cockfights or dogfights, at Delta or Black Belt juke joints, on doddering old riverboats in famous coastal dives in Galveston, New Orleans, Mobile, or Biloxi. Southerners even cooked up grandiose schemes like the famous Louisiana State Lottery. Chartered after the Civil War and cloaked in the patina of Lost Cause righteousness by the presence of former Confederate generals Jubal A. Early and P.G.T. Beauregard, it mushroomed into a national phenomenon earning from twenty to thirty million dollars a year until Congress finally shut it down in 1893. Righteous old Ross Barnett, confronted with reports in 1961 of widespread illegal gambling across the state of Mississippi, particularly on the Gulf Coast between Biloxi and Gulfport, blandly allowed as how he would stick to his campaign pledge not to be "a raiding governor" and did his best to look the other way. Even the cotton-based agriculture of the Delta had always been a highly leveraged big-bucks crapshoot in which fortunes were famously made and lost with stunning speed.

If Vicksburg seemed a little shell-shocked by the casino, Natchez, eighty miles to the south, which was founded in 1714 on the grand alluvial bluffs two hundred feet above the Mississippi, and likes to think of itself as the ultimate unadorned Old South haven of old money, old gentility, and old conventions, seemed, as always, utterly unruffled.

David Cohn, the planter who in the forties and fifties gave us some of the most enduring prose about Mississippi, wrote of Natchez in a famous article in the *Atlantic Monthly*: "People walk in its streets, boats move on its river, newspapers are printed and read and business is transacted. It is cluttered now with the paraphernalia of contemporaneity; the illusion of newness hovers about its bowed head.... But, for all this, Natchez will never be part of the world in which it lives.... Natchez lives with its dead."

Well, yes and no. Natchez today does seem to exist, as always, in an Old South time warp. Dashing Confederate officers and lovely lily-white belles cavort at the famous Natchez Pilgrimage and Confederate Pageant, where the grand finale includes a Confederate soldier running around, waving the flag and giving the rebel yell while everyone in the audience breaks into a spirited rendition of "Dixie." Grand plantation homes like Longwood, an Oriental-style, domed octagonal mansion with Moorish arches; Dunleith, built in Greek Revival style with two-story-tall columns completely encircling the house; or Melrose, built on eighty acres of woods and ponds, with its old slave houses and smoke house still intact, rise up behind iron gates like amazingly well-preserved dowagers. Astounding Old World–style churches rise toward the heavens, like the Gothic Revival St. Mary's Cathedral with its altars of Cararra marble and its soaring spires and elegant stained glass; Trinity Episcopal, built in 1821 and remodeled in 1838 as an almost exact replica of the Theseum in Athens; or the giant First Presbyterian Church, built in 1828 in the Federal Neoclassical style with space for six hundred people and antique swinging doors at the ends of the pews.

In a slightly less elevated vein other visionaries have created one-of-a-kind architectural wonders like Mammy's Cupboard, a restaurant and gift shop in the form of a giant black mammy, or the astounding Hubcap House, where W. E. Whitehead has adorned his house, yard, trees, and fences with hundreds of hubcaps that gleam in the sun like Roman armature. It's a marvel of adaptive-use architecture rivaled perhaps only by the esteemed Beer Can House in Houston, where John and Mary Milkovisch have covered every inch of the outside walls of their house with flattened beer cans and where festive strands of cans dangle from the eaves and rustle like ghostly aluminum wind chimes.

On its face, Natchez is about as politically incorrect as you can get (well, not the Hubcap House), but it has also been home to an old, established, black elite almost as tradition-bound and snobby as the whites; its history includes such black luminaries as the author Richard Wright and Hiram Revels, the nation's first black senator. Natchez is still pretty much as segregated as ever–blacks in north Natchez, whites in south Natchez–but over the years the Pilgrimage has started including more African-American history and a recognition of the city's black past. In fact, the board chairman of the Historic Natchez Foundation was a black brick mason named Duncan Morgan, a development roughly comparable to an Arab running the Jerusalem Chamber of Commerce. Unlike Vicksburg, downtown Natchez was full of life, its antebellum homes all lit up, crowds pouring out of places like the famous King's Tavern on Jefferson Street, the oldest tavern in the Natchez Territory, built in 1787 of ship's timbers from an ancient river flatboat.

I drove over toward the Lady Luck Casino, a mock riverboat at Natchez-Under-the-Hill, the landing that had been famous for its dives and gambling joints for most of Natchez's history. It was a Saturday night, and like every casino in America, it was jammed. I played the slots next to Melvin Cooper, a black retired truck driver from Vidalia, Louisiana, who said he played several times a week and once won one hundred dollars. "I lit out of here like the place was on fire," he said. I returned to my penny-ante guerilla war approach, moving from various slots–Double Cherries, Crazy Cash, Double Jackpot, Black Diamonds, Blast of Bucks–and feeling the brainless stupefication of the casino sucking me in. I got up a few dollars, and feeling sick of the whole thing figured I'd leave. Instead, I wandered around for a while, taking in the numbing robotic sounds and rhythms of the casino, its squadrons of solicitous barmaids, its jovial winners and its hollow-eyed losers. On television was an arena football game (there is always a big game on television in casinos, no matter what time of day or season of the year you're there); Number 46 had just swept around his own right end to score a critical touchdown, putting the Iowa somethings ahead of the Orlando something elses.

Suitably inspired, I wandered over to the poker tables. Around a somewhat ratty green table, a group of blacks and whites were playing a very talky game of poker. There was a rednecky-looking guy with long brown hair and tattooed arms sitting next to a thin, talkative black woman who had the biggest pile of chips, and I sensed bad karma.

When a seat opened up, I sat down between the guy with the tattoos and an attractive blonde Southern belle with braces named Dolly to see what transpired.

Players came and went but the core ones were Dolly, who had a finance business in town; a forty-five-ish white guy named Jim with dark hair and the middle-class, middle-aged look of an accountant or sales manager; a phlegmatic, poker-faced, light-skinned black man named Doc; the black woman with the big pile of chips, whose name was Willie Mae; and the guy with the tattoos.

So much for my racial antenna. It turned out to be about the most convivial game of poker ever played, and I found myself thinking of the blacks and whites sitting around the pool table at the market in Bobo, as if this were only a gaudier, more prosperous variation on the same theme. It turned out that most of the players came every Saturday. Whenever Jim won a hand, he tossed a chip to Willie Mae, who ritual-istically chimed out, "Thank you, Mr. Jim," in a mocking play on the racial conventions of the Old South. There was a running, ribald joke of indeterminate origin about three-legged men that had Dolly howling in delight and then primly telling Willie Mae to hush, because she was embarrassing them all.

Out of curiosity, I asked Doc whether he was indeed a doctor, and he fished a card from his wallet and tossed it across the table with the sly air of a man showing his cards after drawing an inside straight. It read:

DR. BENNY A. WRIGHT. GENERAL DENTISTRY
11 A.M.–8 P.M. BY APPOINTMENT
408 N. PINE ST., NATCHEZ, MISS. 39120

I played for more than two hours and left about two in the morning, finishing exactly one dollar up, in addition to my fabulous $13.75 in slot-machine winnings. I waited by the river, listening to its night sounds of croaking frogs and chirping crickets, for the shuttle bus that took us back to the parking lot, where Willie Mae got into a big blue Cadillac, and I got into my big white Buick.

I woke early the next morning for what I had planned as the penulti-mate stop on my trip, my third visit to the Spring Hill Free Will Baptist Church in Amite County near McComb. It had been the scene of one of those moments of racial grace, like Dick Molpus's speech in Neshoba

County, that stayed with you with the intensity of a vision. On April 4, 1993, the anniversary of Martin Luther King's assassination, the church, which was organized under a large white oak tree by a group of freed slaves in August 1868, burned to the ground. It was just a month after the completion of remodeling work on the sanctuary, built in 1958.

The culprits turned out to be three white teenagers, two from nearby Summit and one from Franklinton, Louisiana. The youths, who had been drinking heavily, kicked in the front door of the old cinder-block church—looking for sound equipment, they later said—used hymnals and a basket of artificial flowers for kindling, and set the place ablaze, while one of them yelled out, "Burn, nigger, burn!" Then they squealed away on the unlit, gravel road. A few hours later, about twenty miles away, they did the same thing at another black church, Rocky Point Missionary Baptist Church near Summit.

Church burnings, like the arson incident that brought Chaney, Goodman, and Schwerner to Neshoba County, were once the signature crimes of Mississippi's violent past. It is shocking that they remain a crime of the present as if the product of free-floating ions of malice still loose in the atmosphere, persisting through time. Still, just as the two fires in Mississippi were almost certainly the result of an indefinable mix of alcohol, malicious stupidity and inchoate racism, the recent rash of church burnings like what happened at Spring Hill Free Will Baptist speak more to the ambiguities of race now than to a repeat perfor-mance of sixties-style Southern white supremacism. Rather than the smug indifference of the past, when such crimes invariably went unpun-ished and barely investigated, the arsons in Mississippi touched a raw nerve among blacks and whites. Jack Honea, a white salesman at the Great American Box Co. in Magnolia, helped organize a Spring Hill rebuilding initiative involving 325 people from seventy-seven different churches. (Rocky Point was fractured by a split within the church and members eventually lawyered themselves into protracted litigation that went to the state Supreme Court to determine who would oversee the rebuilding.) Those who signed up included Bubba Mathis, a black busi-nessman in Summit; Rex Cowart, a white mail carrier from Summit; Carl Young, a black mechanic at the Ford dealership in McComb; and Frank Martin, a white banker from Summit. They began working in December 1993 and by May had finished a $100,000 brick veneer church with gleaming white walls and refinished oak pews. On the day the new church was dedicated, perhaps 250 people–black and white–jammed into the 150 seats in the pews, spilled into the aisles, into the new kitchen behind the pulpit, into the front foyer, and finally into the steamy air outside. They waved their hand-held funeral-home fans to keep cool or just fanned themselves with the program, whose front page read: "Spring Hill Free Will Baptist Church, Amite County, Mississippi. Burned by Fire. Rebuilt by Faith and Love. Dedicated by Members and Christian Friends to the Glory of God. May 15, 1994."

After the service, after an interracial choir sang, "There's a sweet, sweet spirit in this place, There are sweet expressions on each face," after Jack Morgan had even the white folks hollering over his shouting, sweating, stomping gospel rendition of "The Little Country Church on the Hill," after a parade of black and white ministers had said that the service should be a beginning not an end, everyone spilled outside. In the afternoon heat, they milled about, Southerners whose music, manners, and mores flowed from the same stream, and ate from paper plates piled with fried chicken, biscuits, potato salad, chicken casserole, and bread pudding.

I had been there during one day of the rebuilding and for the dedication and wanted to see what had come of it. I drove up just before Sunday school started at ten A.M., reintroduced myself to the pastor, Arelious Robinson, who was dressed in a dazzling double-breasted turquoise suit, white shirt, artful silk tie with matching handkerchief, and two-toned black-and-white shoes. About fifteen people were there for the Sunday-school reading of Isaiah 5: 18–23, "A Catalogue of Evils"; perhaps forty came for the full service.

There was no reason to expect the magic of my last visit, and it was clear that for the most part the two different communities that intersected after the fire had pretty much gone back to their own worlds. There were, however, plans for a joint revival meeting around Thanksgiving, and Reverend Robinson spoke glowingly of the events to come. "I can't do this myself," he proclaimed, amid the shouts of "Yassuh!" and "Tell it!" and "Sweet Jesus!" from the congregation. "But this will be a revival like you've never seen before. We'll stop at everyone's house regardless of race, creed, or color, and it's not going to be traditional. It's going to be just the way the Lord wants it to be, nothing but the pure word of Jesus Christ. Hallelujah! God's going to grant some children new fathers, and some daughters new mothers, because the ones that brought them here are going to get converted. There's going to be homes for the homeless; there's going to be clothes for the naked. There's going to be shoes for the children that don't have any, and there's going to be money for those that need it. And you know who's going to give it? Jesus. Hallelujah! That's right, the Lord Almighty."

I'd been to black churches many times, from Hemphill, Texas, to Meridian, Mississippi, to Atlanta. This service wasn't much different than the others I'd been to, but somehow I felt let down. It went on too long for my taste, and the interminable sermon by the visiting preacher, Quordiniah Lockley, who overdid the rhetorical device of rephrasing every thought three different ways, left me feeling trapped like when I was a young reporter stuck at some endless zoning board meeting. I found myself thinking of the Plaza United Methodist Church in Charlotte and how hard it was to meld everything, from the music to the timetable, to fit both white and black sensibilities, and of the way I felt oddly moved by the music and pageantry of the suburban service Mark Gibbs took me to in Cobb County, even if it didn't fit my self-image. Last time at Spring Hill had been magic. This time was a reminder that the world doesn't change by magic moments alone and of how big the gulf between white and black worlds remains, no matter how much good liberals would like to think it weren't so.

My last stop was the Mississippi coast. Willie Morris and JoAnne Prichard had given me a copy of a beautiful book published by the University Press of Mississippi, *Mississippi Observed,* a collection of photographs from the Mississippi Department of Archives and History, with selections from various Mississippi writers. Accompanying old photographs of seaside gazebos and the Biloxi Yacht Club perched on stilts, looking like a Mississippi pagoda at the end of a rickety wooden pier, was a passage from the introduction to *On the Gulf,* a collection of short stories by Elizabeth Spencer.

> If I could have one part of the world back the way it used to be, I would not choose Dresden before the fire bombing, Rome before Nero, or London before the blitz. I would not resurrect Babylon, Carthage or San Francisco. Let the leaning tower lean and the hanging gardens hang. I want the Mississippi Gulf Coast back the way it was before Hurricane Camille.

Biloxi and Gulfport are not names that immediately evoke such grand images for most people, but in their heyday they were known across the South for their gorgeous old antebellum seaside mansions whose broad front porches looked out toward the sea and whose gardens were filled with camellia japonicas, poinsettias, crape myrtles, and azaleas. Old-time residents remember the days when you could lower nets with chicken necks inside into the warm Gulf waters and within a few hours catch enough crabs to fill a washtub. A graceful canopy of live oaks with thick gray tentacles of Spanish moss hung languorously over Highway 90 along the beach. Modest little mom-and-pop tourist courts and seaside fish joints jutted out into the Gulf on wooden pilings, and people returned each year to grand old Southern institutions like the famous old three-hundred-room Edgewater Hotel, where guests for years were required to wear black tie to dinner and where each place was set with eleven pieces of fine silver.

On August 17, 1969, it was all blown to smithereens by the two-hundred-mile-an-hour winds of Camille, the most powerful hurricane ever recorded on American shores. The storm killed 145 people on the Mississippi coast, did a billion dollars' worth of damage back when a billion dollars was real money, and blew away the existing world of the Gulf every bit as decisively as the bombs blew away Dresden. Jon Nordheimer of *The New York Times* found perhaps the most literate man on the Gulf Coast, a businessman named Andy Anderson, who quoted from Shakespeare's *As You Like It*: " 'Sweet are the uses of adversity, which, like the toad, ugly and venomous, wears yet a precious jewel in his head.' " He mused that perhaps something good could come of the devastation. "Who knows?" he said. "Maybe in the long run this hurricane is going to change a sleepy town into a magnificent resort." Much of it was rebuilt, if often in a diminished form, but for most of the time since then the Mississippi coast had plodded along like a battered boxer who has scars up and down his arms and legs and lumbers punch-drunk around the ring.

Given the coast's parlous state, it seemed like the makings of a good Jeff Foxworthy routine a few years back when some businessmen, taking advantage of a law that allowed gambling offshore, gussied up a boat called the *Europa Star* as a floating casino and promised to make Biloxi the South's answer to Las Vegas. Five years later it didn't seem like a joke at all. Though the *Europa Star* was gone, when the first dock-side casino opened in August 1992, the Gulf Coast came to life in a way that it never had since Camille blew it apart.

Granted, it was not everybody's kind of life. But by the summer of 1995, Biloxi, Gulfport, Bay Saint Louis, all the communities clobbered most by Camille had the feel of boom towns, their growth fueled almost completely by the fourteen casinos built on barges at the edge of the Gulf, each of which had required about $60 million to $70 million in investment and which had combined revenues of $70 million a month. A $100 million casino was set to open, and another $150 million one was on the drawing boards. Within a year the industry titans were engaged in gambling's version of the arms race to build the biggest and best casinos and hotels, topped by Mirage Resorts' planned $475 million, 1,800-room casino/hotel–bigger than anything in Atlantic City. The casinos already employed 15,000 people, not to mention spin-off jobs in hotels or service businesses and thanks to the casinos, total employment on the coast grew a startling 17 percent to 159,270 jobs at the end of 1995 from 136,250 just three years earlier.

Some of the casinos, like the cool pastel neon of the Isle of Capri Casino, with its thunderous indoor waterfall cascading through it, had the classy feel of Miami's South Beach. Some of them, like the goofy Treasure Bay Casino, with its blackjack dealers dressed like out-of-work actors auditioning for parts in the *Pirates of Penzance* and an automated buccaneer who looked like he had Parkinson's disease, seemed just about what you might expect if someone blended Las Vegas and Biloxi.

It's hard to believe you can build a state economy on gambling, and the whole mania in Mississippi had the feel of the South at its most Snopesian: Don't educate people; just go from the cotton fields to the catfish ponds to the blackjack tables or whatever get-rich-quick scheme comes along that can keep people happy without unduly upsetting the existing social order. Some of the social costs were already becoming clear. For example, in just two years, the number of Gamblers Anonymous chapters on the coast had gone from two to eleven and almost everybody knew a story about someone who had lost money at the casinos that he couldn't afford to lose or never even had.

But if gambling isn't going to make everyplace rich, in Gulfport and Biloxi it had the feel of a big bet that was paying off, so much so that gambling in New Orleans was proving to be a bust because everyone was driving to Mississippi instead. Reportorial symmetry demanded one last casino run, so I headed for the Biloxi Grand, which was billed as the world's largest floating casino, with 1,800 slot machines, 84 table games, a 1,900-seat theater, a 500-room hotel and the Kid's Quest day-care center, open until midnight (one A.M. on Fridays and Saturdays), where you could park Junior before a bank of video machines for a mere three dollars per hour per child while you went about your business. Rather than toying with the slots, I went straight to the poker tables. Unlike the Boboesque amity of the casino in Natchez, this was all business, about what you'd expect from people sitting at poker tables in Biloxi, Mississippi, at eleven P.M. on a Sunday night.

I played for about an hour and a half, feeling like a jump shooter in the zone. You won a hundred dollars if you had the best poker hand in the room during any one hour. You won fifty dollars if you had second best. I won them both, with two full houses, aces over nines and aces over sixes. I lost a few hands at the end, so my winnings came to about my two big hands. I finished my four-round bout with the casinos up 4–0. It will never happen again, but it was fun while it lasted. Forget the "Magnolia State" or Vernon Chadwick's funky green state eco-flag. My suggestion for the state slogan: "Mississippi–You Can't Win If You Don't Play."

I had one last place to visit in Biloxi, Beauvoir, the final home of Jefferson Davis. It was built as a seaside planter's retreat in 1851, was sold to Davis in 1879, and in 1903 became a home for Confederate veterans and their wives and widows, who lived in twelve barracks on the grounds. When the last two widows were taken to nursing homes in 1957, the home was returned to the Mississippi Division of the Sons of Confederate Veterans, which operates the property as a shrine to Jefferson Davis and the Lost Cause. It sits today in regal repose behind a marble memorial arch facing out to sea, just up the street from the President Casino, whose name, it turned out, came from the company's original casino, a riverboat in Davenport, Iowa, rather than from the only president of the Confederate States of America.

When I was planning my trip, I had a vague sense that there would be a dour, portentous metaphor here, something about the last vestiges of the Old South, flawed but not without nobility, slowly going to seed amid the Snopesian greed and all-American tackiness of the Las Vegas South.

Instead, like Elvis, Jefferson Davis had never been better. There were bumper stickers all over the South reading DON'T BLAME US. WE VOTED FOR JEFFERSON DAVIS. Mississippi Senator Thad Cochran had just gotten the U.S. Senate to pass a resolution permanently assigning Davis's old mahogany desk to the senior senator from Mississippi. (The only similar assignment was Daniel Webster's desk to the senior senator from New Hampshire.) Beauvoir had obtained $4.5 million in state bond funds to build a 14,000-square-foot, two-story, Palladian Jefferson Davis Presidential Library to put him on a more equal footing with his peers who had operated out of Washington. Governor Fordice had invited all the Southern governors to meet there in September, and instead of representing the New South Democrats of the Clinton-Mabus-Roemer Barge Compact era of just a few years ago, the group was the most conservative in decades and the most Republican in modern history. (Alabama's Fob James and South Carolina's David Beasely both ran at least as far to the right as Fordice.) And 130 years after losing the war, Davis, who was among the most passionate believers in the states' rights doctrine, had the feel of a winner.

"I don't want to make [Davis] a figure on the current political scene, but there's sure a whole lot of talk now about the Tenth Amendment and states' rights and government getting too big and too intrusive and telling folks what to do," said Keith Hardison, director of Beauvoir, echoing Trent Lott's remarks in *Southern Partisan,* and the standard neo-Con line. "Well, this was what Jefferson Davis was talking about. That's why he left the Union. It sounds real good to some people for the textbooks to say the 1861–65 war was a conflict over slavery, and that he led a revolt of slave owners, but it's not true. That was one of a variety of issues being discussed and debated, but the reason Jefferson Davis did what he did was the same reason people elected Newt Gingrich and a Republican Congress in the last election. It's as old as Fort Sumter and Mississippi seceding from the Union and as new as the Contract with America. Jefferson Davis was a staunch defender of limited constitutional government with a strong states' rights component. Davis once said he loved the Union, but he loved the Constitution more, and it was better to leave the Union with the Constitution than to remain in the Union without it.

"I'm not saying Jefferson Davis would believe everything the Republicans believe or everything Newt Gingrich believes, but the bedrock assertion of a very narrowly constructed, very rigidly controlled national government that doesn't intrude unnecessarily on the affairs of its citizens was the hallmark of what Jefferson Davis believed, what the new conservatism believes, and what Ronald Reagan believed. In fact, I remember listening to Reagan's inaugural remarks and thinking, 'Hey, I've heard this before. This is Jefferson Davis.' "

This was a pretty selective reading of history. It's hard to argue with a straight face that the Civil War was essentially an idealistic crusade by the enlightened North against the evils of slavery. For the most part, blacks were looked down upon and viewed as inferiors in the North almost as much as they were in the South. But it's just as hard to argue that slavery wasn't the critical fulcrum around which political, cultural, and economic sectional rivalries revolved, just as it's impossible to disassociate the South's race-based passion for states' rights pre–Civil War or at the time of integration from the national vogue for states' rights now. And as one of the minority of Southerners who owned slaves, passionately believed in the institution of slavery, and whose livelihood was dependent on it, Davis was no more a disinterested advocate of the philosophical principles of limited government than George Wallace was when he stood in front of the Alabama capitol where Davis once stood and invoked Davis's name as he pledged to uphold "segregation now, segregation tomorrow, segregation forever."

Davis remains something of an enigma to this day, "the sphinx of the Confederacy." He was a man of great pride, stubbornness, and reserve, who raised himself from common beginnings to the proto-aristocratic status of the most successful planters. During his life he was alternately praised for pulling together a functioning country and a remarkable army out of fractious farming states and damned as an obstinate despot who feuded with his own generals and failed miserably as a tactician, particularly in his fatal blunders in the Atlanta campaign. While Lincoln, not General Grant, came to symbolize the Union cause, it was General Lee, not Davis, who most came to stand for the Confederacy; significantly, the *Encyclopedia of Southern Culture* gives twice as much space to the general from Virginia as to Davis.

But Davis's imprisonment for two years without trial after the war, and the decision of the Congress to leave him alone as part of the general amnesty offered to all Confederates, made him the original Lost Cause martyr. He artfully positioned himself on both sides of the Southern postwar divide. As for secession and war, he had no apologies. "Remembering, as I must, all which has been suffered, all which has been lost, disappointed hopes and crushed aspirations, yet I deliberately say, if I were to do it all over again, I would again do just as I did in 1861." As for the future, it was time to move on economically: "The past is dead; let it bury its dead, its hopes and aspirations.... Let me beseech you to lay aside all rancor, all bitter sectional feeling, and to take your places in the ranks of those who will bring about a consummation devoutly to be wished—a reunited country."

When he died in 1889, doubts about his presidency long since buried in the warm glow of Lost Cause nostalgia, the funeral in New Orleans—one of the answers to Charles Wilson's Dixie funeral riddle—was the most extravagant show of sectional unity since the Civil War. It was at turns macabre (the undertaker botched the embalming and Davis's face decomposed literally before mourners' eyes in the sticky New Orleans air) and grandiose (seventy thousand people viewed his body, and a dozen militia companies from Georgia, Texas, Mississippi, Alabama, and Louisiana marched in a four-mile-long funeral procession, which ended up at the cemetery in Metairie, the New Orleans suburb that later became David Duke's stomping grounds). In an essay on Southern funerals Wilson said the scene around the open coffin with its Confederate flags and weaponry "gave the impression that the deceased was dug in, ready to fight again."

At Beauvoir, the neo-Cons were still fighting. The cover of the new issue of *Southern Partisan* on sale at the Beauvoir souvenir shop proclaimed, "Two Victories: Confederate Forces Advance," referring to decisions in Danville, Virginia, and Columbia, South Carolina, to continue flying Confederate flags. As ever, the *Partisan* was still refighting the war with ads for books like *North Against South* ("Finally ... the War and Reconstruction from our point of view") and state-by-state political news under the rubric "C.S.A. Today." The wares at the gift shop included such essentials as the 1996 "Confederate calendar," Civil War CDs and tapes like "Homespun Songs of the C.S.A.," black mammy dolls, Civil War cookbooks and playing cards, Battle Flag T-shirts, and neo-Con classics like *The South Was Right!* or *The Confederate Republic: A Revolution Against Politics.* The combination of Biloxi reborn and Davis triumphant was, rather than a metaphor for decline, the story of the South–everything had changed, but the old ghosts still lived, breathed, and dreamed of ultimate victory.

I wandered around the Beauvoir site–the name means "beautiful view"–for two hours. It was a graceful white one-story house built in the Louisiana raised-cottage style: it was elevated so hurricane tides would wash under the house and its roof was built with a high peak and steep slope, so that if it was blown apart during a hurricane, the roof would come down onto the house rather than fly off. The house was damaged by Camille but survived, while many of its neighbors were blown to bits.

In what used to be the old hospital chapel, there was a museum of Civil War memorabilia, its gray walls decorated with verses from the Bible, hand lettered by one of the Confederate veterans. Nearby was a Currier and Ives novelty picture of Confederate heroes that when viewed from the center displayed Jefferson Davis, from the left showed Stonewall Jackson, and from the right showed Robert E. Lee. Outside the museum was the house itself, with its deep rambling front porch where Davis used to sit and view the sea, its reception hall running the building's entire length with rounded corners and rococo-style frescoed walls and Davis's bedroom with a framed needlepoint garland of flowers stitched for him by 350 women when he was imprisoned after the war.

From the front of the house you could see the cars whizzing by on Highway 90 and even the casino signs just to the east. But if you went out back past Keith Hardison's house with the Fordice sticker on his car and kept walking, the casino world drifted away. You could walk through dense groves of longleaf and loblolly pine, water oak and red oak, tulip poplar, laurel, chinaberry and magnolia and the indestructible old live oaks, including one named for Davis that is over seventy feet high with a limb spread of over a hundred eighty feet. A young woman was tending the rose garden behind the house. Just beyond it a man-made lagoon called Oyster Bay Lagoon led to the Confederate Cemetery, which holds the graves of 771 Confederate veterans and their wives and the Confederate version of the Tomb of the Unknown Soldier. Its inscription reads:

Ah! Fearless on many a day for us
They stood in front of the fray for us
And held the foeman at bay for us
And tears should fall
Fore'er o'er all
Who fell while wearing the gray for us.

All you could hear was the rustling of leaves in the moist air, the sound of the mockingbirds, blue jays and kingfishers, and the cackling of distant crows.

Chapter 12

FROM MORELAND TO ATLANTA
Visions of the South from Tobacco Road to the Sad
Ballad of Lewis Grizzard

THE LITTLE TOWN OF MORELAND, GEORGIA, FORTY-FIVE MILES southwest of Atlanta, has about 450 people, no stoplight, one gas station and one convenience store, a Baptist and a Methodist church, and two literary museums. In their own way, they capture the twists and turns the South has taken in the nation's soul and what they say about the South and the nation.

The first is the Erskine Caldwell Birthplace and Museum, "The Little Manse." The rickety, one-story, five-room house where Caldwell was born about three miles southeast of Moreland on the cold, rainy, winter night of December 17, 1903, had been abandoned for years, used only for storing hay, until 1990, when local officials and the local historical society moved it to town, restored it, and reopened it as a museum that's open for a few hours on Saturday and Sunday afternoons.

It's a pretty simple place, all bare floors, old books, movie posters, and family artifacts like Caldwell's old briefcase, typewriter, and childhood copies of *Swiss Family Robinson* and *Molly Cottontail*. The house sits rather forlornly by itself at the edge of the town square and you don't get the sense that anyone much cares about it. You would never guess that for at least three decades, from the thirties into the sixties, Erskine Caldwell was the best-known, bestselling, and most celebrated Southern writer of them all—indeed the bestselling American author of his time. Between 1931 and 1976 he churned out some 150 short stories, twenty novels, and ten nonfiction books. Overall, he produced fifty-six books, which have sold more than 80 million copies and been translated into forty-three languages. By the late 1940s, he had sold more books than any writer in the nation's history. His first novel, *Tobacco Road,* was turned into the most successful Broadway play of its time; it ran for seven and a half years and was staged in Paris by Albert Camus. Later it was made into a successful Hollywood movie. His second novel, *God's Little Acre,* was for years the bestselling Southern book in history, with more than 8 million copies sold, more even than *Gone with the Wind.* When William Faulkner listed the five best novelists of his era he named, in order, Thomas Wolfe, himself, John Dos Passos, Erskine Caldwell, and Ernest Hemingway.

Caldwell was the only son of Ira Sylvester Caldwell, a dogged, courageous Associated Presbyterian minister, and Carolyn Bell Caldwell, a meticulous, austere schoolteacher, and his youth was hardly the stuff of neo-Con agrarian fantasies. His father was more taken with notions of social justice and racial fairness than with the fundamentalist vapors of the South, and he took his son with him to see the threadbare hovels of the poor and what he considered the ignorant excesses of snake handling, blood drinking, speaking in tongues, and self-mutilation common in the fundamentalist churches scattered across the landscape. His mother vacillated between doting on her only son—dressing him in an absurd white linen blouse that hung to his knees as if he were a little Cossack—and completely neglecting him. He was burned so badly in an accident that he almost died, and he grew up an odd, lonely, mirthless youth, animated by his father's disdain for the social mores of the rural South and his mother's chilly reserve. Caldwell tried attending two colleges, picking cotton, playing professional football, and pursuing journalism before leaving the South to write about it. He faced years of rejection before his career finally took off, but eventually he became one of the foremost literary celebrities of his time, as much a fixture on the gossip and news pages as the book section and the most influential, if not the most admired, interpreter of the South.

Still, his museum in Moreland is an unlikely institution for two reasons. First, his reputation has dimmed with time, dragged down by too many years he spent knocking out second-rate work to the point that he is barely read today and is usually omitted from the Faulkner-Welty-McCullers-O'Connor-Styron-Wolfe pantheon of Southern writers. Second, Caldwell came to be seen within the South not as a celebrator of the region but as a traitor to it. The books for which he is best known are antic, obsessively sexual, tragicomic portraits of dirt-poor, rural grotesqueries, like Jeeter Lester, the famous white-trash protagonist of *Tobacco Road,* or Ty Ty Walden, who spends his time digging holes in the Georgia clay looking for gold in *God's Little Acre.* His characters are lewd, crude, half-starved sharecroppers fighting over a sack of turnips, harelipped Jezebels slithering in the dust like dogs in heat, worn-out Depression-era illiterates whose idea of a meal was fatback rinds boiled in a pan of water and whose idea of work was trying to sell blackjack oak that was tougher than iron waterpipes.

The overall picture is not without saving graces. Like most Southerners, his characters had an almost mystical attachment to the land and to the past. And Caldwell wrote about the ravages of racial injustice on both whites and blacks in a way that was ahead of its time. One of his admirers was W. J. Cash, who wrote in the *Charlotte News:* "I like Caldwell a great deal. And for all his faults, he has a sardonic sense of humor that sometimes raises old Jeeter Lester and the rest of his brood to Rabelaisian proportions."

But Caldwell's books, coming when the region's image was trending back toward hookworm and pellagra, the Scopes monkey trial, nightriders and lynching bees, defined the Depression-era Savage South in a way that enraged critics and readers throughout the region. Donald Davidson, one of the Nashville Agrarians and Russell Kirk's favorite summoner of timeless Southern virtues, railed against Caldwell's "libelous and malicious proceedings," grouping him with the Civil War–era abolitionists and Radical Republicans as an enemy of the South. When the play based on *Tobacco Road* became a national sensation, Braswell Deen, a U.S. congressman from southeast Georgia, rose on the floor of the House and thundered: "I open my mouth and resent with all the power of my soul this untruthful, undignified, undiplomatic, and unfair sketch of Southern life. There is not a word of truth in it. I denounce it and resent it." Even today critics argue over how much of his work was his own mix of well-meaning leftist social commentary and the Southern comic tradition and how much was a calculated attempt to use the poverty of the South as a way to pander to Yankee prejudices about Southern depravity.

To some extent Caldwell provided his own best defense in *You Have Seen Their Faces,* a jarring look at real-world Southern poverty using his text and the photographs of the second of his four wives, the celebrated *Life* magazine photographer Margaret Bourke-White. Critics charged that it, too, was loaded, slanted, and calibrated to shock as much as to elucidate. It may not have been a picture of the whole South, but the haunting images of hollow-faced sharecroppers and farmers, like those of James Agee and Walker Evans's *Let Us Now Praise Famous Men,* were bleak, unvarnished testimony to the poverty, sickness, and despair of the real-world Jeeter Lesters of a region that, despite the neo-Con nostalgia for the past, earned the label FDR gave it, "the nation's number one economic problem."

In fact, much of Caldwell's work, like his introduction to *You Have Seen Their Faces,* does walk a fine line between denouncing the economic ravages the region has always endured and denouncing the region and its people. "The South has always been shoved around like a country cousin," he began. "It buys mill ends and hand-me-downs. It sits at second table and is fed short rations. It is the place where the ordinary will do, where the makeshift is good enough. It is that dog-town on the other side of the railroad tracks that smells so badly every time the wind changes." And yet, for all its trouble and toil, it's a place "where anybody may come without an invitation and, before the day is over, be made to feel like one of the homefolks. Scientists with microscopes and theologians with Bibles come to the South to tell it what is wrong with it, and stay to buy a home and raise a family. Gaping tourists come to pick its flesh to pieces and remain to eat fried chicken and watermelon for the rest of their lives."

But such affirmation was the exception, not the norm. Elsewhere in the book he wrote, "The South has been taking a beating for a long time, and the pain and indignity is beginning to tell." The result was a warped economic, political, and cultural wasteland, "a retarded and thwarted civilization," a "worn-out agricultural empire," a loser culture that has "purposely isolated itself from the world in retaliation for defeat, and taken refuge in its feeling of inferiority." It was a place where politicians did little more than instill and generate prejudices, and the church, absent the social conscience of people like his father, had become "a burlesque of religion."

In Caldwell's later years and later books, the excesses of sex and violence remained without the insight and compassion that leavened them in his best books. His books were inevitably marketed with salacious covers of busty, half-dressed women groveling in the red clay like avatars of Southern Gothic porn, and after a while he became associated more with cheap, sex-saturated paperbacks than serious literature. Virtually everything he wrote was out of print for years until the University of Georgia began rereleasing much of it a few years back.

From beginning to end, Caldwell's career reveals two indelible facts about the South. First, the South was America's loser region, a place that at the beginning of the New Deal had a quarter of the nation's population but a tenth of its wealth, a sickly colony of rural poverty where sharecroppers were paid twenty cents for a hundred pounds of cotton, where only half the children under eighteen went to school at all; the fourteen lowest rungs of the nation's educational ladder were all occupied by Southern and border states. Second, for all the richness of its music, literature, and folkways, the South was as much a cultural colony as an economic one. The embryonic music scene in Nashville was able to create music of, by, and for Southerners that had limited appeal outside the region. But the Southern culture that was disseminated nationally was the result of what was filtered through the lens of the literary and cultural capitals on the two coasts. Whether or not Caldwell was a rank panderer or a clever satirist and social reformer, he was taking his literary wares entirely to the cultural marketplace outside the South, at once playing off of stereotypes of Southern life and creating them.

The second literary museum in Moreland is a lot cheerier. Housed in an old frame building that used to be a doctor's office on Main Street, its gleaming white paint is set off by sky-blue trim. Red, white, and blue bunting hangs over the door frames. An American flag flies in the breeze on one side of the front porch and a Georgia flag, with its Confederate Saint Andrews cross, flies from the other. Unlike the Little Manse, it honors a writer who was never considered a serious figure in American letters. Most literary types loathed him, and his books, with their trademark goofy titles like *Elvis Is Dead and I Don't Feel So Good Myself* or *Chili Dawgs Only Bark at Night*, were generally ignored or trashed by literary critics outside the South. But with his book-a-year pace and his newspaper column syndicated in 450 newspapers in the South and beyond, Lewis Grizzard was read and revered in his home region as Caldwell never was. The *Encyclopedia of Southern Culture* gives him roughly as much space as it does Caldwell. In his own way, Lewis

Grizzard was as revealing a Southern writer in his time as Caldwell was in his, a shipwrecked combination of bravado and bathos, past and present, true grit and stale shtick. When he died, in 1994, he was mourned like Martin Luther King, Jr., like Jefferson Davis, like the Bear, like Elvis himself, as the embodiment of a particular vision of the South. Figuring out just what that vision signifies and where it leads is no easy task.

Lewis Grizzard was born in Fort Benning, Georgia, in 1946, the only child of an army lieutenant, Lewis Grizzard, and Christine Grizzard. His father, who was decorated in World War II and Korea and then dishonorably discharged in 1953, was an alcoholic who left his family when his son was six. Lewis Sr. was a big bear of a man with a flattop haircut, a ready smile, a booming voice always ready to break out into a favorite hymn, and had the charm of a born con man. He spent his life going from job to job, bouncing checks, telling tales, and charming, disarming, and amiably torturing those who loved him, most of all his namesake. Until he died penniless of a stroke in 1970, his relationship with Lewis Jr. was a heartbreaking tease in which he periodically popped into his son's life and raised his hopes and then either disappeared or had to be rescued from a drunken stupor in one or another seedy motel.

Most of Grizzard's books are so fluffy and ephemeral as to float away, but his book on his father, *My Daddy Was a Pistol and I'm a Son of a Gun,* despite the cheery Grizzardian title, is a harrowing account of the ties that choke as well as bind, a George Jones crying song elevated to art, full of heartbreaking self-deception and naked bitter truth. "Don't hate me," his father invariably said upon blinking into consciousness after a long drunk, and Grizzard could neither hate him nor fully come to grips with what the relationship did to him. In the end, he lived out his father's life of too much drink and too little truth, outdoing his dad with a fourth marriage to his father's three just before going in for his fourth—ultimately fatal—heart surgery in 1994. He was forty-seven years old when he died.

If the pain of his relationship with his father was one pole of his life, his love for the South was the other. It was almost as if Grizzard invested his home region with all the love, security, constancy, and virtue he wanted so desperately and never received from his father. He grew up with his mother in Moreland, married at the age of nineteen, went to the University of Georgia, where he spent most of his time working as sports editor of the fledgling *Athens Daily News,* and then headed off to the *Atlanta Journal,* where he became executive sports editor at the age of twenty-three; he divorced for the first time a year later. From there he went to the Chicago *Sun-Times,* where he picked up wife and divorce Number 2.

Chicago eventually became great joke fodder as the place where he was held hostage behind enemy lines, where his precinct captain was Frosty the Snowman, where he had to endure its two seasons—winter and the Fourth of July. He missed Georgia. Along with divorce Number 2, he was burned out by various unpleasantnesses, including a successful discrimination suit by a black sportswriter who was dismissed after being demoted by Grizzard. Back home, Jimmy Carter had made it to the White House, the media were falling over themselves to spin the wheel back from the Savage South of Jeeter Lester and Bull Connor to the Sunny South of Billy Beer and Gritz and Fritz, and the time was ripe for a new Southern voice. So Grizzard returned to Atlanta to try writing a column, first about sports, then about whatever he wanted.

Say what you want about Lewis Grizzard's work, but no one ever doubted he had a brilliant sense for what his readers wanted to hear. As an editor and columnist Lewis used to say he wanted "barbershop stories," the kind of stories ordinary folks were talking about over haircuts. And when he started his column, Lewis realized there was a market not just for a Southern voice, but for one that wasn't housebroken. Carter helped spawn plenty of Yankee-leaning Southern writers who sold a still-quirky but no-longer-menacing domesticated South of hot cornbread, fried catfish, Jack Daniels, and racial peace, a South that had shed its old vices and, in the reigning journalistic cliché of the day, "rejoined the Union." Grizzard, partly through calculation and partly from his gut, said, "Screw that." He figured he could sell the South on its own terms, a place of hot cornbread, fried catfish, and Jack Daniels, but one where people still thought the wrong side had won the war, liberals were the enemy, Elvis was King, the rebel flag was still worth flying, and if you didn't like it, well, as Lewis loved to say, "Delta is ready when you are"—if you don't like it, the plane is waiting to fly you back to Cleveland or Buffalo.

Grizzard and Caldwell had a lot in common. Both were grounded in the same Southern comic tradition. Both were born yarn spinners with great ears for the texture of Southern voices. Both were compulsive workers pounding out books the way others pounded in rivets. Both were complicated, incredibly needy people and obsessive womanizers who married four times. Both wrote for the *Atlanta Journal* and drew intense reactions from the folks at home. In the end, though, they were like mirror images, looking at the same text and coming up with entirely different readings, Caldwell seeing the Savage South, Grizzard seeing the Sunny one.

Beyond that, Grizzard turned Caldwell's two truths on their heads. The South was now the nation's winner region, full of fleeing Yankees, instead of the loser region whose people migrated North. And, though many Southerners still rankled at the degree to which American culture was still dominated by the media giants on the two coasts, the nation had changed enough so that Grizzard figured he didn't need to sell a vision of the South that would go over well with critics and cultural pashas in the North. He surmised that what played in the South would probably play pretty well in Peoria as well. Whether he thought it through or not, Grizzard reckoned he could do just fine writing about a world where, instead of the South rejoining the Union, the Union was joining the South.

Not that he began as any kind of a propagandist. Indeed, most of his columns—the best ones—simply reflected his heartfelt joy in being home and the allure of the simple virtues of Southern life. He celebrated University of Georgia football; the Vienna sausage, Home Run cigarettes, and Hollywood candy bars at country general stores; the Hank Williams songs on the jukebox at Steve Smith's truck stop in Moreland; the barbecue sandwich, onion rings, Brunswick stew, and lemon icebox pie at Sprayberry's barbecue in Newnan, up the road from Moreland. Just as he used every twist and turn of his Georgia accent to tell stories, at his best he captured the small moments and telling details of Southern life in a way that evoked the shared culture of the South.

As time went by and his astute marketing instincts sniffed out the dimensions of the nation's rightward drift, he became a professional provocateur as well. Long before the rise of talk radio and the notion of the angry white male, Grizzard, with much of the insight but little of the venom of George Wallace, turned his mythic South into the quintessence of the good old days. It wasn't a new role. Throughout

American history, the region has in its Sunny South guise been turned into a peaceful, orderly, mythic kingdom of stability and values evoked time and again in times of turmoil of national drift. But Grizzard brought the image up to date and added a new twist: not only had the South got it right in terms of values and repose, it was outdoing the rest of the country economically as well.

Grizzard's idealized South was the world before feminists and affirmative action, when gays stayed in the closet where they belonged, where America pretty much meant the world of small-town white folks like him. In his columns and speeches, delivered at twenty thousand dollars a pop, gays were "fruitflies," feminists were "hairy-legged Yankee women" or "sweathogs," and life would be perfect if we could just go back to 1962. A typical column found Grizzard at the Georgia–Ole Miss football game in Oxford. The band played "Dixie." The Mississippi partisans waved their Confederate flags. The Mississippians in front of him were drinking Jim Beam. Grizzard was in heaven: "All of this prompted my friend Bugar Seely, a veteran Georgia fan, to say, 'They still wave the flag, still sing "Dixie," they can still pray and can still bring liquor into the game. No wonder they beat us.' "

When the brief and tumultuous tenure of Bill Kovach, who came to the Atlanta newspapers from *The New York Times* with a disdain for Grizzard's calculated suburban redneck view of the South, ended in a stormy tempest in 1988, Grizzard drew up a manifesto he wanted to run as a paid ad saying the papers would do fine, "with apologies to those who enjoy reading exhaustive series on what's doing in Africa." Particularly in his later years he trafficked in an endless sense of grievance as if nothing in life was so hard as to be a smart-assed white boy from Georgia. "I'm a white man and I'm a Southerner, and I'm sick of being told what is wrong with me from outside critics, and I'm tired of being stereotyped as a refugee from *God's Little Acre*," he complained on behalf of his readers, at least the white men among them.

By the end, he was his own little conglomerate with five million books in print and lucrative speaking engagements, who continuously plumbed and recycled every episode in his life in his columns, books, tapes, and videotapes—dedicated Grizzardologists could come upon the same joke in at least four media. Those in need of a second opinion could read his third wife Kathy Grizzard Schmook's cutting *How to*

Tame a Wild Bore and Other Facts of Life with Lewis–The Semitrue Confessions of the Third Mrs. Grizzard. Those in need of a third opinion could try his stepbrother Ludlow Porch's respectful *Lewis and Me and Skipper Makes 3.*" His personal soap opera was so much a part of Southern life that for a while Atlanta's freeways were dotted with bumper stickers reading HONK IF YOU'VE BEEN MARRIED TO LEWIS GRIZZARD.

Grizzard came by his pining for the past honestly–he wrote on an antique Royal manual typewriter, drank Tab, loved trains, and hated flying in much the way one of Flannery O'Connor's characters dismissed the wonders of modern travel by sneering, "I wouldn't give you nothin' for no airplane. A buzzard can fly." But for all his nostalgia for the good old days, Grizzard no more wanted to move back to Moreland than he wanted to join Act Up or the Rainbow Coalition. Instead, he actually was the patron saint of the new suburban South, where you could have both the values of the old general store and the designer-label wares of the megamalls that serve as the main streets of Atlanta, Charlotte, Birmingham, and Dallas. Lewis dressed for life like a golfer on his way to the clubhouse in his knit shirts reading THE CROSBY or MELROSE, his Dockers pants and Gucci loafers with no socks. He hung out with his card and golf buddies every day at the Men's Grill of the Ansley Golf Club, and drank Stolichnaya vodka, not Budweiser. His books may have evoked a South of faith, love, trust, and old-time values, but he lived most of his life without any of them.

Grizzard sang the song of the South, but lived the life of the Sun Belt, the world of beachfront condos on Hilton Head or in Panama City, of wooded subdivisions full of glistening new Georgian homes, of Peachtree Road singles bars, of pregame tailgate parties at the Florida-Georgia football game. He was a great friend to a lot of people, but no one ever missed how far his own life was from the values he championed and what a cranky, unhappy, insecure, loveless figure lurked just beneath the surface of his world. "Lewis is the loneliest man in the world," said Kathy Grizzard Schmook, wife Number 3. "He has always felt he would die like his father, young and penniless. Lewis is now constant shtick, and there's very little of the man I knew left. I don't know what Lewis represents anymore. He's like a great big plastic fast-food box that sells really well, but I don't know what's inside it anymore."

Every day, weather permitting, you could find Grizzard on the golf

course with his black-and-red Georgia Bulldogs golf bag and matching
Bulldog head covers. I met him once in Gulf Shores, Alabama, where
he was giving a speech. In typical Grizzard fashion, he was more or less
engaged to one woman but had managed to smuggle in another for this
particular expedition. He played eighteen at the Cotton Creek Golf
Club, hung out at the pink-stucco Perdido Beach Hilton, and then gave
his speech, a wonderfully orchestrated paean to all things Southern, to a
claque of appreciative fans.

But it was when the speech ended that the fun really began. Grizzard
hated to fly but loved to travel by bus, particularly in Sonny Williams's
forty-foot-long customized Silver Eagle with the 318 Detroit engine, the
humongous steer horns above the driver's seat, the televisions and
VCRs and tape decks, the shag carpet, and the mirror with the two big-
eyed cocker spaniels. Williams, who owns a truckstop in Fairview, Tennessee, has driven country music stars like Alabama and rock stars like
Bon Jovi. With Sonny's buddy Elvis, also known as Danny Ramm,
riding shotgun, Grizzard got the same treatment as the bus headed for
Atlanta.

Like a lot of people who get paid to be funny, Grizzard seldom
seemed to be having much fun in real life. He could be awkward and
stiff, looking at the floor, mumbling, evading a stranger's eyes, but on
the bus and on the booze he came to life. Two heart surgeries down the
road, he was chain-smoking Marlboros and knocking down screw-
drivers one after another, poured from a half-gallon bottle of Stolichnaya he carried around as if prepared to pour drinks for anyone who
wandered by. Now, on the road, Ricky Van Shelton was soon belting
out Merle Haggard's "Working Man's Blues" from the tape deck and
suddenly the gritty South Grizzard evoked in his columns beckoned.
There was talk of getting off the damn interstates and going to one-
stoplight towns and country stores or canoeing in middle-of-nowhere
mountain streams.

"If this ain't better than flying, there's something wrong with the
world," Grizzard hollered and by one-thirty in the morning the bus felt
like the spirit of the South—not the antiseptic country-club South he
lived in but the rough-edged real thing. Sonny was smiling as
he bounced up and down in the driver's seat. Grizzard had taken the
copilot's seat from Elvis. "Goddamn! We're at Montgomery? This is

great. You just tell Sonny when you want to get there, and he'll get you there. Take it on down the road, Sonny! Take it on down the road! At this rate, we'll be home by four-thirty."

But that was as far as the fantasy went. Grizzard was asleep in the back an hour later when the blower shaft that gets air to the engine cut off and the bus broke down on I-85 outside Auburn, Alabama, about 120 miles from home. Bleary-eyed and hung over, Grizzard finally stumbled into a cab his manager had hustled up, stopped for breakfast at McDonald's, and headed in glum silence up the highway to the comforts of home in Ansley Park, the tony neighborhood around the corner from his club.

Before long, Grizzard's life and body pretty much broke down, too, in a slow-motion train wreck that played out like a Tom T. Hall–era Nashville weeper. In 1993 he had a third heart operation and almost died, hovering in a coma for ten days. Somehow he made it through, but as the year went on everything went wrong. His black lab, Catfish, died on Thanksgiving night; Grizzard eulogized him in a column that ended: "There were times he was all I had. And now he has up and died. My own heart, or what is left of it, is breaking." He had surgery to repair an abscess on his abdominal wall, his spleen began to give out, and on the night after Christmas an artery ruptured and spilled nearly two pints of blood into his liver. His Georgia Bulldogs had a losing football season. "I feel like I'm dying a piece at a time," he told a friend.

Finally, in February 1994, while golfing in Orlando, he was hospitalized with severe pain in his kidneys. He was flown back to Atlanta, where doctors found an infection in his Dacron artificial aortic wall and valve. Facing long odds of surviving a fourth heart operation, sick of hospitals and needles and pills, terrified of death despite being shot up with antidepressant drugs, feeling for the first time like a father to the five-year-old daughter of his girlfriend Dedra Kyle, he married for the fourth time sitting in a wheelchair hooked to an IV at the hospital March 16. Some friends saw it as Lewis's final sad folly. To others, Lewis had finally found true love, and this one would have lasted in much the way Caldwell, after three failed marriages, lasted thirty years with the woman who was at his side when he died. We'll never know. He underwent his fourth heart surgery two days later, and this time his luck ran out. He suffered massive brain damage and died two days later.

Lewis Grizzard probably didn't write anything that will stand the test of time. Newspaper columns, especially those written under tee-time and barroom deadlines as pressing as journalistic ones, are just newspaper columns, and his cranked-out books were more fast food than full meals. But there's no mistaking what an enormous following he had, how much his work meant to hundreds of thousands of fans, and how deeply and genuinely he was loved and mourned. As he lay in a coma in 1993, more than forty thousand cards and letters of support poured into Emory Hospital from all across the nation; when he died a year later, it was as if a part of the South died with him.

In his essay "The Death of Southern Heroes: Historic Funerals of the South" published in 1994, Charles Reagan Wilson gives a quick tour of postbellum Southern mores through the region's most notable funerals. When Robert E. Lee died in 1870, the real-world death and devastation of the war were too fresh for any revisionist nostalgia, and in keeping with his wishes for a simple burial, Lee was accorded the traditional rites of the Episcopal church with no funeral oration. A military escort a mile long, headed by ex-Confederate soldiers, led the way, and he was buried in a simple suit of black after the singing of his favorite hymn, "How Firm a Foundation."

When Jefferson Davis died nineteen years later, Reconstruction had ended, the myth of the Lost Cause was beginning to flower, and the grand funeral pageant in New Orleans, part military ritual, part Confederate Mardi Gras, and part Victorian death ceremony, signaled the South's reborn dreams of sectional glory. When Huey P. Long was assassinated in 1935, one hundred thousand people turned out for his funeral, which reflected his populist appeal to poor whites—the South's road not taken based on economics rather than race—right down to the funeral dirge composed from Long's own "Every Man a King."

When Hank Williams died in the backseat of his powder-blue Cadillac on New Year's Day, 1953, he got the greatest country music burial of his time, broadcast live on two Montgomery radio stations. There were tons of flowers—the largest arrangement in the shape of a Bible with the first notes of Hank's religious song "I Saw the Light" on the cover—and performances by country greats like Ernest Tubb, Roy Acuff, and Red Foley. It was a powerful evocation of the new evolving Southern culture of religious values and country music, which was growing even more powerful as Southern whites moved to the city than it had been when they lived in the country.

Martin Luther King, Jr.'s, funeral in Atlanta in 1968, which brought out an estimated 150,000 to 200,000 blacks and whites, was an event blessed by white city fathers, if not by the segregationist governor, Lester Maddox, and reflected the first stirrings of a truly interracial South. Elvis's funeral in 1977, which brought 80,000 people to Graceland within a day of his death, was one of the biggest the nation has ever seen, with more flowers than any other funeral in American history. He lay in state in Graceland, in a setting every bit as ornate as Jefferson Davis's before eighteen white Cadillacs rolled down Elvis Presley Boulevard in the motor cortège. Hank Williams's funeral was a pageant of an emerging Southern popular culture strictly of, by, and for Southerners. Elvis's was a display of Southern culture for the world.

Lewis Grizzard won't go down in history in quite the same ranks with Lee, Davis, "The Kingfish" Long, Williams, King, or Elvis. In fact, not long after Grizzard's death, Jeff Foxworthy, with his "You might be a redneck if . . ." shtick, took a watered-down, inoffensive version of Grizzardism and achieved the kind of megawealth and megastardom Grizzard only dreamed of. Somewhere, Lewis Grizzard is not laughing. Still, his long good-bye could have continued Wilson's chronology.

The *Atlanta Constitution,* his home paper, for days printed elaborate tributes, special sections, reprints of his columns, and eulogies from readers. Almost every Southern paper gave him something similar to the point that even non-Grizzardians felt obligated to weigh in on what it all meant. One of my favorite contributions was by Vicki Covington, a novelist in Birmingham, who a week after Grizzard's death began by musing, "I wonder what Lewis Grizzard thinks about all this eulogizing that's going on down here. He probably wishes we'd just shut up." She confessed to being a closet fan and gave Grizzard credit for being willing to stand up for the South on its own terms. "Thank the stars, he didn't hate who he was: a Southern boy. We were spared the agony of watching yet another homeboy make good and proceed to tell us just how bigoted and backward and sorry we are."

After being laid out in his black-and-red Georgia Bulldog colors and an open-necked shirt the night before the funeral, he was memorialized on a glorious spring day amid blooming dogwoods, red plums, forsythia, and daffodils at the jammed-to-the-gills Moreland United

Methodist Church just up the street from his boyhood home. Among the eulogizers was, instead of the old Confederate generals who invoked the majesty of the South in Davis's day, University of Georgia football coach Ray Goff, who represented the South's current inspirational caste when he said with a mock shrug of his shoulders, "What can you say about Lewis Grizzard that you can say in a church?"

Grizzard's widow wore a bright red dress and gold shoes. The church was packed with old friends from Moreland, golfing buddies, loyal readers. The hometown choir sang his favorite hymns, including "Precious Memories," which had been sung at Hank Williams's funeral by the gospel group The Statesmen Quartet. Shortly afterward, Grizzard's cremated ashes–or most of them–were buried next to his mother's grave in the little Moreland cemetery, just as Elvis was laid to rest next to his mama in Memphis. His headstone reads A GREAT AMERICAN, LEWIS M. GRIZZARD JR. After the service, three of his golfing buddies, dressed in black golf shirts, played a round in his honor, one golfer short of a foursome, in "the missing man formation."

There was one final private observance. Before his death Grizzard had repeatedly said that when he died he wanted to be cremated and sprinkled on the fifty-yard line at Sanford Stadium in Athens, home of the Georgia Bulldogs. Dedra kept some of his ashes for just that purpose. On a gorgeous late-spring day about three months after his death, she retrieved the ashes and drove with Grizzard's business manager, Steve Enoch, down U.S. 78 toward Athens. They stopped for a six-pack of Bud, visited Grizzard's father's grave at the Zoar Baptist Church in Snellville, and continued on to Athens. When they got there, they scaled the stadium fence with the ashes in a plastic bag and sprinted toward the fifty-yard line. Dedra dug her hand into the bag of ashes, brought up a handful, tossed them into the air and watched as they drifted back to earth. As Flannery O'Connor put it, "Everything that rises must converge."

To this day, the Grizzardian view–the Sunny South evoked from within not from without–has amazing power, like a song you recognize from the first note. It's out there in endless guises, as easy to find as Grizzard's beloved Sprayberry's barbecue, where the Lewis Grizzard Special (barbecue sandwich, Brunswick stew, and fried onion rings) is still a bargain at $6.50, the sweetened ice tea comes in big old Coca-Cola glasses, and Grizzard's visage and columns still grace the walls;

one such column is his remembrance of the first time his mama took him in her '48 Chevy to get his first sliced barbecue pork sandwich at Sprayberry's when he was seven.

A year or so after his death, I drove down to Moreland with my daughter, Emma, for the Lewis Grizzard Storytelling Barbecue and Southern Celebration. It was a chilly April afternoon. We'd missed the nine A.M. Catfish fun run, the fifties and sixties car show, and the Politically Incorrect Players of General Wheeler's Mess Tent and Mansion Museum, and got there just as a bunch of Confederate balladeers were finishing up more neo-Con tributes to the old South and the Moreland Community Singers were beginning a round of hymns: "This is My Story," "Amazing Grace," "What a Friend We Have in Jesus."

Vendors hawked Cokes, hot dogs, and Sprayberry's barbecue at the Lewis Grizzard Bar-B-Que Pavilion, as well as Grizzard T-shirts and memorabilia. The Grizzard museum, featuring Grizzardiana like his high school letter jacket, Aunt Una's recipe for buttermilk pie, and photos of Lewis playing golf, was open and crowded. The Caldwell museum, full of smutty movie posters, out-of-print novels, and photos of Caldwell and busty movie starlets, was open and empty. Outside the Grizzard museum, Nancy Grizzard Jones (wife Number 1) and Camilla Stamps Stevens, divorced from Grizzard's friend Dudley Stamps, were autographing copies of *Photos and Memories of Lewis Grizzard*, which helped give the scene the proper Grizzardian mix of misty nostalgia and make-a-buck commerce. I bought a copy for my son Ben's collection of autographed books. "Ben—Hope you enjoy our little memory book!" wrote Camilla. "To Ben, Thanks so much for liking Lewis," was Nancy's version.

It wasn't exactly my kind of affair. The crafts fair consisted largely of right-wing T-shirts reading VISUALIZE NO LIBERALS—RUSH LIMBAUGH FOR PRESIDENT, or showing Bill Clinton with a huge nose and the words CLINNOCHIO—WILL HE EVER STOP LYING? But it was hard not to be moved by the power of the shared vision, the sense of common values, community, and simpler times. Like all Southern nostalgia it took a selective memory to buy in too far—Grizzard's Moreland was the segregated South and his whole vision rested on the notion of a homogeneous community that never really was and never will be. Still, when I watched Emma wander off to the playground in the square, it was easy to see how almost any parent these days could find this vision of small-town peace pretty alluring. It certainly worked for the Grizzardians there, and when everyone joined in on Grizzard's favorite hymn, singing as one "Precious memories, oh how they linger ..." it was hard to find a dry eye in town.

Of course, if a lot of people loved Lewis Grizzard, plenty of people saw him as nothing more than either the colossus of Southern crapola or a throwback to the bad old days of the segregated South. The most famous Grizzard hater was the novelist Pat Conroy, who during l'affaire Kovach pronounced Grizzard "a syphilis germ before they invented penicillin" and came to see him as the embodiment of every failing of the peckerwood, nitwit, racist, unreconstructed South writ large. "Your South is the one I loathe, Lewis," Conroy wrote in an open letter that berated Grizzard for his famous anti-Kovach ad. "Because I too am a redneck, I want to translate for all your readers and for the Cox chains what you meant by the line, 'with apologies to those who enjoy reading exhaustive series on what's doing in Africa.' Let me translate this in our shared southern vernacular. You wrote it in code but the translation is this: Atlanta doesn't care if niggers starve. It is the word 'nigger,' Lewis, that subliminally disfigures your work, and cheapens your worth as a man. J. B. Stoner, at least, has the guts to use it out loud."

Conroy's engine can run pretty hot in real life, like the intensity level of his prose in print, and it's a pretty big leap from J. B. Stoner, the church bomber and Klan rally orator, to Lewis Grizzard. In fact, though many blacks instinctively disliked his column, at times Grizzard's Southern chauvinism and jibes at the North appealed to black Southerners as well as whites. And one of the most striking things about the contemporary South is how blacks and whites can evoke it with equal fervor, like jewelers looking at a gem from different perspectives. Ralph Ellison, grandson of slaves and the author of *Invisible Man,* acknowledged that shared culture shortly before his death in 1994, when he said, "You can't be Southern without being black, and you can't be a black Southerner without being white." Alex Haley, the author of *Roots,* recognized it a few years back when he said, "I don't know anything I treasure more as a writer than being a Southerner." John Hope Franklin, now a retired professor at Duke, talks about "our beloved South" as the nation's best hope for racial peace.

I once visited Franklin in Durham, still a stinky tobacco town with an airport that looked like a Greyhound bus station back when I went to

Duke; now Durham is one of those citadels of New South prosperity rechristened the City of Medicine. It was two days after the Republican electoral sweep of 1994, and Franklin was still in shock at the familiar tide of white anger, as if the South of the 1890s had been transformed into the nation of the 1990s.

At eighty, Franklin was tall, erect, and impeccably proper as he took me on a tour of his home. His CD rack was full of his favorite Brahms, and the walls were covered with the work of great African-American artists like Jacob Lawrence, Henry O. Tanner, and Aaron Douglas. Downstairs where he works, in what he calls "the slave quarters," every inch of the walls and shelves was covered with books and diplomas and awards and mementos. In the spacious backyard was a grove of bamboo and a goldfish pond and, most important of all, his greenhouse.

"Children, meet Mr. Applebome," he said to his waiting choir of seven hundred orchids and then gave a detailed tour. There was a beautiful lavender *Laelia cattleya* Molly Tyler Black River; a pinkish-orange Malworth Orchidglade, one of the world's great orchid hybrids; and an exotic yellow-and-brown striped *Ansellia gigantea nilotica* from the Nile Valley. And there was his floral namesake, John Hope Franklin, white with red lips, which was developed in his honor by a grower in Illinois, who registered it in 1976.

In an essay entitled "Pursuing Southern History: A Strange Career," Franklin once recounted the odd logistics of being a black scholar in the Jim Crow South: the empty room ceded to him at the Department of Archives and History in Raleigh, being snuck by the state archivist into the segregated archives in Baton Rouge on V-J Day in 1945, allowing him to do his research while the rest of the town celebrated the end of the war. "Strange" is a very genteel word for much of that experience, like that of being crammed with other blacks into a baggage car of a train while coming back from a college graduation, while German prisoners of war laughed at them from the comfort of the nearly empty car behind.

There is an even stranger coda to Franklin's personal Southern history: these days he almost sounds like a Southern chauvinist. Partly this reflects his disenchantment over the years with the the harsh subtleties of discrimination in the North. But much of it reflects the phenomenon, so common particularly in blacks who grew up during Jim Crow, of a coming to terms with the South, like long-feuding siblings who've finally made their peace with each other. With his orchids, his easy amiability, his intense sense of place, his iconlike status in his profession, his endless circle of friends (he sends out six hundred Christmas cards a year), Dr. Franklin at home seems nothing so much as a distinguished Southern gentleman of the old school whose only peculiarity is that he's black, not white.

"The South as a place is as attractive to blacks as it is to whites," he said. "Blacks even when they left the South didn't stop having affection for it. They just couldn't make it there. Then they found the North had its problems too, so you look for a place of real ease and contentment, where you could live as a civilized human being. That's the South. It's more congenial, the pace is better, the races get along better. It's a sense of place. It's home. In rare moments, it's something that blacks and whites have shared. The South in that sense rises above race."

Those moments are indeed rare, but they do suggest another Southern model than the standard one purveyed by Grizzard and the neo-Cons, one where Caldwell's stunted, impoverished South is gone, but its successor is something much broader and richer and inclusive than the neo-Con vision of Dixie triumphant at last. It's a South that has gone through the fire of change and come out redeemed.

Grizzard left himself wide open to the accusations of racism that often came his way. "Y'all take Botswana," he told a reporter from *Vanity Fair,* reprising his line—the one that enraged Conroy—about the paper's coverage, under Kovach, of news from Africa. "We'll take Cobb County." But the real problem with the Grizzardian South—with the Grizzardian America—is not that it's so malevolent or racist or hateful, but that it's so limited, so narrow, in the end so small. If the South's fatal flaw over time has been its tendency to look back instead of forward, Grizzard was nothing if not Dixie nostalgia as a worldview. Grizzard wrote proudly as a defiant white Southerner—as if he were the last white man in America. But as America becomes blacker and browner and more diverse—when you can cruise up the international polyglot of Buford Highway in Atlanta, where Vietnamese noodle joints with big-screen TVs showing Vietnamese music videos butt up next to Mexico City *taquerías* with big-screen TVs showing Mexican game shows—it's a chord that resonates equally inside and outside the South. One of the most famous dictums of Southern scholarship is the historian Ulrich B. Phillips's pronouncement in 1928 that the essence of the South was "a common resolve indomitably maintained" that the South "shall be and remain a white man's country." The South has changed and the nation has changed a lot since 1928. But just as the South was defined and deformed for so long by the painful gyrations white Southerners went through to impose a white culture on a diverse world, the same issues increasingly are shaping the nation's politics and culture, from Proposition 187 in California to the tangled politics of race in New York.

The South that is triumphant now is pretty much the one that both Grizzard and the neo-Cons would buy in to, a place of feel-good nostalgia, easy answers, and painless solutions, forever looking backward through a pale mist and seeing only the soft-focus outlines of what it wants to see. W. J. Cash described it as "perpetually suspended in the great haze of memory ... colossal, shining and incomparably lovely," where the past is somehow all Beauvoir, "Precious Memories," and the Moreland United Methodist Church with the dogwoods in bloom—and never Jeeter Lester, the Edmund Pettus Bridge, or the Chiquola Mill.

It's a place of cheap ranting about states' rights with no mention of the Wallaces, Maddoxes, and Barnetts who marched under that banner; of fashionable tirades about the evils of government with no mention of the enormous role the federal government, from the New Deal to the defense industry, played in transforming Caldwell's Tobacco Road into Grizzard's Peachtree Road. Cash captured the place perfectly in his famous penultimate paragraph a half century ago: "proud, brave, honorable by its lights," but still in thrall to "a too narrow concept of social responsibility, attachment to fictions and false values, above all too great attachment to racial values and a tendency to justify cruelty and injustice in the name of those values." What's most striking now is how true the words ring not just for the South but for the nation.

The South Franklin suggests speaks to the American experience too. What moment in American history, after all, speaks more eloquently to the nation's best instincts than King's "I Have a Dream" speech? Southern whites as well as blacks have hit similar notes, like the prophetic minority of Southerners John Egerton profiled in his *Speak Now Against the Day,* who tried to confront the prison of segregation between the New Deal and the *Brown* decision in 1954. One of the most eloquent of them was Don West, a Georgia mountain boy, radical poet, labor activist, and preacher, who back in 1946 envisioned a South that was hammered "into a beautiful song," a South of "sharecroppers, tenants, Black men and Crackers" leading the nation toward a broader vision of itself. His song concluded:

> *Look here, America.*
> *Bend your head toward me*
> *And listen.*
> *Make your dreaming eyes to look*
> *For I have tales to tell*
> *And little pieces*
> *Of twisted life to show ...*

This redeemed interracial South is more a hypothesis than a caricature—and these days not a hypothesis that many people black or white seem to be buying into. It hovers in the air in magic moments like the rededication of the Spring Hill Free Will Baptist Church or Dick Molpus's speech in Philadelphia. Perhaps more importantly, it exists in the routine courtesies and kindness and daily common ground of Southern life.

But as for its advocates and symbols—its Grizzards, its Beauvoirs, its Southern Leagues, its "Precious Memories," its Willistons, its institutional bases in politics, business or social life—well, that's a house no one has built yet. Maybe no one will. Still, what kind of a nation we become will depend in large part on which Southern vision becomes the nation: the narrow one that's ascendant or the broader one that's hovered just out of reach for so long.

The South's experience has much to teach us. It's a reminder, sadly, that slaying the worst dragons, the Tillmans and Stoners and Barnetts, even converting them à la Wallace, isn't enough to guarantee racial peace. It teaches whites that good intentions—and certainly the mere absence of bad ones—is not enough, and it teaches blacks how tenuous the moral high ground can be, that the hard-won spiritual grandeur of the civil rights workers of Selma in 1964 does not automatically devolve to their children and grandchildren. It's a reminder of the long arm of history and how much the past reverberates into the present, no matter how much the surface changes. Most of all, perhaps, it's a reminder for

cynical times that politics–and particularly the moral dimension of
politics–matters, that the South always had private virtues that never
quite became public ones largely because its politicians too often have
responded to momentous issues of race by offering up only cheap swill.
Sometimes they served it because it fit their tastes. But more often than
not, like George Wallace, they did it because it was easier to whip up
and dish out, and if you got people hooked on it, it worked in the short
run even if it killed over time.

The American political world will not always be a triangle bounded
by moderate Southern Yuppies like Bill Clinton and Al Gore, cultural
conservatives like Pat Buchanan, and states' rights devolutionists like
Newt Gingrich and Dick Armey. Two years after the 1994 Republican
revolution, it's already pretty clear that the easy answers and repackaged nostrums out of the South's past are as hollow as plastic pipe and
that the racial scapegoating and public disinvestment that crippled the
South for so long will do the same thing for the nation.

But at a time of wrenching national change, no place has lived with
change as has the South–defeated in war, turned upside down in
Reconstruction, reconfigured in segregation, turned upside down again
by desegregation. At a time of gnawing economic anxiety, no place has
been shaped by poverty, scarcity, and the bitter competition for jobs
and a piece of prosperity as the South. At a time so desperate for a
sense of community and shared values, no place has them, exalts them,
and flaunts them like the South. And at a time when race, not just black
and white, but the whole emerging, multicultural stew of twenty-first
century America is the underlying social issue in America, no place has
been so defined by race, alternately ennobled and debased by it, as the
South. The South's past may offer up more wrong turns than right
ones, but its experience, West's "little pieces of twisted life," is as good a
distillation of the nation's search for its soul as we are likely to find.

I think we've known it all along, but we couldn't afford to lose the
various Souths–mythologized from within and without–that we have
projected onto the national experience like the nighttime movies flick-
ering outside the Lumina as the waves licked the beach. The South has
been a lightning rod for our fondest hopes and worst fears–a shadow
theater for national guilt–a place to stow the bloody rags we didn't
want to see; a scapegoat for our worst failings; a model of an imagined,
perfect past; a hypothesis for a nation redeemed or a nation damned.

Like the movies at the Lumina, that show is probably over. The Southern pageant will go on, but it has become pretty clear that we're all actors, coconspirators, secret sharers in the drama.

"Jesus, the South is fine, isn't it?" said Shreve McCannon to Quentin Compson in Faulkner's *Absalom, Absalom!* "It's better than the theatre, isn't it? It's better than Ben Hur, isn't it?"

Yes and no. The lines are still better, the chariots gaudier, the plots more Byzantine. But it ain't no theater. It ain't no Ben Hur. It's us.

Notes on Sources

I'm a journalist, not a historian, and this book essentially is an exercise in journalism. It's mostly a result of the people I interviewed, the places I went, and the things I observed. A little of it goes back to the early 1980s when I was in Texas. Some of the reporting, and much of the thinking that led to the book, dates back to 1989 when I moved to Atlanta to become Southern Bureau chief for *The New York Times*. Indeed, much of the book began with or expands upon stories I did for *The Times*, particularly a four-part series I did from July 31 to August 3, 1994, that in many ways proved to be the genesis of this book. The vast majority of the reporting and virtually all of the writing, however, is the result of travel, interviews, and reporting I did over a year and a half beginning in January 1995.

But if this is largely a work of journalism, it is informed throughout by the history, scholarship, theorizing, and journalism of others. It seemed a little pretentious and contrary to the spirit of the book to end with formal footnotes or endnotes. ("Interview with Bruno Fava at Bruno's Quik Mart" seemed a little off.) It would be churlish and misleading not to acknowledge the enormous debts I have to others, both in the specifics of this book and what I've learned from them over the years. As a result, I've chosen to acknowledge my sources below in a form that I hope will allow me to credit those whose work was used directly and those whose work helped inform and shape my own reporting and writing. I've tried to give specific citations for most quotes I've taken from research material or for particularly striking facts. In instances that are well-known (Wallace's "Segregation now, segregation tomorrow ..." speech, for instance) or an unquestioned part of the historical record, I haven't bothered to cite sources.

If there's a simple notion—perhaps a conceit—at the heart of the book it's this: for all the remarkable profusion of great writing about the South, for many years there hasn't been a nonacademic, journalistic voyage across the region that captures in a big way a moment in the South's history and its place in the national imagination—not perhaps since John Egerton's *The Americanization of Dixie: The Southernization of America* in 1974. This book is very different from that one—not least of all because Egerton is a native Southerner, and I am not. But if this book has a model, it's a combination of what Egerton did for the South in 1974 and expansive, journalistic looks at other places like Ian Frazier on the Great Plains, Nicholas D. Kristof and Sheryl WuDunn on China, Thomas Friedman on the Middle East, and Joseph Lelyveld on South Africa. If my reach exceeds my grasp, it's certainly not because of a shortage of material to work with or superb research and scholarship to learn from.

Chapter 1

As noted above, John Egerton's work, particularly *The Americanization of Dixie* and *Speak Now Against the Day* strike me as models of intelligence and humanity in making sense of the South and what it says about the nation. But this first chapter was shaped by the work of many others as well. Anyone who writes on the South these days almost has to start with the work of John Shelton Reed, expert on all things Southern, at the University of North Carolina. The University of Mississippi's William Ferris and Charles Reagan Wilson, coeditors of the *Encyclopedia of Southern Culture,* are in the same league. The section on Southern politics draws heavily on the authoritative work of Merle and Earl Black of Emory and Rice Universities. The sections on the South's place in the national imagination owe much to the best work on that subject, Jack Temple Kirby's *Media-Made Dixie*. Other contemporary scholars and historians whose work is essential to anyone writing about the South include C. Vann Woodward, John Hope Franklin, George Tindall, Dan Carter, James C. Cobb, and Edward L. Ayers. Howard Zinn's *The Southern Mystique* is only one book that tried to make sense of the relationship between North and South. Others that have illuminated similar turf in very different ways include works by Eugene Genovese, Jack Bass, Pat Watters, and the collections edited by Frank Vandiver and Charles Sellers. Carl N. Degler's "Thesis, Antithesis, Synthesis: The South, the North and the Nation" in the February 1987 *Journal of Southern History* is a succint summation of the regional crosswinds.

As for specific references here, my information on the Southern Baptists came from various publications, news releases, and officials at the convention in Atlanta. Particularly helpful was Dr. William O'Brien of Samford University in Birmingham, Alabama. The Frady quote ("The Old Testament...") comes from page xv of his evocative book, *Southerners*. Population figures come from the Census Bureau. The fact that a presidential candidate could now be elected with the states carried by Richard Nixon in 1960 and William Jennings Bryan in 1896 is on page 93 of Kevin P. Phillips's *Post-Conservative America*. The quote from Satchel Paige comes from Reed's *Whistling Dixie,* page 24. Economic figures come from various sources including the Regional Economic Reviews produced by Mark Vitner at First Union Bank in Charlotte. The South as the world's fourth-largest economy comes from Vitner. The figures about half the new jobs in 1993 coming to the South come from the "Survey of the American South" in the December 10–16, 1994, issue of *The Economist*. The rather remarkable migration figures–most people don't realize the white exodus was equal to the black–come from Jack Temple Kirby's "The Southern Exodus, 1910–1960: A Primer for Historians" in *The Journal of Southern History*. The quote from *Absalom, Absalom!* is taken from page 10 of Lisa Howarth's *The South–A Treasury of Art and Literature*. The Mencken quotes are from Egerton's *Speak Now Against the Day,* page 63. The Caldwell quote is from page 1 of his *You Have Seen Their Faces*. Many of the cultural reflections of the South come from Kirby's *Media-Made Dixie,* as is the "So sick ..." quote, on page 62. The Yancey quote is from the essay "As for Our History," by John Hope Franklin on page 3 of *The Southerner as American*. Sources on Calhoun include Charles Potts's *How the South Finally Won*

the Civil War–And Controls the Political Future of the United States (more
on him later), Richard Hofstadter's *The Paranoid Style in American Politics,* and M. L. Coit's *John Calhoun, American Portrait.* The "subtly rendered pastless" quote from Frady comes from page 211 of the essay
"Will Dixie Disappear? Cultural Contours of a Region in Transition" by
Howard L. Preston in Dunn and Preston's *The Future South.* Egerton's
quotes, "exporting vices," and "modern, acquisitive," are on Pages 19
and 25 of *The Americanization of Dixie.* Brother Dave's memorable
quote comes from Reed, *Whistling Dixie,* page 77. The "will-o'-the wisp
Eden" quote is from Charles Roland quoted on page 771 of William J.
Cooper and Thomas E. Terrill's *The American South.* The Margaret
Mitchell quote comes from page 7 of the collection of Southern quotes
On the Night the Hogs Ate Willie.

Chapter 2

I used four sources on the battle of Kennesaw Mountain: Geoffrey C.
Ward's *The Civil War,* the book version of Ken Burns's PBS series;
William R. Scaife's *The Campaign for Atlanta;* Dennis Kelly's tour guide
of the battle site; and Ronald H. Bailey's *Battles for Atlanta, Sherman
Moves East,* one of nineteen books in the Time–Life series on the war.
Sherman's quote that "Kennesaw is the key to the whole country," his
cheery quote on daily slaughters, and the anecdotes about the brushfire
and the truce to bury the dead came from Bailey on pages 60–75.

The most complete look at the Leo Frank Case is Leonard Dinnerstein's *The Leo Frank Case,* first published in 1966 and then reissued with
a new preface in 1987. The quote from the *Marietta Journal and Courier*
is on page 144 of Dinnerstein. Also valuable is a five-part series on the
case done by the Atlanta *Constitution* from February 27 to March 3,
1978, and Steve Oney's "The Lynching of Leo Frank" in the September
1985 *Esquire.* On March 7, 1982, the Nashville *Tennessean* published an
entire section on the case, based on the affidavit of Alonzo Mann, who
as a boy saw Jim Conley carrying away the body. My rendering of the
case comes from those four sources. Mann's affidavit was hailed at the
time as proof of Frank's innocence. But though it provided further proof
that Conley lied repeatedly on the stand, experts on the case such as
Dinnerstein and Oney, who for years has been working on a book
about it, say it only provided more circumstantial evidence tipping the
balance of evidence toward Conley rather than proving Frank's case.

Most observers today would agree with Melissa Fay Greene in *The Temple Bombing* that the defense's case was not airtight, but "the exceedingly slim bit of circumstantial evidence against Frank ought not to have supported a verdict of guilty beyond a reasonable doubt."

The material on Cobb's racial history comes from an affidavit prepared by Brian Sherman, a sociologist with the Southern Regional Council in Atlanta, in connection with a pending death penalty case. Asked to document the history of racism in the county he concluded: "There is no need to speculate about its impact; public officials have openly and repeatedly conceded its prominent influence."

The information on far-right groups draws heavily on two excellent publications prepared for the Cobb Citizens Coalition, "The Shadow of Hatred—Hate Group Activity in Cobb County, Georgia" and "Hidden Agenda—The Influence of Religious Extremism on Politics in Cobb County, Georgia."

For other specifics, William Archer's quote on Southern religion is from Edward Ayers's *The Promise of the New South,* page 160. H. Louis Patrick's is from Egerton's *The Americanization of Dixie,* pages 197–98. Most of the local history came from the predictably upbeat but reliable *Cobb County: At the Heart of Change,* produced by the Cobb County Chamber of Commerce. The material on regional shifts in defense spending came from an April 19, 1995, *New York Times* story by Louis Uchitelle. The quote "Lockheed is immersed . . ." is on page 114 of *Cobb County: At the Heart of Change.* The economic and demographic figures came from the Cobb County Chamber of Commerce. The study for *Common Cause* magazine written by Peter Overby was excerpted in the Atlanta *Constitution* August 8, 1993. Keith L. Maney's quotes came from the *Marietta Daily Journal,* May 26, 1994.

On the all-important Big Chicken issue, I relied on Don Plummer's January 24, 1993, opus in the Atlanta *Journal and Constitution,* complete with Newt Gingrich's endorsement of saving the chicken. The chicken's future was allegedly in doubt at the time, although one doesn't need to be a genius to discern the hand of some KFC PR man in the decision to publicize the bird's endangered status, leading up to the company's gallant decision to save it.

Chapter 3
The Civil Rights Movement in the Black Belt and Bloody Sunday

have, of course, been the subject of brilliant reporting over the years. Books I made particular use of include Howell Raines's invaluable oral history, *My Soul Is Rested;* Dan Carter's *The Politics of Rage,* also widely used in the next chapter; Howard Zinn's *SNCC;* J. L. Chestnut Jr. and Julia Cass's *Black in Selma;* The Southern Poverty Law Center's *Free at Last;* and Alston Fitts III's *Selma.*

The demographic figures on the Black Belt were compiled by the Center for Demographic and Cultural Research at Auburn University, Montgomery. The history of Dicksonia comes from page 150 of Chip Cooper, Harry Knopke and Robert Gamble's *Silent in the Land,* a gorgeous book of photos and Alabama history. The Selma history is from Fitts. The "several large buildings ..." quote is on page 9. The information on Turner is on page 78. The "Why sir ..." quote is on page 90. I've seen Forrest described as the first grand dragon, grand wizard, supreme grand wizard, and imperial wizard of the Ku Klux Klan. I chose the term used by Jack Hurst in his biography, *Nathan Bedford Forrest.* The details and dates on the civil rights murders come from the Southern Poverty Law Center's *Free At Last,* plus Alston Fitts's helpful comments on my manuscript. Sheriff Clark's quote "Get those ..." is from page 249 of Carter. The material from Velariani and Hoffman is from *Raines;* Veleriani is on page 372, and Hoffman is on page 377.

The Chestnut material is from *Black in Selma.* The quote, "Everyone in Selma ..." is on page 416. Chestnut's letter to Al Benn is from the February 26, 1992, *Montgomery Advertiser.* The battles over Dr. Roussell received state, local, and national publicity. A particularly good account, and one that included details like the floating corpses, is by Alston Fitts in the September 14, 1990, issue of *Commonweal.* Fitts, in interviews, also provided details on the bumper-sticker war and the rivalry between the whites who sent their children to Selma High and those whose children went to Morgan Academy. Crisman's quote is also from Fitts in *Commonweal.*

Chapter 4

The definitive account for now of Wallace's political career and its influence on American politics is Dan Carter's merciless *The Politics of Rage,* which cuts through the natural revisionism surrounding the repentant, crippled Wallace of the present and relentlessly chronicles the harsh contours of his career prior to Arthur Bremer's bullets. My view of Wallace's impact on the nation was also shaped enormously by interviews I did with Carter over the years for newspaper stories. Stephan Lesher's *George Wallace–American Populist,* written with Wallace's cooperation, is less damning but a readable, valuable, not uncritical biography. Marshall Frady's *Wallace,* read in serialization in *The Saturday Evening Post* from June 15 to June 29, 1968, is particularly vivid in capturing Wallace during his political heyday.

The work of many writers was useful in chronicling the Wallace legacy, including Earl and Merle Black's *The Vital South,* Jack Bass and Walter De Vries's *The Transformation of Southern Politics,* E. J. Dionne's *Why Americans Hate Politics,* Wayne Greenhaw's *Elephants in the Cotton-fields,* and Michael Kazin's *The Populist Persuasion.* Bass wrote several other pieces that were particularly useful, including "A Prophet of the New Politics," in the December 25, 1988, *Philadelphia Inquirer* magazine.

Carter and Frady provided more details in the chapter than any other sources. The description of the 1965 Montgomery rally and the events leading up to it come from Carter. The freedom song is on page 256, Wallace's quote, "I'm not going to have ..." is on page 247. James Bevel's rallying cry, "We must go to Montgomery ..." is from Fitts, page 146.

Wallace's quote about the politics of the 1970s is from an interview with R. W. Apple Jr. of *The New York Times,* which ran January 2, 1970. Many of Wallace's best-known and most revealing quotes, including the famous one about not being "out-nigguhed," are from Frady. Wallace denied making the remark or making regular use of the "N" word. But, while he did not use the word in his public speeches, it was a regular part of his private vocabulary and the quote is almost certainly accurate. Other quotes in the book that come from Frady include: "They say we gonna hurt 'em ..." "intellectual morons ...," "a bayonet in yo back ...," and "I'm gonna make race the basis ..." Also from Frady is the Folsom quote, "As long as the Negroes ...," "the Number One Do-Gooder" and John Kohn's quote, "Now George Wallace ..." Wallace's campaign ad (Vote right–vote white–...) is on page 106 of Carter.

Lesher's book provided some of the details of Wallace's life and the quotes from Kilpatrick and Scott. Kilpatrick is on page 391 and Scott is on page 401. Jack and Jock–a quote first pointed out to me by Merle Black–is on page 130 of Cash. Talmadge's quote ("I'm just as mean ...")

is from page 163 of *The Vital South*. The quote from Jersey City ("You don't know ...") is from an October 9, 1968, *New York Times* story by Roy Reed. The Kiker quote is from page 344 of Carter. Wallace's account of the rally in Milwaukee is on pages 88 and 89 of *Stand Up for America*. Carter is skeptical about Wallace's crowd count but otherwise sees the event's significance much as Wallace did on pages 206–208. The Thompson quote is from Carter's "Legacy of Rage: George Wallace and the Transformation of American Politics" in the February 1966 *Journal of Southern History*.

The Southern political arithmetic is on page 351 of *The Vital South*. *The Vital South* and Bass and DeVries's *The Transformation of Southern Politics* are among the best sources for the political chronology that follows. The South Carolina as insane asylum quote is on page 23 of Bass's *Porgy Comes Home*. Cotton Ed's "He's as black as ..." is from page 110 of Egerton's *Speak Now Against the Day*. His "When a ..." is from page 681 of Cooper and Terrill. Thurmond's party-switching quotes are from my copy of the full text of his speech. The two Gary Wills quotes are from pages 117 and 144 of Sale's *Power Shift*. The Gingrich campaign flyer on Virginia Shepard is on page 92 of Dick Williams's *Newt!* The Mailer poem is from *The New Yorker*, December 11, 1995. Wallace's quote about, "The first people I saw ..." is from a *New York Times* story by Howell Raines, January 7, 1979. The "I started talking about schools ..." quote is from Carter, page 109. The account of the Montgomery rally at the end of the 1995 Selma to Montgomery march comes from the *New York Times* account by Rick Bragg, March 11, 1995, and from the observations of Alan Weiner, Joseph Lowery, and Charles Bonner.

Chapter 5

Not too much has been written on the neo-Confederate groups. My best resource was a man who prefers to remain anonymous, who lives in a major Southern city and spends much of his time researching the literature of the neo-Cons. Under various pseudonyms he subscribes to more than a dozen neo-Con and related publications and buys tapes and catalogues and books. He writes long, carefully documented analyses of the material and the neo-Con movement, some of which he sends out to selected journalists, professors, or publications. He sent me dozens of excerpts and copies from numerous publications and reports that were of great value.

Many books were of enormous value in doing this chapter. *So Good a Cause,* a collection from *Southern Partisan,* is a serious, often compelling, sometimes repellent collection of pieces from a magazine that doesn't fit my political profile, but is often an intelligent publication. James and Walter Kennedy's *The South Was Right!* summarizes most of the neo-Con themes. There are interesting parts picking apart Northern hypocrisies and then there are chapters like "Race Relations in the Old South," whose philosophy is pretty much summed up by the opening epigraph from a former slave named Charles Stewart: "... we jes' went on peaceful an' happy til de war come an' rooted ebery blessed thing up by de roots." And the neo-Cons can't understand why so many people assume the worst when they see the Battle Flag. At the other extreme of opinionated, semi-pro regional history is Charles Potts's interesting, if hyperventilating, *How the South Finally Won the Civil War–And Controls the Political Future of the United States,* which, like Kirkpatrick Sale's earlier *Power Shift,* views the South as a malignant force that's taken over America. More conventional histories that were valuable include the works of C. Van Woodward, Charles Grier Sellers's collection *The Southerner as American,* and the works of John Egerton and Jack Temple Kirby.

Most of the quotes from neo-Con publications include the dates they were published in the text. The Klan quotes from Grissom are on page 323 of *When the South Was Southern.* The Egerton quote is from page 15 of *The Americanization of Dixie.* The description of the Confederate Constitution comes from *The South Was Right!,* which includes the text of the full Constitution on pages 333–63. Russell Kirk wrote regularly for *Southern Partisan.* A good summation of his affection for the South is "Russell Kirk's Southern Sensibilities: A Celebration," by N. Alan Cornett in the 2nd Quarter 1994 *Southern Partisan.* The quotes "Kirk had found ..." and "The South then has been ..." come from Cornett's article. The Pierce Butler quote ("considered the interests of ...") is from "Americans Below the Potomac," by Thomas P. Govan, on page 23 of *The Southerner as American.* The Franklin quote is on page 9 of his "As for Our History" in the same book. Much of the material on the post-Reconstruction era is from Kirby's *Media-Made Dixie.* "Magnified convictions already there ..." is on page 8. "Every man who comes out ..." is on page 4.

The Cotton Mather anecdote is from James Dabbs's *Who Speaks for the South?*, page 48. The Charles Lyell quote is from the same book, page 49. The de Tocqueville quote is in George Tindall's "The Central Theme Revisited," on page 111 of Sellers. Lincoln's quote is used often. I took this one from page 27 of *The South Was Right!*, but non–Lincoln haters use it as well. Woodward's *The Strange Career of Jim Crow* and *The Burden of Southern History* were especially helpful on the racial mores of the North before and after the Civil War. The quote from Leon F. Litwack's *North of Slavery* in on page 18 of Woodward's *The Strange Career of Jim Crow*. The James Weldon Johnson quote ("No group of . . .") is from Tindall's essay in Sellers, on page 105. The material on the famous sons of Edgefield, South Carolina, is from pages 18 and 19 of *Strom Thurmond and the Politics of Southern Change* by Nadine Cohodas. The rest of the material on Pitchfork Ben is from Howard Dorgan's " 'Pitchfork Ben' Tillman and 'The Race Problem from a Southern Point of View' " on pages 46–65 of *The Oratory of Southern Demagogues.*

I used the same sources on Hood and the Campaign for Atlanta as I used for Kennesaw, plus *The Atlanta Campaign Staff Ride Briefing Book* by Edward P. Shanahan and the essays in Gabor Borrit's *Why the Confederacy Lost*. Hood's class rank at West Point is from B. C. Hall and C. T. Wood's *The South*, page 230. Scaife's reading "Mine eyes have beheld . . ." is from his own *The Campaign for Atlanta*, page 78. An excellent, nuanced report on what the Southern church fires were and were not is Michael Kelly's "Playing with Fire" in the July 15, 1996, *New Yorker*. The quote "as symbols of . . ." is from Randolph Scott-McLaughlin, vice president of the Center for Constitutional Rights, as reported by Kevin Sack in the May 21, 1996 *New York Times*. Most of the material on the liberal tradition is from Egerton's *Speak Now Against the Day*. The material on the Graham-Smith race, one of the most famous and influential in the postwar South, and one that Jesse Helms obviously learned much from, is on pages 531–32 of *Speak Now Against the Day*.

Genovese's quotes are from pages ix, xii, and 9 of *The Southern Tradition*. Bledsoe provided the text of his speech.

Chapter 6

My main source on the New South history is Paul Gaston's definitive *The New South Creed*. DeLeon's quotes are on pages 15 and 33. The

Grady quotes are from my copy of his whole speech. The W. J. Cash "new charge at Gettysburg ..." quote is on page 184 of *The Mind of the South*. "The coming El Dorado of American adventure" is on page 43 of Gaston. The unimpressed *Washington Post* reporter was Henry Allen, whose piece from the *Post*'s Style section was reprinted in the November 9, 1993, *Charlotte Observer* under the headline "Bull's-eye or Just Bull? A Washington Newspaper Says Our City Has an Inferiority Complex."

I used various sources on Charlotte's history. A reliable overview is Mary Norton Kratt's glossy "Charlotte–Spirit of the New South." Also helpful was a ten-part series on Charlotte's history that ran July 9 in the *Observer*. Indeed, the *Observer* is a constant source of ruminations on Charlotte's mania for Big-Timedom. See for instance, "Hey, We're Big-time Now. Readers tell what Charlotte Really needs," on November 6, 1993, in which readers suggest, among other things, a Bloomingdales, a super outlet mall, residential sections where dogs don't bark all day long, and a "real nice NHRA (National Hot Rod Association) drag strip." Former county commissioner Liz Hair opined: "One thing we need to be a world-class city is to call downtown 'downtown.' To me 'uptown' smacks of Podunk." The *Observer*'s best bit of self-analysis was sports columnist Tom Sorenson's November 10, 1993, column that began: "We have a rule at this newspaper called the World Class Rule. If I understand the rule correctly, it states that we have to use the phrase 'world class' or an acceptable substitute such as 'major league' in every edition of the *Observer*." An April 29, 1985, story by Janet Fix in *Forbes* caught Charlotte at a particularly optimistic moment after Gantt's election as mayor.

D. H. Hill's journal comes from Richard Weaver's *The Southern Tradition at Bay*, page 146, although Gaston notes that Hill later had second thoughts about industrialization and the New South movement. The quote from Avery ("Charlotte has passed through ...") is in Kratt and Pamela Grundy's "From Il Travatore to the Crazy Mountaineers: The Rise and Fall of Elevated Culture on WBT-Charlotte, 1922–1930" in the Fall 1994 *Southern Cultures*. The "Let's Go Charlotte!" headline is from the collection of the Museum of the New South.

The standard reference on Cash is Bruce Clayton's excellent *W. J. Cash, a Life*. "Shot into a pulp ..." is on page 13; "After Edinburgh ..." and "murder capital ..." are on pages 136 and 137. The gravestone citation is on page 1. A succinct overview of Cash's life is Clayton's chapter in Paul Escott's *W. J. Cash and the Minds of the South,* a thoroughly engaging collection of essays that grew out of a 1991 conference on Cash at Wake Forest University. King's quote is from his essay on page 85 of Escott. Egerton's quote is from page 277 of *Speak Now Against the Day.* Of the Cash quotes, "tree with many age rings . . ." is from page L of the Preface, "cosmic conspiracy . . ." is on page 46, "Negro entered into white man . . ." is on page 49, "new charge at Gettysburg . . ." is on page 184, "Jeb Stuart's cavalrymen . . ." is on page 219, "hog has for a morning coat . . ." is on page 219, "Strange notes–Yankee notes" is on page 220, "Progress was . . ." is on page 226, and "Proud, brave . . ." is on page 428. The material on Tompkins comes largely from Kratt and Gaston. The anecdote about the Independence Building is from page 102 of Kratt. The quote about the *Observer* ("The only thing I wanted . . .") is on page 104 of Kratt. The material on McColl comes largely from a draft copy Frye Gaillard let me see of a piece that ran in the September issue of *Charlotte* magazine.

Virtually all of the material on the history of school desegregation is from Gaillard's superb *The Dream Long Deferred,* one of the best books written on integration in an American city. The *Charlotte News* editorial is on page 25, Golden and Jim Postell on page 138, the Reagan editorial on page xv of the introduction, and Billy Graham's note to Dorothy Counts on pages 9–10. The *Charlotte Post* article on Plaza United is from November 9, 1995.

Chapter 7

This chapter relies heavily on the research done for the remarkable documentary film *The Uprising of '34* and the information generated by its release. The film itself is a compelling, sensitive account not just of the labor unrest, but also of the positive and negative aspects of the culture of the Southern mill villages.

The film helped generate news coverage, some of it quite ambitious, about the events in Honea Path and across the South. Two particularly good packages of stories on Honea Path were the May 28, 1995, stories by Deb Richardson-Moore and Jim DuPlessis in the Greenville, South Carolina, *News* and the November 13, 1994, stories by Pat Butler in the Columbia, South Carolina, *State.*

The best source on Southern labor history is Ray Marshall's *Labor in the South.* Also valuable for historical context was Gary M. Fink and Merl E. Reed's *Essays in Southern Labor History.* The figures on union membership in South Carolina and other states came from an October 22, 1995, story in *The New York Times* by Steven Greenhouse. The quote "by human legislation ..." from the ubiquitous "Cotton Ed" Smith is from page 100 of Cobb's *The Selling of the South.* Most of the history of the town, and the speculation about the name, is from a history of Honea Path on file at the Honea Path library. The "triple bugaboo" quote is on page 108 of *The Selling of the South.*

The *Greenville News* stories were extremely helpful in putting together the account of what happened that day at the mill. The details from the funeral and the aftermath of the shootings come largely from the September 10, 1934, American Federation of Labor Weekly News Service Special Supplement provided to me by the filmmakers. Many of the details of strikes and violent incidents elsewhere came from Cobb's book. The Senate subcommittee quote "In stopping ..." is from a 1961 report called "... almost unbelievable" put out by the Textile Workers Union of America. The quote on Fieldcrest Cannon is from an Associated Press story that ran on September 6 in *The New York Times.* The Cobb quote on Strom Thurmond is from page 259 of *The Selling of the South.* My main source on the Imperial fire in Hamlet was a four-part series that ran December 8–11, 1991, in the Raleigh, North Carolina, *News and Observer.* The Kunja reporting included National Labor Relations Board hearing records and material from the Marion Star & Mullins Enterprise from June 13, 1990, and March 15, 1991.

The figures on economic and income inequality come from three sources: the July 17, 1995, cover story in *Business Week,* "The Wage Squeeze"; The July/August 1995 cover story in *The Washington Monthly,* "The Case for Unions"; and a February 1996 report by the AFL-CIO Department of Economic Research entitled "America Needs a Raise."

All the quotes from Dr. King come from "Now Is the Time. Dr. Martin Luther King, Jr., on Labor in the South: The Case for Coalition," a fifty-six-page pamphlet published in January 1968 by the Southern Labor Institute, a special project of the Southern Regional Council.

Chapter 8
My main sources on Williston, obviously, were the remembrances of

former students and staff members, including Linda Pearce, Joe McQueen, Kenneth McLaurin, Peter Grear, Billy Fewell, Bertha Todd, Harry Williams, and Caronell Chestnutt, and Linda Pearce's copy of the commemorative Williston video which featured interviews with dozens of former staff members. Other information came from the excellent exhibit put together by the Cape Fear Museum and from a history of Williston written for the museum.

My trip to Annie E. Colbert High School in Dayton was done as part of reporting for a story for *Texas Monthly*. On Wilmington's history and the Lumina I relied on exhibits and materials at the Cape Fear Museum, Daniel W. Barefoot's *Touring the Backroads of North Carolina's Lower Coast*, and Ginny Turner's *North Carolina Traveler*.

I used several accounts of the Wilmington race riot and North Carolina's post-Reconstruction history. They include Edward Ayers's *The Promise of the New South*, Paul Luebke's *Tar Heel Politics*, *The Encyclopedia of Southern Culture*, William S. Powell's *North Carolina Through Four Centuries*, and Catherine W. Bishir's "Landmarks of Power: Building a Southern Past 1885–1915," a particularly thoughtful and engaging account of the post-Reconstruction world, in the inaugural issue of *Southern Cultures*.

Dr. Eaton's book *Every Man Should Try* is a remarkable account of the struggle for integration, a reminder both of how much one remarkable man could achieve and how fragile those achievements turned out to be. The opening anecdote in the chapter about the dedication of Williston is on pages 50–51. The Woolworth's quote ("Nigger! Don't touch me …") is on page 7. The quote "I concluded …" is on page 9. The quote "In time …" is on page 22. The anecdote about the segregated Bibles is on pages 3–4. The quotes from Golden Frinks ("We've come to …") is on page 109. Herrick Roland's quotes are on page 102 and in the illustrations between pages 120 and 121. Dr. Eaton's response ("Fourteen years were lost …") is on page 104. The material on Ben Chavis and the Wilmington Ten comes from Dr. Eaton and from various clips from the *Wilmington Star*, particularly a long two-part retrospective that ran February 9 and 10, 1986.

Chapter 9

Whether or not you like the music (I do), there are few big businesses in America as open and accessible as the country music business in Nashville. This chapter is largely the result of interviews over a five-day period in August 1995 with Tim DuBois of Arista, Tony Brown and Bruce Hinton at MCA, Joe Galante and Thom Schuyler at RCA, Jim Ed Norman at Warner/Reprise, and Bud Wendell at Opryland, all of them among the most powerful people in the industry, who were extremely generous with their time on short notice. Thanks to all of them. Also extremely helpful and gracious were Janis Ian, Marty Stuart, Bill Ivey at the Country Music Foundation, David Ross of *Music Row* magazine, Amy Kurland of the Blue Bird Café, publicist extraordinaire Evelyn Shriver, Billy Ray Hearn, Steve Griffin, Mike Hyland at Opryland, Robert Moore, and BR5-49.

All the gee-whiz numbers on country sales and growth come from the County Music Association. The CMA, in turn, depended largely on the Simmons Study of Media and Markets. Lord knows there are a zillion books on country music. Three volumes I found extremely useful in different ways were Bill Malone's indispensable *Singing Cowboys and Musical Mountaineers,* Nick Tosches' eccentric *Country,* and the succinct and intelligent guide to the Country Music Hall of Fame put together by the Country Music Foundation, a great resource on American culture. The country roots of the early rockers is from Tosches. Most of the other history is Malone and the long quote is from pages 73–74 of Malone. Much of the Nashville trivia after the DuBois section is, amazingly enough, from Karr, Kosten, Flexer, and Stillman's *Nashville Trivia.* (Bonus question: Who coined Maxwell House Coffee's famous slogan, "Good to the last drop"? Answer: President Theodore Roosevelt.) The quote from *Southern Partisan* is from the first quarter 1995 issue ("Two Victories–Confederate Forces Advance") issue.

The Garth Brooks quotes come from a profile by Robert Hilburn in the *Los Angeles Times,* March 3, 1996. My source on the history of Tootsie's and Lower Broadway are stories by Chet Flippo and Jim Bessman in *Billboard,* July 15, 1995.

Chapters 10 and 11

The Mississippi chapters are perhaps the most purely journalistic of any in the book, the result of a week-long drive across Mississippi in August 1995. But, here, as elsewhere, I made use of numerous sources for background and history.

The Phil Ochs material is all from Marc Eliot's *Death of a Rebel.* The song lyrics are on page 89, the quote "Why single out Mississippi..." is also on page 89, and the Carnegie Hall quote "If there's any hope..." is on pages 199–200. The most valuable source on the Delta was James C. Cobb's *The Most Southern Place on Earth,* which provided the Gilchrist (page 312), Welty (page 312), and Faulkner (page 126) quotes at the beginning. His own quote ("behind the seductive and disarming facade...") is on page 326. The Delta's poverty has been amply documented by the Lower Mississippi Delta Commission and in other reports. Benjamin and Christina Schwarz's "Mississippi Monte Carlo" in the January 1996 *Atlantic Monthly* provided an excellent update of what gambling has or hasn't done for Tunica.

"A New Type of Black Ghetto in the Plantation South," by Charles S. Aiken, first printed in *The Annals of the Association of American Geographers,* vol. 80, no. 2, June 1990, pages 223–46, lays out an intriguing case for Delta towns as rural ghettos. Aiken, a geographer at the University of Tennessee, provided the changes in the racial composition of Delta towns from 1950 to 1980. Susan Taylor in the Atlanta Bureau of *The New York Times* did the legwork from new census figures, so I could update them to the 1990 census for a story on rural ghettos that ran in the *Times* on August 21, 1993. The Styron quote on Faulkner's funeral is from "The Death of Southern Heroes: Historic Funerals of the South" by Charles Reagan Wilson in the Fall 1994 edition of the valuable journal *Southern Cultures.* The detail about Elvis's father at Parchman comes from Ron Rosenbaum's story "Among the Believers" in the September 24, 1995, *New York Times Magazine.*

The quote from *The Citizen* is from the September 1962 edition of *The Citizen,* with Ross Barnett on the cover amid a sea of rebel flags. Howard Finster's quote is from *The Birmingham News,* August 9, 1995. Barnett's malapropisms come from a February 7, 1967, article in the Memphis *Commercial Appeal* by William B. Street and Jerry DeLaughter, and a magazine story "According to Ross" by John Corlew in the Summer 1965 issue of *Mississippi* magazine. The Elvis/Jesus parallels circulate around various Elvis internet sites.

The information on the catfish industry comes from an excellent report in the Fall 1991 issue of *Southern Exposure.* The David Cohn quotes on Natchez come from "Paying Homage in Natchez" by Mary

"Mimi" Warren Miller in the Fall 1995 issue of *Reckon*. The account of Hurricane Camille comes from Jon Nordheimer's report in the August 26, 1969, *New York Times*.

Much of the information on Beauvoir came from "Beauvoir–A Walk Through History" sold at the shop there. The account of Jefferson Davis's funeral is from Wilson's *The Death of Southern Heroes*.

Chapter 12

My two main sources on Caldwell's life were his own autobiography, *With All My Might,* and Dan Miller's biography, *Erskine Caldwell: The Journey from Tobacco Road*. Caldwell's autobiography, written near the end of his life, isn't very revealing. Miller's is both readable and informative. Kirby in *Media-Made Dixie* and Egerton in *Speak Now Against the Day* had valuable sections on Caldwell and his role in shaping perceptions of the South. Figures on books published and sold come from Miller and from Caldwell's widow, Virginia Caldwell Hibbs. Cash's quote is from page 118 of Clayton's biography, *W. J. Cash, A Life*. Davidson's quote on Caldwell is from page 240 of Miller. Deen's is from page 208. The quotes from *You Have Seen Their Faces* begin on page 1.

Grizzard's fans know the outlines of his life story by heart. He told it most affectingly in *My Daddy Was a Pistol....* A collection of reminiscences by his friends, *Don't Fence Me In,* pretty much covers the expected, hagiographic ground, although Lewis was such an obviously flawed character that even his admirers almost had to deal with his weaknesses as well as his strengths. Also valuable is the blizzard of stories and tributes that ran in the Atlanta *Constitution* during the week after Grizzard's death on March 20, 1994. An excellent, balanced retrospective of his life is Vincent Coppola's "Laughing Man" in the July 1994 issue of *Atlanta* magazine. A *Constitution* piece by Jim Auchmutey, May 25, 1994, on Lewis's widow and marriage also goes somewhat beyond the usual Grizzard mythmaking. This chapter, more than any other, drew on reporting I did for the *Times*. My interviews with Grizzard and our bus ride to oblivion were part of a story for *The New York Times Magazine* that ran on April 8, 1990. The material from John Hope Franklin is from a November 1994 interview, when I was just starting work on the book, that ran in the *Times Magazine* on April 23, 1995.

The funeral material comes from Charles Wilson's previously cited "The Death of Southern Heroes" piece in the Fall 1994 *Southern Cul-*

tures. The Vicki Covington quotes ("I wonder what ...") are from the March 27, 1994, *Birmingham News*. The Pat Conroy quotes "syphilis germ" and "Your South ..." are from the November 26, 1988, and February 18, 1989, issues of *Creative Loafing,* a weekly Atlanta publication. The "Y'all take Botswana ..." quote is from Peter J. Boyer's "Atlanta Burns" in the February 1989 issue of *Vanity Fair.* Ellison's quote is from a profile by David Remnick in the March 14, 1994, *New Yorker.* Alex Haley's is from page 6 of *The Enduring South.* West's poem is on page 13 of *Clods of Southern Earth.* The final Faulkner quote from *Absalom, Absalom!* was taken from "The Savage South: An Inquiry into the Origins, Endurance and Presumed Demise of an Image" by Fred C. Hobson on page 147 of Gerster and Cord's *Myths and Southern History.*

Bibliography

Ayers, Edward L. *The Promise of the New South: Life after Reconstruction.* New York: Oxford University Press, 1992.

Bailey, Ronald H. *Battles for Atlanta: Sherman Moves East.* Alexandria, Va.: Time-Life Books, 1985.

Barefoot, Daniel W. *Touring the Backroads of North Carolina's Lower Coast.* Winston-Salem, N. C.: John F. Blair, 1995.

Bass, Jack. *Porgy Comes Home: South Carolina after Three Hundred Years.* Columbia, S.C.: R. L. Bryan Company, 1972.

Bass, Jack, and Walter De Vries. *The Transformation of Southern Politics.* New York: Basic Books, 1976.

Binswanger, Barbara, and Jim Charlton, eds. *On the Night the Hogs Ate Willie and Other Quotations On All Things Southern.* New York: Dutton, 1994.

Black, Earl, and Merle Black. *The Vital South: How Presidents Are Elected.* Cambridge, Mass.: Harvard University Press, 1992.

Boritt, Gabor S., ed. *Why the Confederacy Lost.* New York: Oxford University Press, 1992.

Bowles, Billy, and Remer Tyson. *They Love a Man in the Country: Saints and Sinners in the South.* Atlanta: Peachtree Publishers, 1989.

Branch, Taylor. *Parting the Waters: America in the King Years, 1954–1963.* New York: Simon & Schuster, 1988.

Cash, W. J. *The Mind of the South.* New York: Alfred A. Knopf, 1941.

Caldwell, Erskine. *Deep South: Memory and Observation.* Athens, Ga.: Brown Thrasher Books, The University of Georgia Press, 1966.

——. *With All My Might: An Autobiography.* Atlanta: Peachtree Publishers, 1987.

——. *Tobacco Road.* Cambridge, Mass.: Robert Bentley, 1932.

Caldwell, Erskine, and Margaret Bourke-White. *You Have Seen Their Faces.* Athens, Ga.: Brown Thrasher Books, The University of Georgia Press, 1995.

Campbell, Will D. *Providence.* Atlanta: Longstreet Press, 1992.

Carter, Dan T. *The Politics of Rage: George Wallace, the Origins of the New Conservatism, and the Transformation of American Politics.* New York: Simon & Schuster, 1995.

Chestnut, J. L. Jr., and Julia Cass. *Black in Selma: The Uncommon Life of J. L. Chestnut, Jr.: Politics and Power in a Small Southern Town.* New York: Farrar, Straus and Giroux, 1990.

Clayton, Bruce. *W. J. Cash, a Life.* Baton Rouge: Louisiana State University Press, 1991.

Clendinen, Dudley, ed. *The Prevailing South: Life and Politics in a Changing Culture.* Marietta, Ga.: Longstreet Press, 1988.

Cobb, James C. *The Most Southern Place on Earth: The Mississippi Delta and the Roots of Regional Identity.* New York: Oxford University Press, 1992.

———. *The Selling of the South: The Southern Crusade for Industrial Development, 1936–1990.* Urbana, Il.: University of Illinois Press, 1993.

Coit, M. L. *John Calhoun, American Portrait.* Boston: Houghton-Mifflin, 1950.

Cooper, William J. Jr., and Thomas E. Terrill. *The American South: A History.* New York: Alfred A. Knopf, 1990.

Country Music Foundation. *The Country Music Hall of Fame and Museum.* Nashville: Country Music Foundation, 1995.

Cox, Jacob D. *Atlanta.* Wilmington, N.C.: Broadfoot Publishing Co., 1989.

Dabbs, James McBride. *Who Speaks for the South?* New York: Funk & Wagnalls, 1964.

Dionne, E. J., Jr. *Why Americans Hate Politics.* New York: Simon & Schuster, 1991.

Dinnerstein, Leonard. *The Leo Frank Case.* Athens, Ga.: University of Georgia Press, 1987.

Dunn, Joe P., and Howard L. Preston, eds. *The Future South: A Historical Perspective for the Twenty-first Century.* Urbana, Il.: University of Illinois Press, 1991.

Eaton, Hubert A. *Every Man Should Try.* Wilmington, N.C.: Bonaparte Press, 1984.

Egerton, John. *Speak Now Against the Day.* New York: Alfred A. Knopf, 1994.

———. *The Americanization of Dixie: The Southernization of America.* New York: Harper's Magazine Press, 1974.

Eliot, Marc. *Death of a Rebel, Starring Phil Ochs and a Small Circle of Friends.* New York: Anchor Books, 1979.

Escott, Paul D., ed. *W. J. Cash and the Minds of the South.* Baton Rouge: Louisiana State University Press, 1992.

Ferris, William. *Blues from the Delta.* New York: Da Capo Press, 1984.

Fifteen Southerners. *Why the South Will Survive.* Athens, Ga.: University of Georgia Press, 1981.

Fink, Gary M., and Merl E. Reed. *Essays in Southern Labor History.* Westport, Ct.: Greenwood Press, 1977.

Fitts, Alston, III. *Selma, Queen City of the Blackbelt.* Selma, Ala.: Clairmont Press, 1989.

Forman, James. *Sammy Younge, Jr: The First Black College Student to Die in the Black Liberation Movement.* Washington, D.C.: Open Hand Publishing, 1986.

Frady, Marshall. *Southerners: A Journalist's Odyssey.* New York: Meridian, 1980.

———. Frady, Marshall. *Wallace.* 2nd. ed. New York: New American Library, 1976.

Freeman, Criswell, ed. *The Book of Southern Wisdom.* Nashville: Walnut Grove Press, 1994.

Gaillard, Frye. *The Dream Long Deferred.* Chapel Hill, N.C.: The University of North Carolina Press, 1988.

Gaston, Paul M. *The New South Creed: A Study in Southern Mythmaking.* New York: Alfred A. Knopf, 1970.

Genovese, Eugene D. *The Southern Tradition: The Achievement and Limitations of an American Conservatism.* Cambridge, Mass.: Harvard University Press, 1994.

Gerster, Patrick, and Nicholas Cords, eds. *Myth and Southern History, Volume 2: The New South.* Urbana, Il.: University of Illinois Press, 1989.

Golden, Harry. *Only in America.* Westport, Ct.: Greenwood Press. 1973.

Grantham, Dewey W. *The South in Modern America: A Region at Odds.* New York: Harper Perennial, 1994.

Greene, Melissa Fay. *The Temple Bombing.* Reading, Mass.: Addison Wesley, 1996.

Greenhaw, Wayne. *Elephants in the Cottonfields: Ronald Reagan and the New Republican South.* New York: Macmillan, 1982.

Griffin, Larry J., and Don H. Doyle, eds. *The South as an American Problem.* Athens, Ga.: University of Georgia Press, 1995.

Grissom, Michael Andrew. *When the South Was Southern.* Gretna, La.: Pelican Publishing Co., 1994.

Grizzard, Lewis. *Chili Dawgs Always Bark at Night.* New York: Villard Books, 1989.

——. *If I Ever Get Back to Georgia I'm Gonna Nail My Feet to the Ground.* New York: Villard Books, 1990.

——. *If Love Were Oil, I'd Be a Quart Low.* Atlanta: Peachtree Publishers, 1983.

——. *Kathy Sue Loudermilk, I Love You.* Atlanta: Peachtree Publishers, 1979.

——. *The Last Bus to Albuquerque.* Atlanta: Longstreet Press, 1994.

——. *My Daddy Was a Pistol and I'm a Son of a Gun.* New York: Villard Books, 1986.

Hall, B. C., and C. T. Wood. *The South.* New York: Scribner's, 1995.

Hightower, Sheree, Cathie Stanga, and Carol Cox. *Mississippi Observed.* Jackson, Miss.: University Press of Mississippi, 1994.

Hill, Jane. *Cobb County: At the Heart of Change.* Marietta, Ga.: Longstreet Press, 1991.

Hofstadter, Richard. *The Paranoid Style in American Politics and Other Essays.* New York: Alfred A. Knopf, 1965.

Howarth, Lisa, ed. *The South: A Treasury of Art and Literature.* New York: Hugh Lauter Levin Associates, 1993.

Hurst, Jack. *Nathan Bedford Forrest: A Biography.* New York: Alfred A. Knopf, 1993.

Karr, Steve, Jerry Kosten, James Flexer, and Barry Stillman. *Nashville Trivia.* Nashville: Rutledge Hill Press, 1987.

Kazin, Michael. *The Populist Persuasion.* New York: Basic Books, 1995.

Kelly, Dennis. *Kennesaw Mountain and the Atlanta Campaign.* Marietta, Ga. Kennesaw Mountain Historical Association, 1990.

Kennedy, James Ronald, and Walter Donald Kennedy. *The South Was Right!* Gretna, La.: Pelican Publishing Company, 1994.

Kirby, Jack Temple. *Media-Made Dixie.* Athens, Ga.: University of Georgia Press, 1986.

Kratt, Mary Norton. *Charlotte: Spirit of the New South.* Winston-Salem, N.C.: John F. Blair, 1992.

Lemann, Nicholas. *The Promised Land: The Great Black Migration and How It Changed America.* New York: Alfred A. Knopf, 1991.

Lesher, Stephan. *George Wallace, American Populist.* Reading, Mass.: Addison-Wesley, 1994.

Logue, Cal M., and Howard Dorgan, eds. *The Oratory of Southern Demagogues.* Baton Rouge: Louisiana State University Press, 1981.

Luebke, Paul. *Tar Heel Politics.* Chapel Hill, N.C.: University of North Carolina Press, 1990.

Malone, Bill C. *Singing Cowboys and Musical Mountaineers: Southern Culture and the Roots of Country Music.* Athens, Ga.: The University of Georgia Press, 1993.

Marshall, F. Ray. *Labor in the South.* Cambridge, Mass.: Harvard University Press, 1967.

McWhiney, Grady. *Cracker Culture: Celtic Ways in the Old South.* Tuscaloosa, Ala.: University of Alabama Press, 1988.

Miller, Dan B. *Erskine Caldwell: The Journey from Tobacco Road.* New York: Alfred A. Knopf, 1994.

Naipaul, V. S. *A Turn in the South.* New York: Alfred A. Knopf, 1989.

Nossiter, Adam. *Of Long Memory: Mississippi and the Murder of Medgar Evers.* Reading, Mass.: Addison-Wesley, 1994.

Perry, Chuck, ed. *Don't Fence Me In: An Anecdotal Biography of Lewis Grizzard by Those Who Knew Him Best.* Atlanta: Longstreet Press, 1995.

Phillips, Kevin P. *Post-Conservative America: People, Politics and Ideology in a Time of Crisis.* New York: Random House, 1982.

Porch, Ludlow. *Lewis and Me and Skipper Makes 3.* Atlanta: Longstreet Press, 1991.

Potts, Charles. *How the South Finally Won the Civil War and Controls the Political Future of the United States.* Walla Walla, Wash.: Tsunami Press, 1995.

Powell, William S. *North Carolina Through Four Centuries.* Chapel Hill, N.C.: University of North Carolina Press, 1989.

Raines, Howell. *My Soul Is Rested.* New York: G. P. Putnam's Sons, 1977.

Reed, John Shelton. *The Enduring South: Subcultural Persistence in Mass Society.* Chapel Hill, N.C.: University of North Carolina Press, 1974.

——. *Southern Folk Plain and Fancy: Native White Social Types.* Athens, Ga.: University of Georgia Press, 1986.

——. *My Tears Spoiled My Aim and Other Reflections on Southern Culture.* Columbia, Mo.: University of Missouri Press, 1993.

——. *Whistling Dixie: Dispatches from the South.* Columbia, Mo.: University of Missouri Press, 1990.

Rubin, Louis D., Jr., and James Jackson Kilpatrick, eds. *The Lasting South.* Chicago: Henry Regnery Co., 1957.

Sale, Kirkpatrick. *Power Shift: The Rise of the Southern Rim and Its Challenge to the Eastern Establishment.* New York: Random House, 1975.

Scaife, William R. *The Campaign for Atlanta.* Saline, Mich.: McNaughton & Gunn, 1993.

Sellers, Charles Grier, Jr., ed. *The Southerner as American.* New York: Dutton, 1966.

Smith, Oran P., ed. *So Good a Cause: A Decade of* Southern Partisan. Columbia, S.C.: The Foundation for American Education, 1993.

Southern Poverty Law Center. *Free at Last. A History of the Civil Rights Movement and Those Who Died in the Struggle.* Montgomery, Ala.: The Southern Poverty Law Center, n.d.

Spencer, Elizabeth. *On the Gulf.* Jackson, Miss.: University Press of Mississippi, 1991.

Tosches, Nick. *Country: Living Legends and Dying Metaphors in America's Biggest Music.* New York: Charles Scribner's Sons, 1985.

Turner, Ginny, ed. *North Carolina Traveler: A Vacationer's Guide to the Mountains, Piedmont and Coast.* Chapel Hill, N.C.: Ventana Press, 1989.

Vandiver, Frank E., ed. *The Idea of the South: Pursuit of a Central Theme.* Chicago: University of Chicago Press, 1964.

Wallace, George C. *Stand Up for America.* Garden City, N.Y.: Doubleday & Co., 1976.

Ward, Geoffrey C., with Ric Burns and Ken Burns. *The Civil War.* New York: Alfred A. Knopf, 1990.

Warner, Judith, and Max Berley. *Newt Gingrich–Speaker to America.* New York: Signet, 1995.

Watters, Pat. *The South and the Nation.* New York: Pantheon Books, 1969.

Weaver, Richard M. *The Southern Tradition at Bay.* New Rochelle, N.Y.: Arlington House, 1968.

West, Don. *Clods of Southern Earth.* New York: Boni and Gaer, 1946.

Williams, Dick. *Newt! Leader of the Second American Revolution.* Marietta, Ga.: Longstreet Press, 1995.

Wilson, Charles Reagan, William Ferris, et al. *Encyclopedia of Southern Culture.* Chapel Hill: University of North Carolina Press, 1989.

Woodward, C. Vann. *The Burden of Southern History.* Baton Rouge: Louisiana State University Press, 1993.

——. *The Strange Career of Jim Crow.* New York: Oxford University Press, 1955. Revised, with a new preface by the author, 1966.

Wright, Gavin. *Old South, New South: Revolutions in the Southern Economy Since the Civil War.* New York: Basic Books, 1986.

Zinn, Howard. *The Southern Mystique.* New York: Alfred A. Knopf, 1964.

Zinn, Howard. *SNCC: The New Abolitionists.* Boston: Beacon Press, 1964.

Index

About the Author

PETER APPLEBOME has been a reporter in the South since 1976 and has been with *The New York Times* since 1986, first as a correspondent and then Bureau Chief in Houston, then as Atlanta Bureau Chief and now as *The Times*'s National Education Correspondent. Born in New York, he graduated from Duke University in 1971 and then received a Master's Degree in Journalism from Northwestern University's Medill School of Journalism in 1974. He worked for *The Dallas Morning News* and *Texas Monthly* magazine before joining the *Times* and has written articles and reviews for numerous publications including the *New Republic*, the *Washington Monthly, The Wall Street Journal,* and the *Texas Observer.* He lives in Atlanta with his wife and two children.